Reports of the
European Communities
1952–1977
An Index to Authors
and Chairmen

Compiled by JUNE NEILSON

Reports of the European Communities 1952–1977 An Index to Authors and Chairmen

Mansell Publishing

ISBN 0 7201 1592 2

Mansell Publishing Limited, 3 Bloomsbury Place,
London WC1A 2QA

First published 1981

Distributed in the United States and Canada by
The H. W. Wilson Company, 950 University Avenue, Bronx,
New York 10452.

British Library Cataloguing in Publication Data

Neilson, June
  Reports of the European Communities, 1952–1977; an
  index to authors and chairmen.
  1. European Communities—Bibliography
  I. Title
  016.3091'4'055   Z7165.E8
  ISBN 0-7201-1592-2

Text set in 10/12 pt Linotron Century, printed and bound in
Great Britain at The Pitman Press, Bath

Contents

Introduction   vii

Abbreviations and Acronyms   xi

Author Index   3

Subject Index   503

Introduction

In the aftermath of the events of World War II, attempts were made to promote the idea of an integrated Europe to prevent recurrence of a devastating war. Following the spirit of the era, the European Coal and Steel Community was established in 1952 amongst the countries of Belgium, France, Federal Republic of Germany, Luxembourg, Italy and the Netherlands. Two more communities came into being in 1958, the European Economic Community and the European Atomic Energy Community, the three thus becoming known as the European Communities. Expansion resulted from the accession of Denmark, Ireland and United Kingdom to the European Communities in 1973 and negotiations are under way for further enlargement to include Greece, Spain and Portugal.

A complicated framework of institutions has developed over the years to serve the needs of the European Communities. Originally, each Community set up its own Council and its own Commission, the Commission of the European Coal and Steel Community being known as the High Authority, but they shared a common Court of Justice and European Parliament. Rationalization ensued in 1967, when the three separate Councils and Commissions were merged into a single Council and Commission. There are also other bodies, such as the Economic and Social Committee, the Consultative Committee of the European Coal and Steel Community, and the European Investment Bank.

Inevitably, the development of these bodies has been accompanied by a proliferation of publications, of which four types can be detected:

(1) Reports published and put up for sale by the Office of Official Publications, the publishing house and sales agency of the European Communities.

(2) Information publications issued free of charge under the aegis of the Office of Official Publications.

(3) Limited circulation documents issued by the various institutions in mimeograph form and free of charge.

(4) Reports published by commercial publishers, representing a recent practice.

The spread of interests by the Communities and the existence of six official languages further complicate the picture.

Earlier listings of publications issued by the European Communities are incomplete and though there have been some improvements in the recent catalogues, gaps still exist. The lack of subject indexes hampers information retrieval. Many reports of the European Communities have been produced by national experts or by a committee. In the case of the latter, the reports are usually referred to by the name of the chairman who presided over the committee responsible for the work, such as the Tindemans report. It was the absence of any complete listing of these experts and chairmen which motivated the compilation of an index to cover reports issued between 1952 and December 1977.

This index is arranged alphabetically by author with an accompanying subject index. However, one must emphasize that it is not a complete list of publications, as many reports do not have a recognized author but are issued in the name of an institution. Exclusions comprise reports of a scientific and technical nature issued under the prefix EUR and the working documents of the European Parliament, as these are reasonably well indexed by the European Communities themselves. The internal documents known by a COM or SEC number are also, on the whole, not included.

The form of entry is:

(1) Author or chairman's surname and initials (where known).

(2) Title. English precedes French where ( ) around the French title indicates the publication also appears in French or [ ] indicating the publication is not issued in French, but a French rendering of the title is given. French precedes English when the publication does not appear in English. A

title with Dutch, German or Italian put first shows that the
report is not in English or French, but nevertheless an
English and French version is given within [ ].

(3) Issuing institution.

(4) Date of publication, not completion of manuscript, as for the
first version of the title.

(5) Pagination.

(6) Series note if appropriate.

(7) Languages of the publication. E F indicates separate lan-
guage editions. DK/D indicates a multilingual format. D/E,
F/N indicates two reports were published, one in German
and English and one in French and Dutch.

(8) European Communities catalogue number. The use of an
ISBN indicates that the work was published by a commercial publisher.

A work appearing as part of a title or in a periodical is indicated
by *In* and then forms part of element (3).

For example:

(1) GAVANIER, P., chairman

(2) Structure of earnings in wholesale and retail distribution,
banking and insurance in 1974. Methods and definitions
(Structure des salaires dans le commerce, les banques et les
assurances en 1974. Méthodes et définitions).

(3) Eurostat, (4) 1977.   (5) 223p.   (6) Special series, B1.

(7) DK/D/E/F/I/N   (8) 7330/1

In compiling this index, I inevitably had to draw heavily on
the resources of the London Office of the European Communities and I must thank the Librarian, Emma Harte for all the
assistance she has given. The British Library of Political and
Economic Science was another rich source and Donald Ross was
a great help. My colleagues have suffered much and thanks are
due to their forbearance, especially Neil Entwistle for guidance
over the treatment of compound names and Margaret Malt for
much help with translating. Bill Fincham made some helpful
comments, whilst Laurie Craigie also aided me with translating. Mistakes remaining are of course my own. My final thanks
must go to the Librarian of Queen Mary College, Mr. Tony

Bowyer for allowing me time to work on this project, otherwise it would never have been completed.

June Neilson

The Library
Queen Mary College
University of London

April 1980

Abbreviations and Acronyms

AASM	Associated African States and Madagascar
AG	Aktiengesellschaft
Benelux	Belgium, the Netherlands, Luxembourg
BR Deutschland	Bundesrepublik Deutschland
Bureau (B)	Bureau de presse et d'information des Communautés européennes, Bruxelles
Bureau (G)	Bureau de presse et d'information des Communautés européennes, Genève
Bureau (P)	Bureau d'information des Communautés européennes, Paris
CE	Communauté européenne or Communautés européennes
CECA	Communauté européenne du charbon et de l'acier
CEE	Communauté économique européenne
Co	Cobalt
Commission	Commission of the European Communities
Commission EAEC	Commission of the European Atomic Energy Community
Commission EEC	Commission of the European Economic Community
Commission (L)	Commission of the European Communities, London Office
Commission (W)	Commission of the European Communities, Washington Office
COPA	Comité des organisations professionnelles agricoles

Council	Council of Ministers of the European Communities
Court	Court of Justice of the European Communities
Cr	Chromium
D	German
DK	Danish
E	English
EAEC	European Atomic Energy Community
EAMA	États africains et malgache associés
EC	European Community or European Communities
ECSC	European Coal and Steel Community
ECSC CA	Common Assembly of the European Coal and Steel Community
ECSC CC	Consultative Committee of the European Coal and Steel Community
ECSC HA	High Authority of the European Coal and Steel Community
EEC	European Economic Community
EG	Europäische Gemeinschaft
EP	European Parliament
EPA	European Parliamentary Assembly
ES	European Schools
ESC	Economic and Social Committee of the European Communities
Euratom	European Atomic Energy Community
Eurostat	Statistical Office of the European Communities
EWG	Europäische Wirtschaftsgemeinschaft
F	French
FR	Federal Republic
FRG	Federal Republic of Germany
G	Greek
GD	Grand-Duché or Grand Duchy
I	Italian
Inf Ser	Information Service of the European Communities, London

loose-leaf	Loose-leaf format
Mo	Molybdenum
Mon Com	Monetary Committee of the European Communities
MTEPC	Medium-term economic policy committee of the European Communities
N	Dutch
n.d.	No date specified
n.i.	No issuing institution specified
Ni	Nickel
N.I.C.E.	Nomenclature des industries des Communautés européennes
OSCE	Office statistique des Communautés européennes
p.	Pages
pp.	Pages
Pr Inf	Direction générale de la Presse et Information, Commission des Communautés européennes
Pub Dept	Publications Department of the European Communities
RF	République fédérale
RFA	République fédérale d'Allemagne
S	Spanish
Ser Inf ESCC	Information Service of the European Coal and Steel Community
SOEC	Statistical Office of the European Communities
TVA	Taxe sur la valeur ajoutée
Uff ESCC	Ufficio Stampa e Informazione della Comunità europea del carbone e dell'acciaio
Uff St Inf	Ufficio Stampa e Informazione della Comunità europea, Roma
USA	United States of America
V	Vanadium

var. pag.	Various pagings
VAT	Value-added tax
Ver	Verbindungsbüro der Europäischen Gemeinschaften, Bonn
vols.	Volumes
W	Tungsten

Author Index

1 ABEELS, P.
Possibilités de création d'industries exportatrices dans les
États africains et malgache associés. Transformation du
bois et fabrication d'articles en bois. Première
transformation: Sciages, déroulages, tranchages.
Deuxième transformation: Profilés, moulures,
contreplaqués, panneaux, produits finis: pour la
construction et l'ameublement. Rapport de synthèse
[Possibilities for the establishment of exporting industries
in the Associated African States and Madagascar. Wood
processing and manufacture of articles in wood. First
process: Sawing, wood-peeling, slicing. Second process:
Shapes, mouldings, plywood, panels, finished products:
for building and furniture. Summary report].
Commission, 1974.   445p.
F   VIII/227/74

2 ABOU-ZAHR, C.
Social indicators for the European Community 1960–1975
(Indicateurs sociaux pour la Communauté européenne
1960–1975).
Eurostat, 1977.   486p.
DK/D/E/F/I/N   CA-22-77-766-6A-C

3 ABRAHAM, K.
La formation professionnelle des jeunes dans les
entreprises industrielles, artisanales et commerciales des
pays de la C.E.E. [Vocational training of young people in
industrial, craft and commercial firms in the countries of
the E.E.C.].
Commission EEC, 1963.   126p.   Studies: social
policy series, 1.
D F I N   8093

4 ABRAHAMSE, J.
Élaboration d'une méthode macroéconomique pour le
calcul de la charge fiscale indirecte pesant en amont des

exploitations agricoles dans chacun des six pays de la
Communauté [Formulation of a macroeconomic method
for the calculation of an indirect tax on farms in each of the
six countries of the Community].
Commission, 1972.   74p.   Studies: competition–
approximation of legislation series, 18.
D F I N   8337

5 ACHBACH, D.
Prévisions agricoles. 2: Possibilités d'utilisation de
certains modèles, méthodes et techniques dans la
Communauté [Agricultural forecasting. 2: Possibilities of
using certain models, methods and techniques in the
Community].
Commission, 1970.   249p.   Internal information on
agriculture, 63.
D F   8433/VI/69

ADAMO, F. d', *see* D'ADAMO, F.

6 ADER, G.
Confidentiality and business statistics in the European
Communities [Le caractère confidentiel et les statistiques
d'affaire dans les Communautés européennes].
Eurostat, 1977.   159p.
E   7511

7 AGOSTINI, D.
Il contributo delle 'Comunità montane' in Italia allo
sviluppo dell'agricoltura di montagna [The contribution of
'Comunità montane' to the development of hill farming in
Italy / La contribution des 'Comunità montane' au
développement de l'agriculture de montagne en Italie].
Commission, 1976.   209p.   Information on
agriculture, 11.
I   8861

8 AGOSTINI, D.
Gli 'enti di sviluppo agricolo' in Italia nella riforma delle
strutture. Problemi e prospettive de adattamento [The

'enti di sviluppo agricolo' in structural reform in Italy.
Adjustment problems and prospects / Les 'enti di sviluppo
agricolo' en Italie et la réforme des structures. Problèmes
et perspectives d'adaptation].
Commission, 1976.   285p.   Information on
agriculture, 12.
I   8862

9 AIGNER, H.
The case for a European Audit Office (Pour une Cour des
comptes européens).
EP, 1973.   164p.
DK D E F I N   6159

ALAURO, O. d', *see* D'ALAURO, O.

10 ALBERS, J.
Comparative study on the rehabilitation of handicapped
persons in the countries of the Community. Legal,
administrative and technical aspects. Volume 2: Federal
Republic of Germany. Netherlands [Étude comparative
sur la réhabilitation des personnes handicapées dans les
pays de la Communauté. Aspects juridiques,
administratifs et techniques. Volume 2: République
fédérale d'Allemagne. Pays-Bas].
Commission, 1974.   96p.
E   4055/74

11 ALKER
La formation professionnelle dans les houillères des pays
de la Communauté [Vocational training in the coal mines
of the countries of the Community].
ECSC HA, 1956.   514p.
F   1669

12 ALLAIS, M., chairman
Options in transport tariff policy (Options de la politique
tarifaire dans les transports).
Commission EEC, 1966.   189p.   Studies: transport
series, 1.
D E F I N   8146

13 ALLARDT, H.
The tasks and the aims of the European Economic
Community in Africa [Les tâches et les intentions de la
Communauté économique européenne à l'égard de
l'Afrique].
Commission EEC, 1959.   29p.
E   2225

14 ALLAYA, M.
Étude sur l'évolution de la concentration dans la
distribution des produits alimentaires en France [A study
of the evolution of concentration in food distribution in
France].
Commission, 1976.   213p.
F   8763

15 ALLEN, R. I. G.
The United Kingdom economy [L'économie britannique].
Commission, 1975.   155p.   Studies: economic and
financial series, 9.
E   8461

16 ALMELO, van
L'information relative aux revenus et aux patrimoines
dans les pays de la Communauté [Information relating to
incomes and inheritances in the countries of the
Community].
Commission, 1973.   43p.   Studies: social policy
series, 22.
D F I N   8377

17 ALS, G.
Enquête sur les budgets familiaux au Luxembourg
[Survey on family budgets in Luxembourg].
In Budgets familiaux 1963/64. Luxembourg.
Eurostat, 1965.   pp.25–124.   Social statistics:
special series, 1.
F

18 ALS, G.
Étude sur le rôle éventuel de certains revenus primaires
non-salariaux dans le développement de l'inflation au

Grand-Duché de Luxembourg [Study on the possible part
played by certain primary non-employment incomes in the
inflationary process in the Grand Duchy of Luxembourg].
Commission, 1977.   74p.   Series: medium-term
economic policy, 10.
F   CG-ST-77-002-FR-C

ALTARELLI, A. Neltner, *see* NELTNER
ALTARELLI, A.

19 ALVENSLEBEN, R. von
Intégration verticale et contrats en agriculture. 1: R. F.
d'Allemagne [Vertical integration and contracts in
agriculture. 1: F. R. of Germany].
Commission, 1973.   136p.   Internal information on
agriculture, 106.
D F   VI/3359/73

20 AMADUZZI, A.
Analisi generale della concentrazione industriale in Italia
dalla costituzione del Mercato Comune (1959–1968). Gli
indici di concentrazione impiegati nella ricerca [General
analysis of industrial concentration in Italy from the
formation of the Common Market (1959–1968).
Concentration indices used in the research / L'analyse
générale de la concentration industrielle en Italie de la
constitution du Marché commun (1959–1968). Les indices
de concentration utilisés dans la recherche].
Commission, 1973.   34p.
I   IV/345/73

21 AMADUZZI, A.
Studio sull'evoluzione della concentrazione industriale in
Italia (1968–1974). Pneumatici. Candele. Accumulatori [A
study of the evolution of industrial concentration in Italy
(1968–1974). Tyres. Sparking plugs. Batteries / Étude sur
l'évolution de la concentration industrielle en Italie
(1968–1974). Pneumatiques. Bougies. Accumulateurs].
Commission, 1976.   341p.
I   8750

22 AMADUZZI, A.
Studio sull'evoluzione della concentrazione nell'industria
della costruzione elettrica in Italia. Costruzione di
apparecchiature elettroniche ed elettroacustiche e di
apparecchi radio e televisivi (NICE 375). Costruzione di
apparecchi elettrodomestici (NICE 376) [A study of the
evolution of concentration in the electrical engineering
industry in Italy. Manufacture of electronic and audio
equipment and radio and television receivers (NICE 375).
Manufacture of electrical domestic appliances (NICE 376)
/ Étude sur l'évolution de la concentration dans l'industrie
de la construction électrique en Italie. Construction
d'appareils électroniques, radios, télévision,
électro-acoustique (NICE 375). Fabrication d'appareils
électrodomestiques (NICE 376)].
Commission, 1974.   109p.
I   IV/189/74

23 AMADUZZI, A.
Studio sull'evoluzione della concentrazione nell'industria
della costruzione elettrica in Italia (1970–1974).
Costruzione di apparecchi elettrodomestici (NICE 376).
Costruzione di apparecchiature elettroniche ed
elettroacustiche e di apparecchi radio e televisivi (NICE
375) [A study of the evolution of concentration in the
electrical engineering industry in Italy (1970–1974).
Manufacture of electrical domestic appliances (NICE 376).
Manufacture of electronic and audio equipment and radio
and television receivers (NICE 375) / Étude sur
l'évolution de la concentration dans l'industrie de la
construction électrique en Italie (1970–1974). Fabrication
d'appareils électrodomestiques (NICE 376). Construction
d'appareils électroniques, radios, télévision,
électro-acoustique (NICE 375)].
Commission, 1975.   236p.
I   8746

24 AMADUZZI, A.
Studio sull'evoluzione della concentrazione nell'industria
di cicli, motocicli e ciclomotori in Italia 1970–1972 [A study
of the evolution of concentration in the cycles, motorcycles

and power-assisted cycles industry in Italy 1970–1972 /
Étude sur l'évolution de la concentration dans l'industrie
des cycles, motocycles et cyclomoteurs en Italie
1970–1972].
Commission, 1975.   87p.
I   8699

AMBROSIO, M. d', *see* D'AMBROSIO, M.

25 AMELUNG, E.
Les aciéries [The steel-works].
Commission, 1971.   283p.   New technical processes
in the iron and steel industry: a personal training manual,
3.   Studies: vocational training.
D F I N   17433

26 ANDEL, G. van
Rapports sur les premières mesures proposées en vue
d'une coordination des politiques énergétiques [Reports
on the first measures proposed for a coordination of
energy policies].
ECSC CC, 1961.   var. pag.
D F I N   8013

27 ANDERS
Dispositions pour faciliter la création d'activités nouvelles.
Dispositions juridiques et financières en vigueur dans les
États membres et le Royaume-Uni [Arrangements to
facilitate the establishment of new activities. Legal and
financial arrangements in force in the Member States and
United Kingdom].
ECSC HA, 1959.   loose-leaf.
D F I N   2275

28 ANDERSEN, A.
Glossary new transport technologies (Glossaire nouvelles
techniques de transport).
Commission, 1976.   900p.
DK/D/E/F/I/N   IX/2061/74

29 ANDRIES, J. M.
Accès à l'exploitation agricole. Dispositions et pratiques
existant dans les États membres de la CEE en vue de
l'obtention et de l'aménagement d'une exploitation
agricole [Access to the farm. Arrangements and practices
existing in the Member States of the EEC for obtaining
and managing a farm].
Commission, 1967.   var. pag.   Internal information
on agriculture, 21.
D F   8325/VI/66

30 ANNESI, M.
Arrangements to facilitate the establishment of new
economic activities. Legal and financial arrangements in
force in the member states of the Community and the
United Kingdom (Dispositions pour faciliter la création
d'activités nouvelles. Dispositions juridiques et financières
en vigueur dans les États membres et le Royaume-Uni).
ECSC HA, 1962.   loose-leaf.
D E F I N   3019

31 ANNESI, M.
Dispositions pour faciliter la création d'activités
nouvelles. Dispositions juridiques et financières en
vigueur dans les États membres et le Royaume-Uni
[Arrangements to facilitate the establishment of new
activities. Legal and financial arrangements in force in the
Member States and United Kingdom].
ECSC HA, 1959.   loose-leaf.
D F I N   2275

ANNO, P. dell', *see* DELL'ANNO, P.

32 ANZIL, E.
Glossary new transport technologies (Glossaire nouvelles
techniques de transport).
Commission, 1976.   900p.
DK/D/E/F/I/N   IX/2061/74

33 APICELLA, V.
Le financement des investissements et les aspects sociaux
de la reconversion [Financing of investments and social
aspects of conversion].
ECSC HA, 1963.   255p.   Collection: regional
economy and policy. 1: Industrial conversion in
Europe, 3.
D F I N   3323

34 ARMAND, L.
Speech delivered by Monsieur Louis Armand President of
the Commission before the European Parliamentary
Assembly. Ordinary Session 1957–1958. Strasbourg. June
23 1958 (Discours de Monsieur Louis Armand président de
la Commission devant l'Assemblée parlementaire
européenne. Session ordinaire 1957–1958. Strasbourg. 23
Juin 1958).
Commission EAEC, 1958.   23p.
D E F I N   2058

35 ARMAND, L.
A target for Euratom. Report submitted by Mr. Louis
Armand, Mr. Franz Etzel and Mr. Francesco Giordiani at
the request of the governments of Belgium, France,
German Federal Republic, Italy, Luxembourg and the
Netherlands (Un objectif pour Euratom. Rapport
présenté par M. Louis Armand, M. Franz Etzel et M.
Francesco Giordiani sur la demande des Gouvernements
de la République Fédérale d'Allemagne, de la Belgique, de
la France, de l'Italie, du Luxembourg et des Pays-Bas).
EAEC, 1957.   104p.
D E F I N

36 ARNOLD, H.
Rapport sur les nouveaux procédés de mesure et de
contrôle pour les câbles d'extraction et de traction ainsi
que pour les guidages dans les puits et galeries de mines
[Report on the new processes of measurement and control
of extraction and traction cables as well as guide-rails in
the mine shafts and galleries].
Commission, 1970.
D F   16512a

37 ARNOUX, J.
Influence des différents caractères de la carcasse de
bovins sur la détermination de son prix [Influence of
different characteristics of the beef carcass on its price
determination].
In Agricultural statistical studies, 1.
Eurostat, 1968.   33p.
F   14892

38 ATTONATY, J. M.
Modèles d'analyse d'entreprises de polyculture-élevage
bovin. 1: Caractéristiques et possibilités d'utilisation
[Models for analysis of mixed crop and cattle farms. 1:
Characteristics and possibilities of utilization].
Commission, 1973.   261p.   Internal information on
agriculture, 97.
D F   VI/1385/72

39 ATTONATY, J. M.
Modèles d'analyse d'entreprises de polyculture-élevage
bovin. 2: Données technico-économiques de base.
Circonscription Nord-Picardie et région limoneuse du
Limbourg belge [Models for analysis of mixed crop and
cattle farms. 2: Basic technico-economic data.
Nord-Picardie area and the limoneuse region of Belgian
Limbourg].
Commission, 1973.   200p.   Internal information on
agriculture, 111.
D F   VI/1792/73

40 ATTONATY, J. M.
Modèles d'analyse d'entreprises de polyculture-élevage
bovin. 3: Données technico-économiques de base. Région
Noordelijke Bouwstreek (Pays-Bas) [Models for analysis
of mixed crop and cattle farms. 3: Basic technico-economic
data. Noordelijke Bouwstreek region (Netherlands)].
Commission, 1975.   90p.   Internal information on
agriculture, 140.
F N   VI/17751/70

41 AUBERT, J.
Modèles d'analyse d'entreprises de polyculture-élevage
bovin. Données technico-économiques de base. Région du
Bassin de Rennes (France) [Models for analysis of mixed
crop and cattle farms. Basic technico-economic data.
Bassin de Rennes region (France)].
Commission, 1977.   98p.   Information on
agriculture, 37.
F   CB-NA-77-037-FR-C

42 AUBRÉE, M.
Structure of earnings in industry 1972 (Structure des
salaires dans l'industrie 1972).
Eurostat, 1975–1977.   13 vols. Social statistics: special
series.
DK/D/E/F/I/N   6817 (v.1), 6887 (v.2), 6949 (v.3),
                7043 (v.4), 7118 (v.5), 7159 (v.6),
                7289 (v.7)

43 AUBY, J.-M.
Les recours juridictionnels contre les actes administratifs
spécialement économiques dans le droit des États
membres de la Communauté économique européenne.
Rapport final [Legal appeals against administrative
actions, especially economic, in the law of the Member
States of the European Economic Community. Final
report].
Commission, 1971.   63p.   Studies:
competition–approximation of legislation series, 12.
D F I N   8298

44 AUENMÜLLER, H. von
Surfaces agricoles pouvant être mobilisées pour une
réforme de structure [Agricultural areas that could be
mobilised for a structural reform].
Commission, 1973.   336p.   Internal information on
agriculture, 77.
D F   VI/14453/69

45 AUKEMA, S.
Credit to agriculture. 4: The Netherlands [Crédits à
l'agriculture. 4: Pays-Bas].
Commission, 1976.   116p.   Information on
agriculture, 4.
E N   8834

46 AVERMAETE, U.
Projections de la production et de la consommation de
produits agricoles—'1977'. 7: Belgique, Grand-Duché de
Luxembourg [Projections of production and consumption
of agricultural products—'1977'. 7: Belgium, Grand Duchy
of Luxembourg].
Commission, 1974.   199p.   Internal information on
agriculture, 134.
D F   VI/4822/71

47 AYERS, C.
Pesticide residues in tobacco and tobacco products. 1:
General report (Les résidus de pesticides dans le tabac et
les produits de tabac. 1: Rapport général).
Commission, 1976.   145p.   Information on
agriculture, 14.
E F   8864

48 AYERS, C.
Les résidus de pesticides dans le tabac et les produits de
tabac. 2: Substances phytosanitaires employées.
Législations. Méthodes d'analyse [Pesticide residues in
tobacco and tobacco products. 2: Plant health substances
employed. Legislation. Methods of analysis].
Commission, 1977.   157p.   Information on
agriculture, 23.
F   8877

49 AZOUVI
Possibilités de création d'industries exportatrices dans les
États africains et malgache associés. Produits de
l'élevage. Viandes, cuirs et peaux, chaussures, articles en
cuir [Possibilities for the establishment of exporting
industries in the Associated African States and

Madagascar. Products from rearing. Meat, hides and
skins, shoes, leather articles].
Commission, 1974.   5 vols.
F   VIII/223/74

50 AZOUVI
Possibilités de création d'industries exportatrices dans les
États africains et malgache associés. Produits de
l'élevage. Viandes, cuirs et peaux, chaussures, articles en
cuir. Rapport de synthèse [Possibilities for the
establishment of exporting industries in the Associated
African States and Madagascar. Products from rearing.
Meat, hides and skins, shoes, leather articles. Summary
report].
Commission, 1975.   27p.
D E F I N   VIII/223/74

51 BACHELET, D.
Econometric analysis of the market in tropical oils and
oilseeds. Extracts (essential results of the study) (Analyse
économétrique du marché des oléagineux tropicaux.
Extraits (résultats essentiels de l'étude)).
Commission, 1969.   55p.
D E F I N   5190/VIII/B/69

52 BACHELET, D.
Évolution et prévisions de la population active agricole.
[Development and estimates of the working agricultural
population].
Commission, 1970.   var. pag.   Internal information
on agriculture, 61.
D F   4131/VI/70

53 BADIN, G.
Les industries de la confection dans la Communauté
économique européenne. Analyse et perspectives 1975
[The ready-to-wear industry in the European Economic
Community. Analysis and prospects 1975].
Commission, 1970.   2 vols.
D F   12734/III/70

54 BADU, A.-M.
Prix, taux d'équivalence de pouvoir d'achat à la
consommation et revenus réels dans les pays de la
C.E.C.A. 1954–1958 [Prices, equivalent rates of
purchasing power from consumption and real incomes
in the countries of the E.C.S.C. 1954–1958].
In Social statistics, 2/1960.   Eurostat, 1960.   219p.
D F I N   2500

55 BAECK, L.
Critères à la base de la fixation des salaires et problèmes
qui y sont liés pour une politique des salaires et des
revenus [Criteria at the basis for the fixing of wages and
problems connected for a wages and incomes policy].
Commission, 1967.   98p.   Studies: social policy
series, 19.
D F I N   8227

56 BAETS, A. de
Pesticide residues in tobacco and tobacco products. 1:
General report (Les résidus de pesticides dans le tabac et
les produits de tabac. 1: Rapport général).
Commission, 1976.   145p.   Information on
agriculture, 14.
E F   8864

57 BAETS, A. de
Les résidus de pesticides dans le tabac et les produits de
tabac. 2: Substances phytosanitaires employées.
Législations. Méthodes d'analyse [Pesticide residues in
tobacco and tobacco products. 2: Plant health substances
employed. Legislation. Methods of analysis].
Commission, 1977.   157p.   Information on
agriculture, 23.
F   8877

58 BAEYENS, H.
Environmental problems of city centres [Les problèmes
d'environnement des centres de cité].
Commission, 1976.   88p.
E

59 BAILLET, C.
Agricultural incomes for 1975 and 1976 in the European
Economic Community [Les revenus agricoles pour 1975 et
1976 dans la Communauté économique européenne].
Commission, 1977.   9p.
E   413/VI/77

60 BAKER, B.
Latin America—links with the Community [Les liens
entre l'Amérique latine et la Communauté].
In European studies. Teachers' series, 21.
Commission (L), 1975.   4p.
E   U/75/21

61 BALLIANO, P.
Evoluzione della concentrazione dal 1962 al 1969 in alcuni
settori dell'industria italiana. Metodologia [Evolution of
concentration in various sectors of Italian industry from
1962 to 1969. Methodology / L'évolution de la
concentration dans quelques secteurs de l'industrie
italienne de 1962 à 1969. Méthodologie].
Commission, 1973.   24p.
I   IV/344/73

62 BALLIANO, P.
Studio sull'evoluzione della concentrazione dell'industria
cartaria in Italia [A study of the evolution of concentration
of the paper industry in Italy / Étude sur l'évolution de la
concentration de l'industrie du papier en Italie].
Commission, 1977.   189p.
I   8753

63 BALLIANO, P.
Studio sull'evoluzione della concentrazione in alcuni settori
dell'industria tessile in Italia. Lana (NICE 232). Cotone
(NICE 233). Maglieria e calzetteria (NICE 237) [A study
of the evolution of concentration in various sectors of the
textile industry in Italy. Wool (NICE 232). Cotton (NICE
233). Knitted and crocheted goods (NICE 237) / Étude sur
l'évolution de la concentration dans quelques secteurs de
l'industrie du textile en Italie. Laine (NICE 232). Coton

(NICE 233). Bonneterie (NICE 237)].
Commission, 1973.   var. pag.
I   IV/347/73

64 BALLIANO, P.
Studio sull'evoluzione della concentrazione in Italia
dell'industria della carta e della sua trasformazione. Carta
(NICE 271). Cartotecnica (NICE 272) [A study of the
evoluzione of concentration in the paper and paper products
industry in Italy. Paper (NICE 271). Paper processing
(NICE 272) / Étude sur l'évolution de la concentration de
l'industrie du papier et des articles en papier en Italie.
Papier (NICE 271). Transformation du papier (NICE
272)].
Commission, 1973.   103p.
I   IV/348/73

65 BALLIANO, P.
Studio sull'evoluzione della concentrazione nel settore
della costruzione di macchine per l'industria tessile in
Italia [A study of the evolution of concentration in the
sector of the manufacture of machines for the textile
industry in Italy / Étude sur l'évolution de la concentration
dans le secteur de la construction des machines pour
l'industrie textile en Italie].
Commission, 1977.   159p.
I   8755

66 BALLIANO, P.
Studio sull'evoluzione della concentrazione nel settore
della costruzione di macchine per ufficio in Italia [A study
of the evolution of concentration in the sector of the
manufacture of office machinery in Italy / Étude sur
l'évolution de la concentration dans le secteur de la
construction des machines de bureau en Italie].
Commission, 1977.   149p.
I   8754

67 BALLIANO, P.
Studio sull'evoluzione della concentrazione nell'industria
cotoniera italiana (NICE 233) [A study of the evolution of

concentration in the Italian cotton industry (NICE 233) /
Étude sur l'évolution de la concentration dans l'industrie
de coton en Italie (NICE 233)].
Commission, 1975.   149p.
I   8743

68 BALLIANO, P.
Studio sull'evoluzione della concentrazione nell'industria
della costruzione di macchine non elettriche in Italia.
Costruzione di materiale per sollevamento e trasporto.
Costruzione di ascensori [A study of the evolution of
concentration in the mechanical engineering industry in
Italy. Manufacture of hoisting and handling equipment.
Manufacture of lifts / Étude sur l'évolution de la
concentration dans le secteur de la construction de
machines non électriques en Italie. Construction de
matériel de levage et de manutention. Construction des
ascenseurs].
Commission, 1977.   152p.
I   8758

69 BALLIANO, P.
Studio sull'evoluzione della concentrazione nell'industria
delle bevande in Italia [A study of the evolution of
concentration in the beverages industry in Italy / Étude
sur l'évolution de la concentration dans l'industrie des
boissons en Italie].
Commission, 1977.   143p.
I   8770

70 BALS, C.
Étude sur la structure sociale et économique de la région
Sieg-Lahn-Dill [Study on the social and economic
structure of the Sieg-Lahn-Dill region].
Commission, 1968.   160p.   Collection: regional
economy and policy. 2: Development and conversion
programme, 10.
D F   4252

71 BANDT, J. de
L'industrialisation textile d'exportation des États
africains et malgache associés [Textile industrialization for
exporting to the Associated African States and
Madagascar].
Commission, 1972.   2 vols.
F   VIII/210/72

72 BANDT, J. de
L'industrie textile de la C.E.E. Analyse et perspectives
1975 [The textile industry of the E.E.C. Analysis and
prospects 1975].
Commission, 1969.   218p.
D F I N   5885/III/69

73 BAPTIST, A. G.
Nouvelles formes de collaboration dans le domaine de la
production agricole. 2: Benelux [New forms of cooperation
in the field of agricultural production. 2: Benelux].
Commission, 1972.   470p.   Internal information on
agriculture, 94.
D F N   VI/2514/72

74 BARBACK, R. H.
Forms of cooperation in the fishing industry. Denmark,
Ireland, United Kingdom [Formes de coopération dans le
secteur de la pêche. Danemark, Irlande, Royaume-Uni].
Commission, 1976.   var. pag.   Information on
agriculture, 9.
E   8842

75 BARBERO, G.
Les tendances d'évolution des structures des exploitations
agricoles. Causes et motifs d'abandon et de
restructuration [Trends of development in farm
structures. Causes and reasons for desertion and
reconstruction].
Commission, 1967.   386p.   Internal information on
agriculture, 20.
D F   8159/VI/67

76 BARBIN
Essai d'appréciation des conditions d'application et des
résultats d'une politique de réforme en agriculture dans
des régions agricoles difficiles. 2: Queyras [Attempts at
estimating the conditions from the application and results
of a reform policy in agriculture in difficult agricultural
regions. 2: Queyras].
Commission, 1975.   var. pag.   Internal information
on agriculture, 150.
F   VI/1988/75

77 BARETJE, R.
Besoins de détente en tant que facteurs pour le
développement régional et agricole [Needs of detente in so
far as the factors for regional and agricultural
development].
Commission, 1973.   var. pag.   Internal information
on agriculture, 116.
F   VI/3808/73

78 BARSCH, A.-M.
Glossary new transport technologies (Glossaire nouvelles
techniques de transport).
Commission, 1976.   900p.
DK/D/E/F/I/N   IX/2061/74

79 BARTELS, H.
L'information relative aux revenus et aux patrimoines
dans les pays de la Communauté [Information relating to
incomes and inheritances in the countries of the
Community].
Commission, 1973.   43p.   Studies: social policy
series, 22.
D F I N   8377

80 BARTELS, H.
Tableaux 'Entrées-Sorties' pour les pays de la
Communauté Économique Européenne ['Input-Output'
tables for the countries of the European Economic
Community].
Eurostat, 1964.   var. pag.
D F

81 BARTELS, H.
Tableaux 'Entrées-Sorties' pour les pays de la
Communauté Économique Européenne. Seconde version
['Input-Output' tables for the countries of the European
Economic Community. Second version].
Eurostat, 1965.   var. pag.
D F

82 BARTLING, G.
Formes de coopération dans le secteur de la pêche. 1:
Synthèse, R.F. d'Allemagne, Italie [Forms of cooperation
in the fishing industry. 1: Summary, F.R. of Germany,
Italy].
Commission, 1970.   var. pag.   Internal information
on agriculture, 68.
D F   14715/VI/69

83 BARTLING, G.
Volume et degré de l'emploi dans la pêche maritime
[Volume and extent of employment in sea fishing].
Commission, 1968.   var. pag.   Internal information
on agriculture, 32.
D F   6993/VI/68

84 BASEVI, G., chairman
Optica report 1976. Inflation and exchange rates.
Evidence and policy guidelines for the European
Community [Rapport Optica 1976. L'inflation et taux de
change. L'évidence et les lignes de politique pour la
Communauté européenne].
Commission, 1977.   129p.
E   II/855/76

85 BASTIN
Essai d'appréciation des conditions d'application et des
résultats d'une politique de réforme en agriculture dans
des régions agricoles difficiles. 2: Queyras [Attempt at
estimating the conditions from the application and results
of a reform policy in agriculture in difficult agricultural
regions. 2: Queyras].

Commission, 1975.   var. pag.   Internal information
on agriculture, 150.
F   VI/1988/75

86 BATIFFOL, H.
La réparation des conséquences dommageables d'une
violation des articles 85 et 86 du traité instituant la CEE
[Compensation for damage suffered through infringement
of Articles 85 and 86 of the Treaty establishing the EEC].
Commission EEC, 1966.   74p.   Studies: competition
series, 1.
D F I N   8153

87 BATLLE
L'industrie électronique des pays de la Communauté et les
investissements américains [The electronics industry of
the countries of the Community and American
investments].
Commission, 1969.   168p.   Studies: industry
series, 1.
D F I N   8240

88 BATTISTA, E.
Vers l'élection directe de l'Assemblée parlementaire
européenne [Towards the direct election of the European
Parliamentary Assembly].
EPA, 1960.   79p.
F   2516

89 BAUER, W., chairman
Die deutsche Wirtschaft und die EWG [The German
economy and the EEC / L'économie allemande et la CEE].
Ver, 1966.   48p.
D

90 BAZIN
Essai d'appréciation des conditions d'application et des
résultats d'une politique de réforme en agriculture dans
des régions agricoles difficiles. 1: Morvan [Attempt at
estimating the conditions from the application and results

of a reform policy in agriculture in difficult agricultural
regions. 1: Morvan].
Commission, 1974.   183p.   Internal information on
agriculture, 138.
F   VI/4572/74

BEAUMELLE, S. de la, *see* LA BEAUMELLE, S. de

91 BECK
Possibilités de création d'industries exportatrices dans les
États africains et malgache associés. Produits de
l'élevage. Viandes, cuirs et peaux, chaussures, articles en
cuir [Possibilities for the establishment of exporting
industries in the Associated African States and
Madagascar. Products from rearing. Meat, hides and
skins, shoes, leather articles].
Commission, 1974.   5 vols.
F   VIII/223/74

92 BECK
Possibilités de création d'industries exportatrices dans les
États africains et malgache associés. Produits de
l'élevage. Viandes, cuirs et peaux, chaussures, articles en
cuir. Rapport de synthèse [Possibilities for the
establishment of exporting industries in the Associated
African States and Madagascar. Products from rearing.
Meat, hides and skins, shoes, leather articles. Summary
report].
Commission, 1975.   27p.
D E F I N   VIII/223/74

93 BECK, K.-G.
Augmentation de la production de coke par régularisation
de la charge des fours. Rapport final 1970–1972/StBV
[Increasing coke production by regularising the furnace
load. Final report 1970–1972/StBV].
Commission, 1973.   48p.   Technical research: coal,
45. Coal valorisation.
D F   5873

94 BÉGUÉ
Les exportations de biens d'équipement de la
Communauté. Essai et prévisions jusqu'en 1970 [Exports
of capital goods from the Community. Sample and
forecasts until 1970].
ECSC HA, 1967.   249p.   Collection: general
objectives for steel, 3A.
D F I N   12885

95 BEHLER
La collaboration entre l'enseignement et les industries de
la C.E.C.A. [Cooperation between education and the
industries of the E.C.S.C.].
ECSC HA, 1959.   134p.
F   4704

BELLA, M. la, *see* LA BELLA, M.

96 BELLUCCI, V.
Le boisement des terres marginales [The afforestation of
marginal lands].
Commission EEC, 1964.   var. pag.   Internal
information on agriculture, 1.
D F   VI/5221/64

97 BELTRAME, F.
Le rôle des ports de la Communauté pour le trafic de
céréales et de farines. 1: Synthèse pour les principaux
ports français et italiens [List of Community ports for the
cereals and flour trade. 1: Summary for the chief French
and Italian ports].
Commission, 1974.   var. pag.   Internal information
on agriculture, 122.
F   VI/2941/73

98 BELTRAME, F.
Le rôle des ports de la Communauté pour le trafic de
céréales et de farines. 2: Monographies pour les principaux
ports français de la Manche [List of Community ports for
the cereals and flour trade. 2: Monographs for the chief
French Channel ports].

Commission, 1974.   var. pag.   Internal information
on agriculture, 123.
F   VI/1169/74

99 BELTRAME, F.
Le rôle des ports de la Communauté pour le trafic de
céréales et de farines. 3: Monographies pour les principaux
ports français de l'Atlantique [List of Community ports for
the cereals and flour trade. 3: Monographs for the chief
French Atlantic ports].
Commission, 1974.   var. pag.   Internal information
on agriculture, 124.
F   VI/1263/74

100 BELTRAME, F.
Le rôle des ports de la Communauté pour le trafic de
céréales et de farines. 4: Monographies pour les principaux
ports français de la Méditerranée [List of Community
ports for the cereals and flour trade. 4: Monographs for the
chief French Mediterranean ports].
Commission, 1974.   var. pag.   Internal information
on agriculture, 125.
F   VI/1264/74

101 BELTRAME, F.
Le rôle des ports de la Communauté pour le trafic de
céréales et de farines. 5: Monographies pour les principaux
ports italiens de la Côte Ouest [List of Community ports
for the cereals and flour trade. 5: Monographs for the chief
Italian West Coast ports].
Commission, 1974.   var. pag.   Internal information
on agriculture, 126.
F   VI/1265/74

102 BELTRAME, F.
Le rôle des ports de la Communauté pour le trafic de
céréales et de farines. 6: Monographies pour les principaux
ports italiens de la Côte Est [List of Community ports for
the cereals and flour trade. 6: Monographs for the chief
Italian East Coast ports].

Commission, 1974.   var. pag.   Internal information
on agriculture, 127.
F   VI/1266/74

103 BEMPT, P. van den, chairman
The trend of public finance in the Member States of the
Community from 1966 to 1970 (L'évolution des finances
publiques dans les États membres de la Communauté de
1966 à 1970).
Commission, 1977.   236p.   Studies: economic and
financial series, 11.
D E F   8713

104 BENICHI, R.
Les monnaies européennes de 1914 à 1939. 5: La formation
du Bloc-Or [European currencies from 1914 to 1939. 5: The
formation of the Gold Block].
In Dossiers pédagogiques, 43.   Bureau(P),
1971.   4p.
F

105 BENICHI, R.
Les monnaies européennes de 1914 à 1939. 6: La
dislocation du Bloc-Or [European currencies from 1914 to
1939. 6: The breaking-up of the Gold Block].
In Dossiers pédagogiques, 44.   Bureau(P),
1971.   4p.
F

106 BENTHEM, J.B. van
General report (Rapport général).
In Reports on the First preliminary draft convention for a
European system for the grant of patents.
Council, 1971.   pp.5–9.
D E F   16325-B

107 BENTHEM, J.B. van
General Report on the activities of Working Party 1 of the
Inter-Governmental Conference (Rapport général
concernant les activités du Groupe de travail 1 de la
Conférence Intergouvernementale).

In Reports on the Second preliminary draft of a
convention establishing a European system for the grant
of patents.   Council, 1971.   pp.55–58.
D/E/F   17275-B

108 BENTHEM, J.B. van
General Report on the results of the Fourth meeting of the
Inter-Governmental Conference (Rapport général
concernant les résultats de la 4ème session de la
Conférence Intergouvernementale).
In Reports on the Second preliminary draft of a
convention establishing a European system for the grant
of patents.   Council, 1971.   pp.59–64.
D/E/F   17275-B

109 BENVENUTI, B.
Évolution régionale de la population active agricole. 5:
Italie [Regional development of the working agricultural
population. 5: Italy].
Commission, 1969.   var. pag.   Internal information
on agriculture, 43.
D F   11445/VI/69

110 BERENDT, M.
The Common Agricultural Policy. 1 [La politique agricole
commune. 1].
In European studies. Teachers' series, 19.
Commission (L), 1975.   4p.
E   U/74/19

111 BERENDT, M.
The Common Agricultural Policy. 2 [La politique agricole
commune. 2].
In European studies. Teachers' series, 20.
Commission (L), 1975.   4p.
E   U/74/20

112 BERG,A.-M.
Pesticide residues in tobacco and tobacco products. 1:
General report (Les résidus de pesticides dans le tabac et
les produits de tabac. 1: Rapport général).

Commission, 1976.   145p.   Information on
agriculture, 14.
E F   8864

113 BERG, A.-M.
Pesticide residues in tobacco and tobacco products. 3:
Appendix. Pesticide residues found in tobacco.
Toxicological aspects of residues in tobacco (Les résidus
de pesticides dans le tabac et les produits de tabac. 3:
Annexe. Résidus de pesticides trouvés dans le tabac.
Aspects toxicologiques des résidus dans le tabac).
Commission, 1977.   var. pag.   Information on
agriculture, 26.
E F   8882

114 BERG, A.-M.
Les résidus de pesticides dans le tabac et les produits de
tabac. 2: Substances phytosanitaires employées.
Législations. Méthodes d'analyse [Pesticide residues in
tobacco and tobacco products. 2: Plant health substances
employed. Legislation. Methods of analysis].
Commission, 1977.   157p.   Information on
agriculture, 23.
F   8877

115 BERGANS, J.
Surfaces agricoles pouvant être mobilisées pour une
réforme de structure [Agricultural areas that could be
mobilised for a structural reform].
Commission, 1973.   336p.   Internal information on
agriculture, 77.
D F   VI/14453/69

116 BERGER
Essai d'appréciation des conditions d'application et des
résultats d'une politique de réforme en agriculture dans
des régions agricoles difficiles. 2: Queyras [Attempt at
estimating the conditions from the application and results
of a reform policy in agriculture in difficult agricultural
regions. 2: Queyras].

Commission, 1975.   var. pag.   Internal information
on agriculture, 150.
F   VI/1988/75

117 BERGHAUS, F.
Les aciéries [The steel-works].
Commission, 1971.   283p.   New technical processes
in the iron and steel industry: a personal training manual,
3.   Studies: vocational training.
D F I N   17433

118 BERGHAUS, F.
Les laminoirs [The rolling mills].
Commission, 1972.   240p.   New technical processes
in the iron and steel industry: a personal training manual,
4.   Studies: vocational training.
D F I N   8349

119 BERGHAUS, F.
Mécanisation, automatisation et techniques de mesure
dans les services des hauts fourneaux [Mechanisation,
automation and measurement techniques in blast-furnace
works].
Commission, 1969.   172p.   New technical processes
in the iron and steel industry: a personal training manual,
2.   Studies: vocational training.
D F I N   14722

120 BERGHAUS, F.
La technique de mesure et de l'automation [Measurement
and automation technique].
ECSC HA, 1967.   204p.   New technical processes in
the iron and steel industry: a personal training manual,
1.   Studies: vocational training.
D F I N   13233

121 BERGMANN, H.
Analyse des facteurs qui influent sur l'orientation de l'offre
régionale des céréales et de produits transformés dérivés
des céréales [Analysis of the factors influencing the

development of the regional supply of cereals and
cereal-converted products].
Commission EEC, 1965.   73p.   Studies: agricultural
series, 17.
D F I N   8130

122 BERGSTRÖM, P. L.
Étude sur les qualités des carcasses de bovins et porcins
dans les pays de la Communauté Économique Européenne
[Study on the qualities of beef and pork carcasses in the
countries of the European Economic Community].
Eurostat, 1966.   80p.   Agricultural statistics.
D/F   3944

123 BERLIN, A.
Intercomparison of measurement of carboxyhaemoglobin
in different European laboratories and establishment of
the methodology for the assessment of COH_B levels in
exposed populations [Inter-comparaison de la mesure du
carboxyle-hémoglobine dans les laboratoires divers
européens et l'établissement de la méthodologie pour
l'imposition des niveaux COH_B dans les populations
exposées].
Commission, 1977.   118p.
E   V/F/1315/77

124 BERNAND, J.
Conséquences écologiques de l'application des techniques
modernes de production en agriculture [Ecological results
from the application of modern production techniques in
agriculture].
Commission, 1974.   var. pag.   Internal information
on agriculture, 137.
D F   VI/3722/74

125 BERNHARDT, R.
The problems of drawing up a catalogue of fundamental
rights for the European Communities [Les problèmes de
l'indication d'un catalogue des droits fondamentaux pour
les Communautés européennes].

In Bulletin of the European Communities. Supplement,
5/1976.
Commission, 1976.   pp.19–69.
DK D E F I N   7108/S/5

126 BERTAUD, G.
Budgets familiaux des ouvriers de la Communauté
européenne du charbon et de l'acier 1956/57 [Family
budgets of workers of the European Coal and Steel
Community 1956/57].
In Social statistics series, 1/1960.
Eurostat, 1960.   436p.
D F I N   2333

127 BERTAUD, G.
Prix, taux d'équivalence de pouvoir d'achat à la
consommation et revenus réels dans les pays de la
C.E.C.A. 1954–1958 [Prices, equivalent rates of
purchasing power from consumption and real incomes
in the countries of the E.C.S.C. 1954–1958].
In Social statistics, 2/1960.   Eurostat, 1960.   219p.
D F I N   2500

128 BERTAUD, G.
La situation des logements des travailleurs dans les
industries de la C.E.C.A. [The housing situation of
workers in the E.C.S.C. industries].
In Social statistics, 2/1961.   Eurostat, 1961.   285p.
D F I N   2767

129 BERTEN, A.
La formation des formateurs. Problèmes, méthodes et
expériences dans les industries de la C.E.C.A. [Training
of the trainers. Problems, methods and experiments in the
industries of the E.C.S.C.].
ECSC HA, 1962.   127p.
F   8514

130 BERTIN, G.
Étude sur l'évolution de la concentration dans quelques
sous-secteurs de l'industrie chimique en France. Produits

pharmaceutiques (NICE 313.1). Produits
photographiques (NICE 313.2) [A study of the evolution
of concentration in various sub-sectors of the chemical
industry in France. Pharmaceutical products (NICE
313.1). Photographic products (NICE 313.2)].
Commission, 1973.   67p.
F   IV/111/73

131 BERTIN, G.
Étude sur l'évolution de la concentration dans quelques
sous-secteurs de l'industrie de la construction de machines
non électriques en France. Machines et tracteurs agricoles
(NICE 361). Machines de bureau (NICE 362). Machines
textiles et leurs accessoires (NICE 364.1). Matériel de
génie civil (NICE 366.4) et matériel de levage et de
manutention (NICE 366.5) [A study of the evolution of
concentration in various sub-sectors of the mechanical
engineering industry in France. Agricultural machinery
and tractors (NICE 361). Office machinery (NICE 362).
Textile machinery and its accessories (NICE 364.1). Civil
engineering equipment (NICE 366.4) and hoisting and
handling equipment (NICE 366.5)].
Commission, 1973.   var. pag.
F   IV/112/73

132 BERTIN, G.
Étude sur l'évolution de la concentration dans un
sous-secteur de l'industrie de la construction de matériel
de transport en France. Cycles, motocycles et
cyclomoteurs (NICE 385.1) [A study of the evolution of
concentration in a sub-sector of the manufacture of
transport equipment industry in France. Cycles,
motorcycles and power-assisted cycles (NICE 385.1)].
Commission, 1973.   32p.
F

133 BERTINELLI, L.S.
Étude sur la physionomie actuelle de la sécurité sociale
dans les pays de la C.E.E. [Study on the current situation
of social security in the countries of the E.E.C.].

Commission EEC, 1962. 130p. Studies: social
policy series, 3.
D F I N   8058

134 BERTONE, G.
Studio sull'evoluzione della concentrazione nell'industria
cotoniera italiana (NICE 233) [A study of the evolution of
concentration in the Italian cotton industry (NICE 233) /
Étude sur l'évolution de la concentration dans l'industrie
de coton en Italie (NICE 233)].
Commission, 1975.   149p.
I   8743

134A BESCH, M.
Objectif, évidences et limites de l'agrégation de quantités
et de valeurs [Objective, facts and limits of the aggregate
of quantities and values].
In Agricultural statistical studies, 16.
Eurostat, 1974.   82p.
D F   6641

135 BETHAZ
La formation professionnelle dans les mines de fer des pays
de la Communauté [Vocational training in the iron mines
of the countries of the Community].
ECSC HA, 1959.   182p.
F   8149

136 BETHMANN, M. von
Méthodes pour la détermination du taux d'humidité du
tabac [Methods for the determination of the rate of
moisture in tobacco].
Commission, 1972.   var. pag.   Internal information
on agriculture, 91.
D F   VI/31/73/72

137 BEVILAQUA
Les conditions d'installation d'entreprises industrielles
dans les États africains et malgache associés. Volume 14:
République du Zaïre [Conditions for the setting-up of

industrial undertakings in the Associated African States
and Madagascar. Volume 14: Republic of Zaïre].
Commission, 1972.   116p.
F   VIII/1324/72

138 BEVILAQUA
Les conditions d'installation d'entreprises industrielles
dans les États africains et malgache associés. Volume 17:
République démocratique de Somalie [Conditions for the
setting-up of industrial undertakings in the Associated
African States and Madagascar. Volume 17: Democratic
Republic of Somalia].
Commission, 1972.   52p.
F   VIII/1327/72

139 BEYSSEL
Étude sur la physionomie actuelle de la sécurité sociale
dans les pays de la C.E.E. [Study on the current situation
of social security in the countries of the E.E.C.].
Commission EEC, 1962.   130p.   Studies: social
policy series, 3.
D F I N   8058

140 BEZY, F.
Possibilités d'industrialisation des États africains et
malgache associés. Volume 3: République démocratique
du Congo [Possibilities for the industrialization of the
Associated African States and Madagascar. Volume 3:
Democratic Republic of the Congo].
Commission EEC, 1966.   2 vols.
F   13077/VIII/B/66, 13078/VIII/B/66

141 BEZY, F.
Possibilités d'industrialisation des États africains et
malgache associés. Volume 4: Burundi, Rwanda et région
Centre-orientale du Congo (Kinshasa) (région des Grands
Lacs) [Possibilities for the industrialization of the
Associated African States and Madagascar. Volume 4:
Burundi, Rwanda and Centre-eastern region of the Congo
(Kinshasa) (region of the Great Lakes)].
Commission EEC, 1966.   2 vols.
F   13079/VIII/B/66, 13080/VIII/B/66

142 BEZY, F.
Possibilités d'industrialisation des États africains et
malgache associés. Volume 5: Madagascar [Possibilities
for the industrialization of the Associated African States
and Madagascar. Volume 5: Madagascar].
Commission EEC, 1966.   2 vols.
F   13081/VIII/B/66, 13082/VIII/B/66

143 BEZY, F.
Possibilités d'industrialisation des États africains et
malgache associés. Volume 6: Somalie [Possibilities for the
industrialization of the Associated African States and
Madagascar. Volume 6: Somalia].
Commission EEC, 1966.   2 vols.
F   13083/VIII/B/66, 13084/VIII/B/66

144 BIAGOLI
La formation professionnelle dans les mines de fer des
pays de la Communauté [Vocational training in the iron
mines of the countries of the Community].
ECSC HA, 1959.   182p.
F   8149

BIANCHI, M. Cesa-, *see* CESA-BIANCHI, M.

145 BIELIG, H. J.
Teneur en métaux lourds des jus de fruits et produits
similaires [Heavy metal content of fruit juices and similar
products].
Commission, 1975.   215p.   Internal information on
agriculture, 148.
D F   VI/1594/75

146 BIELLI, C.
Le condizioni di lavoro della donne salariate nei sei stati
membri della Comunità europea. Italia [The conditions of
work for wage-earning women in the six Member States of
the European Community. Italy / Les conditions de travail
des femmes salariées dans les six États membres de la
Communauté européenne. Italie].
Commission, 1972.   186p.
I   V/167/73

147 BIERMA, J.
Population and employment 1968–1972 (Population et
emploi 1968–1972).
In Social statistics, 2/1973.   Eurostat, 1974.   168p.
D/E/F   6310

148 BIGI, F.
Production and marketing of bananas from the Associated
African States and Madagascar. Summary (La production
et l'écoulement des bananes originaires des États africains
et malgache associés. Synthèse).
Commission, 1972.   133p.   Studies: development aid
series, 4.
D E F I N   8346

BIHAN, J. le, *see* LE BIHAN, J.

149 BIKKER, F.
La production de produits animaux dans des entreprises à
grande capacité de la CEE. Nombre et formes dans le
secteur de l'engraissement de porcs, de veaux et de jeunes
bovins [The production of animal products in large scale
enterprises in the EEC. Number and types in the pig, calf
and store cattle fattening industry].
Commission, 1968.   158p.   Internal information on
agriculture, 23.
D F   11974/1/VI/67

150 BIKKER, F.
La spéculation ovine. 3: R.F. d'Allemagne, Pays-Bas
[Sheep specialization 3: F.R. of Germany, the
Netherlands].
Commission, 1973.   var. pag.   Internal information
on agriculture, 103.
D F   VI/1509/73

151 BILOTTI, E.
Méthodes de lutte intégrée et de lutte biologique en
agriculture. Conditions et possibilités de développement
[Methods of integrated and biological pest control in
agriculture. Conditions and possibilities for development].

Commission, 1975.   106p.   Internal information on
agriculture, 149.
D F   VI/1595/75

152 BLACKABY, F. T.
The United Kingdom economy [L'économie britannique].
Commission, 1975.   155p.   Studies: economic and
financial series, 9.
E   8461

153 BLANPAIN, H.
Les effectifs scolaires et universitaires dans les pays de la
Communauté [The school and university numbers in the
countries of the Community].
In Statistical studies and surveys, 3/1968.
Eurostat, 1968.   pp.178–297.
D/F/I/N   4515

154 BLANPAIN, H.
Labour costs in industry 1972–1975. Results of the
surveys of 1972 and 1973. Updating of the costs to 1975
(Coût de la main-d'œuvre dans l'industrie 1972–1975.
Résultats des enquêtes de 1972–1973. Actualisation des
coûts jusqu'en 1975).
In Social statistics, 6/1975.   Eurostat, 1976.   456p.
DK/D/E/F/I/N   6936/6

155 BLANPAIN, H.
Population et forces de travail. L'évolution de la
population et de la population active dans les pays de la
Communauté 1970–1980 [Population and labour forces.
The development of population and working population in
the countries of the Community 1970–1980].
In Social statistics, 4/1970.
Eurostat, 1970.   pp.1–59.
D/F/I/N   4930

156 BLANPAIN, H.
Population et forces de travail 1968 [Population and labour
forces 1968].
In Social statistics, 6/1969.   Eurostat, 1969.   355p.
D/F/I/N   4820

157 BLED, P.
Nouvelles formes de collaboration dans le domaine de la
production agricole. 5: France [New forms of cooperation
in the field of agricultural production, 5: France].
Commission, 1973.   514p.   Internal information on
agriculture, 118.
D F   VI/2511/72

158 BLOIS, J.
Premier seminaire pour cadres dirigeants de la formation
dans l'agriculture et en milieu rural. Rapport final [First
seminar for executivé officials about training in
agriculture and the rural environment. Final report].
Commission, 1970.   var. pag.
F

159 BLUME, F.
La formation des formateurs. Problèmes, méthodes et
expériences dans les industries de la C.E.C.A. [Training
of the trainers. Problems, methods and experiments in the
industries of the E.C.S.C.].
ECSC HA, 1962.   127p.
F   8514

160 BLUNDEN, K.
Étude sur l'évolution de la concentration dans l'industrie
pharmaceutique en France [A study of the evolution of
concentration in the pharmaceutical industry in France].
Commission, 1976.   126p.
F   8741

BO, D. del, *see* DEL BO, D.

161 BOBBA, F.
Rapport sur la capacité concurrentielle de la Communauté
européenne [Report on the competitive capacity of the
European Community].
Commission, 1972.   3 vols.
D F   II/481/72

162 BÖCKER, W.
Les investissements américains en Europe [American
investments in Europe].
ECSC HA, 1967.   40p.
F   13353

163 BOCHKOLTZ, F.
Possibilités d'industrialisation des États africains et
malgache associés. Volume 5: Madagascar [Possibilities
for the industrialization of the Associated African States
and Madagascar. Volume 5: Madagascar].
Commission EEC, 1966. 2 vols.
F   13081/VIII/B/66, 13082/VIII/B/66

164 BODDEZ, G.
Prévisions agricoles. 2: Possibilités d'utilisation de
certains modèles, méthodes et techniques dans la
Communauté [Agricultural forecasting. 2: Possibilities of
using certain models, methods and techniques in the
Community].
Commission, 1970.   249p.   Internal information on
agriculture, 63.
D F   8433/VI/69

165 BODDEZ, G.
Projections de la production et de la consommation de
produits agricoles—'1977'. 7: Belgique, Grand-Duché de
Luxembourg [Projections of production and consumption
of agricultural products—'1977'. 7: Belgium, Grand Duchy
of Luxembourg].
Commission, 1974.   199p.   Internal information on
agriculture, 134.
D F   VI/4822/71

166 BODDEZ, G.
Les tendances d'évolution des structures des exploitations
agricoles. Causes et motifs d'abandon et de
restructuration [Trends of development in farm
structures. Causes and reasons for desertion and
reconstruction].

Commission, 1967.   386p.   Internal information on
agriculture, 20.
D F   8159/VI/67

167 BOER, H. de
Étude sur les qualités des carcasses de bovins et porcins
dans les pays de la Communauté Économique Européenne
[Study on the qualities of beef and pork carcasses in the
countries of the European Economic Community].
Eurostat, 1966.   80p.   Agricultural statistics.
D/F   3944

168 BOES, W.
Le chômage et la main-d'œuvre sous-employée. Mise en
œuvre d'une méthode de recherche. Belgique
[Unemployment and underemployed manpower.
Implementing of a research method. Belgium].
Commission EEC, 1965.   176p.   Studies: social
policy series, 9.
D F I N   8135

169 BOISSEAU, J.
Comparative study on the rehabilitation of handicapped
persons in the countries of the Community. Legal,
administrative and technical aspects. Volume 1:
Introduction. Belgium. France. Italy. Luxembourg
[Étude comparative sur la réhabilitation des personnes
handicapées dans les pays de la Communauté. Aspects
juridiques, administratifs et techniques. Volume 1:
Introduction. Belgique. France. Italie. Luxembourg].
Commission, 1974.   207p.
E   3229/74

170 BÖKER, H.
La consommation des engrais dans les pays de la C.E.E.
[Fertilizer consumption in the countries of the E.E.C.].
Commission EEC, 1962.   119p.   Studies:
agricultural series, 8.
D F   8054

171 BOLDT, G.
Le contrat de travail dans le droit des pays membres de la
CECA [The employment contract in the law of the
member countries of the ECSC].
ECSC HA, 1966.   727p.   Collection: labour law.
D F I N   3568

172 BOLDT, G.
Grève et lock-out [Strike and lock-out].
ECSC HA, 1961.   399p.   Collection: labour law. 2:
Labour law in the Community, 5.
D F I N   2367

173 BOLDT, G.
La juridiction du travail et la juridiction de la sécurité
sociale dans les pays de la Communauté européenne
[Employment and social security jurisdiction in the
countries of the European Community].
Commission, 1972.   615p.   Collection: labour law.
D F I N   8341

174 BOLDT, G.
La protection des travailleurs en cas de perte de l'emploi
[Protection of workers in the event of loss of employment].
ECSC HA, 1961.   489p.   Collection: labour law. 2:
Labour law in the Community, 11.
D F I N   2626

175 BOLDT, G.
Le régime juridique des organisations professionnelles
dans les pays membres de la C.E.C.A. [Legal
administration of professional organisations in the
member countries of the E.C.S.C.].
ECSC HA, 1968.   666p.   Collection: labour law.
D F I N   13879

176 BOLDT, G.
La représentation des travailleurs sur le plan de
l'entreprise dans le droit des pays membres de la
C.E.C.A. [Workers' representation at management level
in the law of the member countries of the E.C.S.C.].

ECSC HA, 1959.   348p.   Collection: labour law, 3.
D F I N   2104

176A BOLDT, G.
Les sources du droit du travail [Sources of labour law].
ECSC HA, 1962.   192p.   Collection: labour law.
2: Labour law in the Community, 1.
D F I N   2773

177 BOLDT, G.
La stabilité de l'emploi dans le droit des pays membres de
la C.E.C.A. [Stability of employment in the law of the
member countries of the E.C.S.C.].
ECSC HA, 1958.   311p.   Collection: labour law, 2.
D F I N   1999

178 BOLOPION, R.
Volume et degré de l'emploi dans la pêche maritime
[Volume and extent of employment in sea fishing].
Commission, 1968.   var. pag.   Internal information
on agriculture, 32.
D F   6993/VI/68

179 BOMBACH, G.
Critères à la base de la fixation des salaires et problèmes
qui y sont liés pour une politique des salaires et des
revenus [Criteria at the basis for the fixing of wages and
problems connected for a wages and incomes policy].
Commission, 1967.   98p.   Studies: social policy
series, 19.
D F I N   8227

180 BONACCI, G.
Les échanges indirects d'acier de la Communauté.
Analyse rétrospective 1955–1966 [Indirect trade of steel of
the Community. Retrospective analysis 1955–1966].
In Statistical studies and surveys, 3/1969.
Eurostat, 1969.   94p.
D/F   4764

181 BONETTI, M.
Forms of cooperation in the fishing industry. Denmark,
Ireland, United Kingdom [Formes de coopération dans le
secteur de la pêche. Danemark, Irlande, Royaume-Uni].
Commission, 1976.   var. pag.   Information on
agriculture, 9.
E   8842

182 BONETY, R.
Community nuclear safety code. Study (Code com-
munautaire de sécurité nucléaire. Étude).
ESC, 1977.   48p.
DK D E F I N

182A BONJER, F.
Aide-mémoire pour la pratique des épreuves d'exercice en
médecine du travail [Manual for the practice of exercise
tests in industrial medicine].
Commission, 1971.   49p.   Collection: industrial
health and medicine, 12.
D F I N   16741

183 BONN, F.
Economic and monetary union (L'union économique et
monétaire).
In Information: economy and finance 43/1973.
Pr Inf, 1973.   23p.
D E F I N   BG 43-73

184 BONNET, P.
Problèmes des huileries d'olive. Contribution à l'étude de
leur rationalisation [Problems of olive oil refineries.
Contribution to the study of their rationalization].
Commission, 1971.   132p.   Internal information on
agriculture, 78.
F I   VI/1633/71

185 BONNET, R.
The effects of the reduction of manpower in the mining
industry on mining social security systems and pension
systems in particular (Les effets des réductions d'effectifs

dans l'industrie charbonnière sur les régimes de sécurité
sociale des mines et spécialement sur les régimes de
pension).
Commission, 1973.   94p.   Studies: social policy
series, 23.
D E F I N   8410

186 BONNET, R.
Practical handbook of social security for employed persons
and their families moving within the Community
(Répertoire pratique de la sécurité sociale des travailleurs
salariés et de leurs familles qui se déplacent à l'intérieur
de la Communauté).
Commission, 1975.   loose-leaf.
DK D E F I N   8443

187 BONNET, R.
Practical handbook of social security for employed persons
and their families moving within the Community. Revised
as at 1 January 1975 (Répertoire pratique de la sécurité
sociale des travailleurs salariés et de leurs familles qui se
déplacent à l'intérieur de la Communauté. Mise à jour au
1er janvier 1975).
Commission, 1976.   loose-leaf.
DK D E F I N   8443

188 BORNARD, J.
Rapports sur les premières mesures proposées en vue
d'une coordination des politiques énergétiques [Reports
on the first measures proposed for a coordination of
energy policies].
ECSC CC, 1961.   var. pag.
D F I N   8013

189 BOS, C.
Prévisions agricoles. 2: Possibilités d'utilisation de
certains modèles, méthodes et techniques dans la
Communauté [Agricultural forecasting. 2: Possibilities of
using certain models, methods and techniques in the
Community].

Commission, 1970.   249p.   Internal information on agriculture, 63.
D F   8433/VI/69

190 BOS, C.
Projections de la production et de la consommation de produits agricoles—'1977'. 5: Pays-Bas [Projections of production and consumption of agricultural products—'1977'. 5: The Netherlands].
Commission, 1974.   76p.   Internal information on agriculture, 128.
D F   VI/3721/74

191 BOUBLI, B.
L'apprentissage en France [Apprenticeships in France].
Commission, 1976.   108p.   Studies: social policy series, 29.
F   CB-NN-76-029-FR-C

192 BOULET, D.
Étude sur l'évolution de la concentration dans l'industrie des spiritueux en France [A study of the evolution of concentration in the spirits industry in France].
Commission, 1977.   163p.
F   8751

193 BOULET, D.
Étude sur l'évolution de la concentration dans les industries des boissons et des boissons non alcoolisées en France [A study of the evolution of concentration in the beverages and soft drinks industries in France].
Commission, 1977.   284p.
F   8768

194 BOULET, D.
L'évolution de la concentration dans l'industrie de la brasserie en France [The evolution of concentration in the brewing industry in France].
Commission, 1976.   99p.
F   8705

195 BOULET, D.
L'évolution de la concentration dans l'industrie des
champagnes et mousseux en France [The evolution of
concentration in the champagne and sparkling wines
industry in France].
Commission, 1977.   127p.
F   8752

196 BOUQUIAUX, J.
Non-organic micropollutants of the environment [Les
micro-pollutants non-organiques de l'environnement].
Commission, 1974.   4 vols.
E   V/F/1966/74

197 BOUREL, F.
Progress report on the Common Agricultural Policy.
Study (Bilan de la politique agricole commune. Étude).
ESC, 1975.   47p.
DK D E F I N   7112

198 BOUREL, F.
The situation of small and medium-sized undertakings in
the European Community. Study (La situation des petites
et moyennes entreprises dans la Communauté
européenne. Étude).
ESC, 1976.   66p.
DK D E F I N   6688

199 BOURRIER, A.
Le rôle des ports de la Communauté pour le trafic de
céréales et de farines. 1: Synthèse pour les principaux
ports français et italiens [List of Community ports for the
cereals and flour trade. 1: Summary for the chief French
and Italian ports].
Commission, 1974.   var. pag.   Internal information
on agriculture, 122.
F   VI/2941/73

200 BOURRIER, A.
Le rôle des ports de la Communauté pour le trafic de
céréales et de farines. 2: Monographies pour les principaux

ports français de la Manche [List of Community ports for the cereals and flour trade. 2: Monographs for the chief French Channel ports].
Commission, 1974.   var. pag.   Internal information on agriculture, 123.
F   VI/1169/74

201 BOURRIER, A.
Le rôle des ports de la Communauté pour le trafic de céréales et de farines. 3: Monographies pour les principaux ports français de l'Atlantique [List of Community ports for the cereals and flour trade. 3: Monographs for the chief French Atlantic ports].
Commission, 1974.   var. pag.   Internal information on agriculture, 124.
F   VI/1263/74

202 BOURRIER, A.
Le rôle des ports de la Communauté pour le trafic de céréales et de farines. 4: Monographies pour les principaux ports français de la Méditerranée [List of Community ports for the cereals and flour trade. 4: Monographs for the chief French Mediterranean ports].
Commission, 1974.   var. pag.   Internal information on agriculture, 125.
F   VI/1264/74

203 BOURRIER, A.
Le rôle des ports de la Communauté pour le trafic de céréales et de farines. 5: Monographies pour les principaux ports italiens de la Côte Ouest [List of Community ports for the cereals and flour trade. 5: Monographs for the chief Italian West Coast ports].
Commission, 1974.   var. pag.   Internal information on agriculture, 126.
F   VI/1265/74

204 BOURRIER, A.
Le rôle des ports de la Communauté pour le trafic de céréales et de farines. 6: Monographies pour les principaux ports italiens de la Côte Est [List of Community ports for

the cereals and flour trade. 6: Monographs for the chief
Italian East Coast ports].
Commission, 1974.   var. pag.   Internal information
on agriculture, 127.
F   VI/1266/74

205 BOURS, E.
Rapport sur l'application de la TVA aux opérations
immobilières au sein de la Communauté [Report on the
application of VAT to real estate operations within the
Community].
Commission, 1975.   157p.   Studies: competition–
approximation of legislation series, 21.
D F I N   8433

206 BOUTHOORN, T. M.
Tableaux 'Entrées-Sorties' pour les pays de la
Communauté Économique Européenne ['Input-Output'
tables for the countries of the European Economic
Community].
Eurostat, 1964.   var. pag.
D F

207 BOUTHOORN, T. M.
Tableaux 'Entrées-Sorties' pour les pays de la
Communauté Économique Européenne. Seconde version
['Input-Output' tables for the countries of the European
Economic Community. Second version].
Eurostat, 1965.   var. pag.
D F

208 BOUTONNET, J. P.
La spéculation ovine. 2: France, Belgique [Sheep
specialization. 2: France, Belgium].
Commission, 1973.   185p.   Internal information on
agriculture, 99.
D F   VI/734/73

209 BRAAM, A. van
Enquête sur les budgets familiaux aux Pays-Bas [Survey
on family budgets in the Netherlands].

In Budgets familiaux 1963/64. Nederland.   Eurostat,
1966.   pp.25–173.   Social statistics special series, 3.
F

210 BRADBEER, J.
Energy in the EEC [L'énergie dans la CEE].
In European studies. Teachers' series, 18.
Commission(L), 1974.   4p.
E   U/74/18

211 BRADER, L.
Méthodes de lutte intégrée et de lutte biologique en
agriculture. Conditions et possibilités de développement
[Methods of integrated and biological pest control in
agriculture. Conditions and possibilities for development].
Commission, 1975.   106p.   Internal information on
agriculture, 149.
D F   VI/1595/75

212 BRADER, L.
Modalités pratiques d'application de méthodes de lutte
intégrée [Practical means for the application of méthods
of integrated pest control].
Commission, 1977.   154p.   Information on
agriculture, 24.
F   8879

213 BRAINE
Essai d'appréciation des conditions d'application et des
résultats d'une politique de réforme en agriculture dans
des régions agricoles difficiles. 2: Queyras [Attempt at
estimating the conditions from the application and results
of a reform policy in agriculture in difficult agricultural
regions. 2: Queyras].
Commission, 1975.   var. pag.   Internal information
on agriculture, 150.
F   VI/1988/75

214 BRANDINI, M.
Critères à la base de la fixation des salaires et problèmes
qui y sont liés pour une politique des salaires et des

revenus [Criteria at the basis for the fixing of wages and
problems connected for a wages and incomes policy].
Commission, 1967.   98p.   Studies: social policy
series, 19.
D F I N   8227

215 BRÄNDLI, P.
Report on the First Preliminary Draft of the Rules
relating to Fees (Rapport concernant le premier
Avant-projet de Règlement relatif aux taxes).
In Reports on the Second preliminary draft of a convention
establishing a European system for the grant of patents.
Council, 1971.   pp.91–92.
D/E/F   17275-B

216 BRANDTNER, E.
Carte de la durée de la période de végétation dans les
États membres des Communautés européennes [Map of
the duration of the vegetation period in the Member
States of the European Communities].
Commission, 1976.   17p.   Information on
agriculture, 5.
D F   8839

217 BRAUN, W.
La concentration des entreprises [The concentration of
firms].
In Documentation européenne. Série syndicale et
ouvrière, 1/1974.   Pr Inf, 1974.   4p.
D F I N   S/74/1

218 BREGONZIO, E.
Possibilités de création d'industries exportatrices dans les
États africains et malgache associés. Production
sidérurgique [Possibilities for the establishment of
exporting industries in the Associated African States and
Madagascar. Iron and steel production].
Commission, 1975.   3 vols.
F   VIII/228/74

219 BREGONZIO, E.
Possibilités de création d'industries exportatrices dans les
États africains et malgache associés. La production
sidérurgique. Pelletisation du minerai de fer et
électro-sidérurgie. Ferro-alliages (ferro-silicium,
-manganèse et -nickel). Rapport de synthèse [Possibilities
for the establishment of exporting industries in the
Associated African States and Madagascar. Iron and steel
production. Pelletisation of iron ore and electro-siderurgy.
Ferro-alloys (ferro-silicon, -manganese and -nickel).
Summary report].
Commission, 1975.   40p.
D E F I N   VIII/228/74

220 BREGUET, P.E., chairman
Le financement public de la recherche et du
développement dans les pays de la Communauté. Analyse
par objectifs 1967–1970 [Public expenditure on Research
and Development in the countries of the Community.
Analysis by objectives 1967–1970].
In Statistical studies and surveys, 2/1970.
Eurostat, 1970.   var. pag.
D/F   5048

221 BREGUET, P. E.
Le financement public de la recherche et du
développement dans les pays de la Communauté. Analyse
par objectifs 1967–1971 [Public expenditure on Research
and Development in the countries of the Community.
Analysis by objectives 1967–1971].
In Statistical studies and surveys, 2/1971.
Eurostat, 1971.   var. pag.
D/F   5510

222 BREITENACHER, M.
Possibilités de création d'industries exportatrices dans les
États africains et malgache associés. Produits de
l'élevage. Viandes, cuirs et peaux, chaussures, articles en
cuirs [Possibilities for the establishment of exporting
industries in the Associated African States and

Madagascar. Products from rearing. Meat, hides and
skins, shoes, leather articles].
Commission, 1974.   5 vols.
F   VIII/223/74

223 BREITENACHER, M.
Possibilités de création d'industries exportatrices dans les
États africains et malgache associés. Produits de
l'élevage. Viandes, cuirs et peaux, chaussures, articles en
cuir. Rapport de synthèse [Possibilities for the
establishment of exporting industries in the Associated
African States and Madagascar. Products from rearing.
Meat, hides and skins, shoes, leather articles. Summary
report].
Commission, 1975.   27p.
D E F I N   VIII/223/74

224 BREITENACHER, M.
Untersuchung zur Konzentrationsentwicklung in
ausgewählten Branchen und Produktgruppen der
Ernährungsindustrie in Deutschland [A study of the
evolution of concentration in selected lines and product
groups in the food industry in Germany / Étude sur
l'évolution de la concentration dans quelques branches et
les groupes de produit de l'industrie alimentaire en
Allemagne].
Commission, 1977.   331p.
D   8769

225 BREITENACHER, M.
Untersuchung zur Konzentrationsentwicklung in der
Getränke-Industrie in Deutschland [A study of the
evolution of concentration in the beverages industry in
Germany / Étude sur l'évolution de la concentration dans
l'industrie des boissons en Allemagne].
Commission, 1977.   156p.
D   8759

226 BRELOH, P.
Le marché foncier et les baux ruraux. Effets des mesures
de réforme des structures agricoles. 2: R.F. d'Allemagne,

France [The land market and rural leases. Effects of
reform measures of agricultural structures. 2: F.R. of
Germany, France].
Commission, 1972.   var. pag.   Internal information
on agriculture, 82.
F   VI/537/72

227 BREYNE, P.
Educational leave in Member States (Les congés culturels
dans les États membres).
Commission, 1977.   416p.   Studies: social policy
series, 26.
D E F I N   CH-SN-76-026-EN-C

228 BROCKHAUS, A.
Le travail de la soudure. Monographie des aspects
technologiques et pathologiques [Suture work.
Monograph of technological and pathological aspects].
Commission, 1969.   88p.   Collection: industrial
health and medicine, 9.
D F I N   4613

229 BROUWER, M.
A study of the evolution of concentration in the Dutch
beverages industry [Étude sur l'évolution de la
concentration dans l'industrie des boissons aux Pays-Bas].
Commission, 1977.   149p.
E   8764

230 BROUWER, W. J. C.
A study of the evolution of concentration in the Dutch
paper products industry [Étude sur l'évolution de la
concentration dans l'industrie des articles en papier aux
Pays-Bas].
Commission, 1977.   89p.
E   8765

231 BROVELLI, F.
Crédits à l'agriculture. 3: Italie [Credit to agriculture. 3:
Italy].

Commission, 1976.   155p.   Information on
agriculture, 3.
F I   8833

232 BROWN, A. J.
The United Kingdom economy [L'économie britannique].
Commission, 1975.   155p.   Studies: economic and
financial series, 9.
E   8461

233 BRUGHIERA
La formation professionnelle dans l'industrie sidérurgique
des pays de la Communauté [Vocational training in the
iron and steel industry of the countries of the
Community].
ECSC HA, 1954.   264p.
F

234 BRUN, A.
Surfaces agricoles pouvant être mobilisées pour une
réforme de structure [Agricultural areas that could be
mobilised for a structural reform].
Commission, 1973.   336p.   Internal information on
agriculture, 77.
D F   VI/14453/69

BRUN, O. le, *see* LE BRUN, O.

235 BRUNNÉE, H.
La conduite sur place des opérations de conversion
industrielle [On-the-spot direction of industrial conversion
operations].
ECSC HA, 1963.   352p.   Collection: regional
economy and policy. 1: Industrial conversion in Europe, 4.
D F I N   3324

236 BRUNNER, G.
Address delivered to the Parliamentary and Scientific
Committee in London on 19 October 1976 by Dr. Guido
Brunner [Discours prononcé par Dr. Guido Brunner,

devant le Comité parlementaire et scientifique à Londres,
le 19 octobre 1976].
In Information: research policy, 140/1976.
Pr Inf, 1976.   11p.
E   X/693/76

237 BRUTON, R.
The Irish economy [L'économie irlandaise].
Commission, 1975.   168p.   Studies: economic and
financial series, 10.
E   8462

238 BRUYN, J. de
European Union. Opinion (Union européenne. Avis).
ESC, 1975.   33p.
DK D E F I N   6937

239 BUBLOT, G.
Tendances de la production et de la consommation en
denrées alimentaires dans la C.E.E. 1956–1965 [Trends in
food production and consumption in the E.E.C.
1956–1965].
Commission EEC, 1960.   266p.   Studies:
agricultural series, 2.
D F I N   8005

240 BUES
Dispositions pour faciliter la création d'activités nouvelles.
Dispositions juridiques et financières en vigueur dans les
États membres et le Royaume-Uni [Arrangements to
facilitate the establishment of new activities. Legal and
financial arrangements in force in the Member States and
United Kingdom].
ECSC HA, 1959.   loose-leaf.
D F I N   2275

241 BUIATTI, P. G.
Étude sur les qualités des carcasses de bovins en Italie
[Study on the qualities of beef carcasses in Italy].
In Agricultural statistical studies, 7.
Eurostat, 1970.   52p.
D F I   16843

242 BUITER, H., chairman
Readaptation and re-employment of workers. Report on
the visit to the United States by a team of trade-union
representatives from the Community [Réadaptation et
réemploi des travailleurs. Rapport sur la visite faite aux
États-Unis par l'équipe des représentants de syndicat de
la Communauté].
ECSC, 1956. 149p. Studies and documents.
D E F I N 1724

243 BÜLOW, A., chairman
Avant-projet de convention concernant la compétence
judiciaire, la reconnaissance et l'exécution des décisions en
matière civile et commerciale et l'exécution des actes
authentiques. Texte adopté par les experts
gouvernementaux lors de la quinzième réunion plénière,
tenue à Bruxelles du 7 au 11 décembre 1964 sous la
présidence de M. le professeur A. Bülow, secrétaire
d'État au ministère de la justice de la république fédérale
d'Allemagne [Draft convention on jurisdiction, recognition
and enforcement of judgments in civil and commercial
matters and the enforcement of instruments. Text
adopted by government experts when at the 15th full
meeting, held in Brussels from 7 to 11 December 1964
under the chairmanship of Professor A. Bülow, Secretary
of State in the Ministry of Justice of the Federal Republic
of Germany].
Commission EEC, 1964. 30p.
F 14371

244 BÜLOW, A., chairman
Report on the Convention on jurisdiction and the
enforcement of judgments in civil and commercial matters
(Rapport sur la Convention concernant la compétence
judiciaire et l'exécution des décisions en matière civile et
commerciale).
In Bulletin of the European Communities. Supplement,
12/1972. Council and Commission, 1972. 113p.
D E F I N 4001/S/12/72

245 BUREAU
Essai d'appréciation des conditions d'application et des
résultats d'une politique de réforme en agriculture dans
des régions agricoles difficiles. 1: Morvan [Attempt at
estimating the conditions from the application and results
of a reform policy in agriculture in difficult agricultural
regions. 1: Morvan].
Commission, 1974.   183p.   Internal information on
agriculture, 138.
F   VI/4572/74

246 BURNS, L.
Localisation et aménagement de terrains industriels. 1re
partie: Expériences dans les pays de la Communauté
européenne, en Grande-Bretagne et aux États-Unis. 2e
partie: Complexes industriels planifiés aux États-Unis
[Selection and planning of industrial sites. Part 1:
Experiments in the countries of the European
Community, in Great Britain and in the United States.
Part 2: Planned industrial complexes in the United
States].
ECSC HA, 1966–1967.   2 vols.   Collection: regional
economy and policy. 1: Industrial conversion in Europe, 7.
D F I N   3693

247 BUSCH, W.
Standardisation des produits horticoles non comestibles
[Standardization of inedible horticultural products].
Commission EEC, 1967.   215p.   Studies:
agricultural series, 23.
D F I N   8178

248 BUTTERWICK, M.
Vertical integration and the use of contracts in
agriculture. 4: Synoptic summary [Intégration verticale et
contrats en agriculture. 4: Aperçu synoptique].
Commission, 1975.   117p.   Internal information on
agriculture, 145.
E F   VI/1590/75

249 BUWALDA, G.
Enquête sur les budgets familiaux aux Pays-Bas [Survey
on family budgets in the Netherlands].
In Budgets familiaux 1963/64. Nederland.
Eurostat, 1966.   pp.25–173.   Social statistics:
special series, 3.
F

250 BUYSE, R.
Budgets familiaux 1963/64. Résultats pour la
Communauté [Family budgets 1963/64. Results for the
Community].
Eurostat, 1967.   257p.   Social statistics: special
series, 7.
D/F, I/N   4233

251 BUYSE, R.
Les diplômés et les enseignants dans les pays de la
Communauté [Graduates and teachers in the countries of
the Community].
In Social statistics, 3/1969.   Eurostat, 1969.
pp.1–165.
D/F/I/N   4691

252 BUYSE, R.
Les effectifs scolaires et universitaires dans les pays de la
Communauté [The school and university numbers in the
countries of the Community].
In Statistical studies and surveys, 3/1968.
Eurostat, 1968.   pp.178–297.
D/F/I/N   4515

253 BYÉ, M.
Expériences de conversion industrielle [Experiments in
industrial conversion].
ECSC HA, 1960.   34p.   Intergovernmental
Conference on Industrial Redevelopment: general report.
F   5319

254 BYÉ, M.
Voies et moyens de la conversion industrielle [Ways and
means of industrial conversion].

ECSC HA, 1961.   136p.   Collection: regional
economy and policy. 1: Industrial conversion in Europe, 2.
F   2775

255 CACCURI, S.
Le travail de la soudure. Monographie des aspects
technologiques et pathologiques [Suture work.
Monograph of technological and pathological aspects].
Commission, 1969.   88p.   Collection: industrial
health and medicine, 9.
D F I N   4613

256 CADILLAT, R. M.
L'agrumiculture dans les pays du Bassin méditerranéen.
Production, commerce, débouchés [Citrus cultivation in
the countries of the Mediterranean Basin. Production,
trade, markets].
Commission, 1967.   320p.   Internal information on
agriculture, 22.
D F   8740/3/VI/66

CAEN, G. Lyon-, *see* LYON-CAEN, G.

257 CALEMBERT, J.
Conséquences écologiques de l'application des techniques
modernes de production en agriculture [Ecological results
from the application of modern production techniques in
agriculture].
Commission, 1974.   var. pag.   Internal information
on agriculture, 137.
D F   VI/3722/74

258 CALISSANO, F.
The aeronautical and space industries of the Community
compared with those of the United Kingdom and the
United States (Les industries aéronautiques et spatiales
de la Communauté, comparées à celles de la
Grande-Bretagne et des États-Unis).
Commission, 1971.   5 vols.   Studies: industry
series, 4.
D E F I N   8284

259 CALISSANO, F.
Evoluzione della concentrazione dal 1962 al 1969 in alcuni
settori dell'industria italiana. Metodologia [Evolution of
concentration in various sectors of Italian industry from
1962 to 1969. Methodology / L'évolution de la
concentration dans quelques secteurs de l'industrie
italienne de 1962 à 1969. Méthodologie].
Commission, 1973.   24p.
I   IV/344/73

260 CALISSANO, F.
Les industries aéronautiques et spatiales de la
Communauté, comparées à celles de la Grande-Bretagne
et des États-Unis. Annexe au Rapport Général [The
aeronautical and space industries of the Community
compared with those of the United Kingdom and the
United States. Appendix to General Report].
Commission, 1969.   10 vols.
F

261 CALISSANO, F.
Studio sull'evoluzione della concentrazione in alcuni settori
dell'industria tessile in Italia. Lana (NICE 232). Cotone
(NICE 233). Maglieria e calzetteria (NICE 237) [A study
of the evolution of concentration in various sectors of the
textile industry in Italy. Wool (NICE 232). Cotton (NICE
233). Knitted and crocheted goods (NICE 237) / Étude sur
l'évolution de la concentration dans quelques secteurs de
l'industrie du textile en Italie. Laine (NICE 232). Coton
(NICE 233). Bonneterie (NICE 237)].
Commission, 1973.   var. pag.
I   IV/347/73

262 CALISSANO, F.
Studio sull'evoluzione della concentrazione in Italia
dell'industria della carta e della sua trasformazione. Carta
(NICE 271). Cartotecnica (NICE 272) [A study of the
evolution of concentration in the paper and paper products
industry in Italy. Paper (NICE 271). Paper processing
(NICE 272) / Étude sur l'évolution de la concentration de
l'industrie du papier et des articles en papier en Italie.

Papier (NICE 271). Transformation du papier (NICE 272)].
Commission, 1973.   103p.
I   IV/348/73

263 CALLIER, C.
Projections de la production et de la consommation de produits agricoles—'1977'. 7: Belgique, Grand-Duché de Luxembourg [Projections of production and consumption of agricultural products—'1977'. 7: Belgium, Grand Duchy of Luxembourg].
Commission, 1974.   199p.   Internal information on agriculture, 134.
D F   VI/4822/71

264 CAMAGNI, R.
Analisi generale della concentrazione industriale in Italia dalla costituzione del Mercato Comune (1959–1968). Gli indici di concentrazione impiegati nella ricerca [General analysis of industrial concentration in Italy from the formation of the Common Market (1959–1968). Concentration indices used in the research / L'analyse générale de la concentration industrielle en Italie de la constitution du Marché commun (1959–1968). Les indices de concentration utilisés dans la recherche].
Commission, 1973.   34p.
I   IV/345/73

265 CAMAGNI, R.
Studio sull'evoluzione della concentrazione industriale in Italia (1968–1974). Pneumatici. Candele. Accumulatori [A study of the evolution of industrial concentration in Italy (1968–1974). Tyres. Sparking plugs. Batteries / Étude sur l'évolution de la concentration industrielle en Italie (1968–1974). Pneumatiques. Bougies. Accumulateurs].
Commission, 1976.   341p.
I   8750

266 CAMAGNI, R.
Studio sull'evoluzione della concentrazione nell'industria della costruzione elettrica in Italia. Costruzione di

apparecchiature elettroniche ed elettroacustiche e di
apparecchi radio e televisivi (NICE 375). Costruzione di
apparecchi elettrodomestici (NICE 376) [A study of the
evolution of concentration in the electrical engineering
industry in Italy. Manufacture of electronic and audio
equipment and radio and television receivers (NICE 375).
Manufacture of electrical domestic appliances (NICE 376)
/ Étude sur l'évolution de la concentration dans l'industrie
de la construction électrique en Italie. Construction
d'appareils électroniques, radios, télévision,
électro-acoustique (NICE 375). Fabrication d'appareils
électrodomestiques (NICE 376)].
Commission, 1974.   109p.
I   IV/189/74

267 CAMAGNI, R.
Studio sull'evoluzione della concentrazione nell'industria
della costruzione elettrica in Italia (1970–1974).
Costruzione di apparecchi elettrodomestici (NICE 376).
Costruzione di apparecchiature elettroniche ed
elettroacustiche e di apparecchi radio e televisivi (NICE
375) [A study of the evolution of concentration in the
electrical engineering industry in Italy (1970–1974).
Manufacture of electrical domestic appliances (NICE 376).
Manufacture of electronic and audio equipment and radio
and television receivers (NICE 375) / Étude sur
l'évolution de la concentration dans l'industrie de la
construction électrique en Italie. Fabrication d'appareils
électrodomestiques (NICE 376). Construction d'appareils
électroniques, radios, télévision, électro-acoustique
(NICE 375)].
Commission, 1975.   236p.
I   8746

268 CAMAGNI, R.
Studio sull'evoluzione della concentrazione nell'industria
di cicli, motocicli e ciclomotori in Italia 1970–1972 [A study
of the evolution of concentration in the cycles, motorcycles
and power-assisted cycles industry in Italy 1970–1972 /
Étude sur l'évolution de la concentration dans l'industrie

des cycles, motocycles et cyclomoteurs en Italie
1970–1972].
Commission, 1975.   87p.
I   8699

269 CAMERLYNCK, G. H.
Le contrat de travail dans le droit des pays membres de la
CECA [The employment contract in the law of the
member countries of the ECSC].
ECSC HA, 1966.   727p.   Collection: labour law.
D F I N   3568

270 CAMERLYNCK, G. H.
La juridiction du travail et la juridiction de la sécurité
sociale dans les pays de la Communauté européenne
[Employment and social security jurisdiction in the
countries of the European Community].
Commission, 1972.   615p.   Collection: labour law.
D F I N   8341

271 CAMPOLONGO, A.
The European Investment Bank and redevelopment [La
Banque européenne d'investissement et la reconversion].
ECSC HA, 1960.   2p.   Intergovernmental
Conference on Industrial Redevelopment: report of the
European Investment Bank.
E   3914

272 CAMPOLONGO, A.
Le financement des investissements et les aspects sociaux
de la reconversion [Financing of investments and social
aspects of conversion].
ECSC HA, 1963.   255p.   Collection: regional
economy and policy. 1: Industrial conversion in Europe, 3.
D F I N   3323

273 CAMY, P.
Arrangements to facilitate the establishment of new
economic activities. Legal and financial arrangements in
force in the member states of the Community and the
United Kingdom (Dispositions pour faciliter la création

d'activités nouvelles. Dispositions juridiques et financières
en vigueur dans les États membres et le Royaume-Uni).
ECSC HA, 1962.   loose-leaf.
D E F I N   3019

274 CAMY, P.
La politique de reconversion industrielle du Grand-Duché
de Luxembourg [Industrial conversion policy of the Grand
Duchy of Luxembourg].
ECSC HA, 1960.   8p.   Intergovernmental
Conference on Industrial Redevelopment: Luxembourg
national report.
F   5025

275 CAMY, P.
Les politiques nationales de développement régional et de
conversion [National policies of regional development and
conversion].
ECSC HA, 1961.   195p.   Collection: regional
economy and policy. 1: Industrial conversion in Europe, 1.
F   2626

276 CANCELIER
Les conditions d'installation d'entreprises industrielles
dans les États africains et malgache associés. Volume 4:
République du Mali [Conditions for the setting-up of
industrial undertakings in the Associated African States
and Madagascar. Volume 4: Republic of Mali].
Commission, 1975.   97p.
F   VIII/1252/74

277 CANCELIER
Les conditions d'installation d'entreprises industrielles
dans les États africains et malgache associés. Volume 5:
République islamique de Mauritanie [Conditions for the
setting-up of industrial undertakings in the Associated
African States and Madagascar. Volume 5: Islamic
Republic of Mauritania]; 2nd ed.
Commission, 1975.   112p.
F   VIII/1254/74

278 CANCELIER
Les conditions d'installation d'entreprises industrielles
dans les États africains et malgache associés. Volume 18:
République du Sénégal [Conditions for the setting-up of
industrial undertakings in the Associated African States
and Madagascar. Volume 18: Republic of Senegal]; 2nd ed.
Commission, 1975.   111p.
F   VIII/1257/74

279 CANGUILHEM, A.
Étude de l'harmonisation des statistiques bovines des
États membres de la Communauté. Étude 1: Description
de la situation en France et en Italie [Study of the
harmonization of beef statistics in the Member States of
the Community. Study 1: Description of the situation in
France and Italy].
In Agricultural statistical studies, 12.
Eurostat, 1974.   197p.
D F   18026

280 CANNAS, M. D.
Possibilités d'industrialisation des États africains et
malgache associés. Volume 3: République démocratique
du Congo [Possibilities for the industrialization of the
Associated African States and Madagascar. Volume 3:
Democratic Republic of the Congo].
Commission EEC, 1966.   2 vols.
F   13077/VIII/B/66, 13078/VIII/B/66

281 CANONICI, A.
Les aciéries [The steel-works].
Commission, 1971.   283p.   New technical processes
in the iron and steel industry: a personal training manual,
3. Studies: vocational training.
D F I N   17433

282 CANONICI, A.
Les laminoirs [The rolling mills].
Commission, 1972.   240p.   New technical processes
in the iron and steel industry: a personal training manual,
4. Studies: vocational training.
D F I N   8349

283 CANONICI, A.
Mécanisation, automatisation et techniques de mesure
dans les services des hauts fourneaux [Mechanisation,
automation and measurement techniques in
blast-furnace works].
Commission, 1969.   172p.   New technical processes
in the iron and steel industry: a personal training manual,
2. Studies: vocational training.
D F I N   14722

284 CANONICI, A.
La technique de mesure et de l'automation [Measurement
and automation technique].
ECSC HA, 1967.   204p.   New technical processes in
the iron and steel industry: a personal training manual, 1.
Studies: vocational training.
D F I N   13233

285 CAO-PINNA, V.
Tableaux 'Entrées-Sorties' pour les pays de la
Communauté Économique Européenne ['Input-Output'
tables for the countries of the European Economic
Community].
Eurostat, 1964.   var. pag.
D F

286 CAO-PINNA, V.
Tableaux 'Entrées-Sorties' pour les pays de la
Communauté Économique Européenne. Seconde version
['Input-Output' tables for the countries of the European
Economic Community. Second version].
Eurostat, 1965.   var. pag.
D F

287 CAO-PINNA, A.
Tendances de la production et de la consommation en
denrées alimentaires dans la C.E.E. 1956–1965 [Trends in
food production and consumption in the E.E.C.
1956–1965].
Commission EEC, 1960.   266p.   Studies:
agricultural series, 2.
D F I N   8005

288 CAPRIO, I.
Enlarging the Community (Rapport d'information sur
l'élargissement de la Communauté).
ESC, 1970.   12p.
D E F I N   16682

288A CARA, M.
Aide-mémoire pour la pratique des épreuves d'exercice en
médecine du travail [Manual for the practice of exercise
tests in industrial medicine].
Commission, 1971.   49p.   Collection: industrial
health and medicine, 12.
D F I N   16741

289 CARAYON
Effets du prix et du revenu sur la consommation des
boissons dans les États membres des Communautés
[Effects of price and income on the consumption of
beverages in the Member States of the Communities].
Commission, 1973.   var. pag.   Studies:
competition–approximation of legislation series, 19.
D F I N   8380

290 CARBALLO, J.
Environmental problems of city centres [Les problèmes
d'environnement des centres de cité].
Commission, 1976.   88p.
E

291 CAREW, A.
Shop-floor trade unionism in Western Europe [Le
syndicalisme du tablier d'atelier dans l'Europe
occidentale].
In European studies. Teachers' series, 18.
Commission(L), 1974.   4p.
E   U/74/18

292 CAROSIO, G. B.
La reconversion dans l'industrie charbonnière et
sidérurgique en Italie [Conversion in the coal and iron and
steel industry in Italy].

Commission, 1973.   69p.   Pamphlets on industrial
conversion, 21.
D F I N   8388

293 CARRANTE, V.
Économie de la production, transformation, et
consommation du blé dur dans la CEE [Economics of the
production, processing and consumption of durum wheat
in the EEC].
Commission EEC, 1965.   233p.   Studies:
agricultural series, 18.
D F I N   8138

294 CARSTAIRS, E. J. C.
Report on the economic law of the United Kingdom
(Rapport sur le droit économique du Royaume-Uni).
Commission, 1976.   134p.   Studies:
competition–approximation of legislation series, 20/5.
D E F   8429

295 CARTA
La formation professionnelle dans les houillères des pays
de la Communauté [Vocational training in the coal mines
of the countries of the Community].
ECSC HA, 1956.   514p.
F   1669

296 CARTA, M.
Le financement des investissements et les aspects sociaux
de la reconversion [Financing of investments and social
aspects of conversion].
ECSC HA, 1963.   255p.   Collection: regional
economy and policy. 1: Industrial conversion in Europe, 3.
D F I N   3323

297 CARTON, P.
Le financement des investissements et les aspects sociaux
de la reconversion [Financing of investments and social
aspects of conversion].
ECSC HA, 1963.   255p.   Collection: regional
economy and policy. 1: Industrial conversion in Europe, 3.
D F I N   3323

298 CARUGNO, N.
Méthodes pour la détermination du taux d'humidité du
tabac [Methods for the determination of the rate of
moisture in tobacco].
Commission, 1972.   var. pag.   Internal information
on agriculture, 91.
D F   VI/31/73/72

299 CARUGNO, N.
Pesticide residues in tobacco and tobacco products. 1:
General report (Les résidus de pesticides dans le tabac et
les produits de tabac. 1: Rapport général).
Commission, 1976.   145p.   Information on
agriculture, 14.
E F   8864

300 CARUGNO, N.
Les résidus de pesticides dans le tabac et les produits de
tabac. 2: Substances phytosanitaires employées.
Législations. Méthodes d'analyse [Pesticide residues in
tobacco and tobacco products. 2: Plant health substances
employed. Legislation. Methods of analysis].
Commission, 1977.   157p.   Information on
agriculture, 23.
E F   8877

301 CARUSI, P.
Analyse de certaines expériences d'aménagement et de
gestion de 'zones industrielles' dans les pays de la
Communauté économique européenne (Belgique, France,
république fédérale d'Allemagne, Italie, Pays-Bas)
[Analysis of some schemes for planning and administration
of 'industrial zones' in the countries of the European
Economic Community (Belgium, France, Federal
Republic of Germany, Italy, the Netherlands)].
Commission, 1972.   175p.   Collection: regional
economy and policy. 1: Industrial conversion in Europe, 9.
D F I N   8362

302 CASCIOTTI, C. M.
Statistiques fiscales 1965–1969 [Tax statistics 1965–1969].
Eurostat, 1971.   111p.
D/F/I/N   5326

303 CASSESE, S.
Il contributo delle 'Comunità montane' in Italia allo
sviluppo dell'agricoltura di montagna [The contribution of
'Comunità montane' to the development of hill farming in
Italy / La contribution des 'Comunità montane' au
développement de l'agriculture de montagne en Italie].
Commission, 1976.   209p.   Information on
agriculture, 11.
I   8861

304 CASSESE, S.
Gli 'enti di sviluppo agicolo' in Italia nella riforma delle
strutture. Problemi e prospettive di adattamento [The
'enti di sviluppo agricolo' in structural reform in Italy.
Adjustment problems and prospects / Les 'enti di sviluppo
agricolo' en Italie et la réforme des structures. Problèmes
et perspectives d'adaptation].
Commission, 1976.   285p.   Information on
agriculture, 12.
I   8862

305 CASTAGNOS, M.
Étude sur l'évolution de la concentration dans la
distribution des produits alimentaires en France [A study
of the evolution of concentration in food distribution in
France].
Commission, 1976.   213p.
F   8763

306 CASTAGNOS, M.
Étude sur l'évolution de la concentration dans l'industrie
alimentaire en France [A study of the evolution of
concentration in the food industry in France].
Commission, 1975.   238p.
F   6912

307 CASTAGNOS, M.
Étude sur l'évolution de la concentration dans l'industrie
alimentaire en France. Tableaux de concentration [A
study of the evolution of concentration in the food industry
in France. Concentration tables].
Commission, 1975.   307p.
F   8706

308 CATALANO, A.
Étude sur les qualités des carcasses de bovins en Italie
[Study on the qualities of beef carcasses in Italy].
In Agricultural statistical studies, 7.
Eurostat, 1970.   52p.
D F I   16843

309 CATELLA, F.
La production de produits animaux dans des entreprises à
grande capacité de la CEE. Nombre et formes dans le
secteur de l'engraissement de porcs, de veaux et de jeunes
bovines [The production of animal products in large scale
enterprises in the EEC. Number and types in the pig, calf
and store cattle fattening industry].
Commission, 1968.   158p.   Internal information on
agriculture, 23.
D F   11974/1/VI/67

310 CATELLA, F.
La production et la commercialisation de parties de
volaille [The production and marketing of poultry cuts].
Commission, 1974.   var. pag.   Internal information
on agriculture, 136.
D F   VI/3723/74

311 CAUBEL, H.
La formation des formateurs. Problèmes, méthodes et
expériences dans les industries de la C.E.C.A. [Training
of the trainers. Problems, methods and experiments in the
industries of the E.C.S.C.].
ECSC HA, 1962.   127p.
F   8514

312 CAUBEL, H.
La formation professionnelle dans les mines de fer des
pays de la Communauté [Vocational training in the iron
mines of the countries of the Community].
ECSC HA, 1959.   182p.
F   8149

313 CAUSSIN, R.
Conséquences écologiques de l'application des techniques
modernes de production en agriculture [Ecological results
from the application of modern production techniques in
agriculture].
Commission, 1974.   var. pag.   Internal information
on agriculture, 137.
D F   VI/3722/74

314 CÉPÈDE, D.
Évolution de la productivité de l'agriculture dans la CEE
[Development of agricultural productivity in the EEC].
Commission, 1969.   509p.   Internal information on
agriculture, 44.
D F   11774/VI/69

315 CÉPÈDE, M.
L'aide alimentaire de la C.E.E. aux pays en voie de
développement problèmes posés et possibilités réelles. 1:
Étude régionale. Afrique du Nord [Food aid from the
E.E.C. to the developing countries. Problems and
possibilities. 1: Regional study. North Africa].
Commission EEC, 1963.   14p.
F   7829

316 CÉPÈDE, M.
L'aide alimentaire de la C.E.E. aux pays en voie de
développement problèmes posés et possibilités réelles. 3:
Étude régionale. Afrique occidentale et centrale [Food aid
from the E.E.C. to the developing countries. Problems
and possibilities. 3: Regional study. West and Central
Africa].
Commission EEC, 1963.   19p.
F   7829

317 CÉPÈDE, M.
Food aid from the EEC to developing countries. Problems and possibilities (L'aide alimentaire de la C.E.E. aux pays en voie de développement. Problèmes posés et possibilités réelles).
Commission EEC, 1964.   233p.   Studies: agricultural series, 14.
D E F I N   8102

318 CERUTTI, F. F. X.
Accès à l'exploitation agricole. Dispositions et pratiques existant dans les États membres de la CEE en vue de l'obtention et de l'aménagement d'une exploitation agricole [Access to the farm. Arrangements and practices existing in the Member States of the EEC for obtaining and managing a farm].
Commission, 1967.   var. pag.   Internal information on agriculture, 21.
D F   8325/VI/66

319 CESA-BIANCHI, M.
Ricerca nell'industria siderurgica italiana [Research in the Italian iron and steel industry / Recherche dans la sidérurgie italienne].
Commission, 1967.   180p.   Collection: occupational physiology and psychology, 3/10.
I   13749

320 CESARINI, G.
Nouvelles formes de collaboration dans le domaine de la production agricole. 1: Italie [New forms of cooperation in the field of agricultural production. 1: Italy].
Commission, 1972.   266p.   Internal information on agriculture, 93.
D F I   VI/2513/72

321 CEYRAC, M.
La conduite sur place des opérations de conversion industrielle [On-the-spot direction of industrial conversion operations].

ECSC HA, 1963.   352p.   Collection: regional
economy and policy. 1: Industrial conversion in Europe, 4.
D F I N   3324

322 CHABRAT, L.
Crédits à l'agriculture [Credit to agriculture].
Commission, 1973.   var. pag.   Internal information
on agriculture, 102.
D F   VI/18121/70

323 CHABRAT, L.
Crédits à l'agriculture. 1: France, Belgique, Grand-Duché
de Luxembourg [Credit to agriculture. 1: France,
Belgium, Grand Duchy of Luxembourg].
Commission, 1976.   var. pag.   Information on
agriculture, 1.
F   8831

324 CHAMBARD, C.
La promotion commerciale des cuirs et peaux originaires
des États africains associés de la zone soudano-sahelienne
sur le marché de la CEE [Commercial promotion of hides
and skins originating from the Sudan-Sahara area of the
Associated African States on the EEC market].
Commission, 1968.   3 vols.
F   14455/VIII/B/68

325 CHAMBARD, C.
La promotion commerciale des cuirs et peaux originaires
des États africains associés de la zone soudano-sahelienne
sur le marché de la CEE. Résumé [Commercial promotion
of hides and skins originating from the Sudan-Sahara area
of the Associated African States on the EEC market.
Summary].
Commission, 1968.   18p.
D E F I   14455/VIII/B/68

326 CHANTRAINE, A.
Méthodologie communautaire des tableaux
Entrées-Sorties 1965 [Community input-ouput tables 1965
methodology].

Eurostat, 1970.   222p.   Special series: input-output tables 1965,1.
D F   4963

327 CHARLET, P.
Dispositions en matière de zootechnie bovine [Provisions concerning bovine husbandry].
Commission, 1976.   138p.   Information on agriculture, 8.
F   8840

328 CHARPENTIER, G.
Public purchasing in the Common Market [L'achat public dans le Marché Commun].
Commission, 1975.   113p.
E   SEC (74) 4272

329 CHARRAYRE, J.
Mémorandum sur les objectifs de 1965. Méthodes d'élaboration et résultats détaillés [Memorandum on the 1965 objectives. Methods of elaboration and detailed results].
ECSC HA, 1962.   540p.   Collection: general objectives for steel, 1.
D F I N   3017

330 CHATENET, P.
Discours de Monsieur Pierre Chatenet Président de la Commission devant l'Assemblée Parlementaire Européenne Strasbourg. Session de février 1962 [Speech by Mr. Pierre Chatenet President of the Commission before the European Parliamentary Assembly Strasbourg. Session of February 1962].
Commission EAEC, 1962.   19p.
F

331 CHATENET, P.
L'énergie nucléaire et la politique européenne [Nuclear energy and European policy].
Bureau (P), 1964.   7p.   Les documents de Communauté européenne, 24.
F

332 CHATENET, P.
Speech by Mr. Pierre Chatenet President of the
Commission before the European Parliament Strasbourg.
Session of June 1964 [Discours de M. Pierre Chatenet
Président de la Commission devant le Parlement européen
Strasbourg. Session de juin 1964].
Commission EAEC, 1964.   23p.
E

333 CHAUVET, J.-P.
Cartes des pentes moyennes. Italie [Maps of average
slopes. Italy].
Commission, 1975.   var. pag.   Internal information
on agriculture, 143.
F I   VI/1600/75

334 CHAUVET, J.-P.
Cartes des pentes moyennes. 2: France, Belgique,
Grand-Duché de Luxembourg [Maps of average slopes. 2:
France, Belgium, Grand Duchy of Luxembourg].
Commission, 1975.   var. pag.   Internal information
on agriculture, 166.
F   VI/511/76

335 CHAUVET, J.-P.
The European Community in maps (La Communauté
européenne. Cartes).
Commission, 1974.   14 maps.
DK D E F I N   6574

336 CHENOIX, F.
Possibilités d'industrialisation des États africains et
malgache associés. Volume 3: République démocratique
du Congo [Possibilities for the industrialization of the
Associated African States and Madagascar. Volume 3:
Democratic Republic of the Congo].
Commission EEC, 1966.   2 vols.
F   13077/VIII/B/66, 13078/VIII/B/66

337 CHENOIX, F.
Possibilités d'industrialisation des États africains et
malgache associés. Volume 4: Burundi, Rwanda et région
Centre-orientale du Congo (Kinshasa) (région des Grands
Lacs) [Possibilities for the industrialization of the
Associated African States and Madagascar. Volume 4:
Burundi, Rwanda and Centre-eastern region of the Congo
(Kinshasa) (region of the Great Lakes)].
Commission EEC, 1966.   2 vols.
F   13079/VIII/B/66, 13080/VIII/B/66

338 CHENOIX, F.
Possibilités d'industrialisation des États africains et
malgache associés. Volume 5: Madagascar [Possibilities
for the industrialization of the Associated African States
and Madagascar. Volume 5: Madagascar].
Commission EEC, 1966.   2 vols
F   13081/VIII/B/66, 13082/VIII/B/66

339 CHEYSSON, C.
The European Community and the Third World [La
Communauté européenne et le tiers monde].
Commission (L), 1975.   pp.1–9.
E

340 CHILLIARD
Essai d'appréciation des conditions d'application et des
résultats d'une politique de réforme en agriculture dans
des régions agricoles difficiles. 2: Queyras [Attempt at
estimating the conditions from the application and results
of a reform policy in agriculture in difficult agricultural
regions. 2: Queyras].
Commission, 1975.   var. pag.   Internal information
on agriculture, 150.
F   VI/1988/75

341 CHOUTEAU, J.
Pesticide residues in tobacco and tobacco products. 1:
General report (Les résidus de pesticides dans le tabac et
les produits de tabac. 1: Rapport général).

Commission, 1976.   145p.   Information on
agriculture, 14.
E F   8864

342 CHOUTEAU, J.
Les résidus de pesticides dans le tabac et les produits de
tabac. 2: Substances phytosanitaires employées.
Législations. Méthodes d'analyse [Pesticide residues in
tobacco and tobacco products. 2: Plant health substances
employed. Legislation. Methods of analysis].
Commission, 1977.   157p.   Information on
agriculture, 23.
F   8877

343 CHRISTIAANSE, J. H., chairman
Tax policy and investment in the European Community
[La politique fiscale et les investissements dans la
Communauté européenne].
Commission, 1975.   var. pag.   Studies: taxation
series, 1.
E   8457

344 CICUREL, M.
Évolution et prévisions de la population active agricole
[Development and estimates of the working agricultural
population].
Commission, 1970.   var. pag.   Internal information
on agriculture, 61.
D F   4131/VI/70

345 CLAPPIER, B., chairman
Monetary policy in the countries of the European
Economic Community. Institutions and instruments (La
politique monétaire dans les pays de la Communauté
économique européenne. Institutions et instruments).
Mon Com, 1974.   436p.
D E F I N   8355

346 CLARKE, R.
Public purchasing in the Common Market [L'achat public
dans le Marché Commun].
Commission, 1975.   113p.
E   SEC (74) 4272

347 CLEFF, R.
Les laminoirs [The rolling mills].
Commission, 1972.   240p.   New technical processes
in the iron and steel industry: a personal training manual,
4.   Studies: vocational training.
D F I N   8349

348 CLEVERING-LOMBARDI, L.
Les produits dérivés de la pomme de terre [Products
derived from the potato].
Commission, 1974.   176p.   Internal information on
agriculture, 133.
F   VI/2886/74

349 CLUZEL, H.
Aides apportées aux agriculteurs migrants dans les pays
de la CEE [Aid provided to migrant farmworkers in the
countries of the EEC].
Commission EEC, 1966.   91p.   Studies: agricultural
series, 22.
D F I N   8159

COCCO, E. di, *see* DI COCCO, E.

350 COHEN, S. D.
The European Community and the General Agreement on
Tariffs and Trade [La Communauté européenne et l'accord
général sur les tarifs douaniers et le commerce].
Commission (W), 1976.   30p.
E   CE/GATT

351 COING
La réparation des conséquences dommageables d'une
violation des articles 85 et 86 du traité instituant la CEE
[Compensation for damage suffered through infringement

of Articles 85 and 86 of the Treaty establishing the EEC].
Commission EEC, 1966. 74p. Studies: competition
series, 1.
D F I N 8153

352 COLEOU, J.
Orientation de la production communautaire de viande
bovine. Facteurs ayant une incidence sur la décision des
agriculteurs de produire de la viande bovine [Direction of
Community beef production. Factors having an effect on
the decision of farmers to produce beef].
Commission, 1970. 382p. Internal information on
agriculture, 60.
D F 6667/VI/70

353 COLITTI, G.
Evoluzione della concentrazione dal 1962 al 1969 in alcuni
settori dell'industria italiana. Metodologia [Evolution of
concentration in various sectors of Italian industry from
1962 to 1969. Methodology / L'évolution de la
concentration dans quelques secteurs de l'industrie
italienne de 1962 à 1969. Méthodologie].
Commission, 1973. 24p.
I IV/344/73

354 COLITTI, G.
Studio sull'evoluzione della concentrazione in alcuni settori
dell'industria tessile in Italia. Lana (NICE 232). Cotone
(NICE 233). Magliera e calzetteria (NICE 237) [A study of
the evolution of concentration in various sectors of the
textile industry in Italy. Wool (NICE 232). Cotton (NICE
233). Knitted and crocheted goods (NICE 237) / Étude sur
l'évolution de la concentration dans quelques secteurs de
l'industrie du textile en Italie. Laine (NICE 232). Coton
(NICE 233). Bonneterie (NICE 237)].
Commission, 1973. var. pag.
I IV/347/73

355 COLITTI, G.
Studio sull'evoluzione della concentrazione in Italia
dell'industria della carta e della sua trasformazione. Carta

(NICE 271). Cartotecnica (NICE 272) [A study of the
evolution of concentration in the paper and paper products
industry in Italy. Paper (NICE 271). Paper processing
(NICE 272) / Étude sur l'évolution de la concentration de
l'industrie du papier et des articles en papier en Italie.
Papier (NICE 271). Transformation du papier (NICE
272).].
Commission, 1973.   103p.
I   IV/348/73

356 COLLEAUX, J.
Possibilités de création d'industries exportatrices dans les
États africains et malgache associés. Transformation du
bois et fabrication d'articles en bois. Première
transformation: Sciages, déroulages, tranchages.
Deuxième transformation: Profilés, moulures,
contreplaqués, panneaux, produits finis: pour la
construction et l'ameublement. Rapport de synthèse
[Possibilities for the establishment of exporting industries
in the Associated African States and Madagascar. Wood
processing and manufacture of articles in wood. First
process: Sawing, wood-peeling, slicing. Second process:
Shapes, mouldings, plywood, panels, finished products:
for building and furniture. Summary report].
Commission, 1974.   445p.
F   VIII/227/74

357 COLLIARD, C.A.
The law and practice relating to pollution control in
France (Loi et usage concernant le contrôle de la pollution
en France).
Commission, 1976.   190p.
E F   0 86010 033 2

358 COLLIDÀ, A.
Analyse de certaines expériences d'aménagement et de
gestion de 'zones industrielles' dans les pays de la
Communauté économique européenne. (Belgique, France,
république fédérale d'Allemagne, Italie, Pays-Bas)
[Analysis of some schemes for planning and administration
of 'industrial zones' in the countries of the European

Economic Community. (Belgium, France, Federal
Republic of Germany, Italy, the Netherlands)].
Commission, 1972.   175p.   Collection: regional
economy and policy. 1: Industrial conversion in Europe, 9.
D F I N   8362

359 COLLIGNON, E.
Glossaire des normes de l'acier. Normes d'essai, de qualité
et de dimensions établi sur la base des EURONORM et
des normes nationales [Glossary of steel standards.
Standards of testing, quality and dimensions established
on the basis of EURONORM and national standards].
Commission, n.d.   307p.
D/F/I/N

360 COLLIGNON, E.
Glossary new transport technologies (Glossaire nouvelles
techniques de transport).
Commission, 1976.   900p.
DK/D/E/F/I/N   IX/2061/74

361 COLONNA DI PALIANO, G., chairman
Principles and general datelines of an industrial policy for
the Community (Principes et orientations générales d'une
politique industrielle de la Communauté).
In Bulletin of the European Communities. Supplement,
4/1970.   Commission, 1970.   26p.
D E F I N   4001

362 COMMINS, B.T.
Intercomparison of measurement of carboxyhaemoglobin
in different European laboratories and establishment of
the methodology for the assessment of COH_B levels in
exposed populations [Inter-comparaison de la mesure du
carboxyle-hémoglobine dans les laboratories divers
européens et l'établissement de la méthodologie pour
l'imposition des niveaux COH_B dans les populations
exposées].
Commission, 1977.   118p.
E   V/F/1315/77

363 COMOGLIO, G.
Studio sull'evoluzione della concentrazione nel settore dei
detersivi per uso domestico in Italia dal 1968 al 1975 [A
study of the evolution of concentration in the sector of
detergents for domestic use from 1968 to 1975 in Italy /
Étude sur l'évolution de la concentration dans le secteur
des détergents pour la maison de 1968 à 1975 en Italie].
Commission, 1977.   249p.
I   CB-NL-77-012-IT-C

364 COOREMANS, L.
W. Hallstein and J. Rey, Freemen of the City of Brussels.
Speeches given on 2 December 1971 at the conferring of
the Freedom of the City of Brussels on the former
Presidents of the Commission of the European Economic
Community and of the Commission of the European
Communities (W. Hallstein et J. Rey, citoyens de la ville
de Bruxelles. Discours prononcés le 2 décembre 1971 à
l'occasion de la remise du diplôme de citoyen d'honneur de
la ville de Bruxelles aux anciens présidents de la
Commission de la Communauté économique européenne et
de la Commission des Communautés européennes).
Commission, 1972.   20p.
D E F I N   8368

365 COPPÉ, A.
Address delivered to the European Parliament by Mr.
Albert Coppé Vice-President of the High Authority of the
European Coal and Steel Community at Strasbourg 14
May 1963 [Discours prononcé par M. Albert Coppé,
Vice-président de la Haute Autorité de la Communauté
européenne du charbon et de l'acier, devant le Parlement
européen, à Strasbourg, 14 mai 1963].
ECSC HA, 1963.   25p.
D E F I N   3314

366 COPPÉ, A.
Le coût social, le coût économique. Discours prononcé à
l'occasion de la 57e Conférence internationale du travail.
Genève, le 22 juin 1972 [Social cost, economic cost.

Address on the occasion of the 57th International Labour
Conference, Geneva, 22 June 1972.].
Commission, 1972.   10p.
D F I N   8394

367 COPPÉ, A.
Déclaration faite par M. Albert Coppé vice-président de la
Haute Autorité devant le Parlement européen à la veille
de la fusion des exécutifs et dans la perspective de la
fusion des traités le 20 juin 1967 [Speech by Mr. Albert
Coppé vice-president of the High Authority to the
European Parliament, before the merger of the
Executives and in the light of the merger of the Treaties
June 20 1967].
ECSC HA, 1967.   11p.
D F I N   13727

368 COPPÉ, A.
From Schuman Plan to European Economic Community.
An address delivered by Albert Coppé Vice-President of
the High Authority of the European Coal and Steel
Community [Du plan Schuman à la Communauté
économique européenne. Discours prononcé par Albert
Coppé Vice-président de la Haute Autorité de la
Communauté européenne du charbon et de l'acier].
Pub Dept, 1957.   22p.
E   1962

369 COPPÉ, A.
El Mercado Común del carbón y del acero. Orientación y
coordinación de las inversiones [The Common Market of
coal and steel. Direction and coordination of investments /
Le marché commun du charbon et de l'acier. L'orientation
et la coordination des investissements].
Pr Inf, 1966.   8p.   Documentos de la Comunidad
Europea, 5.
S

370 COPPÉ, A.
New Europe: unity for expansion. An address delivered
by Albert Coppé Vice-President of the High Authority of

the European Coal and Steel Community New York April
10 1956 [L'Europe nouvelle: unité pour l'expansion.
Discours prononcé par Albert Coppé Vice-président de la
Haute Autorité de la Communauté européenne du charbon
et de l'acier New York 10 avril 1956].
ECSC, 1956.   19p.
E   1765

371 COPPÉ, A.
On the threshold of a new stage in the Communities'
development. Address delivered by Mr. Albert Coppé
Vice-president of the High Authority of the European
Coal and Steel Community to the European Parliament at
Strasbourg. May 8 1967 (Au seuil d'une nouvelle étape de
l'évolution de nos Communautés. Discours de M. Albert
Coppé Vice-président de la Haute Autorité de la
Communauté européenne du charbon et de l'acier devant le
Parlement européen à Strasbourg. 8 mai 1967).
ECSC HA, 1967.   12p.
D E F I N   13642

372 COPPINI, A., chairman
The economic impact of social security (Les incidences
économiques de la sécurité sociale).
Commission, 1972.   193p.   Studies: social policy
series, 21.
D E F I N   8275

373 COPPO, D.
Le financement des investissements et les aspects sociaux
de la reconversion [Financing of investments and social
aspects of conversion].
ECSC HA, 1963.   255p.   Collection: regional
economy and policy. 1: Industrial conversion in Europe, 3.
D F I N   3323

374 CORBINO, E., chairman
Comunità sopranazionale contributo all'integrazione
economica generale [The supranational community
contribution to a general economic integration / La

contribution de la communauté supranationale à
l'intégration économique générale].
Ser Inf ESCC, 1955.   214p.
I

375 CORDONNIER, P.
Modèles d'analyse d'entreprises de polyculture-élevage
bovin. Données technico-économiques de base. Région du
Bassin de Rennes (France) [Models for analysis of mixed
crop and cattle farms. Basic technico-economic data.
Bassin de Rennes region (France)].
Commission, 1977.   98p.   Information on
agriculture, 37.
F   CB-NA-77-037-FR-C

376 CORDONNIER, P.
Modèles d'analyse d'entreprises de polyculture-élevage
bovin. Données technico-économiques de base. Région
Volvestre (France) [Models for analysis of mixed crop and
cattle farms. Basic technico-economic data. Volvestre
region (France)].
Commission, 1977.   102p.   Information on
agriculture, 39.
F   CB-NA-77-039-FR-C

377 CORDONNIER, P.
Modèles d'analyse d'entreprises de polyculture-élevage
bovin. 1: Caractéristiques et possibilités d'utilisation
[Models for analysis of mixed crop and cattle farms. 1:
Characteristics and possibilities of utilization].
Commission, 1973.   261p.   Internal information on
agriculture, 97.
D F   VI/1385/72

378 CORDONNIER, P.
Modèles d'analyse d'entreprises de polyculture-élevage
bovin. 2: Données technico-économiques de base.
Circonscription Nord-Picardie et région limoneuse du
Limbourg belge [Models for analysis of mixed crop and
cattle farms. 2: Basic technico-economic data.

Nord-Picardie area and the limoneuse region of Belgian Limbourg].
Commission, 1973.   200p.   Internal information on agriculture, 111.
D F   VI/1792/73

379 CORDONNIER, P.
Modèles d'analyse d'entreprises de polyculture-élevage bovin. 3: Données technico-économiques de base. Région Noordelijke Bouwstreek (Pays-Bas) [Models for analysis of mixed crop and cattle farms. 3: Basic technico-economic data. Noordelijke Bouwstreek region (Netherlands)].
Commission, 1975.   90p.   Internal information on agriculture, 140.
F N   VI/17751/70

380 CORDONNIER, P.
Modelle zur Analyse von Ackerbau-Rindviehhaltungsbetrieben. Technisch-wirtschaftliche Grundangaben. Schwäbisch-Bayerisches Hügelland (B.R. Deutschland) [Models for analysis of mixed crop and cattle farms. Basic technico-economic data. Schwäbisch-bayerisches Hügelland (F.R. Germany) / Modèles d'analyse d'entreprises de polyculture-élevage bovin. Données technico-économiques de base. Schwäbisch-bayerisches Hügelland (R.F. Allemagne)].
Commission, 1976.   86p.   Information on agriculture, 6.
D   8835

381 CORDONNIER, P.
Models for analysis mixed crop and cattle farms. Basic techno-economic data. South-East Leinster (Ireland), West Cambridgeshire (United Kingdom), Fünen (Denmark) [Modèles d'analyse d'entreprises de polyculture-élevage bovin. Données technico-économiques de base. South-East Leinster (Irlande), West Cambridgeshire (Royaume-Uni), Fünen (Danemark)].
Commission, 1976.   var. pag.   Information on agriculture, 7.
E   8836

382 CORDONNIER, P.
Models for analysis mixed crop and cattle farms. 6:
Characteristics and possible applications. South-East
Leinster (Ireland), West Cambridgeshire (United
Kingdom), Fünen (Denmark), Schwäbisch-bayerisches
Hügelland (F.R. Germany) (Modèles d'analyse
d'entreprises de polyculture-élevage bovin. 6:
Caractéristiques et possibilités d'utilisation. South-East
Leinster (Irlande), West Cambridgeshire (Royaume-Uni),
Fünen (Danemark), Schwäbisch-bayerisches Hügelland
(R.F. d'Allemagne)).
Commission, 1976.   47p.   Internal information on
agriculture, 152.
E F   VI/3715/1/74

383 CORNU, R.B.
A study of the evolution of concentration in the United
Kingdom textile industry [Étude sur l'évolution de la
concentration dans l'industrie du textile au
Royaume-Uni].
Commission, 1976.   226p.
E   8701

384 CORNU, R. B.
Women and employment in the United Kingdom, Ireland
and Denmark [Les femmes et l'emploi au Royaume-Uni,
en Irlande et au Danemark].
Commission, 1975.   var. pag.
E   V/649/75

385 COSCIANI, C.
Dispositions fiscales en matière de coopération et de fusion
d'exploitations agricoles. 4: Italie [Tax arrangements
concerning cooperation and amalgamation of farms. 4:
Italy].
Commission, 1973.   175p.   Internal information on
agriculture, 98.
F I   VI/16341/69

385A COSTER, A. de
Aide-mémoire pour la pratique des épreuves d'exercice en
médecine du travail [Manual for the practice of exercise
tests in industrial medicine].
Commission, 1971.   49p.   Collection: industrial
health and medicine, 12.
D F I N   16741

386 COULON, R.
L'évolution des prix du gaz dans les pays de la
Communauté européenne de 1955 à 1970 [The
development of gas prices in the countries of the European
Community from 1955 to 1970].
In Statistical studies and surveys, 3/1971.
Eurostat, 1971.   261p.
D/F   5509

387 COUREL
Les conditions d'installation d'entreprises industrielles
dans les États africains et malgache associés. Volume 2:
République de Haute Volta [Conditions for the setting-up
of industrial undertakings in the Associated African
States and Madagascar. Volume 2: Republic of Upper
Volta]; 2nd ed.
Commission, 1975.   82p.
F   VIII/1250/74

388 COUREL
Les conditions d'installation d'entreprises industrielles
dans les États africains et malgache associés. Volume 8:
République togolaise [Conditions for the setting-up of
industrial undertakings in the Associated African States
and Madagascar. Volume 8: Republic of Togo]; 2nd ed.
Commission, 1975.   86p.
F   VIII/1260/74

389 COUREL
Les conditions d'installation d'entreprises industrielles
dans les États africains et malgache associés. Volume 19:
République de Côte-d'Ivoire [Conditions for the
setting-up of industrial undertakings in the Associated

African States and Madagascar. Volume 19: Republic of
Ivory Coast]; 2nd ed.
Commission, 1975.   80p.
F   VIII/1247/74

390 COUSIN, J.-M.
Population and employment 1950–1976 (Population et
emploi 1950–1976).
Eurostat, 1977.   201p.
E/F   CA-22-77-031-2A-C

391 COUSSY, P.
Élaboration d'une méthode macroéconomique pour le
calcul de la charge fiscale indirecte pesant en amont des
exploitations agricoles dans chacun des six pays de la
Communauté [Formulation of a macroeconomic method
for the calculation of an indirect tax on farms in each of the
six countries of the Community].
Commission, 1972.   74p.   Studies:
competition–approximation of legislation series, 18.
D F I N   8337

392 CRAMER
Dispositions pour faciliter la création d'activités nouvelles.
Dispositions juridiques et financières en vigueur dans les
États membres et le Royaume-Uni [Arrangements to
facilitate the establishment of new activities. Legal and
financial arrangements in force in the Member States and
United Kingdom].
ECSC HA, 1959.   loose-leaf.
D F I N   2275

393 CREVEL
Essai d'appréciation des conditions d'application et des
résultats d'une politique de réforme en agriculture dans
des régions agricoles difficiles. 2: Queyras [Attempt at
estimating the conditions from the application and results
of a reform policy in agriculture in difficult agricultural
regions. 2: Queyras].
Commission, 1975.   var. pag.   Internal information
on agriculture, 150.
F   VI/1988/75

394 CRISPOLTI, G.
Premier séminaire pour cadres dirigeants de la formation
dans l'agriculture et en milieu rural. Rapport final [First
seminar for executive officials about training in
agriculture and the rural environment. Final report].
Commission, 1970.   var. pag.
F

395 CROHAIN, A.
Conséquences écologiques de l'application des techniques
modernes de production en agriculture [Ecological results
from the application of modern production techniques in
agriculture].
Commission, 1974.   var. pag.   Internal information
on agriculture, 137.
D F   VI/3722/74

396 CROISIER, A.
Les services de la main-d'œuvre des États membres de la
Communauté. Exposé de synthèse [Employment
exchanges in the Member States of the Community.
Summary].
Commission EEC, 1967.   131p.   Studies: social
policy series, 16.
D F I N   8193

397 CURRAN, D. W.
L'énergie et l'Europe [Energy and Europe].
Bureau (P), 1974.   loose-leaf.   Les grands
problèmes européens.
F

398 CURRAN, D. W.
Le pétrole dans la CEE. 3: Le raffinage [Petroleum in the
EEC. 3: Refining].
In Dossiers pédagogiques, 41.
Bureau (P), 1971.   4p.
F

399 CURZON, V.
The 4th World Congress of the International Economic
Association, Budapest, August 19–24 1974 [Le congrès

mondial quatrième de l'Association Internationale des sciences économiques, Budapest, 19–24 août 1974].
Bureau (G), 1977.   26p.
E

400 CUSIMANO, G.
Incidence du rapport des prix de l'huile de graines et de l'huile d'olive sur la consommation de ces huiles [The effect of the report of linseed and olive oil prices on their consumption].
Commission, 1968.   139p.   Internal information on agriculture, 30.
D F   4785/VI/67

401 D'ADAMO, F.
Crédits à l'agriculture. 3: Italie [Credit to agriculture. 3: Italy].
Commission, 1973.   135p.   Internal information on agriculture, 113.
D F I   VI/3350/73

402 D'ADAMO, F.
Crédits à l'agriculture. 3: Italie [Credit to agriculture. 3: Italy].
Commission, 1976.   155p.   Information on agriculture, 3.
F I   8833

403 D'ALAURO, O.
Liguria [Liguria / Liguria].
ECSC, 1958.   74p.   Studies and documents.
Regional studies of employment.
I   2034

404 D'AMBROSIO, M.
Educational leave in Member States (Les congés culturels dans les États membres).
Commission, 1977.   416p.   Studies: social policy series, 26.
D E F I N   CH-SN-76-026-EN-C

D'HARMANT, A. F., *see* HARMANT, A. F. d'

405 DABIN
La réparation des conséquences dommageables d'une
violation des articles 85 et 86 du traité instituant la CEE
[Compensation for damage suffered through infringement
of Articles 85 and 86 of the Treaty establishing the EEC].
Commission EEC, 1966.   74p.   Studies: competition
series, 1.
D F I N   8153

406 DAHRENDORF, R.
Research, science and education. Scientific and technical
information. Programme of work proposed by Mr. Ralf
Dahrendorf (Recherche, science et éducation. Information
scientifique et technique. Programme de travail de M.
Ralf Dahrendorf).
Commission, 1973.   27p.
D E F I N

407 DAINTITH, T.
Report on the economic law of the United Kingdom
(Rapport sur le droit économique du Royaume-Uni).
Commission, 1976.   134p.   Studies:
competition–approximation of legislation series, 20/5.
D E F   8429

408 DALLEMAGNE, V.
La commune et les structures locales dans la CEE [The
commune and local structures in the EEC].
In Documentation européenne. Série pédagogique; série
agricole; série syndicale et ouvrière, 2/1974.
Pr Inf, 1974.   4p.
D F I N   U/A/S/74/2

409 DANZIN, A.
Science and the renaissance of Europe [Science et la
renaissance de l'Europe].
Commission, 1977.   168p.
E

410 DARCHEVILLE, M.
Conséquences écologiques de l'application des techniques
modernes de production en agriculture [Ecological results

from the application of modern production techniques in
agriculture].
Commission, 1974.   var. pag.   Internal information
on agriculture, 137.
D F   VI/3722/74

411 DAUBACH, P.
Aussenhandel und Versorgung an Manganerz,
Hochofen-Ferromangan und Spiegeleisen in der
Gemeinschaft [Foreign trade and supply of manganese
ore, high-carbon ferro-manganese and spiegeleisen in the
Community / Commerce extérieur et approvisionnements
du minerai de manganèse, du ferromanganèse carburé et
du spiegel dans la Communauté].
In Statistical studies and surveys, 1/1970.
Eurostat, 1970.   pp.1–61.
D   16543

412 DAUPHIN, J.
Économie de la production, transformation, et
consommation du blé dur dans la CEE [Economics of the
production, processing and consumption of durum wheat
in the EEC].
Commission EEC, 1965.   233p.   Studies:
agricultural series, 18.
D F I N   8138

413 DAUPHIN, J.
Possibilités d'introduire un système de gradation pour le
blé et l'orge produits dans la CEE [Possibilities for
introducing a grading system for wheat and barley
products in the EEC].
Commission, 1968.   193p.   Internal information on
agriculture, 35.
D F   21863/VI/68

414 DAUTEL, H.
La région d'Amberg. Tendances et possibilités de
développement économique [The Amberg region. Trends
and possibilities for economic development].
ECSC HA, 1966.   184p.   Collection: regional

economy and policy. 2: Development and conversion
programme, 7.
D F   3898

415 DAUVIN, J. P.
Étude sur l'évolution de la concentration dans l'industrie
de la construction électrique en France. Construction
d'appareils électriques, radios, télévision,
électro-acoustique (NICE 375). Fabrication d'appareils
électrodomestiques (NICE 376) [A study of the evolution
of concentration in the electrical engineering industry in
France. Manufacture of electrical and audio equipment,
radio and television receivers (NICE 375). Manufacture of
electrical domestic appliances (NICE 376)].
Commission, 1974.   93p.
F   IV/25/74

416 DAUVIN, J. P.
L'industrie électronique des pays de la Communauté et les
investissements américains [The electronics industry of
the countries of the Community and American
investments].
Commission, 1969.   168p.   Studies: industry
series, 1.
D F I N   8240

417 DAVIDSON, I.
Bretton Woods and after. 1 [Bretton Woods et les
suites. 1].
In European studies. Teachers' series, 16.
Inf Ser, 1973.   4p.
E   U 73/16

418 DAVIDSON, I.
Bretton Woods and after. 2 [Bretton Woods et les
suites. 2].
In European studies. Teachers' series, 17.
Inf Ser, 1973.   4p.
E   U/73/17

419 DAVIGNON, E., chairman
Report by the Foreign Ministers of the Member States on
the problems of political unification [Rapport des ministres
des affaires étrangères des États membres sur les
problèmes de l'unification politique].
In Bulletin of the European Communities, 11/1970.
Commission, 1970.   pp.9–14.
D E F I N S   4001

DE BAETS, A., *see* BAETS, A. de

DE BANDT, J., *see* BANDT, J. de

DE BOER, H., *see* BOER, H. de

DE BRUYN, J., *see* BRUYN, J. de

DE COSTER, A., *see* COSTER, A. de

DE FERRANTI, B., *see* FERRANTI, B. de

DE GAAY FORTMAN, W. F., *see* GAAY FORTMAN,
W. F. de

DE GHELLINCK, E., *see* GHELLINCK, E. de

DE GONNEVILLE, *see* GONNEVILLE, de

DE GRAEFF, J. J., *see* GRAEFF, J. J. de

DE GROOTE, P. *see* GROOTE, P. de

DE HAAN, *see* HAAN, de

DE HAAN, P., *see* HAAN, P. de

DE JASAY, A., *see* JASAY, A. de

DE JONG, H. W., *see* JONG, H. W. de

DE KIMPE, *see* KIMPE, de

DE KIMPE, M., *see* KIMPE, M. de

DE KINDER, R., *see* KINDER, R. de

DE LA BEAUMELLE, S., *see* LA BEAUMELLE, S. de

DE LA VALLEE POUSSIN, C. *see* POUSSIN, C. de la
Vallee

DE LA VINELLE, L. Duquesne, *see* DUQUESNE DE LA VINELLE, L.

DE LA VINELLE, M. Duquesne, *see* DUQUESNE DE LA VINELLE, M.

DE LANGE, R., *see* LANGE, R. de

DE LEEUW, A., *see* LEEUW, A. de

DE LETTENHOVE, K., *see* LETTENHOVE, K. de

DE LOO, J. W. H. van, *see* LOO, J. W. H. van de

DE MARCILLAC, *see* MARCILLAC, de

DE MAS LATRIE, *see* MAS LATRIE, de

DE MIEULLE, *see* MIEULLE, de

DE MOT, M., *see* MOT, M. de

DE POUS, J. W., *see* POUS, J. W. de

DE PUTTE, R. van, *see* PUTTE, R. van de

DE ROSA, L., *see* ROSA, L. de

DE RUITER, T., *see* RUITER, T. de

DE STAERCKE, J., *see* STAERCKE, J. de

DE STEEN, J. van, *see* STEEN, J. van de

DE STEENE, *see* STEENE, de

DE SUTTER, R., *see* SUTTER, R. de

DE VEER, J., *see* VEER, J. de

DE VEN, A. C. M. van, *see* VEN, A. C. M. van de

DE VISSCHER, G., *see* VISSCHER, G. de

DE VOGHEL, F., *see* VOGHEL, F. de

DE VOS, I., *see* VOS, I. de

DE WANDELEER, R., *see* WANDELEER, R. de

DE WILMARS, C. Mertens, *see* MERTENS DE WILMARS, C.

DE WOLFF, P., *see* WOLFF, P. de

420 DEAN, A. J. H.
The United Kingdom economy [L'économie britannique].
Commission, 1975.   155p.   Studies: economic and
financial series, 9.
E   8461

421 DEBLON
Les conditions d'installation d'entreprises industrielles
dans les États africains et malgache associés. Volume 9:
République unie du Cameroun [Conditions for the
setting-up of industrial undertakings in the Associated
African States and Madagascar. Volume 9: United
Republic of Cameroon].
Commission, 1972.   94p.
F   VIII/1319/72

422 DEBLON
Les conditions d'installation d'entreprises industrielles
dans les États africains et malgache associés. Volume 11:
République Centrafricaine [Conditions for the setting-up
of industrial undertakings in the Associated African
States and Madagascar. Volume 11: Central African
Republic].
Commission, 1972.   68p.
F   VIII/1321/72

423 DEBLON
Les conditions d'installation d'entreprises industrielles
dans les États africains et malgache associés. Volume 12:
République gabonaise [Conditions for the setting-up of
industrial undertakings in the Associated African States
and Madagascar. Volume 12: Republic of Gabon].
Commission, 1972.   84p.
F   VIII/1322/72

424 DEBLON
Les conditions d'installation d'entreprises industrielles
dans les États africains et malgache associés. Volume 13:
République populaire du Congo [Conditions for the
setting-up of industrial undertakings in the Associated

African States and Madagascar. Volume 13: Popular
Republic of the Congo].
Commission, 1972.   80p.
F   VIII/1323/72

425 DECANNIÈRE, R.
Le lin textile dans la CEE [Flax in the EEC].
Commission, 1969.   75p.   Internal information on
agriculture, 50.
D F   13635/VI/69

426 DEENEN, B. van
Le marché foncier et les baux ruraux. Effets des mesures
de réforme des structures agricoles. 2: R.F. d'Allemagne,
France [The land market and rural leases. Effects of
reform measures of agricultural structures. 2: F.R. of
Germany, France].
Commission, 1972.   var. pag.   Internal information
on agriculture, 82.
F   VI/537/72

427 DEFAY, J., chairman
Public expenditure on Research and Development
1974–1976 (Le Financement public de la recherche et du
développement 1974–1976).
Eurostat, 1977.   133p.
DK/D/E/F/I/N   CA-22-76-003-6A-C

428 DEGGELLER, L.
De arbeidsomstandigheden en -voorwaarden van vrouwen
in loodienst in de zes lid-staten van de Europese
Gemeenschap. Nederland [The conditions of work for
wage-earning women in the six Member States of the
European Community. Netherlands / Les conditions de
travail des femmes salariées dans les six États membres
de la Communauté européenne. Pays-Bas].
Commission, 1972.   104p.
N   V/169/73

428A DEGRE, S.
Aide-mémoire pour la pratique des épreuves d'exercice en médecine du travail [Manual for the practice of exercise tests in industrial medicine].
Commission, 1971.   49p.   Collection: industrial health and medicine, 12.
D F I N   16741

429 DEHOUSSE, F.
The case for elections to the European Parliament by direct universal suffrage (Pour l'élection du Parlement européen au suffrage universel direct).
EP, 1969.   350p.
D E F I N   4736

430 DEHOUSSE, F.
Vers l'élection directe de l'Assemblée parlementaire européenne [Towards the direct election of the European Parliamentary Assembly].
EPA, 1960.   79p.
F   2516

431 DEHOVE, G.
Le droit et la pratique des conventions collectives dans les six pays de la C.E.E. [The law and practice of collective agreements in the six countries of the E.E.C.].
Commission EEC, 1963.   63p.   Studies: social policy series, 6.
D F I N   8091

432 DEKKER, D. J.
La reconversion des charbonnages dans le Limburg néerlandais [Conversion of coalfields in the Dutch Limburg].
Commission, 1971.   39p.   Pamphlets on industrial conversion, 17.
F   8339

433 DEL BO, D.
Address delivered by Mr. Dino Del Bo, President of the High Authority of the European Coal and Steel

Community, to the European Parliament in Strasbourg,
May 10, 1966 (Discours de M. Dino Del Bo, Président de la
Haute Autorité de la Communauté européenne du charbon
et de l'acier, devant le Parlement européen à Strasbourg,
10 mai 1966).
ECSC HA, 1966.   14p.
D E F I N   3902

434 DEL BO, D.
Address delivered by Sig. Dino Del Bo, President of the
High Authority of the European Coal and Steel
Community, to the European Parliament in Strasbourg.
May 12, 1964 [Discours prononcé par M. Dino Del Bo,
Président de la Haute Autorité de la Communauté
européenne du charbon et de l'acier, devant le Parlement
européen à Strasbourg. 12 mai 1964].
ECSC HA, 1964.   18p.
E   3541

435 DEL BO, D.
Addresses delivered by Sig. Dino Del Bo, President of the
High Authority of the European Coal and Steel
Community, to the European Parliament in Strasbourg.
March 24 and May 11 1965 (Discours de M. Dino Del Bo,
Président de la Haute Autorité de la Communauté
européenne du charbon et de l'acier, devant le Parlement
européen à Strasbourg. 24 mars et 11 mai 1965).
ECSC HA, 1965.   26p.
D E F I N   3711

436 DEL BO, D.
ECSC and the merger [La CECA et la fusion].
Inf Ser, 1964.   7p.   Community topics, 14.
E

437 DEL BO, D.
L'expérience de la C.E.C.A. [The E.C.S.C.'s experience].
Bureau (P), 1964.   7p.   Les documents de
Communauté européenne, 21.
F

438 DEL MARMOL
La réparation des conséquences dommageables d'une
violation des articles 85 et 86 du traité instituant la CEE
[Compensation for damage suffered through infringement
of Articles 85 and 86 of the Treaty establishing the EEC].
Commission EEC, 1966.   74p.   Studies: competition
series, 1.
D F I N   8153

439 DEL VISCOVO, M.
Options in transport tariff policy (Options de la politique
tarifaire dans les transports).
Commission EEC, 1966.   189p.   Studies: transport
series, 1.
D E F I N   8146

440 DELANOE
Possibilités de création d'industries exportatrices dans les
États africains et malgache associés. Conserves et
préparation de fruits tropicaux. Dattes. Bananes.
Agrumes et huiles essentielles. Ananas et conserves au
sirop. Anacardes et amandes cajou. Arachides de bouche.
Fruits exotiques divers [Possibilities for the
establishment of exporting industries in the Associated
African States and Madagascar. Preserving and
preparation of tropical fruits. Dates. Bananas. Citrus
fruits and aromatic oils. Pineapples and preserves in
syrup. Cashew nuts and almonds. Edible groundnuts.
Various tropical fruits].
Commission, 1974.   560p.
F   VIII/225/74

441 DELANOE
Possibilités de création d'industries exportatrices dans les
États africains et malgache associés. Conserves et
préparation de fruits tropicaux. Dattes. Bananes.
Agrumes et huiles essentielles. Ananas et conserves au
sirop. Anarcardes et amandes cajou. Arachides de bouche.
Fruits exotiques divers. Rapport de synthèse
[Possibilities for the establishment of exporting industries
in the Associated African States and Madagascar.

Preserving and preparation of tropical fruits. Dates.
Bananas. Citrus fruits and aromatic oils. Pineapples and
preserves in syrup. Cashew nuts and almonds. Edible
groundnuts. Various tropical fruits. Summary report].
Commission, 1975.   22p.
D E F I N   VIII/225/74

442 DELANOË, G.
Étude sur l'évolution de la concentration dans l'industrie
du textile en France. Coton (NICE 233). Laine (NICE
232) [A study of the evolution of concentration in the
textile industry in France. Cotton (NICE 233). Wool
(NICE 232)].
Commission, 1976.   201p.
F   8716

443 DELARGE, M.
Rapport sur les résultats d'une enquête effectuée en
janvier 1956 sur la situation des coûts et recettes des
charbonnages de la Ruhr [Report on the results of a
survey carried out in January 1956 on the situation of costs
and returns of the Ruhr coalfields].
ECSC HA, 1956.   48p.
F   729

444 DELL'ANNO, P.
The law and practice relating to pollution control in Italy
[Loi et usage concernant le contrôle de la pollution en
Italie].
Commission, 1976.   342p.
E I   0 86010 039 1

445 DELORME, P.
Projections de la production et de la consommation de
produits agricoles—'1977'. 8: France [Projections of
production and consumption of agricultural
products—'1977'. 8: France].
Commission, 1975.   173p.   Internal information on
agriculture, 164.
F   VI/1123/72

446 DELVAUX, B.
Accès à l'exploitation agricole. Dispositions et pratiques
existant dans les États membres de la CEE en vue de
l'obtention et de l'aménagement d'une exploitation
agricole [Access to the farm. Arrangements and practices
existing in the Member States of the EEC for obtaining
and managing a farm].
Commission, 1967.   var. pag.   Internal information
on agriculture, 21.
D F   8325/VI/66

447 DEMEESTER, J.
Evaluation of the hygienic problems related to the chilling
of poultry carcasses [Évaluation des problèmes d'hygiène
en rapport avec le refroidissement des carcasses de
volaille].
Commission, 1977.   108p.   Information on
agriculture, 22.
E   8878

448 DEMUYNCK, J.
Modèles d'analyse d'entreprises de polyculture-élevage
bovin. 2: Données technico-économiques de base.
Circonscription Nord-Picardie et région limoneuse du
Limbourg belge [Models for analysis of mixed crop and
cattle farms. 2: Basic technico-economic data.
Nord-Picardie area and the limoneuse region of Belgian
Limbourg].
Commission, 1973.   200p.   Internal information on
agriculture, 111.
D F   VI/1792/73

DEN BEMPT, P. van, *see* BEMPT, P. van den

DEN TEMPEL, A. J. van, *see* TEMPEL, A. J. van den

449 DENDAS, J.
Conséquences écologiques de l'application des techniques
modernes de production en agriculture [Ecological results
from the application of modern production techniques in
agriculture].

Commission, 1974.   var. pag.   Internal information
on agriculture, 137.
D F   VI/3722/74

450 DENIAU, J.-F.
The future before the enlarged Community [Le futur
devant la Communauté élargie].
In Bulletin of the European Communities. Supplement,
1/1972.   Commission, 1972.   pp.11–12.
D E F I N   4001/S/1/72

450A DENOLIN, H.
Aide-mémoire pour la pratique des épreuves d'exercice en
médecine du travail [Manual for the practice of exercise
tests in industrial medicine].
Commission, 1971.   49p.   Collection: industrial
health and medicine, 12.
D F I N   16741

451 DEPREZ, L.
Le financement des investissements et les aspects sociaux
de la reconversion [Financing of investments and social
aspects of conversion].
ECSC HA, 1963.   255p.   Collection: regional
economy and policy. 1: Industrial conversion in Europe, 3.
D F I N   3323

DER GIESSEN, H. B. van, *see* GIESSEN, H. B. van der

DER GOES VAN NATERS, J. van, *see* GOES VAN
NATERS, J. van der

DER GROEBEN, H. von, *see* GROEBEN, H. von der

DER HEYDE, M. van, *see* HEYDE, M. van der

DER STRAATEN, C. van, *see* STRAATEN, C. van der

DER VAEREN, C. van, *see* VAEREN, C. van der

DER WEERDEN, W. van, *see* WEERDEN, W. van der

452 DEREYMAEKER, R.
Tableaux 'Entrées-Sorties' pour les pays de la
Communauté Économique Européenne ['Input-Output'
tables for the countries of the European Economic
Community].
Eurostat, 1964.   var. pag.
D F

453 DEREYMAEKER, R.
Tableaux 'Entrées-Sorties' pour les pays de la
Communauté Économique Européenne. Seconde version
['Input-Output' tables for the countries of the European
Economic Community. Second version].
Eurostat, 1965.   var. pag.
D F

454 DERNEDEN, F.
L'emploi agricole dans les pays de la C.E.E. Tome 1:
Structure [Agricultural employment in the countries of
the E.E.C. Volume 1: Structure].
Commission EEC, 1964.   61p.   Studies: social policy
series, 7.
D F I N   8108

455 DERNEDEN, F.
L'emploi agricole dans les pays de la C.E.E. Tome 2:
Évolution et perspectives [Agricultural employment in
the countries of the E.E.C. Volume 2: Development and
prospects].
Commission EEC, 1964.   51p.   Studies: social policy
series, 8.
D F I N   8123

456 DERNEDEN, F.
Évolution de la productivité de l'agriculture dans la CEE
[Development of agricultural productivity in the EEC].
Commission, 1969.   509p.   Internal information on
agriculture, 44.
D F   11774/VI/69

457 DERNEDEN, F.
Surfaces agricoles pouvant être mobilisées pour une
réforme de structure [Agricultural areas that could be
mobilised for a structural reform].
Commission, 1973. 336p. Internal information on
agriculture, 77.
D F VI/14453/69

458 DEROO, J.
Les services de la main-d'œuvre des États membres de la
Communauté. Exposé de synthèse [Employment
exchanges in the Member States of the Community.
Summary].
Commission EEC, 1967. 131p. Studies: social
policy series, 16.
D F I N 8193

459 DEROSSI, F. Z.
Étude sur la zone de Carbonia. Les conséquences sociales
de la crise minière dans le bassin de Sulcis (Sardaigne)
[Study on the Carbonia area. Social consequences of the
coal crisis in the Sulcis coalfield (Sardinia)].
ECSC HA, 1966. 255p. Collection: regional
economy and policy. 2: Development and conversion
programme, 6.
D F I N 3710

460 DESABIE, J.
Enquêtes sur les budgets familiaux en France [Surveys on
family budgets in France].
In Budgets familiaux 1963/64. France.
Eurostat, 1966. pp.27–183. Social statistics:
special series, 6.
F 3979

461 DESIDERI, C.
Il contributo delle 'Comunità montane' in Italia allo
sviluppo dell'agricoltura di montagna [The contribution of
'Comunità montane' to the development of hill farming in
Italy / La contribution des 'Comunità montane' au
développement de l'agriculture de montagne en Italie].

Commission, 1976.   209p.   Information on
agriculture, 11.
I   8861

462 DESIDERI, C.
Gli 'enti di sviluppo agricolo' in Italia nella riforma delle
strutture. Problemi e prospettive di adattamento [The
'enti di sviluppo agricolo' in structural reform in Italy.
Adjustment problems and prospects / Les 'enti di sviluppo
agricolo' en Italie et la réforme des structures. Problèmes
et perspectives d'adaptation].
Commission, 1976.   285p.   Information on
agriculture, 12.
I   8862

463 DESSEINE, J.
Inflammation et combustion de charbon gras sur grille
[Ignition and combustion of soft coal on grate].
ECSC HA, 1966.   65p.   Technical research: coal, 3.
Coal combustion.
D F I N   11735

464 DETIGER, J. G.
Conséquences budgétaires, économiques et sociales de
l'harmonisation des taux de la TVA dans la CEE avec une
analyse quantitative pour les Pays-Bas [Budgetary,
economic and social results of the harmonisation of VAT
rates in the EEC with a quantitative analysis for the
Netherlands].
Commission, 1970.   92p.   Studies:
competition–approximation of legislation series, 16.
D F I N   8316

465 DETROZ, A.
Arrangements to facilitate the establishment of new
economic activities. Legal and financial arrangements in
force in the member states of the Community and the
United Kingdom (Dispositions pour faciliter la création
d'activités nouvelles. Dispositions juridiques et financières
en vigueur dans les États membres et le Royaume-Uni).
ECSC HA, 1962.   loose-leaf.
D E F I N   3019

466 DETROZ, A.
La conduite sur place des opérations de conversion
industrielle [On-the-spot direction of industrial conversion
operations].
ECSC HA, 1963.   352p.   Collection: regional
economy and policy. 1: Industrial conversion in Europe, 4.
D F I N   3324

467 DETROZ, A.
Dispositions pour faciliter la création d'activités nouvelles.
Dispositions juridiques et financières en vigueur dans les
États membres et le Royaume-Uni [Arrangements to
facilitate the establishment of new activities. Legal and
financial arrangements in force in the Member States and
United Kingdom].
ECSC HA, 1959.   loose-leaf.
D F I N   2275

468 DETROZ, A.
Les organismes d'action régionale [Bodies for regional
action].
ECSC HA, 1966.   119p.   Collection: regional
economy and policy. 1: Industrial conversion in Europe, 6.
D F I N   3823

469 DEUTSCH, K. W.
Contrôle des armements et efforts d'intégration dans le
complexe de la politique européenne [Arms control and
efforts at integration in the complex of European policy].
Pr Inf, 1966.   47p.
F

470 DEUTZMANN, W.
Review of studies carried out in the producer countries on
the forecast consumption of the alloying elements Ni, Cr,
Mo, V, W and Co for special steel production in the years
1980 and 1985 (Synthèse des études effectuées dans les
pays producteurs sur les prévisions de consommation des
éléments d'alliage Ni, Cr, Mo, V, W, Co pour la
production d'aciers spéciaux pour les années 1980 et 1985).

Commission, 1977.   33p.   Series: raw material
supply for the iron and steel industry, 1.
D E F I   8935

471 DEVAUX, M.
Étude sur l'évolution de la concentration dans l'industrie
des pneumatiques en France [A study of the evolution of
concentration in the tyre industry in France].
Commission, 1977.   113p.
F   CB-NL-77-007-FR-C

472 DEVEAUX-PAYEN, M. L.
Le rôle des ports de la Communauté pour le trafic de
céréales et de farines. 1: Synthèse pour les principaux
ports français et italiens [List of Community ports for the
cereals and flour trade. 1: Summary for the chief French
and Italian ports].
Commission, 1974.   var. pag.   Internal information
on agriculture, 122.
F   VI/2941/73

473 DEVEAUX-PAYEN, M. L.
Le rôle des ports de la Communauté pour le trafic de
céréales et de farines. 2: Monographies pour les principaux
ports français de la Manche [List of Community ports for
the cereals and flour trade. 2: Monographs for the chief
French Channel ports].
Commission, 1974.   var. pag.   Internal information
on agriculture, 123.
F   VI/1169/74

474 DEVEAUX-PAYEN, M. L.
Le rôle des ports de la Communauté pour le trafic de
céréales et de farines. 3: Monographies pour les principaux
ports français de l'Atlantique [List of Community ports for
the cereals and flour trade. 3: Monographs for the chief
French Atlantic ports].
Commission, 1974.   var. pag.   Internal information
on agriculture, 124.
F   VI/1263/74

475 DEVEAUX-PAYEN, M. L.
Le rôle des ports de la Communauté pour le trafic de
céréales et de farines. 4: Monographies pour les principaux
ports français de la Méditerranée [List of Community
ports for the cereals and flour trade. 4: Monographs for the
chief French Mediterranean ports].
Commission, 1974.   var. pag.   Internal information
on agriculture, 125.
F   VI/1264/74

476 DEVEAUX-PAYEN, M. L.
Le rôle des ports de la Communauté pour le trafic de
céréales et de farines. 5: Monographies pour les principaux
ports italiens de la Côte Ouest [List of Community ports
for the cereals and flour trade. 5: Monographs for the chief
Italian West Coast ports].
Commission, 1974.   var. pag.   Internal information
on agriculture, 126.
F   VI/1265/74

477 DEVEAUX-PAYEN, M. L.
Le rôle des ports de la Communauté pour le trafic de
céréales et de farines. 6: Monographies pour les principaux
ports italiens de la Côte Est [List of Community ports for
the cereals and flour trade. 6: Monographs for the chief
Italian East Coast ports].
Commission, 1974.   var. pag.   Internal information
on agriculture, 127.
F   VI/1266/74

478 DEVEAUX-PAYEN, M. L.
Le rôle des ports de la Communauté pour le trafic de
céréales et de farines. 7: Synthèse pour les principaux
ports de la R.F. d'Allemagne, du Royaume-Uni, des
Pays-Bas, de la Belgique, de l'Irlande et du Danemark
[List of Community ports for the cereals and flour trade. 7:
Summary for the chief ports of F.R. of Germany, United
Kingdom, the Netherlands, Belgium, Ireland and
Denmark].
Commission, 1975.   var. pag.   Internal information
on agriculture, 155.
F   VI/3170/75

479 DEVEAUX-PAYEN, M. L.
Le rôle des ports de la Communauté pour le trafic de
céréales et de farines. 8: Monographies pour les principaux
ports de la R.F. d'Allemagne [List of Community ports for
the cereals and flour trade. 8: Monographs for the chief
ports of the F.R. of Germany].
Commission, 1975.   var. pag.   Internal information
on agriculture, 156.
F   VI/3171/75

480 DEVEAUX-PAYEN, M. L.
Le rôle des ports de la Communauté pour le trafic de
céréales et de farines. 9: Monographies pour les principaux
ports du Royaume-Uni [List of Community ports for the
cereals and flour trade. 9: Monographs for the chief ports
of the United Kingdom].
Commission, 1975.   var. pag.   Internal information
on agriculture, 157.
F   VI/3172/75

481 DEVEAUX-PAYEN, M. L.
Le rôle des ports de la Communauté pour le trafic de
céréales et de farines. 10: Monographies pour les
principaux ports des Pays-Bas [List of Community ports
for the cereals and flour trade. 10: Monographs for the
chief ports of the Netherlands].
Commission, 1975.   var. pag.   Internal information
on agriculture, 158.
F   VI/3173/75

482 DEVEAUX-PAYEN, M. L.
Le rôle des ports de la Communauté pour le trafic de
céréales et de farines. 11: Monographies pour les
principaux ports de la Belgique [List of Community ports
for the cereals and flour trade. 11: Monographs for the
chief ports of Belgium].
Commission, 1975.   var. pag.   Internal information
on agriculture, 159.
F   VI/3174/75

483 DEVEAUX-PAYEN, M. L.
Le rôle des ports de la Communauté pour le trafic de
céréales et de farines. 12: Monographies pour les
principaux ports de l'Irlande et du Danemark [List of
Community ports for the cereals and flour trade. 12:
Monographs for the chief ports of Ireland and Denmark].
Commission, 1975.   var. pag.   Internal information
on agriculture, 160.
F   VI/3175/75

484 DEVEAUX-PAYEN, M. L.
Le rôle des ports de la Communauté pour le trafic de
céréales et de farines. 13: Résumé et conclusions [List of
Community ports for the cereals and flour trade. 13:
Summary and conclusions].
Commission, 1975.   var. pag.   Internal information
on agriculture, 161.
F   VI/3791/75

485 DEVOS, M.
Glossaire des normes de l'acier. Normes d'essai, de qualité
et de dimensions établi sur la base des EURONORM et
des normes nationales [Glossary of steel standards.
Standards of testing, quality and dimensions established
on the basis of EURONORM and national standards].
Commission, n.d.   307p.
D/F/I/N

486 DI COCCO, E.
Agricultural forecasting. 1: Methods, techniques and
models (Prévisions agricoles. 1: Méthodes, techniques et
modèles).
Commission, 1969.   259p.   Internal information on
agriculture, 48.
D E F   6736/VI/69

487 DI NARDI, G.
Les moyens d'intervention pour la création d'activités
nouvelles [Means of intervention for the creation of new
activities].

ECSC HA, 1960.   67p.   Intergovernmental
Conference on Industrial Redevelopment: general report.
F   5281

488 DI NARDI, G.
Voies et moyens de la conversion industrielle [Ways and
means of industrial conversion].
ECSC HA, 1961.   136p.   Collection: regional
economy and policy. 1: Industrial conversion in Europe, 2.
F   2775

DI PALIANO, G. Colonna, *see* COLONNA DI
PALIANO, G.

489 DI ROSSI, G.
Évolution de la productivité de l'agriculture dans la CEE
[Development of agricultural productivity in the EEC].
Commission, 1969.   509p.   Internal information on
agriculture, 44.
D F   11774/VI/69

490 DICK, G.
La conduite sur place des opérations de conversion
industrielle [On-the-spot direction of industrial conversion
operations].
ECSC HA, 1963.   352p.   Collection: regional
economy and policy. 1: Industrial conversion in Europe, 4.
D F I N   3324

491 DICKERTMANN, D.
Enseignements à tirer en agriculture d'expérience des
'Revolving funds' [Lessons to learn in agriculture from the
experience of 'Revolving funds'].
Commission, 1970.   97p.   Internal information on
agriculture, 62.
D F   VI/11144/70

492 DIEHL, H.
Modell und Methoden zur Vorausrechnung von
Rinderprozzessen [Model and methods of forecasts of the
beef process/Modèle et méthodes des prévisions de
processus bovin].

In Agricultural statistical studies, 8.
Eurostat, 1970.　89p.
D E　　16753

493 DIEHL, L.
Indice CE des prix agricoles à la production. Description
de la méthode [EC index of agricultural production prices.
Description of the method].
In Agricultural prices. Supplement, 5/1971.
Eurostat, 1971.　37p.
D/F　　17435

494 DIELS
Tableaux 'Entrées-Sorties' pour les pays de la
Communauté Économique Européenne. Seconde version
['Input-Output' tables for the countries of the European
Economic Community. Second version].
Eurostat, 1965.　var. pag.
D F

495 DIENA
La formation professionnelle dans les houillères des pays
de la Communauté [Vocational training in the coal mines
of the countries of the Community].
ECSC HA, 1956.　514p.
F　　1669

496 DITTRICH, E.
Étude sur la structure sociale et économique de la région
Sieg-Lahn-Dill [Study on the social and economic
structure of the Sieg-Lahn-Dill region].
Commission, 1968.　160p.　Collection: regional
economy and policy. 2: Development and conversion
programme, 10.
D F　　4252

497 DOERR, W.
La technique de mesure et de l'automation [Measurement
and automation technique].
ECSC HA, 1967.　204p.　New technical processes in
the iron and steel industry: a personal training manual, 1.
Studies: vocational training.
D F I N　　13233

498 DOHRENDORF
Enlarging the Community (Rapport d'information sur
l'élargissement de la Communauté).
ESC, 1970.   12p.
D E F I N   16682

499 DOMINICI, G.
Le financement des investissements et les aspects sociaux
de la reconversion [Financing of investments and social
aspects of conversion].
ECSC HA, 1963.   255p.   Collection: regional
economy and policy. 1: Industrial conversion in Europe, 3.
D F I N   3323

500 DONDELINGER, J., chairman
Rapport du groupe mixte d'experts pour l'écoulement des
produits originaires des E.A.M.A. [Report of a mixed
group of experts on the marketing of products from the
A.A.S.M.].
Council, 1967.   186p.   Association between the
EEC and the Associated African States and Malagasy.
D F I N

501 DOUBLET
Étude sur la physionomie actuelle de la sécurité sociale
dans les pays de la C.E.E. [Study on the current situation
of social security in the countries of the E.E.C.].
Commission EEC, 1962.   130p.   Studies: social
policy series, 3.
D F I N   8058

502 DOVE, A.
A study of the evolution of concentration in the mechanical
engineering sector for the United Kingdom [Étude sur
l'évolution de la concentration dans le secteur de la
construction de machines non électriques au
Royaume-Uni].
Commission, 1976.   264p.
E   8708

503 DOVE, A.
A study of the evolution of concentration in the
pharmaceutical industry for the United Kingdom [Étude
sur l'évolution de la concentration dans l'industrie
pharmaceutique au Royaume-Uni].
Commission, 1977.   168p.
E   8707

504 DOYLE, F.
Forms of cooperation in the fishing industry. Denmark,
Ireland, United Kingdom [Formes de coopération dans le
secteur de la pêche. Danemark, Irlande, Royaume-Uni].
Commission, 1976.   var. pag.   Information on
agriculture, 9.
E   8842

505 DRECHSEL, M.
La conduite sur place des opérations de conversion
industrielle [On-the-spot direction of industrial conversion
operations].
ECSC HA, 1963.   352p.   Collection: regional
economy and policy. 1: Industrial conversion in Europe, 4.
D F I N   3324

506 DRESEN, M. P.
Rapport sur les résultats d'une enquête effectuée en
janvier 1956 sur la situation des coûts et recettes des
charbonnages de la Ruhr [Report on the results of a
survey carried out in January 1956 on the situation of costs
and returns of the Ruhr coalfields].
ECSC HA, 1956.   48p.
F   729

507 DREWER, S.
The economic impact of immigrant workers in Western
Europe [L'impact économique des travailleurs immigrants
dans l'Europe occidentale].
In European studies. Teachers' series, 18.
Commission (L), 1974.   4p.
E   U/74/18

508 DREYER, H.
Teneur en métaux lourds des jus de fruits et produits
similaires [Heavy metal content of fruit juices and similar
products].
Commission, 1975.   215p.   Internal information on
agriculture, 148.
D F   VI/1594/75

509 DRIESPRONG, C. P.
Les organismes groupant les producteurs pour la vente
des fruits et légumes frais dans les États membres de la
CEE. Aspects juridiques. Importance. Rôle économique
[Growers' associations for the sale of fresh fruit and
vegetables in the Member States of the EEC. Legal
aspects. Importance. Economic role].
Commission EEC, 1965.   123p.   Studies:
agricultural series, 19.
D F I N   8139

510 DRIEUX, H.
Résistance des virus dans les produits d'origine animale
[Virus resistance in products of animal origin].
Commission, 1975.   305p.   Internal information on
agriculture, 165.
F   VI/5000/75

511 DRION, H.
La réparation des conséquences dommageables d'une
violation des articles 85 et 86 du traité instituant la CEE
[Compensation for damage suffered through infringement
of Articles 85 and 86 of the Treaty establishing the EEC].
Commission EEC, 1966.   74p.   Studies: competition
series, 1.
D F I N   8153

512 DRION, J.
La réparation des conséquences dommageables d'une
violation des articles 85 et 86 du traité instituant la CEE
[Compensation for damage suffered through infringement
of Articles 85 and 86 of the Treaty establishing the EEC].
Commission EEC, 1966.   74p.   Studies: competition
series, 1.
D F I N   8153

513 DROBNIG
The suretyship in the law of the Member States of the
European Communities (Le cautionnement dans le droit
des États membres des Communautés européennes).
Commission, 1974.   115p.   Studies:
competition–approximation of legislation series, 14.
D E F I N   8301

514 DROESCH, M.
Évolution et prévisions de la population active agricole
[Development and estimates of the working agricultural
population].
Commission, 1970.   var. pag.   Internal information
on agriculture, 61.
D F   4131/VI/70

515 DROEVEN, G.
Conséquences écologiques de l'application des techniques
modernes de production en agriculture [Ecological results
from the application of modern production techniques in
agriculture].
Commission, 1974.   var. pag.   Internal information
on agriculture, 137.
D F   VI/3722/74

516 DRÖSCHER, W.
Exposé sur les conditions politiques de la réalisation
intégrale et de l'élargissement des Communautés [Report
on the political conditions of the full realization and
enlargement of the Communities].
EP, 1968.   12p.
D F I N

517 DROUIN, P.
French industry and the Common Market [L'industrie
française et le Marché Commun].
Inf Ser, 1962.   55p.   Community topics, 5.
E

518 DU GRANRUT, C.
Vocational guidance and training for women workers
[Orientation et formation professionnelle pour les
travailleurs féminins].
Commission, 1976.   65p.
E   CB-22-76-164-EN-C

519 DUBOIS, N., chairman
Le secours et le sauvetage [Assistance and rescue].
Commission, 1973.   88p.   General Commission on
safety and health in the iron and steel industry.
D F I N   1524

520 DUCHEMIN, J. M.
Essai d'appréciation des conditions d'application et des
résultats d'une politique de réforme en agriculture dans
des régions agricoles difficiles. 1: Morvan [Attempt at
estimating the conditions from the application and results
of a reform policy in agriculture in difficult agricultural
regions. 1: Morvan].
Commission, 1974.   183p.   Internal information on
agriculture, 138.
F   VI/4572/74

521 DUCHEMIN, J. M.
Essai d'appréciation des conditions d'application et des
résultats d'une politique de réforme en agriculture dans
des régions agricoles difficiles. 2: Queyras [Attempt at
estimating the conditions from the application and results
of a reform policy in agriculture in difficult agricultural
regions. 2: Queyras].
Commission, 1975.   var. pag.   Internal information
on agriculture, 150.
F   VI/1988/75

522 DUDZIAK
La formation professionnelle dans l'industrie sidérurgique
des pays de la Communauté [Vocational training in the
iron and steel industry of the countries of the
Community].
ECSC HA, 1954.   264p.
F

523 DUFF, A.
The development of summit meetings [Le développement
des réunions de sommet].
In European studies. Teachers' series, 22.
Commission (L), 1975.   3p.
E   U/75/22

524 DÜKER, H.
Forschung in der deutschen Eisen- und Stahlindustrie
[Research in the German iron and steel industry /
Recherche dans la sidérurgie allemande].
Commission, 1967.   104p.   Collection:
occupational physiology and psychology, 3/7.
D   13749

525 DUMARD
Effets du prix et du revenu sur la consommation des
boissons dans les États membres des Communautés
[Effects of price and income on the consumption of
beverages in the Member States of the Communities].
Commission, 1973.   var. pag.
Studies: competition–approximation of legislation
series, 19.
D F I N   8380

526 DUMAY, M.
Le financement des investissements et les aspects sociaux
de la reconversion [Financing of investments and social
aspects of conversion].
ECSC HA, 1963.   255p.   Collection: regional
economy and policy. 1: Industrial conversion in Europe, 3.
D F I N   3323

527 DUMONCEAU, H.
La conduite sur place des opérations de conversion
industrielle [On-the-spot direction of industrial conversion
operations].
ECSC HA, 1963.   352p.   Collection: regional
economy and policy. 1: Industrial conversion in Europe, 4.
D F I N   3324

528 DUMONT, B. L.
Étude sur les qualités des carcasses de bovins en France
[Study on the qualities of beef carcasses in France].
In Agricultural statistical studies, 4.
Eurostat, 1969.   76p.
D F N

529 DUMONT, B. L.
Étude sur les qualités des carcasses de bovins et porcins
dans les pays de la Communauté Économique Européenne
[Study on the qualities of beef and pork carcasses in the
countries of the European Economic Community].
Eurostat, 1966.   80p.   Agricultural statistics.
D/F   3944

530 DUMONT, B. L.
Influence des différents caractères de la carcasse de
bovins sur la détermination de son prix [Influence of
different characteristics of the beef carcass on its price
determination].
In Agricultural statistical studies, 1.
Eurostat, 1968.   33p.
F   14892

531 DUMOUTET, P.
Inflammation et combustion de charbon gras sur grille
[Ignition and combustion of soft coal on grate].
ECSC HA, 1966.   65p.   Technical research: coal, 3.
Coal combustion.
D F I N   11735

532 DUMSER
La formation des formateurs. Problèmes, méthodes et
expériences dans les industries de la C.E.C.A. [Training
of the trainers. Problems, methods and experiments in the
industries of the E.C.S.C.].
ECSC HA, 1962.   127p.
F   8514

533 DUPEYROUX, J.-J.
Étude sur la physionomie actuelle de la sécurité sociale
dans les pays de la C.E.E. [Study on the current situation
of social security in the countries of the E.E.C.].
Commission EEC, 1962.   130p.   Studies: social
policy series, 3.
D F I N   8058

534 DUPEYROUX, J.-J.
Évolution et tendances des systèmes de sécurité sociale
des pays membres des Communautés européennes et de la
Grande-Bretagne [Development and trends in the social
security systems of the member countries of the European
Communities and Great Britain].
ECSC HA, 1967.   169p.
D F I N   13601

535 DUPEYROUX, J.-J.
Le régime juridique des organisations professionnelles
dans les pays membres de la C.E.C.A. [Legal
administration of professional organisations in the
member countries of the E.C.S.C.].
ECSC HA, 1968.   666p.   Collection: labour law.
D F I N   13879

536 DUPONT, H.
La reconversion des bassins houillers en France
[Conversion of coalfields in France].
Commission, 1973.   185p.   Pamphlets on industrial
conversion, 22.
D F I N   8386

537 DUQUESNE DE LA VINELLE, L.
Options in transport tariff policy (Options de la politique
tarifaire dans les transports).
Commission EEC, 1966.   189p.   Studies: transport
series, 1.
D E F I N   8146

538 DUQUESNE DE LA VINELLE, M.
La conduite sur place des opérations de conversion
industrielle [On-the-spot direction of industrial conversion
operations].
ECSC HA, 1963.   352p.   Collection: regional
economy and policy. 1: Industrial conversion in Europe, 4.
D F I N   3324

539 DUQUESNE DE LA VINELLE, M.
Travaux de la Commission de la C.E.E. en matière de
développement régional [The work of the Commission of
the E.E.C. with regard to regional development].
ECSC HA, 1960.   3p.   Intergovernmental
Conference on Industrial Redevelopment: report of the
Commission of the E.E.C.
F   904

540 DURAND, P., chairman
Étude comparative des sources du droit du travail dans les
pays de la Communauté européenne du charbon et de
l'acier [Comparative study of the sources of labour law in
the countries of the European Coal and Steel Community].
ECSC, 1957.   180p.   Collection: labour law, 1.
F   1880

541 DURAND, P.
Grève et lock-out [Strike and lock-out].
ECSC HA, 1961.   399p.   Collection: labour law. 2:
Labour law in the Community, 5.
D F I N   2367

542 DURAND, P.
La participation des travailleurs à l'organisation de la vie
économique et sociale en France [Participation of workers
in the organisation of economic and social life in France].
ECSC HA, 1962.   62p.   Collection: labour law, 1.
D F I N   2887

543 DURAND, P.
La protection des travailleurs en cas de perte de l'emploi
[Protection of workers in the event of loss of employment].

ECSC HA, 1961.   489p.   Collection: labour law. 2:
Labour law in the Community, 11.
D F I N   2626

544 DURAND, P.
La représentation des travailleurs sur le plan de
l'entreprise dans le droit des pays membres de la
C.E.C.A. [Workers' representation at management level
in the law of the member countries of the E.C.S.C.].
ECSC HA, 1959.   348p.   Collection: labour law, 3.
D F I N   2104

544A DURAND, P.
Les sources du droit du travail [Sources of labour law].
ECSC HA, 1962.   192p.   Collection: labour law. 2:
Labour law in the Community, 1.
D F I N   2773

545 DURAND, P.
La stabilité de l'emploi dans le droit des pays membres de
la C.E.C.A. [Stability of employment in the law of the
member countries of the E.C.S.C.].
ECSC HA, 1958.   311p.   Collection: labour law, 2.
D F I N   1999

546 DURAZZO, C.
Formes de coopération dans le secteur de la pêche. 1:
Synthèse, R.F. d'Allemagne, Italie [Forms of cooperation
in the fishing industry. 1: Summary, F.R. of Germany,
Italy].
Commission, 1970.   var. pag.   Internal information
on agriculture, 68.
D F   14715/VI/69

547 DURAZZO, C.
Gestion économique des bateaux pour la pêche à la
sardine. Recherche des conditions optimales Italie, Côte
méditerranéenne française. 1: Synthèse [Economic
administration of sardine fishing boats. Research into the

optimum conditions, Italy, French Mediterranean Coast.
1: Summary].
Commission, 1971.   178p.   Internal information on
agriculture, 79.
F I   VI/3012/71

548 DURAZZO, C.
Gestion économique des bateaux pour la pêche à la
sardine. Recherche des conditions optimales Italie, Côte
méditerranéenne française. 2: Résultats des enquêtes
dans les zones de pêche [Economic administration of
sardine fishing boats. Research into the optimum
conditions, Italy, French Mediterranean coast. 2: Results
of the fishing zone surveys].
Commission, 1971.   334p.   Internal information on
agriculture, 80.
F I   VI/3012/71

549 DURAZZO, C.
Volume et degré de l'emploi dans la pêche maritime
[Volume and extent of employment in sea fishing].
Commission, 1968.   var. pag.   Internal information
on agriculture, 32.
D F   6993/VI/68

550 EHRLICH, K.
Phraseological vocabulary compiled on the basis of the
Treaties establishing the European Communities
(Vocabulaire phraséologique établi sur la base des Traités
instituant les Communautés européennes); 2nd ed.
Commission, 1974.   var. pag.
DK/D/E/F/I/N   IX/1572/73

551 EHRLICH, K.
Vocabulary of the staff regulations of officials of the
European Communities and the conditions of employment
of other servants, plus other relevant Community
documents (Vocabulaire du statut des fonctionnaires des
Communautés européennes et du régime applicable aux

autres agents ainsi que de documents administratifs s'y rapportant).
Commission, 1975.   var. pag.
DK/D/E/F/I/N   IX/1435/1975

552 EICKELPASCH, D.
Les aciéries [The steel-works].
Commission, 1971.   283p.   New technical processes in the iron and steel industry: a personal training manual, 3. Studies: vocational training.
D F I N   17433

553 EIJCK, van
Tendances de la production et de la consommation en denrées alimentaires dans la C.E.E. 1956–1965 [Trends in food production and consumption in the E.E.C. 1956–1965].
Commission EEC, 1960.   266p.   Studies: agricultural series, 2.
D F I N   8005

554 ELLIS, F.
The European Community and the Third World [La Communauté européenne et le tiers monde].
In European studies. Teachers' series, 19.
Commission (L), 1975.   4p.
E   U/74/19

555 ELLIS, F.
The European Community and the Third World 2 [La Communauté européenne et le tiers monde 2].
In European studies. Teachers' series, 20.
Commission (L), 1975.   pp.5–8.
E   U/74/20

556 ENGEL. A.
Les aciéries [The steel-works].
Commission, 1971.   283p.   New technical processes in the iron and steel industry: a personal training manual, 3. Studies: vocational training.
D F I N   17433

557 ENGELKE, F.
Étude sur les qualités des carcasses de bovins et porcins
dans les pays de la Communauté Économique Européenne
[Study on the qualities of beef and pork carcasses in the
countries of the European Economic Community].
Eurostat, 1966.   80p.   Agricultural statistics.
D/F   3944

558 ESSEIMANN, W.
Intégration verticale et contrats en agriculture. 1: R.F.
d'Allemagne [Vertical integration and contracts in
agriculture. 1: F.R. of Germany].
Commission, 1973.   136p.   Internal information on
agriculture, 106.
D F   VI/3359/73

559 ESSELMANN, W.
Analyse du marché du porcelet dans l'optique d'une
stabilisation du marché du porc [Analysis of the piglet
market in the perspective of a stabilization of the pork
market].
Commission, 1973.   143p.   Internal information on
agriculture, 115.
D F   VI/3423/73

560 ETZEL, F.
Statements by Herr Franz Etzel Vice-President of the
High Authority, to the Common Assembly on the changes
in the coal-selling and importing organizations in the
Community. May 11, 1955 and November 23, 1955
Strasbourg (Déclarations de Monsieur Franz Etzel
Vice-président de la Haute Autorité devant l'Assemblée
Commune concernant la modification des organisations de
vente et d'achat du charbon dans la Communauté. 11 mai
1955–23 novembre 1955 Strasbourg].
ECSC, 1955.   40p.
D E F   1663

561 ETZEL, F.
A target for Euratom. Report submitted by Mr. Louis
Armand, Mr. Franz Etzel and Mr. Francesco Giordiani at

the request of the governments of Belgium, France,
German Federal Republic, Italy, Luxembourg and the
Netherlands (Un objectif pour Euratom. Rapport
présenté par M. Louis Armand, M. Franz Etzel et M.
Francesco Giordiani sur la demande des Gouvernements
de la République Fédérale d'Allemagne, de la Belgique, de
la France, de l'Italie, du Luxembourg et des Pays-Bas).
EAEC, 1957.   104p.
D E F I N

562 ETZEL, F.
Zur europäischen Integration. Auszüge aus der Rede des
Vizepräsidenten der Hohen Behörde des Europäischen
Gemeinschaft für Kohle and Stahl vor der Industrie- und
Handelskammer Essen am 7. Juni 1955 [Towards
European integration. Extract from a speech of the
Vice-President of the High Authority of the European
Coal and Steel Community to the Essen Industry and
Chamber of Commerce on 7 June 1955 / Vers l'intégration
européenne. Extrait du discours du Vice-Président de la
Haute Autorité de la Communauté européenne du charbon
et de l'acier devant l'industrie et la chambre de commerce
d'Essen, 7 juin 1955].
ECSC, 1955.   23p.
D

563 EULER, M.
Enquête sur les budgets familiaux an Allemagne fédérale
[Survey on family budgets in Federal Germany].
In Budgets familiaux 1962/63. Deutschland (BR).
Eurostat, 1966.   pp.25–129.   Social statistics:
special series, 5.
F   3953

564 EVAIN
European Union. Opinion (Union européenne. Avis).
ESC, 1975.   33p.
DK D E F I N   6937

565 EVANS, J., chairman
Progress report on the Common Agricultural Policy.
Study (Bilan de la politique agricole commune. Étude).
ESC, 1975.   47p.
DK D E F I N   7112

566 EVANS, M. E.
A study of the evolution of concentration in the electrical
appliances industry for the United Kingdom. Electrical
appliances primarily for domestic use. Broadcast receiving
and sound reproducing equipment [Étude sur l'évolution
de la concentration dans l'industrie des appareils
électriques au Royaume-Uni. Appareils
électrodomestiques. Appareils électriques, radios,
télévision, électro-acoustique].
Commission, 1977.   366p.
E   CH-SL-77-002-EN-C

567 EVELY, R. W.
A study of the evolution of concentration in the beverages
industry for the United Kingdom. Part one: Industry
structure and concentration, 1969–1974 [Étude sur
l'évolution de la concentration dans l'industrie des
boissons au Royaume-Uni. Partie première: La structure
industrielle et la concentration, 1969–1974].
Commission, 1977.   263p.
E   8942

568 EVELY, R. W.
A study of the evolution of concentration in the food
distribution industry for the United Kingdom. Volume 2:
Price surveys [Étude sur l'évolution de la concentration
dans l'industrie de la distribution des produits
alimentaires au Royaume-Uni. Tome 2: Enquêtes de prix].
Commission, 1977.   152p.
E   8762

569 EVELY, R. W.
A study of the evolution of concentration in the food
industry for the United Kingdom. Product market
structure [Étude sur l'évolution de la concentration dans

l'industrie alimentaire au Royaume-Uni. Structure des
marchés de produit].
Commission, 1976.   2 vols.
E   8827, 8709

570 EVERSEN, H. J.
Recueil de textes. Organisation, compétences et
procédure de la Cour [Collected texts. Organization,
jurisdiction and procedure of the Court].
Court, 1963.   332p.
D F I N   3306

571 EYQUEM, B.
Les comptes sociaux des Pays Membres de la Communauté
Économique Européenne 1962–1963 [Social accounts of
the Member Countries of the European Economic
Community 1962–1963].
In Social statistics, 5/1967.   Eurostat, 1967.   184p.
D/F, I/N   4145

572 EYQUEM, B.
Indicateurs de sécurité sociale [Social security indicators].
Commission, 1971.   122p.
D F I N   8292

573 FABER, J.
Constatation des cours des vins de table à la production. 1:
France et RF d'Allemagne [Ascertaining the production
prices of table wines. 1: France and FR of Germany].
Commission, 1970.   171p.   Internal information on
agriculture, 59.
D F   2565/VI/70

574 FABER, J.
Constatation des cours des vins de table à la production. 2:
Italie, GD de Luxembourg [Ascertaining the production
prices of table wines. 2: Italy, GD of Luxembourg].
Commission, 1971.   var. pag.   Internal information
on agriculture, 75.
D F   VI/17662/69

575 FABER, M.
The European Community in maps (La Communauté
européenne. Cartes).
Commission, 1974.   14 maps.
DK D E F I N   6574

576 FABRA, P.
French industry and the Common Market [L'industrie
française et le Marché Commun].
Inf Ser, 1962.   55p.   Community topics, 5.
E

577 FACCA, U.
L'emploi agricole dans les pays de la C.E.E. Tome 1:
Structure [Agricultural employment in the countries of
the E.E.C. Volume 1: Structure].
Commission EEC, 1964.   61p.   Studies: social policy
series, 7.
D F I N   8108

578 FACCA, U.
L'emploi agricole dans les pays de la C.E.E. Tome 2:
Évolution et perspectives [Agricultural employment in
the countries of the E.E.C. Volume 2: Development and
prospects].
Commission EEC, 1964.   51p.   Studies: social policy
series, 8.
D F I N   8123

579 FAES, J.
Enquête sur les salaires dans les industries de la
Communauté économique européenne. Année 1959
[Survey on wages in the industries of the European
Economic Community. 1959].
In Social statistics, 3/1961.   Eurostat, 1961.   170p.
D F I N

580 FALKENBERG, K.-F.
Growing scarcity of resources. A temporary phenomenon
or a question of survival. Approaches to food policy in the
USA and the European Community. A comparative study

(Raréfaction des ressources, phénomène temporaire ou
problème d'existence. Voies empruntées pour les
États-Unis et la Communauté européenne pour une
politique alimentaire. Examen comparatif).
In Newsletter on the common agricultural policy,
2/1976.   Pr Inf, 1976.   8p.
D E F I N   X/316/76

581 FANO, D.
Il contributo delle 'Comunità montane' in Italia allo
sviluppo dell'agricoltura di montagna [The contribution of
'Comunità montane' to the development of hill farming in
Italy / La contribution des 'Comunità montane' au
développement de l'agriculture de montagne en Italie].
Commission, 1976.   209p.   Information on
agriculture, 11.
I   8861

582 FANO, D.
Gli 'enti de sviluppo agricolo' in Italia nella riforma delle
strutture. Problemi e prospettive di adattamento [The
'enti di sviluppo agricolo' in structural reform in Italy.
Adjustment problems and prospects / Les 'enti di sviluppo
agricolo' en Italie et la réforme des structures. Problèmes
et perspectives d'adaptation].
Commission, 1976.   285p.   Information on
agriculture, 12.
I   8862

583 FANO, P. L.
Analyse de certaines expériences d'aménagement et de
gestion de 'zones industrielles' dans les pays de la
Communauté économique européenne (Belgique, France,
république fédérale d'Allemagne, Italie, Pays-Bas)
[Analysis of some schemes for planning and administration
of 'industrial zones' in the countries of the European
Economic Community (Belgium, France, Federal
Republic of Germany, Italy, the Netherlands)].
Commission, 1972.   175p.   Collection: regional
economy and policy. 1: Industrial conversion in Europe, 9.
D F I N   8362

584 FANTOLI, A.
La reconversion dans l'industrie charbonnière et
sidérurgique en Italie [Conversion in the coal and iron and
steel industry in Italy].
Commission, 1973.   69p.   Pamphlets on industrial
conversion, 21.
D F I N   8388

585 FANTOZZI, A.
Dispositions fiscales en matière de coopération et de fusion
d'exploitations agricoles. 4: Italie [Tax arrangements
concerning cooperation and amalgamation of farms. 4:
Italy].
Commission, 1973.   175p.   Internal information on
agriculture, 98.
F I   VI/16341/69

586 FASSINA, B., chairman
The situation of small and medium-sized undertakings in
the European Community. Study (La situation des petites
et moyennes entreprises dans la Communauté
européenne. Étude).
ESC, 1976.   66p.
DK D E F I N   6688

587 FASSINA, B., chairman
Study of the Section for Industry, Commerce, Crafts and
Services on 'the situation of small and medium-sized
undertakings in the European Community' [Étude de la
section pour l'industrie, le commerce, les métiers et les
services sur 'la situation des petites et moyennes
entreprises dans la Communauté européenne].
ESC, 1974.   92p.
E   CES 232/73

588 FASSINOTTI, J.L.
Possibilités de création d'industries exportatrices dans les
États africains et malgache associés. Conserves et
préparation de fruits tropicaux. Dattes. Bananes.
Agrumes et huiles essentielles. Ananas et conserves au
sirop. Anacardes et amandes cajou. Arachides de bouche.

Fruits exotiques divers [Possibilities for the
establishment of exporting industries in the Associated
African States and Madagascar. Preserving and
preparation of tropical fruits. Dates. Bananas. Citrus
fruits and aromatic oils. Pineapples and preserves in
syrup. Cashew nuts and almonds. Edible groundnuts.
Various tropical fruits].
Commission, 1974.   560p.
F   VIII/225/74

589 FASSINOTTI, J. L.
Possibilités de création d'industries exportatrices dans les
États africains et malgache associés. Conserves et
préparation de fruits tropicaux. Dattes. Bananes.
Agrumes et huiles essentielles. Ananas et conserves au
sirop. Anacardes et amandes cajou. Arachides de bouche.
Fruits exotiques divers. Rapport de synthèse
[Possibilities for the establishment of exporting industries
in the Associated African States and Madagascar.
Preserving and preparation of tropical fruits. Dates.
Bananas. Citrus fruits and aromatic oils. Pineapples and
preserves in syrup. Cashew nuts and almonds. Edible
groundnuts. Various tropical fruits. Summary report].
Commission, 1975.   22p.
D E F I N   VIII/225/74

590 FASSINOTTI, J. L.
Possibilités de création d'industries exportatrices dans les
États africains et malgache associés. Fabrication de
cigares et cigarillos [Possibilities for the establishment of
exporting industries in the Associated African States and
Madagascar. Manufacture of cigars and cigarillos].
Commission, 1974.   158p.
F   VIII/226/74

591 FASSINOTTI, J. L.
Possibilités de création d'industries exportatrices dans les
États africains et malgache associés. Fabrication de
cigares et cigarillos. Rapport de synthèse [Possibilities for
the establishment of exporting industries in the

Associated African States and Madagascar. Manufacture
of cigars and cigarillos. Summary report].
Commission, 1975.　　19p.
D E F I N　　VIII/226/74

592 FASSINOTTI, J. L.
Possibilités de création d'industries exportatrices dans les
États africains et malgache associés. Produits
électro-mécaniques. Produits électroniques [Possibilities
for the establishment of exporting industries in the
Associated African States and Madagascar.
Electro-mechanical products. Electronic products].
Commission, 1975.　　3 vols.
F　　VIII/224/74

593 FASSINOTTI, J. L.
Possibilités de création d'industries exportatrices dans les
États africains et malgache associés. Produits
électro-mécaniques. Produits électroniques. Rapport de
synthèse [Possibilities for the establishment of exporting
industries in the Associated African States and
Madagascar. Electro-mechanical products. Electronic
products. Summary report].
Commission, 1975.　　23p.
D E F I N　　VIII/224/74

594 FAUCHER, F.
Le marché foncier et les baux ruraux. Effets des mesures
de réforme des structures agricoles. 2: R.F. d'Allemagne,
France [The land market and rural leases. Effects of
reform measures of agricultural structures. 2: F.R. of
Germany, France].
Commission, 1972.　　var. pag.　　Internal information
on agriculture, 82.
F　　VI/537/72

595 FAURE, M.
Vers l'élection directe de l'Assemblée parlementaire
européenne [Towards the direct election of the European
Parliamentary Assembly].
EPA, 1960.　　79p.
F　　2516

596 FAVERGE, J. M.
Recherche dans les charbonnages belges [Research in the
Belgian coalmines].
Commission, 1967.   139p.   Collection: occupational
physiology and psychology, 3/2.
F   13749

597 FAVERGE, J. M.
Recherche dans les charbonnages français [Research in
the French coalmines].
Commission, 1967.   146p.   Collection: occupational
physiology and psychology, 3/3.
F   12427

598 FAVERGE, J. M.
Recherche dans les mines de fer françaises [Research in
the French iron mines].
Commission, 1967.   97p.   Collection: occupational
physiology and psychology, 3/6.
F   13749

599 FEDERICI, N.
Le condizioni di lavoro delle donne salariate nei sei stati
membri della Comunità europea. Italia [The conditions of
work for wage-earning women in the six Member States of
the European Community. Italy / Les conditions de travail
des femmes salariées dans les six États membres de la
Communauté européenne. Italie].
Commission, 1972.   186p.
I   V/167/73

600 FERRANDI, J.
L'action de la Communauté économique européenne à
l'égard des pays associés. Discours prononcé par M.
Jacques Ferrandi, directeur des programmes de la
recherche et du développement, à l'occasion de la
conférence économique africaine et malgache, à Marseille,
octobre 1962 [The action of the European Economic
Community in the associated countries. Address delivered
to the African and Malagasy Economic Conference at
Marseilles, October 1962, by Mr. Jacques Ferrandi,

Director of Research and Development Programmes].
Commission EEC, 1962.   32p.
D F   8074

601 FERRANTI, B. de, chairman
EEC's transport problems with East European
Countries. Opinion [Les problèmes des transports de la
CEE avec les pays européens de l'est. Avis].
ESC, 1977.   164p.
DK D E F I N

602 FERRO, O.
Prévisions agricoles. 2: Possibilités d'utilisation de
certains modèles, méthodes et techniques dans la
Communauté [Agricultural forecasting. 2: Possibilities of
using certain models, methods and techniques in the
Community].
Commission, 1970.   249p.   Internal information on
agriculture, 63.
D F   8433/VI/69

603 FERRO, O.
Projections de la production et de la consommation de
produits agricoles—'1977'. 3: Italie [Projections of
production and consumption of agricultural
products—'1977'. 3' Italy].
Commission, 1973.   186p.   Internal information on
agriculture, 117.
D F   VI/815/72

604 FILIPPI, F.
The aeronautical and space industries of the Community
compared with those of the United Kingdom and the
United States (Les industries aéronautiques et spatiales
de la Communauté, comparées à celles de la
Grande-Bretagne et des États-Unis).
Commission, 1971.   5 vols.   Studies: industry
series, 4.
D E F I N   8284

605 FILIPPI, F.
Les conditions d'installation d'entreprises industrielles
dans les États africains et malgache associés. Volume 7:
République du Tchad [Conditions for the setting-up of
industrial undertakings in the Associated African States
and Madagascar. Volume 7: Republic of Chad]. 2nd ed.
Commission, 1975.   83p.
F   VIII/1259/74

606 FILIPPI, F.
Les conditions d'installation d'entreprises industrielles
dans les États africains et malgache associés. Volume 9:
République du Burundi [Conditions for the setting-up of
industrial undertakings in the Associated African States
and Madagascar. Volume 9: Republic of Burundi]; 2nd ed.
Commission, 1975.   79p.
F   VIII/1243/74

607 FILIPPI, F.
Les conditions d'installation d'entreprises industrielles
dans les États africains et malgache associés. Volume 10:
République du Rwanda [Conditions for the setting-up of
industrial undertakings in the Associated African States
and Madagascar. Volume 10: Republic of Rwanda]; 2nd
ed.
Commission, 1975.   72p.
F   VIII/1256/74

608 FILIPPI, F.
Les conditions d'installation d'entreprises industrielles
dans les États africains et malgache associés. Volume 11:
République du Zaïre [Conditions for the setting-up of
industrial undertakings in the Associated African States
and Madagascar. Volume 11: Republic of Zaïre]; 2nd ed.
Commission, 1975.   104p.
F   VIII/1261/74

609 FILIPPI, F.
Conditions for the setting-up of industrial undertakings in
the associated African states and Madagascar. Volume 13:
Democratic Republic of Somalia (Les conditions

d'installation d'entreprises industrielles dans les États
africains et malgache associés. Volume 13: République
démocratique de Somalie); 2nd ed.
Commission, 1975.   71p.
E F I   VIII/1258/74

610 FILIPPI, F.
Les industries aéronautiques et spatiales de la
Communauté, comparées à celles de la Grande-Bretagne et
des États-Unis. Annexe au Rapport Général [The
aeronautical and space industries of the Community
compared with those of the United Kingdom and the
United States. Appendix to General Report].
Commission, 1969.   10 vols.
F

611 FILIPPI, F.
Possibilités de création d'industries exportatrices dans les
États africains et malgache associés. Produits de
l'élevage. Viandes, cuirs et peaux, chaussures, articles en
cuir [Possibilities for the establishment of exporting
industries in the Associated African States and
Madagascar. Products from rearing. Meat, hides and
skins, shoes, leather articles].
Commission, 1974.   5 vols.
F   VIII/223/74

612 FILIPPI, F.
Possibilités de création d'industries exportatrices dans les
États africains et malgache associés. Produits de
l'élevage. Viandes, cuirs et peaux, chaussures, articles en
cuir. Rapport de synthèse [Possibilities for the
establishment of exporting industries in the Associated
African States and Madagascar. Products from rearing.
Meat, hides and skins, shoes, leather articles. Summary
report].
Commission, 1975.   27p.
D E F I N   VIII/223/74

613 FINALDI, D.
L'information relative aux revenus et aux patrimoines
dans les pays de la Communauté [Information relating to

incomes and inheritances in the countries of the
Community].
Commission, 1973.   43p.   Studies: social policy
series, 22.
D F I N   8377

614 FINET, P.
Address by M. Paul Finet President of the High Authority
to the European Parliamentary Assembly. Ordinary
Session 1957–1958 Strasbourg. May 13 1958 [Discours de
M. Paul Finet Président de la Haute Autorité devant
l'Assemblée parlementaire européenne. Session ordinaire
1957–1958 Strasbourg. 13 mai 1958].
ECSC HA, 1958.   33p.
D E   2047

615 FISHWICK, F.
A study of the evolution of concentration in the United
Kingdom textile industry [Étude sur l'évolution de la
concentration dans l'industrie du textile au
Royaume-Uni].
Commission, 1976.   226p.
E   8701

616 FLESSELLES, J.
Méthodes pour la détermination du taux d'humidité du
tabac [Methods for the determination of the rate of
moisture in tobacco].
Commission, 1972.   var. pag.   Internal information
on agriculture, 91.
D F   VI/31/73/72

617 FOCCROULLE, C.
Les aciéries [The steel-works].
Commission, 1971.   283p.   New technical processes
in the iron and steel industry: a personal training manual,
3.   Studies: vocational training.
D F I N   17433

618 FOCCROULLE, C.
Les laminoirs [The rolling mills].
Commission, 1972.   240p.   New technical processes

in the iron and steel industry: a personal training manual,
4. Studies: vocational training.
D F I N 8349

619 FOCCROULLE, C.
Mécanisation, automatisation et techniques de mesure
dans les services des hauts fourneaux [Mechanisation,
automation and measurement techniques in blast-furnace
works].
Commission, 1969. 172p. New technical processes
in the iron and steel industry: a personal training manual,
2. Studies: vocational training.
D F I N 14722

620 FOCCROULLE, C.
La technique de mesure et de l'automation [Measurement
and automation technique].
ECSC HA, 1967. 204p. New technical processes in
the iron and steel industry: a personal training manual,
1. Studies: vocational training.
D F I N 13233

621 FONTAINE, A.
La C.E.E. L'Europe de l'Est [The E.E.C. East Europe].
Bureau (P), 1975. loose-leaf. Les documents de
Communauté européenne informations. L'Europe
par les textes.
F

622 FONTANA, A.
Gestion économique des bateaux pour la pêche à la
sardine. Recherche des conditions optimales Italie, Côte
méditerranéenne française. 1: Synthèse [Economic
administration of sardine fishing boats. Research into the
optimum conditions, Italy, French Mediterrranean coast.
1: Summary].
Commission, 1971. 178p. Internal information on
agriculture, 79.
F I VI/3012/71

623 FONTANA, A.
Gestion économique des bateaux pour la pêche à la
sardine. Recherche des conditions optimales Italie, Côte
méditerranéenne française. 2: Résultats des enquêtes
dans les zones de pêche [Economic administration of
sardine fishing boats. Research into the optimum
conditions, Italy, French Mediterranean coast. 2: Results
of the fishing zone surveys].
Commission, 1971.   334p.   Internal information on
agriculture, 80.
F I   VI/3012/71

FORSTER, A. Sadler-, *see* SADLER-FORSTER, A.

624 FÖRSTER, W.
Détermination des erreurs lors des recensements du bétail
au moyen de sondages [Determination of errors in sample
livestock censuses].
Commission, 1967.   62p.   Internal information on
agriculture, 16.
F

625 FORTE, F.
The aeronautical and space industries of the Community
compared with those of the United Kingdom and the
United States (Les industries aéronautiques et spatiales
de la Communauté, comparées à celles de la
Grande-Bretagne et des États-Unis).
Commission, 1971.   5 vols.   Studies: industry
series, 4.
D E F I N   8284

626 FORTE, F.
Les industries aéronautiques et spatiales de la
Communauté, comparées à celles de la Grande-Bretagne
et des États-Unis. Annexe au Rapport Général [The
aeronautical and space industries of the Community
compared with those of the United Kingdom and the
United States. Appendix to General Report].
Commission,1969.   10 vols.
F

FORTMAN, W. F. de Gaay, *see* GAAY FORTMAN, W. F. de

627 FOUGERON
Essai d'appréciation des conditions d'application et des résultats d'une politique de réforme en agriculture dans des régions agricoles difficiles. 1: Morvan [Attempt at estimating the conditions from the application and results of a reform policy in agriculture in difficult agricultural regions. 1: Morvan].
Commission, 1974.   183p.   Internal information on agriculture, 138.
F   VI/4572/74

628 FOUQUET
Projections de la production et de la consommation de produits agricoles—'1977'. 8: France [Projections of production and consumption of agricultural products—'1977'. 8: France].
Commission, 1975.   173p.   Internal information on agriculture, 164.
F   VI/1123/72

629 FOURNIER, E.
Le travail de la soudure. Monographie des aspects technologiques et pathologiques [Suture work. Monograph of technological and pathological aspects].
Commission, 1969.   88p.   Collection: industrial health and medicine, 9.
D F I N   4613

630 FOYER, H. A.
Les exportations de biens d'équipement de la Communauté. Essai et prévisions jusqu'en 1970 [Exports of capital goods from the Community. Sample and forecasts until 1970].
ECSC HA, 1967.   249p.   Collection: general objectives for steel, 3A.
D F I N   12885

631 FOYER, H. A.
Mémorandum sur les objectifs de 1965. Méthodes
d'élaboration et résultats détaillés [Memorandum on the
1965 objectives. Methods of elaboration and detailed
results].
ECSC HA, 1962.   540p.   Collection: general
objectives for steel, 1.
D F I N   3017

632 FRAIGNEAUD, R.
Aides apportées aux agriculteurs migrants dans les pays
de la CEE [Aid provided to migrant farmworkers in the
countries of the EEC].
Commission EEC, 1966.   91p.   Studies: agricultural
series, 22.
D F I N   8159

633 FRANCHI, M.
Labour force sample survey (Enquête par sondage sur les
forces de travail).
In Social statistics, 1/1975.   Eurostat, 1975.   233p.
DK/D/E/F/I/N   6936/1

634 FRANCHI, M.
Labour force sample survey 1975 (Enquête par sondage
sur les forces de travail 1975).
Eurostat, 1977.   221p.
DK/D/E/F/I/N   7353

635 FRANÇOIS, H.
Dispositions fiscales en matière de coopération et de fusion
d'exploitations agricoles. 1: Belgique, France, G.D. de
Luxembourg [Tax arrangements concerning cooperation
and amalgamation of farms. 1: Belgium, France, G.D. of
Luxembourg].
Commission, 1972.   var. pag.   Internal information
on agriculture, 83.
F   VI/894/71

636 FRANK, W.
Einführung in die Diskussion über die Klassifizierung
landwirtschaftlicher Betriebe [Introduction to the

discussion over classifying farms / Introduction à la
discussion de la classification des entreprises agricoles].
In Agricultural statistical studies, 18.
Eurostat, 1975.   78p.
D   6972

637 FRESSONNET, P.
Introductory Report on the First Preliminary Draft of the
Implementing Regulations to the Convention (Rapport
introductif concernant le premier Avant-projet de
Règlement d'exécution de la Convention).
In Reports on the Second preliminary draft of a
convention establishing a European system for the grant
of patents.   Council, 1971.   pp.81–2.
D/E/F   17275-B

638 FRIX, P.
Possibilités d'industrialisation des États africains et
malgache associés. Volume 3: République démocratique
du Congo [Possibilities for the industrialization of the
Associated African States and Madagascar. Volume 3:
Democratic Republic of the Congo].
Commission EEC, 1966.   2 vols.
F   13077/VIII/B/66, 13078/VIII/B/66

639 FRIX, P.
Possibilités d'industrialisation des États africains et
malgache associés. Volume 4: Burundi, Rwanda et région
Centre-orientale du Congo (Kinshasa) (région des Grands
Lacs) [Possibilities for the industrialization of the
Associated African States and Madagascar. Volume 4:
Burundi, Rwanda and Centre-eastern region of the Congo
(Kinshasa) (region of the Great Lakes)].
Commission EEC, 1966.   2 vols.
F   13079/VIII/B/66, 13080/VIII/B/66

640 FROMONT, M.
Rapport sur le droit économique français [Report on
French economic law].
Commission, 1974.   85p.   Studies:
competition–approximation of legislation series, 20/2.
D F   8426

641 FROMONT, M.
Les recours juridictionnels contre les actes administratifs spécialement économiques dans le droit des États membres de la Communauté économique européenne. Rapport final [Legal appeals against administrative actions, especially economic in the law of the Member States of the European Economic Community. Final report].
Commission, 1971.   63p.   Studies: competition–approximation of legislation series, 12.
D F I N   8298

642 FÜRST, G.
Über die Berechnung von Produktions-Indexziffern für die Europäische Wirtschaftsgemeinschaft [Problems concerning the calculation of industrial production indexes for the European Economic Community / Problèmes concernant le calcul d'indices de production industrielle pour la Communauté économique européenne].
In Statistical studies and surveys, 1/1968.
Eurostat, 1968.   pp.79–116.
D   4407

643 FÜRST, H.
Les conditions de logement dans la Communauté [Housing conditions in the Community].
In Social statistics, 3/1967.   Eurostat, 1967.   162p.
D/F, I/N   4143

644 FÜRST, H.
Education statistics 1970–1975 (Statistiques de l'enseignement 1970–1975).
Eurostat, 1977.   194p.
DK/D/E/F/I/N   CA-22-76-043-6A-C

645 FÜRST, H.
L'emploi dans les pays de la Communauté 1963–1964 [Employment in the countries of the Community 1963–1964].
In Social statistics, 4/1965.   Eurostat, 1965.   167p.
D/F/I/N

646 FÜRST, H.
L'emploi salarié dans l'industrie avril 1966 [Employees in industry April 1966].
In Social statistics, 6/1967.   Eurostat, 1967.   31p.
D/F/I/N   4234

647 FÜRST, H.
General and vocational training 1973 (Formation générale et professionnelle 1973).
In Social statistics, 4, 1975.   Eurostat, 1976.   126p.
D/E/F/I/N   6936/4

648 FÜRST, H.
Labour force sample survey (Enquête par sondage sur les forces de travail).
In Social statistics, 1/1975.   Eurostat, 1975.   233p.
DK/D/E/F/I/N   6936/1

649 FÜRST, H.
Population and employment 1950–1976 (Population et emploi 1950–1976)
Eurostat, 1977.   201p.
E/F   CA-22-77-031-2A-C

650 FÜRST, H.
Population and employment 1968–1972 (Population et emploi 1968–1972).
In Social statistics, 2/1973.   Eurostat, 1974.   168p.
D/E/F   6310

651 FÜRST, H.
Population et forces de travail. Résultats de l'enquête communautaire par sondage sur les forces de travail 1969 [Population and labour forces. Results of a Community labour force sample survey 1969].
In Social statistics, 4/1970.
Eurostat, 1970.   pp.1–229.
D/F/I/N   4930

652 FÜRST, H.
Population et forces de travail 1968 [Population and labour forces 1968].
In Social statistics, 6/1969.　　Eurostat, 1969.　　355p.
D/F/I/N　　4820

653 FÜRST, H.
La situation des logements des travailleurs dans les industries de la C.E.C.A. [The housing situation of workers in the E.C.S.C. industries].
In Social statistics, 2/1961.　　Eurostat, 1961.　　285p.
D F I N　　2767

654 FÜRST, H.
Statistiques harmonisées de la durée hebdomadaire moyenne du travail offerte par ouvrier octobre 1965 et avril 1966 [Harmonized statistics of the average weekly hours of work per manual worker October 1965 and April 1966].
In Social statistics, 2/1967.　　Eurostat, 1967.　　39p.
D/F/I/N　　4142

655 FÜRST, H.
Statistiques harmonisées des gains horaires bruts, de la durée hebdomadaire du travail offerte et de l'emploi salarié dans l'industrie Avril 1967 [Harmonized statistics of gross hourly wages, weekly hours of work and employees in industry April 1967].
In Statistical studies and surveys, 2/1968.
Eurostat, 1968.　　222p.
D/F/I/N　　4411

656 GAARLANDT, K. H.
La conduite sur place des opérations de conversion industrielle [On-the-spot direction of industrial conversion operations].
ECSC HA, 1963.　　352p.　　Collection: regional economy and policy. 1: Industrial conversion in Europe, 4.
D F I N　　3324

657 GAAY FORTMAN, W. F. de
La juridiction du travail et la juridiction de la sécurité
sociale dans les pays de la Communauté européenne
[Employment and social security jurisdiction in the
countries of the European Community].
Commission, 1972.   615p.   Collection: labour law.
D F I N   8341

658 GAISCH, P.
Pesticide residues in tobacco and tobacco products. 1:
General report (Les résidus de pesticides dans le tabac et
les produits de tabac. 1: Rapport général).
Commission, 1976.   145p.   Information on
agriculture, 14.
E F   8864

659 GAISCH, P.
Les résidus de pesticides dans le tabac et les produits de
tabac. 2: Substances phytosanitaires employées.
Législations. Méthodes d'analyse [Pesticide residues in
tobacco and tobacco products. 2: Plant health substances
employed. Legislation. Methods of analysis].
Commission, 1977.   157p.   Information on
agriculture, 23.
F   8877

GALL, le, *see* LE GALL

660 GALLER, H.-P.
Study on the possible part played by certain primary
non-employment incomes in the inflationary process in the
Federal Republic of Germany (Étude sur le rôle éventuel
de certains revenus primaires non-salariaux dans le
développement de l'inflation en Allemagne).
Commission, 1976.   101p.   Series: medium-term
economic policy, 5.
D E F I N   8860

661 GÄLLI
Les conditions d'installation d'entreprises industrielles
dans les États africains et malgache associés. Volume 18:

République Malgache [Conditions for the setting-up of
industrial undertakings in the Associated African States
and Madagascar. Volume 18: Malagasy Republic].
Commission, 1973.   96p.
F   VIII/1328/72

662 GARDENT, P.
Rapports sur les premières mesures proposées en vue
d'une coordination des politiques énergétiques [Reports
on the first measures proposed for a coordination of
energy policies].
ECSC CC, 1961.   var. pag.
D F I N   8013

663 GASTALDI, M. J.
Incidences économiques de certains types
d'investissements structurels en agriculture.
Remembrement, irrigation [Economic effects of certain
types of structural investments in agriculture.
Reparcelling, irrigation].
Commission, 1969.   136p.   Internal information on
agriculture, 53.
D F   13527/VI/69

664 GATZ, W.
Points de départ pour une politique agricole internationale
[Points of departure for an international agricultural
policy].
Commission, 1968.   167p.   Internal information on
agriculture, 31.
D F   13906/VI/68

665 GAUDET, M.
The Common Market and the law [Le Marché commun et
le droit].
Inf Ser, 1961.   Community topics, 4.
E

666 GAUDET, M.
La préparation des juristes dans la nouvelle dimension
européenne [The preparation of jurists in the new
European dimension].
Commission EEC, 1967.   21p.
F   97

667 GAUDY, P.
Auditor's report for the year 1973 (Rapport du
Commissaire aux comptes pour l'exercice 1973).
ECSC, 1974.   172p.
DK D E F I N   18260

668 GAUDY, P.
Auditor's report for the year 1974 (Rapport du
Commissaire aux comptes pour l'exercice 1974).
ECSC, 1975.   147p.
DK D E F I N   6825

669 GAUDY, P.
Auditor's report for the year 1975 (Rapport du
Commissaire aux comptes pour l'exercice 1975).
ECSC, 1976.   156p.
DK D E F I N   7198

670 GAUDY, P.
Auditor's report for the year 1976 (Rapport du
Commissaire aux comptes pour l'exercice 1976).
ECSC, 1977.   145p.
DK D E F I N   GX-22-77-104-EN-C

671 GAUDY, P.
Rapport du Commissaire aux comptes pour l'exercice 1971
[Auditor's report for the year 1971].
ECSC, 1972   173p.
D F I N   17590

672 GAUDY, P.
Rapport du Commissaire aux comptes pour l'exercice 1972
[Auditor's report for the year 1972].
ECSC, 1973.   178p.
D F I N   17980

673 GAVANIER, P.
Les accidents du travail dans l'industrie sidérurgique 1960
[Work accidents in the iron and steel industry 1960].
In Social statistics, 2/1962.   Eurostat, 1962.   53p.
D/F, I/N   3006

674 GAVANIER, P.
Budgets familiaux des ouvriers de la Communauté
européenne du charbon et de l'acier 1956/57 [Family
budgets of workers of the European Coal and Steel
Community 1956/57].
In Social statistics series, 1/1960.
Eurostat, 1960.   436p.
D F I N   2333

675 GAVANIER, P.
Budgets familiaux 1963/64 [Family budgets 1963/64].
Eurostat, 1965–1966.   6 vols.   Social statistics:
special series.
D/F/I/N   3953 (v.5), 3979 (v.6)

676 GAVANIER, P.
Les conditions de logement dans la Communauté [Housing
conditions in the Community].
In Social statistics, 3/1967.   Eurostat, 1967.   162p.
D/F, I/N   4143

677 GAVANIER, P., chairman
Le coût de la main-d'œuvre dans les industries de la
Communauté 1969 [The cost of labour in the industries of
the Community 1969].
In Social statistics, 3/1971.   Eurostat, 1971.   533p.
D/F, I/N   5456

678 GAVANIER, P., chairman
Les coûts de la main-d'œuvre dans les banques, les
assurances et le commerce de détail 1970 [Labour costs in
banks, insurance and the retail trade 1970].
In Social statistics, 4/1972.   Eurostat, 1973.   247p.
D/F/I/N   5785

679 GAVANIER, P., chairman
Earnings in agriculture 1974 (Gains dans l'agriculture
1974).
In Social statistics, 5/1975.   Eurostat, 1976.   107p.
D/E/F/I/N   6936/5

680 GAVANIER, P.
L'emploi dans les pays de la Communauté 1963–1964
[Employment in the countries of the Community
1963–1964].
In Social statistics, 4/1965.   Eurostat, 1965.   167p.
D/F/I/N

681 GAVANIER, P.
Enquête sur les salaires dans les industries de la
Communauté économique européenne. Année 1959
[Survey on wages in the industries of the European
Economic Community. 1959].
In Social statistics, 3/1961.   Eurostat, 1961.   170p.
D F I N

682 GAVANIER, P.
Enquête sur les salaires dans les industries de la
Communauté économique européenne. Année 1959. Étude
sur les revenus des ouvriers [Survey on wages in the
industries of the European Economic Community. 1959.
Study on the incomes of workers].
In Social statistics, 3/1962.   Eurostat, 1962.   144p.
D/F, I/N

683 GAVANIER, P.
Enquête sur les salaires dans les industries de la
Communauté économique européenne. Année 1960.
[Survey on wages in the industries of the European
Economic Community. 1960].
In Social statistics, 1/1963.   Eurostat, 1963.   383p.
D/F, I/N   3285

684 GAVANIER, P.
Enquête sur les salaires dans les industries de la
Communauté économique européenne 1961 [Survey on

wages in the industries of the European Economic
Community 1961].
In Social statistics, 2/1964.   Eurostat, 1964.   495p.
D/F, I/N   3484

685 GAVANIER, P.
Enquête sur les salaires dans les industries de la
Communauté économique européenne 1962 [Survey on
wages in the industries of the European Economic
Community 1962].
In Social statistics, 5/1964.   Eurostat, 1964.   519p.
D/F, I/N

686 GAVANIER, P.
Enquête sur les salaires dans les industries de la
Communauté économique européenne 1963 [Survey on
wages in the industries of the European Economic
Community 1963].
In Social statistics, 6/1965.   Eurostat, 1965.   365p.
D/F, I/N

687 GAVANIER, P.
Enquête sur les salaires dans les industries de la
Communauté économique européenne 1964 [Survey on
wages in the industries of the European Economic
Community 1964].
In Social statistics, 5/1966.   Eurostat, 1966.   445p.
D/F, I/N   3996

688 GAVANIER, P.
Harmonized statistics of average hourly gross wages in
the industries of the European Communities April 1964
(Statistiques harmonisées des gains horaires moyens
bruts dans les industries des Communautés européennes
avril 1964).
In Social statistics, 3/1965.   Eurostat, 1965.   105p.
D E F I N

689 GAVANIER, P.
Prix, taux d'équivalence de pouvoir d'achat à la
consommation et revenus réels dans les pays de la

C.E.C.A. 1954–1958 [Prices, equivalent rates of
purchasing power from consumption and real incomes
in the countries of the E.C.S.C. 1954–1958].
In Social statistics, 2/1960.　　Eurostat, 1960.　　219p.
D F I N　　2500

690 GAVANIER, P.
Salaires C.E.C.A. 1961. Les coûts de la main-d'œuvre et
les revenus des ouvriers dans les industries de la
C.E.C.A. Année 1961 et évolution 1954–1961 [E.C.S.C.
wages 1961. Labour costs and the incomes of workers in
the industries of the E.C.S.C. 1961 and development
1954–1961].
In Social statistics, 2/1963.　　Eurostat, 1963.　　201p.
D/F, I/N

691 GAVANIER, P.
La situation des logements des travailleurs dans les
industries de la C.E.C.A. [The housing situation of
workers in the E.C.S.C. industries].
In Social statistics, 2/1961.　　Eurostat, 1961.　　285p.
D F I N　　2767

692 GAVANIER, P.
Les statistiques sociales, leur degré de comparabilité et
les difficultés rencontrées dans le domaine de leur
harmonisation [The degree of comparability and the
difficulties encountered in the field of the harmonization of
social statistics].
In Statistical studies and surveys, 3/1968.
Eurostat, 1968.　　pp.9–63.
D/F/I/N　　4515

693 GAVANIER, P., chairman
Structure of earnings in wholesale and retail distribution,
banking and insurance in 1974. Methods and definitions
(Structure des salaires dans le commerce, les banques et
les assurances en 1974. Méthodes et définitions).
Eurostat, 1977.　　223p.　　Special series, B1.
DK/D/E/F/I/N　　7330/1

694 GAY, J.
Structure et évolution de l'industrie de transformation du
lait dans la CEE [Structure and development of the milk
processing industry in the EEC].
Commission, 1968.   335p.   Internal information on
agriculture, 34.
D F   16194/VI/67

695 GEARY, R. C.
Study on the possible part played by certain primary
non-employment incomes in the inflationary process in
Ireland (Étude sur le rôle éventuel de certains revenus
primaires non-salariaux dans le développement de
l'inflation en Irlande).
Commission, 1977.   110p.   Series: medium-term
economic policy, 9.
E F   CD-ST-77-001-EN-C

696 GEELHOED, L. A.
Rapport sur le droit économique néerlandais [Report on
Dutch economic law].
Commission, 1974.   190p.   Studies:
competition–approximation of legislation series, 20/4.
D F N   8428

697 GEENS, V.
La collaboration entre l'enseignement et les industries de
la C.E.C.A. [Cooperation between education and the
industries of the E.C.S.C.].
ECSC HA, 1959.   134p.
F   4704

698 GEISSLER, B.
Modelle zur Analyse von
Ackerbau-Rindviehhaltungsbetrieben
Technisch-wirtschaftliche Grundangaben.
Schwäbisch-Bayerisches Hügelland (B.R. Deutschland)
[Models for analysis of mixed crop and cattle farms. Basic
technico-economic data. Schwäbisch-bayerisches
Hügelland (F.R. Germany / Modèles d'analyse
d'entreprises de polyculture-élevage bovin. Données

technico-économiques de base. Schwäbisch-bayerisches
Hügelland (R.F. Allemagne)].
Commission, 1976.   86p.   Information on
agriculture, 6.
D   8835

699 GEISSLER, B.
Models for analysis mixed crop and cattle farms. 6:
Characteristics and possible applications. South-East
Leinster (Ireland), West Cambridgeshire (United
Kingdom), Fünen (Denmark), Schwäbisch-bayerisches
Hügelland (F.R. Germany) (Modèles d'analyse
d'entreprises de polyculture-élevage bovin. 6:
Caractéristiques et possibilités d'utilisation. South-East
Leinster (Irlande), West Cambridgeshire (Royaume-Uni),
Fünen (Danemark), Schwäbisch-bayerisches Hügelland
(R.F. d'Allemagne).
Commission, 1976.   47p.   Internal information on
agriculture, 152.
E F   VI/3715/1/74

700 GENET
L'industrie électronique des pays de la Communauté et les
investissements américains [The electronics industry of
the countries of the Community and American
investments].
Commission, 1969.   168p.   Studies: industry
series, 1.
D F I N   8240

701 GENTZ, H.
La polyvalence dans la formation professionnelle dans les
pays de la Communauté [Polyvalency in vocational
training in the countries of the Community].
Commission, 1971.   66p.
D F I N   8363

GEOURS, J. Saint-, *see* SAINT-GEOURS, J.

702 GERL, F.
La consommation du vin et les facteurs qui la déterminent.
RF d'Allemagne [Wine consumption and the factors which
determine it. FR of Germany].
Commission, 1969.   117p.   Internal information on
agriculture, 46.
D F   13859/VI/69

703 GHAZZALI, A.
Educational leave in Member States (Les congés culturels
dans les États membres).
Commission, 1977.   416p.   Studies: social policy
series, 26.
D E F I N   CH-SN-76-026-EN-C

704 GHELLINCK, E. de
L'évolution de la concentration dans l'industrie de la
brasserie et des boissons en Belgique [The evolution of
concentration in the brewing and beverages industry in
Belgium].
Commission, 1977.   108p.
F   8760

705 GHELUWE, G. van
The development of Flemish economy in the international
perspective. Synthesis and options of policy (L'évolution
de l'économie flamande considérée dans une perspective
internationale. Synthèse et options politiques).
Commission, 1974.   83p.   Studies: regional policy
series, 1.
DK D E F I N   8419

706 GHERSI, G.
Étude sur l'évolution de la concentration dans la
distribution des produits alimentaires en France [A study
of the evolution of concentration in food distribution in
France].
Commission, 1976.   213p.
F   8763

707 GHERSI, G.
Étude sur l'évolution de la concentration dans l'industrie
alimentaire en France [A study of the evolution of
concentration in the food industry in France].
Commission, 1975.   238p.
F   6912

708 GHERSI, G.
Étude sur l'évolution de la concentration dans l'industrie
alimentaire en France. Tableaux de concentration [A
study of the evolution of concentration in the food industry
in France. Concentration tables].
Commission, 1975.   307p.
F   8706

709 GHIGLIA, G.
Evoluzione della concentrazione dal 1962 al 1969 in alcuni
settori dell'industria italiana. Metodologia [Evolution of
concentration in various sectors of Italian industry from
1962 to 1969. Methodology / L'évolution de la
concentration dans quelques secteurs de l'industrie
italienne de 1962 à 1969. Méthodologie].
Commission, 1973.   24p.
I   IV/344/73

710 GHIGLIA, G.
Studio sull'evoluzione della concentrazione in alcuni settori
dell'industria tessile in Italia. Lana (N.I.C.E. 232).
Cotone (N.I.C.E. 233). Maglieria e calzetteria (N.I.C.E.
237) [A study of the evolution of concentration in various
sectors of the textile industry in Italy. Wool (N.I.C.E.
232). Cotton (N.I.C.E. 233). Knitted and crocheted goods
(N.I.C.E. 237) / Étude sur l'évolution de la concentration
dans quelques secteurs de l'industrie du textile en Italie.
Laine (N.I.C.E. 232). Coton (N.I.C.E. 233). Bonneterie
(N.I.C.E. 237)].
Commission, 1973.   var. pag.
I   IV/347/73

711 GHIGLIA, G.
Studio sull'evoluzione della concentrazione in Italia
dell'industria della carta e della sua trasformazione. Carta

(N.I.C.E. 271). Cartotecnica (N.I.C.E. 272) [A study of
the evolution of concentration in the paper and paper
products industry in Italy. Paper (N.I.C.E. 271). Paper
processing (N.I.C.E. 272) / Étude sur l'évolution de la
concentration de l'industrie du papier et des articles en
papier en Italie. Papier (N.I.C.E. 271). Transformation du
papier (N.I.C.E. 272)].
Commission, 1973.   103p.
I   IV/348/73

712 GIACCHERO, E.
Verso il mercato comune europeo. Il Mezzogiorno nel
mercato italiano. Raccolta di testimonianze [Towards a
European common market. The Mezzogiorno in the Italian
market. Collection of documents / Vers un marché
commun européen. Le Mezzogiorno dans le marché italien.
Collection des documents].
ECSC, 1957.   81p.
I   1935

713 GIAMPIERI, G.
Studio sull'evoluzione della concentrazione nel settore dei
detersivi per uso domestico in Italia dal 1968 al 1975 [A
study of the evolution of concentration in the sector of
detergents for domestic use from 1968 to 1975 in Italy /
Étude sur l'évolution de la concentration dans le secteur
des détergents pour la maison de 1968 à 1975 en Italie].
Commission, 1977.   249p.
I   CB-NL-77-012-IT-C

714 GIANNICCHI, G.
Evoluzione della concentrazione dal 1962 al 1969 in alcuni
settori dell'industria italiana. Metodologia [Evolution of
concentration in various sectors of Italian industry from
1962 to 1969. Methodology / L'évolution de la
concentration dans quelques secteurs de l'industrie
italienne de 1962 à 1969. Méthodologie].
Commission, 1973.   24p.
I   IV/344/73

715 GIANNICCHI, G.
Studio sull'evoluzione della concentrazione in alcuni settori
dell'industria tessile in Italia. Lana (N.I.C.E. 232).
Cotone (N.I.C.E. 233). Maglieria e calzetteria (N.I.C.E.
237) [A study of the evolution of concentration in various
sectors of the textile industry in Italy. Wool (N.I.C.E.
232). Cotton (N.I.C.E. 233). Knitted and crocheted goods
(N.I.C.E. 237) / Étude sur l'évolution de la concentration
dans quelques secteurs de l'industrie du textile en Italie.
Laine (N.I.C.E. 232). Coton (N.I.C.E. 233). Bonneterie
(N.I.C.E. 237)].
Commission, 1973.   var. pag.
I   IV/347/73

716 GIANNICCHI, G.
Studio sull'evoluzione della concentrazione in Italia
dell'industria della carta e della sua trasformazione. Carta
(N.I.C.E. 271). Cartotecnica (N.I.C.E. 272) [A study of
the evolution of concentration in the paper and paper
products industry in Italy. Paper (N.I.C.E. 271). Paper
processing (N.I.C.E. 272) / Étude sur l'évolution de la
concentration de l'industrie du papier et des articles en
papier en Italie. Papier (N.I.C.E. 271). Transformation du
papier (N.I.C.E. 272)].
Commission, 1973.   103p.
I   IV/348/73

717 GIEL, W.
Arrangements to facilitate the establishment of new
economic activities. Legal and financial arrangements in
force in the member states of the Community and the
United Kingdom (Dispositions pour faciliter la création
d'activités nouvelles. Dispositions juridiques et financières
en vigueur dans les États membres et le Royaume-Uni).
ECSC HA, 1962.   loose-leaf.
D E F I N   3019

718 GIEL, W.
Implantation d'entreprises industrielles dans les régions
affectées par la fermeture de mines [Development of

industrial undertakings in those regions affected by mine closure].
ECSC HA, 1960.   25p.   Intergovernmental Conference on Industrial Redevelopment: German national report.
F   5163

719 GIEL, W.
Les politiques nationales de développement régional et de conversion [National policies of regional development and conversion].
ECSC HA, 1961.   195p.   Collection: regional economy and policy. 1: Industrial conversion in Europe, 1.
F   2626

720 GIERSCH, H.
Die voraussichtliche Entwicklung der internationalen Versorgung mit landwirtschaftlichen Erzeugnissen und ihre Folgen für die Gemeinschaft. 3: Öle und Fette, Eiweissfuttermittel [The foreseeable trend in world availabilities of agricultural products and the consequences for the Community. 3: Oils and fats, protein products / L'évolution prévisible de l'approvisionnement international en produits agricoles et ses conséquences pour la Communauté. 3: Huiles et graisses, aliments azotés pour animaux].
Commission, 1977.   200p.   Information on agriculture, 36.
D   CB-NA-77-036-DE-C

721 GIESSEN, H. B. van der
Production laitière dans les exploitations ne disposant pas de ressources fourragères propres suffisantes [Milk production in the farms without its own sufficient fodder resources].
Commission, 1974.   117p.   Internal information on agriculture, 121.
D F N   VI/634/74

722 GILES, A. K.
Gross margins of agricultural products in the E.C.
(Marges brutes pour les produits agricoles dans la C.E.).
Commission, 1975.   var. pag.   Internal information
on agriculture, 162.
E F   VI/564/73   .

723 GILROY, S.
Forms of cooperation between farms for production and
marketing in the new Member States [Formes de
collaboration entre exploitations agricoles dans les
nouveaux États membres].
Commission, 1976.   340p.   Information on
agriculture, 20.
E   8876

724 GIORDAN, M.
Education of consumers: an extensive documentary search
and a report on pedagogic experiments in the United
Kingdom [L'education des consommateurs: un recherche
authentique ample et un rapport sur les expériences
pédagogiques au Royaume-Uni].
Commission, 1977.   92p.
E   ENV/286/75

725 GIORDANO
Recherche sur la réduction directe des minerais de fer
dans le four à cuve [Research on direct reduction of iron
ore in a shaft furnace].
ECSC HA, 1964.   70p.
D F   10991

726 GIORDIANI, F.
A target for Euratom. Report submitted by Mr. Louis
Armand, Mr. Franz Etzel and Mr. Francesco Giordiani at
the request of the governments of Belgium, France,
German Federal Republic, Italy, Luxembourg and the
Netherlands (Un objectif pour Euratom. Rapport
présenté par M. Louis Armand, M. Franz Etzel et M.
Francesco Giordiani sur la demande des Gouvernements
de la République Fédérale d'Allemagne, de la Belgique, de

la France, de l'Italie, du Luxembourg et des Pays-Bas).
EAEC, 1957.   104p.
D E F I N

727 GIORGI, E.
Conditions de commercialisation et de formation des prix
des vins de consommation courante au niveau de la
première vente. France, Italie [Conditions for marketing
and price formation of ordinary wines at the first sale.
France, Italy].
Commission, 1969.   474p.   Internal information on
agriculture, 52.
D F   1789/VI/70

728 GIORGI, E.
Il contributo delle 'Comunità montane' in Italia allo
sviluppo dell'agricoltura di montagna [The contribution of
'Comunità montane' to the development of hill farming in
Italy / La contribution des 'Comunità montane' au
développement de l'agriculture de montagne en Italie].
Commission, 1976.   209p.   Information on
agriculture, 11.
I   8861

729 GIORGI, E.
Gli 'enti di sviluppo agricolo' in Italia nella riforma delle
strutture. Problemi e prospettive di adattamento [The
'enti di sviluppo agricolo' in structural reform in Italy.
Adjustment problems and prospects / Les 'enti di sviluppo
agricolo' en Italie et la réforme des structures. Problèmes
et perspectives d'adaptation].
Commission, 1976.   285p.   Information on
agriculture, 12.
I   8862

730 GIRARD, A.
Le financement des investissements et les aspects sociaux
de la reconversion [Financing of investments and social
aspects of conversion].
ECSC HA, 1963.   255p.   Collection: regional
economy and policy. 1: Industrial conversion in Europe, 3.
D F I N   3323

731 GIUGNI, G.
L'évolution de la négociation collective dans les industries
de la Communauté 1953–1963 [The development of
collective bargaining in the industries of the Community
1953–1963].
ECSC HA, 1967.   264p.
D F I N   14021

732 GLEIZES, C.
Incidences économiques de certains types
d'investissements structurels en agriculture.
Remembrement, irrigation [Economic effects of certain
types of structural investments in agriculture.
Reparcelling, irrigation].
Commission, 1969.   136p.   Internal information on
agriculture, 53.
D F   13527/VI/69

733 GLESKE, chairman
Les recettes et les dépenses des administrations publiques
dans les pays membres de la CEE [Government revenue
and expenditure in the member countries of the EEC].
Commission EEC, 1964.   304p.   Studies: economic
and financial series, 2.
D F I N   8125

734 GLODEK, P.
Étude sur les qualités des carcasses de bovins et porcins
dans les pays de la Communauté Économique Européenne
[Study on the qualities of beef and pork carcasses in the
countries of the European Economic Community].
Eurostat, 1966.   80p.   Agricultural statistics.
D/F   3944

735 GLODEN, J.
Dispositions fiscales en matière de coopération et de fusion
d'exploitations agricoles. 1: Belgique, France, G.D. de
Luxembourg [Tax arrangements concerning cooperation
and amalgamation of farms. 1: Belgium, France, G.D. of
Luxembourg].

Commission, 1972.   var. pag.   Internal information
on agriculture, 83.
F   VI/894/71

736 GNAD, F. J.
Aussenhandel und Versorgung an Manganerz,
Hochofen-Ferromangan und Spiegeleisen in der
Gemeinschaft [Foreign trade and supply of manganese
ore, high-carbon ferro-manganese and spiegeleisen in the
Community / Commerce extérieur et approvisionnements
du minerai de manganèse, du ferromanganèse carburé et
du spiegel dans la Communauté].
In Statistical studies and surveys, 1/1970.
Eurostat, 1970.   pp.1–61.
D   16543

737 GÖBEN, H.
Le marché de poissons frais en république fédérale
d'Allemagne et aux Pays-Bas et les facteurs qui
interviennent dans la formation du prix du hareng frais
[The wet fish market in the Federal Republic of Germany
and the Netherlands and the factors which determine the
formation of fresh herring prices].
Commission EEC, 1965.   200p.   Internal
information on agriculture, 3.
D F   8701/VI/63

738 GOCHT, H.
Le marché des produits d'œufs dans la CEE [The market
for egg products in the EEC].
Commission EEC, 1966.   var. pag.   Internal
information on agriculture, 10.
D F   13736/VI/64

739 GOCHT, H.
La statistique des prix des œufs dans les États membres
de la CEE [Egg price statistics in the Member States of
the EEC].
In Agricultural statistical studies, 6.
Eurostat, 1969.   80p.
D F   15852

740 GOES VAN NATERS, J. van der
Le développement de l'intégration économique de
l'Europe [The development of economic integration of
Europe].
ECSC CA, 1955.   114p.
F

741 GOETGHELUCK
Essai d'appréciation des conditions d'application et des
résultats d'une politique de réforme en agriculture dans
des régions agricoles difficiles. 2: Queyras [Attempt at
estimating the conditions from the application and results
of a reform policy in agriculture in difficult agricultural
regions. 2: Queyras].
Commission, 1975.   var. pag.   Internal information
on agriculture, 150.
F   VI/1988/75

742 GOETZ, M.
Formes de coopération dans le secteur de la pêche. 1:
Synthèse, R.F. d'Allemagne, Italie [Forms of cooperation
in the fishing industry. 1: Summary, F.R. of Germany,
Italy].
Commission, 1970.   var. pag.   Internal information
on agriculture, 68.
D F   14715/VI/69

743 GOETZ, M.
Formes de coopération dans le secteur de la pêche. 2:
France, Belgique, Pays-Bas [Forms of cooperation in the
fishing industry. 2: France, Belgium, the Netherlands].
Commission, 1970.   var. pag.   Internal information
on agriculture, 69.
D F   14715/VI/69

744 GOFFIN, R.
Glossaire des normes de l'acier. Normes d'essai, de qualité
et de dimensions établi sur la base des EURONORM et
des normes nationales [Glossary of steel standards.
Standards of testing, quality and dimensions established
on the basis of EURONORM and national standards].
Commission, n.d.   307p.
D/F/I/N

745 GOFFIN, R.
Glossary new transport technologies (Glossaire nouvelles
techniques de transport).
Commission, 1976.   900p.
DK/D/E/F/I/N   IX/2061/74

746 GOLDMAN, B.
Rapport concernant le projet de convention sur la
reconnaissance mutuelle des sociétés et personnes morales
[Report on the draft convention on the mutual recognition
of companies and corporate bodies].
Commission EEC, 1965.   32p.
D F I N   8106/1/IV/65

747 GOLDMAN, B.
Report on the Draft Convention on the international
merger of sociétés anonymes (Rapport concernant le
projet de convention sur la fusion internationale de
sociétés anonymes).
In Bulletin of the European Communities. Supplement,
13/1973.   Commission, 1973.   pp.31–123.
D E F I N   4001/S/13/73

748 GOLLNICK, H.
Problèmes de la stabilisation du marché du beurre à l'aide
de mesures de l'État dans les pays de la Communauté
économique européenne [Problems of stabilizing the
butter market by State aid measures in the countries of
the European Economic Community].
Commission EEC, 1965.   113p.   Internal
information on agriculture, 5.
D F   8185/VI/63

749 GOLLNICK, H.
Tendances de la production et de la consommation en
denrées alimentaires dans la C.E.E. 1956–1965 [Trends in
food production and consumption in the E.E.C.
1956–1965].
Commission EEC, 1960.   266p.   Studies:
agricultural series, 2.
D F I N   8005

750 GONNEVILLE, de
Possibilités de création d'industries exportatrices dans les
États africains et malgache associés. Produits de
l'élevage. Viandes, cuirs et peaux, chaussures, articles en
cuir [Possibilities for the establishment of exporting
industries in the Associated African States and
Madagascar. Products from rearing. Meat, hides and
skins, shoes, leather articles].
Commission, 1974.   5 vols.
F   VIII/223/74

751 GONNEVILLE, de
Possibilités de création d'industries exportatrices dans les
États africains et malgache associés. Produits de
l'élevage. Viandes, cuirs et peaux, chaussures, articles en
cuir. Rapport de synthèse [Possibilities for the
establishment of exporting industries in the Associated
African States and Madagascar. Products from rearing.
Meat, hides and skins, shoes, leather articles. Summary
report].
Commission, 1975.   27p.
D E F I N   VIII/223/74

752 GONOD, P.
Évolution de la productivité de l'agriculture dans la CEE
[Development of agricultural productivity in the EEC].
Commission, 1969.   509p.   Internal information on
agriculture, 44.
D F   11774/VI/69

753 GONOD, P.
Problèmes et méthodes de mesure de la productivité dans
les industries de la Communauté [Problems and methods
of measuring productivity in the industries of the
Community].
ECSC HA, 1964.   81p.   Collection: industrial
economics, 2.
D F I N   3535

754 GOODANEW, T. F.
Le rôle des ports de la Communauté pour le trafic de
céréales et de farines. 7: Synthèse pour les principaux

ports de la R.F. d'Allemagne, du Royaume-Uni, des
Pays-Bas, de la Belgique, de l'Irlande et du Danemark
[List of Community ports for the cereals and flour trade. 7:
Summary for the chief ports of F.R. of Germany, United
Kingdom, the Netherlands, Belgium, Ireland and
Denmark].
Commission, 1975.   var. pag.   Internal information
on agriculture, 155.
F   VI/3170/75

755 GOODANEW, T. F.
Le rôle des ports de la Communauté pour le trafic de
céréales et de farines. 8: Monographies pour les principaux
ports de la R.F. d'Allemagne [List of Community ports for
the cereals and flour trade. 8: Monographs for the chief
ports of the F.R. of Germany].
Commission, 1975.   var. pag.   Internal information
on agriculture, 156.
F   VI/3171/75

756 GOODANEW, T. F.
Le rôle des ports de la Communauté pour le trafic de
céréales et de farines. 9: Monographies pour les principaux
ports de Royaume-Uni [List of Community ports for the
cereals and flour trade. 9: Monographs for the chief ports
of the United Kingdom].
Commission, 1975.   var. pag.   Internal information
on agriculture, 157.
F   VI/3172/75

757 GOODANEW, T. F.
Le rôle des ports de la Communauté pour le trafic de
céréales et de farines. 10: Monographies pour les
principaux ports des Pays-Bas [List of Community ports
for the cereals and flour trade. 10: Monographs for the
chief ports of the Netherlands].
Commission, 1975.   var. pag.   Internal information
on agriculture, 158.
F   VI/3173/75

758 GOODANEW, T. F.
Le rôle des ports de la Communauté pour le trafic de
céréales et de farines. 11: Monographies pour les
principaux ports de la Belgique [List of Community ports
for the cereals and flour trade. 11: Monographs for the
chief ports of Belgium].
Commission, 1975.   var. pag.   Internal information
on agriculture, 159.
F   VI/3174/75

759 GOODANEW, T. F.
Le rôle des ports de la Communauté pour le trafic de
céréales et de farines. 12: Monographies pour les
principaux ports de l'Irlande et du Danemark [List of
Community ports for the cereals and flour trade. 12:
Monographs for the chief ports of Ireland and Denmark].
Commission, 1975.   var. pag.   Internal information
on agriculture, 160.
F   VI/3175/75

760 GOODANEW, T. F.
Le rôle des ports de la Communauté pour le trafic de
céréales et de farines. 13: Résumé et conclusions [List of
Community ports for the cereals and flour trade. 13:
Summary and conclusions].
Commission, 1975.   var. pag.   Internal information
on agriculture, 161.
F   VI/3791/75

761 GOOSSENS, R.
Le chômage et la main-d'œuvre sous-employée. Mise en
œuvre d'une méthode de recherche. Belgique
[Unemployment and underemployed manpower.
Implementing of a research method. Belgium].
Commission EEC, 1965.   176p.   Studies: social
policy series, 9.
D F I N   8135

762 GOUAULT, J.-M.
Educational leave in Member States (Les congés culturels
dans les États membres).

Commission, 1977. 416p. Studies: social policy
series, 26.
D E F I N   CH-SN-76-026-EN-C

763 GOUDZWAARD, M. B.
Politique économique et problèmes de la concurrence dans
la CEE et dans les pays membres de la CEE [Economic
policy and competition problems in the EEC and the
member countries of the EEC].
Commission EEC, 1966. 68p. Studies: competition
series, 2.
D F I N   8176

764 GOUX, C.
General survey of the world situation regarding fats and
oils (Document synthétique sur l'économie mondiale des
matières grasses).
Commission EEC, 1964. 63p. Studies: overseas
development series, 2.
D E F I N   8116

765 GOVAERTS
Tableaux 'Entrées-Sorties' pour les pays de la
Communauté Économique Européenne. Seconde version
['Input-Output' tables for the countries of the European
Economic Community. Second version].
Eurostat, 1965. var. pag.
D F

766 GOYBET, P.
Méthodologie communautaire des tableaux
Entrées-Sorties 1965 [Community input-output tables
1965 methodology].
Eurostat, 1970. 222p. Special series: input-output
tables 1965, 1.
D F   4963

767 GRAEFF, J. J. de
The law and practice relating to pollution control in the
Netherlands [Loi et usage concernant le contrôle de la
pollution aux Pays-Bas].
Commission, 1976. 184p.
E   0 86010 030 8

768 GRANDCLAUDE, L.
Modèles d'analyse d'entreprises de polyculture-élevage
bovin. Données technico-économiques de base. Région du
Bassin de Rennes (France) [Models for analysis of mixed
crop and cattle farms. Basic technico-economic data.
Bassin de Rennes region (France)].
Commission, 1977.   98p.   Information on
agriculture, 37.
F   CB-NA-77-037-FR-C

769 GRANDCLAUDE, L.
Modèles d'analyse d'entreprises de polyculture-élevage
bovin. Données technico-économiques de base. Région
Volvestre (France) [Models for analysis of mixed crop and
cattle farms. Basic technico-economic data. Volvestre
region (France)].
Commission, 1977.   102p.   Information on
agriculture, 39.
F   CB-NA-77-039-FR-C

770 GRANDCLAUDE, L.
Modèles d'analyse d'entreprises de polyculture-élevage
bovin. 1: Caractéristiques et possibilités d'utilisation
[Models for analysis of mixed crop and cattle farms. 1:
Characteristics and possibilities of utilization].
Commission, 1973.   261p.   Internal information on
agriculture, 97.
D F   VI/1385/72

771 GRANDCLAUDE, L.
Modèles d'analyse d'entreprises de polyculture-élevage
bovin. 2: Données technico-économiques de base.
Circonscription Nord-Picardie et région limoneuse du
Limbourg belge [Models for analysis of mixed crop and
cattle farms. 2: Basic technico-economic data.
Nord-Picardie area and the limoneuse region of Belgian
Limbourg].
Commission, 1973.   200p.   Internal information on
agriculture, 111.
D F   VI/1792/73

772 GRANDCLAUDE, L.
Modèles d'analyse d'entreprises de polyculture-élevage
bovin. 3: Données technico-économiques de base. Région
Noordelijke Bouwstreek (Pays-Bas) [Models for analysis
of mixed crop and cattle farms. 3: Basic technico-economic
data. Noordelijke Bouwstreek region (Netherlands)].
Commission, 1975.   90p.   Internal information on
agriculture, 140.
F N   VI/17751/70

773 GRANDCLAUDE, L.
Modelle zur Analyse von
Ackerbau-Rindviehhaltungsbetrieben.
Technisch-wirtschaftliche Grundangaben.
Schwäbisch-Bayerisches Hügelland (B.R. Deutschland)
[Models for analysis of mixed crop and cattle farms. Basic
technico-economic data. Schwäbisch-bayerisches
Hügelland (F.R. Germany) / Modèles d'analyse
d'entreprises de polyculture-élevage bovin. Données
technico-économiques de base. Schwäbisch-bayerisches
Hügelland (R.F. Allemagne)].
Commission, 1976.   86p.   Information on
agriculture, 6.
D   8835

774 GRANDCLAUDE, L.
Models for analysis mixed crop and cattle farms. Basic
techno-economic data. South-East Leinster (Ireland),
West Cambridgeshire (United Kingdom), Fünen
(Denmark) [Modèles d'analyse d'entreprises de
polyculture-élevage bovin. Données technico-économiques
de base. South-East Leinster (Irlande), West
Cambridgeshire (Royaume-Uni), Fünen (Danemark)].
Commission, 1976.   var. pag.   Information on
agriculture, 7.
E   8836

775 GRANDCLAUDE, L.
Models for analysis mixed crop and cattle farms. 6:
Characteristics and possible applications. South-East
Leinster (Ireland), West Cambridgeshire (United

Kingdom), Fünen (Denmark), Schwäbisch-bayerisches
Hügelland (F.R. Germany) (Modèles d'analyse
d'entreprises de polyculture-élevage bovin. 6:
Caractéristiques et possibilités d'utilisation. South-East
Leinster (Irlande), West Cambridgeshire (Royaume-Uni),
Fünen (Danemark), Schwäbisch-bayerisches Hügelland
(R.F. d'Allemagne)).
Commission, 1976.   47p.   Internal information on
agriculture, 152.
E F   VI/3715/1/74

GRANRUT, C. du, *see* DU GRANRUT, C.

776 GRAVENHORST, W.
The law of property in the European Community [Le droit
de la propriété dans la Communauté européenne].
Commission, 1977.   305p.   Studies:
competition–approximation of legislation series, 27.
E   8727

777 GRAVIER, J. F.
Auvergne-Aquitaine [Auvergne-Aquitaine].
ECSC, 1957.   68p.   Studies and documents.
Regional studies of employment.
F   1949

778 GREEN, M. J.
Community input-output tables 1970–1975 methodology
(Méthodologie des tableaux entrées-sorties
communautaires 1970–1975).
Eurostat, 1977.   38p.   Special series, 1.
DK D E F I N   7197/1

779 GREIPL, E.
Untersuchung zur Konzentrationsentwicklung in der
Nahrungsmitteldistribution in Deutschland [A study of
the evolution of concentration in food distribution in
Germany / Étude sur l'évolution de la concentration dans
la distribution des produits alimentaires en Allemagne].
Commission, 1977.   307p.
D   8767

780 GROEBEN, H. von der
Approximation of legislation: the policy of the Commission
of the European Communities. Address by Dr. Hans von
der Groeben, Member of the Commission of the European
Communities to the European Parliament, Strasbourg, 27
November 1969 (La politique de la Commission
européenne dans le domaine du rapprochement des
législations. Discours prononcé par M. Hans von der
Groeben, membre de la Commission des Communautés
européennes, devant le Parlement européen à Strasbourg,
le 27 novembre 1969).
Commission, 1970. 16p.
D E F I N 8289

781 GROEBEN, H. von der
Competition in the Common Market. Speech made by Mr.
von der Groeben during the debate of the draft regulation
pursuant to Articles 85 and 86 of the EEC Treaty in the
European Parliament [La concurrence dans le Marché
commun. Discours prononcé par M. von der Groeben
pendant le débat du projet de règlement concernant les
Articles 85 et 86 du traité de la CEE dans le Parlement
européen].
Commission, 1961. 12p.
D E F I N 8035

782 GROEBEN, H. von der
Competition policy as part of economic policy in the
Common Market. Address by M. von der Groeben,
Member of the Commission of the European Economic
Community, President of the Competition Group, to the
European Parliament, Strasbourg 16 June 1965 (La
politique de concurrence, partie intégrante de la politique
économique dans le Marché commun. Discours prononcé
par Hans von der Groeben, membre de la Commission de
la Communauté économique européenne, président du
groupe 'concurrence', devant le Parlement européen à
Strasbourg, le 16 juin 1965).
Commission EEC, 1965. 21p.
D E F I N 8158

783 GROEBEN, H. von der
Competition policy in the Common Market. [La politique
de la concurrence dans le Marché commun].
Inf Ser, 1965.   15p.   Community topics, 19.
E

784 GROEBEN, H. von der
Competition policy in the European Economic Community
(La politique de la concurrence dans la Communauté
économique européenne).
In Bulletin of the European Economic Community.
Supplement, 7–8/1961.
Commission EEC, 1961.   32p.
D E F I N S   8032

785 GROEBEN, H. von der
European monetary policy. Towards the gradual
establishment of a European monetary system (Problèmes
de politique monétaire européenne. Pour l'établissement
graduel d'un système monétaire européen).
Commission, 1968.   18p.
D E F I N   8252

786 GROEBEN, H. von der
Harmonizing taxes. A step to European integration
[L'harmonisation fiscale. Un pas vers l'intégration
européenne].
Inf Ser, 1968.   Community topics, 30.
E

787 GROEBEN, H. von der
La politique de concurrence dans le Marché Commun
[Competition policy in the Common Market].
Bureau (P), 1965.   19p.   Les documents de
Communauté européenne, 31.
F

788 GROEBEN, H. von der, chairman
Rapport concernant l' 'assiette des impôts' sur les
bénéfices des entreprises [Report on the 'state of taxes' on
company profits].
Commission EEC, 1964.   78p.
D F I N   5833

789 GROEBEN, H. von der
Regional policy in an integrated Europe [La politique
régionale dans une Europe intégrale].
Inf Ser, 1969.   Community topics, 33.
E

GRONTEC, P. le, *see* LE GRONTEC, P.

790 GROOT, J. P.
L'emploi agricole dans les pays de la C.E.E. Tome 1:
Structure [Agricultural employment in the countries of
the E.E.C. Volume 1: Structure].
Commission EEC, 1964.   61p.   Studies: social policy
series, 7.
D F I N   8108

791 GROOT, J. P.
L'emploi agricole dans les pays de la C.E.E. Tome 2:
Évolution et perspectives [Agricultural employment in
the countries of the E.E.C. Volume 2: Development and
prospects].
Commission EEC, 1964.   51p.   Studies: social policy
series, 8.
D F I N   8123

792 GROOT, J. P.
Évolution régionale de la population active agricole. 3:
Benelux [Regional development of the working
agricultural population. 3: Benelux].
Commission, 1969.   151p.   Internal information on
agriculture, 41.
D F   8837/VI/69

793 GROOTE, P. de
Gedenken an Robert Schuman Ehrenpräsident des
Europäischen Parlaments [In memory of Robert Schuman
honorary president of the European Parliament / En
souvenir de Robert Schuman président honoraire du
parlement européen].
EP, 1963.   23p.
D   3371

794 GROOTE, P. de
Réflexions sur des expériences acquises par Euratom en
matière de politique communautaire de recherche
scientifique et technique [Reflections on the experiences
gained by Euratom concerning community policy of
scientific and technical research].
Commission EAEC, 1967.   49p.
F

795 GRÜNEISEN, M.
Incidences économiques de certains types
d'investissements structurels en agriculture.
Remembrement, irrigation [Economic effects of certain
types of structural investments in agriculture.
Reparcelling, irrigation].
Commission, 1969.   136p.   Internal information on
agriculture, 53.
D F   13527/VI/69

796 GRÜNEWALD, F.
Les laminoirs [The rolling mills].
Commission, 1972.   240p.   New technical processes
in the iron and steel industry: a personal training manual,
4.   Studies: vocational training.
D F I N   8349

797 GRUNEWALD, L.
Possibilités de création d'industries exportatrices dans les
États africains et malgache associés. Produits de
l'élevage. Viandes, cuirs et peaux, chaussures, articles en
cuir [Possibilities for the establishment of exporting
industries in the Associated African States and
Madagascar. Products from rearing. Meat, hides and
skins, shoes, leather articles].
Commission, 1974.   5 vols.
F   VIII/223/74

798 GRUNEWALD, L.
Possibilités de création d'industries exportatrices dans les
États africains et malgache associés. Produits de
l'élevage. Viandes, cuirs et peaux, chaussures, articles en

cuir. Rapport de synthèse [Possibilities for the
establishment of exporting industries in the Associated
African States and Madagascar. Products from rearing.
Meat, hides and skins, shoes, leather articles. Summary
report].
Commission, 1975.   27p.
D E F I N   VIII/223/74

799 GUCKES, S.
Un système de statistiques des prix agricoles pour la CE
[A system of agricultural price statistics for the EC].
In Agricultural statistical studies, 9.
Eurostat, 1970.   58p.
D F   17224

800 GUERBER
Essai d'appréciation des conditions d'application et des
résultats d'une politique de réforme en agriculture dans
des régions agricoles difficiles. 1: Morvan [Attempt at
estimating the conditions from the application and results
of a reform policy in agriculture in difficult agricultural
regions. 1: Morvan].
Commission, 1974.   183p.   Internal information on
agriculture, 138.
F   VI/4572/74

801 GUIDO, A.
Studio sull'evoluzione della concentrazione nel settore dei
detersivi per uso domestico in Italia dal 1968 al 1975 [A
study of the evolution of concentration in the sector of
detergents for domestic use from 1968 to 1975 in Italy /
Étude sur l'évolution de la concentration dans le secteur
des détergents pour la maison de 1968 à 1975 en Italie].
Commission, 1977.   249p.
I   CB-NL-77-012-IT-C

802 GUINET, A.
Modèles d'analyse d'entreprises de polyculture-élevage
bovin. Données technico-économiques de base. Région du
Bassin de Rennes (France) [Models for analysis of mixed
crop and cattle farms. Basic technico-economic data.

Bassin de Rennes region (France)].
Commission, 1977.   98p.   Information on
agriculture, 37.
F   CB-NA-77-037-FR-C

803 GUINET, A.
Modèles d'analyse d'entreprises de polyculture-élevage
bovin. Données technico-économiques de base. Région
Volvestre (France) [Models for analysis of mixed crop and
cattle farms. Basic technico-economic data. Volvestre
region (France)].
Commission, 1977.   102p.   Information on
agriculture, 39.
F   CB-NA-77-039-FR-C

804 GUINET, A.
Modèles d'analyse d'entreprises de polyculture-élevage
bovin. 1: Caractéristiques et possibilités d'utilisation
[Models for analysis of mixed crop and cattle farms. 1:
Characteristics and possibilities of utilization].
Commission, 1973.   261p.   Internal information on
agriculture, 97.
D F   VI/1385/72

805 GUINET, A.
Modèles d'analyse d'entreprises de polyculture-élevage
bovin. 2: Données technico-économiques de base.
Circonscription Nord-Picardie et région limoneuse du
Limbourg belge [Models for analysis of mixed crop and
cattle farms. 2: Basic technico-economic data.
Nord-Picardie area and the limoneuse region of Belgian
Limbourg].
Commission, 1973.   200p.   Internal information on
agriculture, 111.
D F   VI/1792/73

806 GUINET, A.
Modèles d'analyse d'entreprises de polyculture-élevage
bovin. 3: Données technico-économiques de base. Région
Noordelijke Bouwstreek (Pays-Bas) [Models for analysis
of mixed crop and cattle farms. 3: Basic technico-economic

data. Noordelijke Bouwstreek region (Netherlands)].
Commission, 1975.   90p.   Internal information on
agriculture, 140.
F N   VI/17751/70

807 GUINET, A.
Modelle zur Analyse von
Ackerbau-Rindviehhaltungsbetrieben.
Technisch-wirtschaftliche Grundangaben.
Schwäbisch-Bayerisches Hügelland (B.R. Deutschland)
[Models for analysis of mixed crop and cattle farms. Basic
technico-economic data. Schwäbisch-bayerisches
Hügelland (F.R. Germany) / Modèles d'analyse
d'entreprises de polyculture-élevage bovin. Données
technico-économiques de base. Schwäbisch-bayerisches
Hügelland (R.F. Allemagne)].
Commission, 1976.   86p.   Information on
agriculture, 6.
D   8835

808 GUINET, A.
Models for analysis mixed crop and cattle farms. Basic
techno-economic data. South-East Leinster (Ireland),
West Cambridgeshire (United Kingdom), Fünen
(Denmark) [Modèles d'analyse d'entreprises de
polyculture-élevage bovin. Données technico-économiques
de base. South-East Leinster (Irlande), West
Cambridgeshire (Royaume-Uni), Fünen (Danemark)].
Commission, 1976.   var. pag.   Information on
agriculture, 7.
E   8836

809 GUINET, A.
Models for analysis mixed crop and cattle farms. 6:
Characteristics and possible applications. South-East
Leinster (Ireland), West Cambridgeshire (United
Kingdom), Fünen (Denmark), Schwäbisch-bayerisches
Hügelland (F.R. Germany) (Modèles d'analyse
d'entreprises de polyculture-élevage bovin. 6:
Caractéristiques et possibilités d'utilisation. South-East
Leinster (Irlande), West Cambridgeshire (Royaume-Uni),

Fünen (Danemark), Schwäbisch-bayerisches Hügelland
(R.F. d'Allemagne)).
Commission, 1976.   47p.   Internal information on
agriculture, 152.
E F   VI/3715/1/74

810 GUNDELACH, F. O.
A new approach to the approximation of legislation (Une
approche nouvelle à l'harmonisation des législations).
In Information: interior market, 59/1974.
Pr Inf, 1974.   5p.
D E F I N   124/X/74

811 GUNDELACH, F. O.
The new Commission's views on the common agricultural
policy (Les orientations de la nouvelle Commission sur
l'Europe verte).
In Newsletter on the common agricultural policy,
2/1977.   Pr Inf, 1977.   9p.
DK D E F I N   X/102/77

812 GUNDELACH, F. O.
Progress towards an internal common market (Progrès
dans la voie d'un marché intérieur commun).
In Information: internal market, 108/1975.
Pr Inf, 1975.   pp.1–4.
D E F I N   493/X/75

813 GÜSTEN, R.
Possibilités de création d'industries exportatrices dans les
États africains et malgache associés. Produits de
l'élevage. Viandes, cuirs et peaux, chaussures, articles en
cuir [Possibilities for the establishment of exporting
industries in the Associated African States and
Madagascar. Products from rearing. Meat, hides and
skins, shoes, leather articles].
Commission, 1974.   5 vols.
F   VIII/223/74

814 GÜSTEN, R.
Possibilités de création d'industries exportatrices dans les
États africains et malgache associés. Produits de

l'élevage. Viandes, cuirs et peaux, chaussures, articles en
cuir. Rapport de synthèse [Possibilities for the
establishment of exporting industries in the Associated
African States and Madagascar. Products from rearing.
Meat, hides and skins, shoes, leather articles. Summary
report].
Commission, 1975.   27p.
D E F I N   VIII/223/74

815 GÜSTEN, R.
Possibilités de création d'industries exportatrices dans les
États africains et malgache associés. Produits
électro-mécaniques. Produits électroniques [Possibilities
for the establishment of exporting industries in the
Associated African States and Madagascar.
Electro-mechanical products. Electronic products].
Commission, 1975.   3 vols.
F   VIII/224/74

816 GÜSTEN, R.
Possibilités de création d'industries exportatrices dans les
États africains et malgache associés. Produits
électro-mécaniques. Produits électroniques. Rapport de
synthèse [Possibilities for the establishment of exporting
industries in the Associated African States and
Madagascar. Electro-mechanical products. Electronic
products. Summary report].
Commission, 1975.   23p.
D E F I N   VIII/224/74

817 GUTHMANN, K.
Technical measures of air pollution control in the iron and
steel industry. Reports and information on research work
subsidized by the ECSC as at June 1968 [Mesures
techniques contre la pollution atmosphérique dans la
sidérurgie. Rapports et information sur le travail de la
recherche subsidié par la CECA à juin 1968].
Commission, 1969.   71p.
E   15444

818 GUY

Essai d'appréciation des conditions d'application et des résultats d'une politique de réforme en agriculture dans des régions agricoles difficiles. 2: Queyras [Attempt at estimating the conditions from the application and results of a reform policy in agriculture in difficult agricultural regions. 2: Queryras].
Commission, 1975.   var. pag.   Internal information on agriculture, 150.
F   VI/1988/75

819 GWILLIAM, K. M.

Coordination of investments in transport infrastructures. Analysis. Recommendations. Procedures (Coordination des investissements en infrastructure de transport. Analyse. Recommandations. Procédures).
Commission, 1974.   85p.   Studies: transport series, 3.
D E F I N   8423

820 HAAN, de, chairman

Avant-projet de convention relatif à un droit européen des marques [Preliminary draft of a convention relating to an European law for trademarks].
Commission, 1973.   187p.
D/F/I/N   8381

821 HAAN, P. de

Étude de droit comparé sur les rapports entre bailleur et preneur à ferme dans les pays de la C.E.E. [Legal study comparing the relations between the landlord and lessee of farmland in the countries of the E.E.C.].
Commission EEC, 1961.   48p.   Studies: agricultural series, 6.
D F I N   8025

822 HAASE, H. M. J. M.

The mobility of cultural workers within the Community (La mobilité des travailleurs culturels dans la Communauté).
Commission, 1977.   98p.   Studies: cultural matters series, 1.
D E F   8732

823 HACCOÛ, J. F.
Le financement de la reconversion industrielle. Formes
particulières de financement [Financing of industrial
conversion. Particular forms of financing].
ECSC HA, 1965.   107p.   Collection: regional
economy and policy. 1: Industrial conversion in Europe,
10.
D F I N   3708

824 HAGE, K.
Nouvelles formes de collaboration dans le domaine de la
production agricole. 3: R.F. d'Allemagne [New forms of
cooperation in the field of agricultural production. 3: F.R.
of Germany].
Commission, 1972.   174p.   Internal information on
agriculture, 95.
D F   VI/2512/72

825 HAGEMANN, G.
Élaboration d'une méthode macroéconomique pour le
calcul de la charge fiscale indirecte pesant en amont des
exploitations agricoles dans chacun des six pays de la
Communauté [Formulation of a macroeconomic method
for the calculation of an indirect tax on farms in each of the
six countries of the Community].
Commission, 1972.   74p.   Studies:
competition–approximation of legislation series, 18.
D F I N   8337

826 HALLET, J.
Étude sur l'évolution de la concentration dans l'industrie
alimentaire en Belgique [A study of the evolution of
concentration in the food industry in Belgium].
Commission, 1976.   93p.
F   8899

827 HALLET, J.
Étude sur l'évolution de la concentration dans l'industrie
de la construction électrique en Belgique. Construction
d'appareils électriques, radios, télévision,
électro-acoustique (N.I.C.E. 375). Fabrication d'appareils

électrodomestiques (N.I.C.E. 376) [A study of the
evolution of concentration in the electrical engineering
industry in Belgium. Manufacture of electrical and audio
equipment, radio and television receivers (N.I.C.E. 375).
Manufacture of electrical domestic appliances (N.I.C.E.
376)].
Commission, 1973.   82p.
F   IV/578/73

828 HALLET, J.
Étude sur l'évolution de la concentration dans quelques
sous-secteurs de l'industrie chimique en Belgique.
Pharmaceutique (N.I.C.E. 313.1). Photographique
(N.I.C.E. 313.2). Produits d'entretien (N.I.C.E. 313.5)
[A study of the evolution of concentration in various
sub-sectors of the chemical industry in Belgium.
Pharmaceuticals (N.I.C.E. 313.1). Photography
(N.I.C.E. 313.2). Cleaning and maintenance products
(N.I.C.E. 313.5)].
Commission, 1973.   var. pag.
F   IV/581/73

829 HALLET, J.
Étude sur l'évolution de la concentration dans quelques
sous-secteurs de l'industrie du textile en Belgique. Laine
(N.I.C.E. 232). Coton (N.I.C.E. 233). Bonneterie
(N.I.C.E. 237) [A study of the evolution of concentration
in various sub-sectors of the textile industry in Belgium.
Wool (N.I.C.E. 232). Cotton (N.I.C.E. 233). Knitted and
crocheted goods (N.I.C.E. 237)].
Commission, 1973.   var. pag.
F   IV/577/73

830 HALLSTEIN, W.
La Communauté européenne. Un nouvel ordre juridique
[The European Community. A new legal system].
Bureau (P), 1964.   11p.   Les documents de
Communauté européenne, 27.
F

831 HALLSTEIN, W.
La Communauté européenne et la formation d'un droit
communautaire. Recueil des exposés prononcés devant
une délégation de magistrats français [The European
Community and the formation of a Community law.
Collection of reports delivered to a delegation of French
judges].
Pr Inf, 1965.   66p.
F

832 HALLSTEIN, W.
Déclaration prononcé par M. le Prof. Dr. Walter
Hallstein, Président de la Commission de la Communauté
économique européenne, devant le Parlement européen à
Strasbourg 21 octobre 1958 [Statement by Prof. Dr.
Walter Hallstein, President of the Commission of the
European Economic Community, to the European
Parliament at Strasbourg 21 October 1958].
Commission EEC, 1958.   38p.
D F I N   2089

833 HALLSTEIN, W.
Economic integration and political unity in Europe
[Intégration économique et unité politique en Europe].
Inf Ser, 1961.   8p.   Community topics, 2.
E

834 HALLSTEIN, W.
Les progrès de l'Europe communautaire [The progress of
Community Europe].
Bureau (P), 1964.   12p.   Les documents de
Communauté européenne, 22.
F

835 HALLSTEIN, W.
Le rôle des institutions communautaires dans la
construction européenne [The role of Community
institutions in European integration].
Bureau (P), 1960.   12p.   Les documents de
Communauté européenne, 6.
F

836 HALLSTEIN, W.
Some of our 'faux problèmes' [Quelques des 'faux
problèmes' notres].
Inf Ser, 1965.   15p.   Community topics, 17.
E

837 HALLSTEIN, W.
Statement by Prof. Dr. Walter Hallstein, President of
the Commission, to the European Parliamentary
Assembly at Strasbourg 20th March 1958 [Déclaration
prononcé par M. le Prof. Dr. Walter Hallstein, Président
de la Commission, devant l'Assemblée du Parlement
européen à Strasbourg, 20 mars 1958].
Commission EEC, 1958.   42p.
D E F I N   2033

838 HALLSTEIN, W.
W. Hallstein and J. Rey, Freemen of the City of Brussels.
Speeches given on 2 December 1971 at the conferring of
the Freedom of the City of Brussels on the former
Presidents of the Commission of the European Economic
Community and of the Commission of the European
Communities (W. Hallstein et J. Rey, citoyens de la ville
de Bruxelles. Discours prononcés le 2 décembre 1971 à
l'occasion de la remise du diplôme de citoyen d'honneur de
la ville de Bruxelles aux anciens présidents de la
Commission de la Communauté économique européenne et
de la Commission des Communautés européennes).
Commission, 1972.   20p.
D E F I N   8368

839 HALLSTEIN, W.
Where the Common Market stands today [Quelle est la
position du Marché commun aujourd'hui].
Inf Ser, 1964.   15p.   Community topics, 13.
E

840 HAMELIN
Possibilités de création d'industries exportatrices dans les
États africains et malgache associés. Produits de
l'élevage. Viandes, cuirs et peaux, chaussures, articles en

cuir [Possibilities for the establishment of exporting
industries in the Associated African States and
Madagascar. Products from rearing. Meat, hides and
skins, shoes, leather articles].
Commission, 1974.   5 vols.
F   VIII/223/74

841 HAMELIN
Possibilités de création d'industries exportatrices dans les
États africains et malgache associés. Produits de
l'élevage. Viandes, cuirs et peaux, chaussures, articles en
cuir. Rapport de synthèse [Possibilities for the
establishment of exporting industries in the Associated
African States and Madagascar. Products from rearing.
Meat, hides and skins, shoes, leather articles. Summary
report].
Commission, 1975.   27p.
D E F IN   VIII/223/74

842 HANISCH, G.
Tableaux 'Entrées-Sorties' pour les pays de la
Communauté Économique Européenne ['Input-Output'
tables for the countries of the European Economic
Community].
Eurostat, 1964.   var. pag.
D F

843 HANISCH, G.
Tableaux 'Entrées-Sorties' pour les pays de la
Communauté Économique Européenne. Seconde version
['Input-Output' tables for the countries of the European
Economic Community. Second version].
Eurostat, 1965.   var. pag.
D F

844 HANSMEYER, K.-H.
Enseignements à tirer en agriculture d'expérience des
'Revolving funds' [Lessons to learn in agriculture from the
experience of 'Revolving funds'].
Commission, 1970.   97p.   Internal information on
agriculture, 62.
D F   VI/11144/70

845 HARMANT, A. F. d'
Les services de la main-d'œuvre des États membres de la
Communauté. Exposé de synthèse [Employment
exchanges in the Member States of the Community.
Summary].
Commission EEC, 1967.   131p.   Studies: social
policy series, 16.
D F I N   8193

846 HARRIS, D., chairman
Earnings in agriculture 1974 (Gains dans l'agriculture
1974).
In Social statistics, 5/1975.   Eurostat, 1976.   107p.
D/E/F/I/N   6936/5

847 HARRIS, D.
Social accounts. Accounts of social protection in the EC
1970–1975 (Comptes sociaux. Comptes de la protection
sociale dans la CE 1970–1975).
Eurostat, 1977.   201p.
DK/D/E/F/I/N   CA-23-77-001-6A-C

848 HARRIS, D.
Social accounts 1970–1973 (Comptes sociaux 1970–1973).
In Social statistics, 3/1975.   Eurostat, 1976.   121p.
DK/D/E/F/I/N   6936/3

849 HART, M.
Secondary schools in Europe [Les écoles secondaires en
Europe].
In European studies. Teachers' series, 21.
Commission (L), 1975.   4p.
E   U/75/21

850 HART, P. E.
A study of the evolution of concentration in the beverages
industry for the United Kingdom. Part one: Industry
structure and concentration, 1969–1974 [Étude sur
l'évolution de la concentration dans l'industrie des
boissons au Royaume-Uni. Partie première: La structure
industrielle et la concentration, 1969–1974].
Commission, 1977.   263p.
E   8942

851 HART, P. E.
A study of the evolution of concentration in the food
distribution industry for the United Kingdom. Volume 2:
Price surveys [Étude sur l'évolution de la concentration
dans l'industrie de la distribution des produits
alimentaires au Royaume-Uni. Tome 2: Enquêtes de prix].
Commission, 1977.   152p.
E   8762

852 HART, P. E.
A study of the evolution of concentration in the food
industry for the United Kingdom. Product market
structure [Étude sur l'évolution de la concentration dans
l'industrie alimentaire au Royaume-Uni. Structure des
marchés de produit].
Commission, 1976.   2 vols.
E   8827, 8709

853 HARTLEY, T. C.
The law of property in the European Community [Le droit
de la propriété dans la Communauté européenne].
Commission, 1977.   305p.   Studies:
competition–approximation of legislation series, 27.
E   8727

854 HARTLEY, T. C.
The law of suretyship and indemnity in the United
Kingdom of Great Britain and Northern Ireland and
Ireland (Le droit du cautionnement et de la garantie au
Royaume-Uni et en Irlande).
Commission, 1977.   64p.   Studies:
competition–approximation of legislation series, 28.
D E F   8729

855 HARTMANN, F.
Les aciéries [The steel-works].
Commission, 1971.   283p.   New technical processes
in the iron and steel industry: a personal training manual,
3. Studies: vocational training.
D F I N   17433

856 HARVENG, I.
Recherches sur l'automatisation de la bande
d'agglomération de l'usine de Marchienne de la Société des
Forges de la Providence (Belgique). (Rapport final)
[Researches on the automation of the sinter strand at the
Marchienne factory of the Forges de la Providence
company (Belgium). (Final report)].
ECSC HA, 1966.   35p.
D F

857 HARVENG, L.
L'automatisation d'agglomération à Forges de la
Providence. Marchienne-au-Pont, Belgique [Automated
sintering at Forges de la Providence,
Marchienne-au-Pont, Belgium].
ECSC HA, 1965.   8p.
D F   12009

858 HARVENG, L.
Le contrôle automatique et continu de l'humidité du
mélange d'agglomération. Application de la mesure par la
conductivité électrique [Automatic continuous control of
the humidity of the sinter blend. Application of the
electrical conductivity measurement].
ECSC HA, 1964.   20p.
D F'   10403

859 HASSON, G. D.
La formation des formateurs. Problèmes, méthodes et
expériences dans les industries de la C.E.C.A. [Training
of the trainers. Problems, methods and experiments in the
industries of the E.C.S.C.].
ECSC HA, 1962.   127p.
F   8514

860 HASSON, G. D.
La formation professionnelle dans les houillères des pays
de la Communauté [Vocational training in the coal mines
of the countries of the Community].
ECSC HA, 1956.   514p.
F   1669

861 HATER, M.
Les aciéries [The steel-works].
Commission, 1971.   283p.   New technical processes
in the iron and steel industry: a personal training manual,
3.   Studies: vocational training.
D F I N   17433

862 HAVEMAN, J.
De quelques problèmes socio-psychologiques posés par le
passage de mineurs à d'autres industries [Several
socio-psychological problems posed by the traffic of miners
to other industries].
ECSC HA, 1960.   6p.   Intergovernmental
Conference on Industrial Redevelopment.
F   5460

863 HAVEMAN, J.
Le financement des investissements et les aspects sociaux
de la reconversion [Financing of investments and social
aspects of conversion].
ECSC HA, 1963.   255p.   Collection: regional
economy and policy. 1: Industrial conversion in Europe, 3.
D F I N   3323

864 HEATH, J. B.
A study of the evolution of concentration in the mechanical
engineering sector for the United Kingdom [Étude sur
l'évolution de la concentration dans le secteur de la
construction de machines non électriques au
Royaume-Uni].
Commission, 1976.   264p.
E   8708

865 HEATH, J. B.
A study of the evolution of concentration in the
pharmaceutical industry for the United Kingdom [Étude
sur l'évolution de la concentration dans l'industrie
pharmaceutique au Royaume-Uni].
Commission, 1977.   168p.
E   8707

866 HEATH, J. B.
A study of the evolution of concentration in the United
Kingdom mechanical engineering industry. Concentration
tables [Étude sur l'évolution de la concentration dans
l'industrie de la construction de machines non électriques
au Royaume-Uni. Tableaux de concentration].
Commission, 1976.   198p.
E   8704

867 HEESCHEN, W.
Dispositions législatives et administratives concernant les
résidus dans le lait, les produits laitiers et les aliments
pour le cheptel laitier [Legislative and administrative
provisions concerning residues in milk, dairy produce and
food for the dairy herd].
Commission, 1973.   198p.   Internal information on
agriculture, 114.
D F   VI/3359/73

868 HEESCHEN, W.
Objectivation of the bacteriological and organoleptic
quality of milk for consumption [Critères objectifs pour
l'appréciation de la qualité bactériologique et
organoleptique du lait de consommation].
Commission, 1977.   161p.   Information on
agriculture, 21.
E   8875

869 HEIDA, H.
Air sulphur dioxide concentrations in the European
Community. Yearly report: April 1971–March 1972
(Concentration d'anhydride sulfureux atmosphérique dans
la Communauté européenne. Rapport annuel: Avril
1971–Mars 1972).
Commission, 1974.   46p.
D/E/F/I/N

870 HEIDE, H.
Situation et tendances des marchés mondiaux des
principaux produits agricoles. Céréales [Position and

trends of world markets for the chief agricultural
products. Cereals].
Commission, 1968.   342p.   Internal information on
agriculture, 24.
D F   4518/VI/68

871 HEILIGER, H. G.
La reconversion des charbonnages dans les bassins de la
République fédérale. Aix-la-Chapelle [The conversion of
coalmines in the basins of the Federal Republic.
Aix-la-Chapelle].
Commission, 1973.   84p.   Pamphlets on industrial
conversion, 20.
D F I N   8390

872 HELL, W.
Les aciéries [The steel-works].
Commission, 1971.   283p.   New technical processes
in the iron and steel industry: a personal training manual,
3.   Studies: vocational training.
D F I N   17433

873 HELLMANN, R.
L'Amérique sur le marché européen. Les investissements
directs des États-Unis dans le Marché commun [America
on the European market. The direct investments of the
United States in the Common Market].
n.i., 1966.   59p.
F   16166/PI/66

874 HELME, W. H.
Models for analysis mixed crop and cattle farms. Basic
techno-economic data. South-East Leinster (Ireland),
West Cambridgeshire (United Kingdom), Fünen
(Denmark) [Modèles d'analyse d'entreprises de
polyculture-élevage bovin. Données technico-économiques
de base. South-East Leinster (Irlande), West
Cambridgeshire (Royaume-Uni), Fünen (Danemark)].
Commission, 1976.   var. pag.   Information on
agriculture, 7.
E   8836

875 HELME, W. H.
Models for analysis mixed crop and cattle farms. 6:
Characteristics and possible applications. South-East
Leinster (Ireland), West Cambridgeshire (United
Kingdom), Fünen (Denmark), Schwäbisch-bayerisches
Hügelland (F.R. Germany) (Modèles d'analyse
d'entreprises de polyculture-élevage bovin. 6:
Caractéristiques et possibilités d'utilisation. South-East
Leinster (Irlande), West Cambridgeshire (Royaume-Uni),
Fünen (Danemark), Schwäbisch-bayerisches Hügelland
(R.F. d'Allemagne)).
Commission, 1976. 47p. Internal information on
agriculture, 152.
E F VI/3715/1/74

876 HENDUS, H.
Africa and the Common Market. Address by M. Heinrich
Hendus, Director General for Overseas Development, to
the meeting of ambassadors of the Congo Republic at
Leopoldville on 25 January 1963 [L'Afrique et le Marché
commun. Discours de M. Heinrich Hendus, Directeur
général du développement de l'outre-mer, à l'assemblée
des ambassadeurs de la République du Congo à
Léopoldville, le 25 janvier 1963].
Commission EEC, 1963. 18p.
D E F I N 8097

877 HENNIG, W.
EEC's transport problems with East European
Countries. Opinion [Les problèmes des transports de la
CEE avec les pays européens de l'est. Avis].
ESC, 1977. 164p.
DKD E F I N

878 HENSCHEL, H.
Les services de la main-d'œuvre des États membres de la
Communauté. Exposé de synthèse [Employment
exchanges in the Member States of the Community.
Summary].
Commission EEC, 1967. 131p. Studies: social
policy series, 16.
D F I N 8193

878A HENTZ, P.
Aide-mémoire pour la pratique des épreuves d'exercice en
médecine du travail [Manual for the practice of exercise
tests in industrial medicine].
Commission, 1971.   49p.   Collection: industrial
health and medicine, 12.
D F I N   16741

879 HERBORG-NIELSEN, T.
A study of the evolution of concentration in the Danish
food distribution industry. Part one: Concentration in the
Danish food distribution system. Part two: The first and
the second price surveys in Denmark [Étude sur
l'évolution de la concentration dans l'industrie de la
distribution des produits alimentaires au Denmark. Partie
première: La concentration dans le système de la
distribution des produits alimentaires au Danemark.
Partie deuxième: Les enquêtes des prix premières et
deuxièmes au Danemark].
Commission, 1977.   292p.
E

880 HERBORG-NIELSEN, T.
A study of the evolution of concentration in the Danish
food processing industry [Étude sur l'évolution de la
concentration dans l'industrie de la transformation des
produits alimentaires au Danemark].
Commission, 1977.   252p.
E   8761

881 HESSE, M.-D.
Méthodes et moyens pour établir une nouvelle
classification des impôts en se basant sur les principes mis
en lumière lors de l'harmonisation des systèmes fiscaux
des États membres de la CEE [Ways and means of
establishing a new classification of taxes based on the
principles brought out when the fiscal systems of the
Member States of the EEC were harmonized].
Commission, 1970.   42p.   Studies:
competition–approximation of legislation series, 13.
D F I N   8304

882 HEYDE, M. van der
Fiskale beschikkingen op het gebied van de samenwerking
en de fusie van landbouwbedrijven. 3: Nederland [Tax
arrangements concerning cooperation and amalgamation
of farms. 3: The Netherlands / Dispositions fiscales en
matière de coopération et de fusion d'exploitations
agricoles. 3: Pays-Bas].
Commission, 1972.   106p.   Internal information on
agriculture, 85.
N   VI/1127/72

883 HIEB, K.
Agriculture de montagne dans la région alpine de la
Communauté. 3: R.F. d'Allemagne [Hill farming in the
alpine region of the Community. 3: F.R. of Germany].
Commission, 1973.   196p.   Internal information on
agriculture, 107.
D F   VI/2316/73

884 HIFFS, G.
Comparaison des bilans d'énergie du Royaume-Uni et de
la Communauté [Comparison of energy balances between
the United Kingdom and the Community].
In Bulletin de la Communauté européenne du charbon et
de l'acier, 12–3/1967.
ECSC HA, 1967.   pp.38–52.
F   4125

885 HILDEBRANDT, A. G. U.
Le marché de poissons frais [The wet fish market].
Commission, 1969.   120p.   Internal information on
agriculture, 47.
D F   14483/VI/69

886 HILDEBRANDT, A. G. U.
Le marché de poissons frais en république fédérale
d'Allemagne et aux Pays-Bas et les facteurs qui
interviennent dans la formation du prix du hareng frais
[The wet fish market in the Federal Republic of Germany
and the Netherlands and the factors which determine the
formation of fresh herring prices].

Commission EEC, 1965.   200p.   Internal
information on agriculture, 3.
D F   8701/VI/63

887 HILDEBRANDT, A. G. U.
Volume et degré de l'emploi dans la pêche maritime
[Volume and extent of employment in sea fishing].
Commission, 1968.   var. pag.   Internal information
on agriculture, 32.
D F   6993/VI/68

888 HILF
Statistiques dans le domaine de la production de porcs
dans les États membres des Communautés européennes
1968–1971 [Statistics in the domain of pork production in
the Member States of the European Communities
1968–1971].
In Agricultural statistical studies, 14.
Eurostat, 1974.   2 vols.
D F   6654

889 HILF, G.
Labour costs in industry 1972–1975. Results of the
surveys of 1972 and 1973. Updating of the costs to 1975
(Coût de la main-d'œuvre dans l'industrie 1972–1975.
Résultats des enquêtes de 1972–1973. Actualisation des
coûts jusqu'en 1975).
In Social statistics, 6/1975.   Eurostat, 1976.   456p.
DK/D/E/F/I/N   6936/6

890 HILL, T. P.
A system of integrated price and volume measures
(indices) [Un système des mesures de prix et volume
intégré (indices)].
In Statistical studies and surveys, 3/1972.
Eurostat, 1973.   pp.7–43.
E   5842

891 HILLERY, P. J.
European social policies. Problems and prospects
(Politique sociale européenne. Problèmes et perspectives).

In Information: social policy, 98/1975.
Pr Inf, 1975.   11p.
D E F I N   278/X/75

892 HINDERFELD, H.
Nouvelles formes de collaboration dans le domaine de la
production agricole. 3: R.F. d'Allemagne [New forms of
co-operation in the field of agricultural production. 3: F.R.
of Germany].
Commission, 1972.   174p.   Internal information on
agriculture, 95.
D F   VI/2512/72

893 HIRSCH, É.
Le rôle des institutions communautaires dans la
construction européenne [The role of Community
institutions in European integration].
Bureau (P), 1960.   12p.   Les documents de
Communauté européenne, 6.
F

894 HIRSCH, É.
Speech delivered to the European Parliament by Mr.
Étienne Hirsch President of the Euratom Commission at
Strasbourg. June 1961. [Discours prononcé par M.
Étienne Hirsch Président de la Commission de l'Euratom
devant le Parlement européen à Strasbourg. Juin 1961].
Commission EAEC, 1961.   16p.
E

895 HIRSCH, É.
Speech delivered to the European Parliament by Mr.
Étienne Hirsch President of the Euratom Commission at
Strasbourg. May 1960 [Discours prononcé par M. Étienne
Hirsch Président de la Commission de l'Euratom devant le
Parlement européen à Strasbourg. Mai 1960].
Commission EAEC, 1960.   26p.
E   2461

896 HÖDL, E.
Study of the characteristics of a Community programme
on the environment and its effect on employment [Étude
des traits d'un programme communautaire sur
l'environnement et son effet sur l'emploi].
n.i., 1977.   225p.
D E   ENV/223/74

897 HOFFMANN, G.
Les aciéries [The steel-works].
Commission, 1971.   283p.   New technical processes
in the iron and steel industry: a personal training manual,
3.   Studies: vocational training.
D F I N   17433

898 HOFFMANN, G.
Les laminoirs [The rolling mills].
Commission, 1972.   240p.   New technical processes
in the iron and steel industry: a personal training manual,
4.   Studies: vocational training.
D F I N   8349

899 HOFFMEYER, M.
Agriculture et politique agricole de quelques pays de
l'Europe occidentale. 1: Autriche [Agriculture and
agricultural policy of several Western European
countries. 1: Austria].
Commission, 1970.   var. pag.   Internal information
on agriculture, 56.
D F   12396/VI/69

900 HOFFMEYER, M.
Agriculture et politique agricole de quelques pays de
l'Europe occidentale. 2: Danemark [Agriculture and
agricultural policy of several Western European
countries. 2: Denmark].
Commission, 1970.   var. pag.   Internal information
on agriculture, 57.
D F   VI/12396/69

901 HOFFMEYER, M.
Agriculture et politique agricole de quelques pays de
l'Europe occidentale. 3: Norvège [Agriculture and
agricultural policy of several Western European
countries. 3: Norway].
Commission, 1970.   246p.   Internal information on
agriculture, 58.
D F   7308/VI/70

902 HOFFMEYER, M.
Agriculture et politique agricole de quelques pays de
l'Europe occidentale. 4: Suède [Agriculture and
agricultural policy of several Western European
countries. 4: Sweden].
Commission, 1970.   var. pag.   Internal information
on agriculture, 64.
D F   23003/VI/69

903 HOFFMEYER, M.
Agriculture et politique agricole de quelques pays de
l'Europe occidentale. 5: Royaume-Uni [Agriculture and
agricultural policy of several Western European
countries. 5: United Kingdom].
Commission, 1970.   308p.   Internal information on
agriculture, 66.
D F   VI/4808/69

904 HOFFMEYER, M.
Agriculture et politique agricole de quelques pays de
l'Europe occidentale. 6: Suisse [Agriculture and
agricultural policy of several Western European
countries. 6: Switzerland].
Commission, 1970.   var. pag.   Internal information
on agriculture, 67.
D F   VI/21229/69

905 HOFFMEYER, M.
Agriculture et politique agricole de quelques pays de
l'Europe occidentale. 7: Portugal [Agriculture and
agricultural policy of several Western European
countries. 7: Portugal].

Commission, 1971.   var. pag.   Internal information
on agriculture, 71.
D F   VI/705/71

906 HOFFMEYER, M.
Agriculture et politique agricole de quelques pays de
l'Europe occidentale. 8: Irlande [Agriculture and
agricultural policy of several Western European
countries. 8: Ireland].
Commission, 1971.   400p.   Internal information on
agriculture, 73.
D F   VI/1898/72

907 HOFFMEYER, M.
Agriculture et politique agricole de quelques pays de
l'Europe occidentale. 9: Finlande [Agriculture and
agricultural policy of several Western European
countries. 9: Finland].
Commission, 1973.   152p.   Internal information on
agriculture, 86.
D F   VI/611/72

908 HOFFMEYER, M.
Agriculture et politique agricole de quelques pays de
l'Europe occidentale. 10: Aperçu synoptique [Agriculture
and agricultural policy of several Western European
countries. 10: Synoptic summary].
Commission, 1972.   196p.   Internal information on
agriculture, 89.
D F   VI/3168/72

909 HOFFMEYER, M.
Projection of production and consumption of agricultural
products—'1977'. 1: United Kingdom (Projections de la
production et de la consommation de produits
agricoles—'1977'. 1: Royaume-Uni).
Commission, 1973.   253p.   Internal information on
agriculture, 108.
D E F   VI/3709/74

910 HOFFMEYER, M.
Projection of production and consumption of agricultural products—'1977'. 2: Denmark, Ireland (Projections de la production et de la consommation de produits agricoles—'1977'. 2: Danemark, Irlande).
Commission, 1973.   137p.   Internal information on agriculture, 109.
D E F   VI/2942/72

911 HOFFMEYER, M.
Situation et tendances des marchés mondiaux des principaux produits agricoles. Céréales [Position and trends of world markets for the chief agricultural products. Cereals].
Commission, 1968.   342p.   Internal information on agriculture, 24.
D F   4518/VI/68

912 HOFFMEYER, M.
Situation et tendances des marchés mondiaux des principaux produits agricoles. Produits laitiers [Position and trends of world markets for the chief agricultural products. Milk products].
Commission, 1967.   356p.   Internal information on agriculture, 19.
D F   10564/VI/67

913 HOFFMEYER, M.
Die voraussichtliche Entwicklung der internationalen Versorgung mit landwirtschaftlichen Erzeugnissen und ihre Folgen für die Gemeinschaft. 1: Weizen, Futtergetreide, Zucker, Gesamtzussammenfassung [The foreseeable trend in world availabilities of agricultural products and the consequences for the Community. 1: Wheat, feed grain, sugar, summary / L'évolution prévisible de l'approvisionnement international en produits agricoles et ses conséquences pour la Communauté. 1: Blé, céréales fourragères, sucre, résumé].
Commission, 1977.   244p.   Information on agriculture, 18.
D   8874

914 HOFFMEYER, M.
Die voraussichtliche Entwicklung der internationalen
Versorgung mit landwirtschaftlichen Erzeugnissen und
ihre Folgen für die Gemeinschaft. 3: Öle und Fette,
Eiweissfuttermittel [The foreseeable trend in world
availabilities of agricultural products and the
consequences for the Community. 3: Oils and fats, protein
products / L'évolution prévisible de l'approvisionnement
international en produits agricoles et ses conséquences
pour la Communauté. 3: Huiles et graisses, aliments
azotés pour animaux].
Commission, 1977.   200p.   Information on
agriculture, 36.
D   CB-NA-77-036-DE-C

915 HOFFNAGELS, H.
L'Europe à la lumière des programmes électoraux aux
Pays-Bas [Europe in the light of electoral programmes in
the Netherlands].
Pr Inf, 1967.   14p.
F

916 HOFSTEE, E. H.
L'emploi agricole dans les pays de la C.E.E. Tome 1:
Structure [Agricultural employment in the countries of
the E.E.C. Volume 1: Structure].
Commission EEC, 1964.   61p.   Studies: social policy
series, 7.
D F I N   8108

917 HOFSTEE, E. H.
L'emploi agricole dans les pays de la C.E.E. Tome 2:
Évolution et perspectives [Agricultural employment in
the countries of the E.E.C. 2: Development and
prospects].
Commision EEC, 1964.   51p.   Studies: social policy
series, 8.
D F I N   8123

918 HOLLAND, P.
Glossary new transport technologies (Glossaire nouvelles
techniques de transport).
Commission, 1976.   900p.
DK/D/E/F/I/N   IX/2061/74

919 HOLSCHUH
La formation professionnelle dans l'industrie sidérurgique
des pays de la Communauté [Vocational training in the
iron and steel industry of the countries of the
Community].
ECSC HA, 1954.   264p.
F

920 HONOUT, J. A.
La consommation du vin et les facteurs qui la déterminent.
3: Pays-Bas [Wine consumption and the factors which
determine it. 3: The Netherlands].
Commission, 1974.   206p.   Internal information on
agriculture, 132.
F N   VI/1045/75

921 HOOF, J. van
Evaluation of the hygienic problems related to the chilling
of poultry carcasses [Évaluation des problèmes d'hygiène
en rapport avec le refroidissement des carcasses de
volaille].
Commission, 1977.   108p.   Information on
agriculture, 22.
E   8878

922 HÖPFNER, K.
La région d'Amberg. Tendances et possibilités de
développement économique [The Amberg region. Trends
and possibilities for economic development].
ECSC HA, 1966.   184p.   Collection: regional
economy and policy. 2: Development and conversion
programme, 7.
D F   3898

923 HORION, P.
Le contrat de travail dans le droit des pays membres de la
CECA [The employment contract in the law of the
member countries of the ECSC].
ECSC HA, 1966.   727p.   Collection: labour law.
D F I N   3568

924 HORION, P.
Grève et lock-out [Strike and lock-out].
ECSC HA, 1961.   399p.   Collection: labour law.
2: Labour law in the Community, 5.
D F I N   2367

925 HORION, P.
La juridiction du travail et la juridiction de la sécurité
sociale dans les pays de la Communauté européenne
[Employment and social security jurisdiction in the
countries of the European Community].
Commission, 1972.   615p.   Collection: labour law.
D F I N   8341

926 HORION, P.
La protection des travailleurs en cas de perte de l'emploi
[Protection of workers in the event of loss of employment].
ECSC HA, 1961.   489p.   Collection: labour law.
2: Labour law in the Community, 11.
D F I N   2626

927 HORION, P.
Le régime juridique des organisations professionnelles
dans les pays membres de la C.E.C.A. [Legal
administration of professional organisations in the
member countries of the E.C.S.C.].
ECSC HA, 1968.   666p.   Collection: labour law.
D F I N   13879

928 HORION, P.
La représentation des travailleurs sur le plan de
l'entreprise dans le droit des pays membres de la
C.E.C.A. [Workers' representation at management level
in the law of the member countries of the E.C.S.C.].
ECSC HA, 1959.   348p.   Collection: labour law, 3.
D F I N   2104

928A HORION, P.
Les sources du droit du travail [Sources of labour law].
ECSC HA, 1962.　　192p.　　Collection: labour law.
2: Labour law in the Community, 1.
D F I N　　2773

929 HORION, P.
La stabilité de l'emploi dans le droit des pays membres de
la C.E.C.A. [Stability of employment in the law of the
member countries of the E.C.S.C.].
ECSC HA, 1958.　　311p.　　Collection: labour law, 2.
D F I N　　1999

930 HOTTELMANN, F.
Les établissements de stockage de céréales dans la CEE.
Partie 1 [The establishment of cereal storage in the EEC.
Part 1].
Commission, 1968.　　281p.　　Internal information on
agriculture, 28.
D F　　12751/VI/68

931 HOUGHTON, J.
The European Parliament [Le Parlement européen].
In European studies. Teachers' series, 19.
Commission (L), 1975.　　4p.
E　　U/74/19

932 HOUIN, R.
La réparation des conséquences dommageables d'une
violation des articles 85 et 86 du traité instituant la CEE
[Compensation for damage suffered through infringement
of Articles 85 and 86 of the Treaty establishing the EEC].
Commission EEC, 1966.　　74p.　　Studies: competition
series, 1.
D F I N　　8153

933 HOUT, T. J. G. van
Les grandes régions agricoles dans la C.E.E. [The main
agricultural regions in the E.E.C.].
Commission EEC, 1960.　　57p.　　Studies: agricultural
series, 1.
D F　　VI/707

934 HOUTTE, A. van
La Communauté Européenne du Charbon et de l'Acier
Communauté Supranationale. Conference faite au
'Convegno di studio per professori d'Università' à
l'Université de Naples, le 15 décembre 1955 [The
European Coal and Steel Community, a supranational
community. Conference held by the 'Convegno di studio
per professori d'Università' at the University of Naples,
15th December 1955].
ECSC, 1955.   36p.
F

935 HOVELAQUE, R.
Modèles d'analyse d'entreprises de polyculture-élevage
bovin. Données technico-économiques de base. Région du
Bassin de Rennes (France) [Models for analysis of mixed
crop and cattle farms. Basic technico-economic data.
Bassin de Rennes region (France)].
Commission, 1977.   98p.   Information on
agriculture, 37.
F   CB-NA-77-037-FR-C

936 HOWE, B.
The preparation of young people for work and for
transition from education to working life [La préparation
des jeunes à l'activité professionnelle et pour le passage de
l'éducation à la vie active].
In Bulletin of the European Communities. Supplement,
12/1976.   Commission, 1977.   pp.13–63.
DK D E F I N   4001/S/76/13

937 HOYOIS, G.
L'emploi agricole dans les pays de la C.E.E. Tome 1:
Structure [Agricultural employment in the countries of
the E.E.C. Volume 1: Structure].
Commission EEC, 1964.   61p.   Studies: social policy
series, 7.
D F I N   8108

938 HOYOIS, G.
L'emploi agricole dans les pays de la C.E.E. Tome 2:
Évolution et perspectives [Agricultural employment in

the countries of the E.E.C. Volume 2: Development and
prospects].
Commission EEC, 1964.   51p.   Studies: social policy
series, 8.
D F I N   8123

939 HÜBNER, J.
Untersuchung der Konzentrationsentwicklung in der
Reifenindustrie sowie ein Branchenbild der
Kraftfahrzeug-Elektrikindustrie in Deutschland [A study
of the evolution of concentration in the tyre industry, as
well as a survey of electrical equipment for the motor
vehicle industry in Germany / Étude sur l'évolution de la
concentration dans l'industrie des pneumatiques, aussi
que un éxamen des appareils électriques pour l'industrie
des véhicules à moteur en Allemagne].
Commission, 1977.   190p.
D   8757

940 HÜBNER, J.
Untersuchung zur Konzentrationsentwicklung in
verschiedenen Untersektoren der Papier- und
Pappeindustrie in Deutschland. Herstellung (N.I.C.E.
271). Verarbeitung (N.I.C.E. 272) [A study of the
evolution of concentration in various sub-sectors of the
paper and paperboard industry in Germany. Manufacture
(N.I.C.E. 271). Processing (N.I.C.E. 272) / Étude sur
l'évolution de la concentration dans quelques
sous-secteurs de l'industrie du papier et du carton en
Allemagne. Fabrication (N.I.C.E. 271). Transformation
(N.I.C.E. 272)].
Commission, 1976.   88p.
D   7195

HUGUET, N. Lilti-, *see* LILTI-HUGUET, N.

941 HÜLSEMEYER, F.
La production et la commercialisation de parties de
volaille [The production and marketing of poultry cuts].
Commission, 1974.   var. pag.   Internal information
on agriculture, 136.
D F   VI/3723/74

942 HUTCHINGS, G.
Les opérations financières et bancaires et la taxe sur la
valeur ajoutée [Financial and banking operations and the
value-added tax].
Commission, 1974.   49p.   Studies:
competition–approximation of legislation series, 22.
D F I N   8434

943 HYLAND, M. L.
Credit to agriculture. 6: Ireland [Crédits à l'agriculture. 6:
Irlande].
Commission, 1975.   224p.   Internal information on
agriculture, 167.
E   VI/510/76

944 IMMENGA, U.
Participation by banks in other branches of the economy
(Participations des banques dans d'autres secteurs
économiques).
Commission, 1975.   190p.   Studies:
competition–approximation of legislation series, 25.
DK D E F I N   7147

945 INDETZKI, H.-D.
La reconversion des charbonnages dans les bassins de la
République fédérale. Aix-la-Chapelle [The conversion of
coalmines in the basins of the Federal Republic.
Aix-la-Chapelle].
Commission, 1973.   84p.   Pamphlets on industrial
conversion, 20.
D F I N   8390

946 INDOVINA, F.
Study on the possible part played by certain primary
non-employment incomes in the inflationary process in
Italy (Étude sur le rôle éventuel de certains revenus
primaires non-salariaux dans le développement de
l'inflation en Italie).
Commission, 1977.   138p.   Series: medium-term
economic policy, 8.
D E F I N   8871

947 JACOB
Les conditions d'installation d'entreprises industrielles
dans les États africains et malgache associés. Volume 1:
République islamique de Mauritanie [Conditions for the
setting-up of industrial undertakings in the Associated
African States and Madagascar. Volume 1: Islamic
Republic of Mauritania].
Commission, 1972.   92p.
F   VIII/1311/72

948 JACOB
Les conditions d'installation d'entreprises industrielles
dans les États africains et malgache associés. Volume 2:
République du Sénégal [Conditions for the setting-up of
industrial undertakings in the Associated African States
and Madagascar. Volume 2: Republic of Senegal].
Commission, 1972.   100p.
F   VIII/1312/72

949 JACOB
Les conditions d'installation d'entreprises industrielles
dans les États africains et malgache associés. Volume 6:
République de Côte-d'Ivoire [Conditions for the
setting-up of industrial undertakings in the Associated
African States and Madagascar. Volume 6: Republic of
Ivory Coast].
Commission, 1972.   100p.
F   VIII/1316/72

950 JACOB
Les conditions d'installation d'entreprises industrielles
dans les États africains et malgache associés. Volume 7:
République togolaise [Conditions for the setting-up of
industrial undertakings in the Associated African States
and Madagascar. Volume 7: Republic of Togo].
Commission, 1972.   100p.
F   VIII/1317/72

951 JACOB
Les conditions d'installation d'entreprises industrielles
dans les États africains et malgache associés. Volume 8:

République du Dahomey [Conditions for the setting-up of
industrial undertakings in the Associated African States
and Madagascar. Volume 8: Republic of Dahomey].
Commission, 1972.   88p.
F   VIII/1318/72

952 JACOBS, H.
Les différences dans les prix des terrains agricoles. Une
étude sur les possibilités d'améliorer les statistiques des
prix des terres [Differences in the prices of agricultural
lands. A study on the possibilities of improving the
statistics of land prices].
In Agricultural statistical studies, 17.
Eurostat, 1974.   91p.
D F   6671

953 JACQUEMART
La formation professionnelle dans l'industrie sidérurgique
des pays de la Communauté [Vocational training in the
iron and steel industry of the countries of the
Community].
ECSC HA, 1954.   264p.
F

954 JACQUEMIN, A.
L'évolution de la concentration dans l'industrie de la
brasserie et des boissons en Belgique [The evolution of
concentration in the brewing and beverages industry in
Belgium].
Commission, 1977.   108p.
F   8760

955 JANNE, H.
For a Community policy on education (Pour une politique
communautaire de l'éducation).
In Bulletin of the European Communities. Supplement,
10/1973.   Commission, 1973.   61p.
D E F I N   4001/S/10/73

956 JANSEN, A. J.
Évolution régionale de la population active agricole. 1:
Synthèse [Regional development of the working
agricultural population. 1: Summary].
Commission, 1969.   74p.   Internal information on
agriculture, 39.
D F   6297/VI/69

957 JANSEN, A. J.
Évolution régionale de la population active agricole. 5:
Italie [Regional development of the working agricultural
population. 5: Italy].
Commission, 1969.   var. pag.   Internal information
on agriculture, 43.
D F   11445/VI/69

958 JANSSEN, J.
Mémorandum sur les objectifs de 1965. Méthodes
d'élaboration et résultats détaillés [Memorandum on the
1965 objectives. Methods of elaboration and detailed
results].
ECSC HA, 1962.   540p.   Collection: general
objectives for steel, 1.
D F I N   3017

959 JANTZ, K.
Étude sur la physionomie actuelle de la sécurité sociale
dans les pays de la C.E.E. [Study on the current situation
of social security in the countries of the E.E.C.].
Commission EEC, 1962.   130p.   Studies: social
policy series, 3.
D F I N   8058

960 JANTZ, K.
L'évolution financière de la sécurité sociale dans les États
membres de la Communauté. 1965–1970–1975. 1ère
Partie: Rapport de synthèse [Financial development of
social security in the Member States of the Community.
1965–1970–1975. First Part: Summary report].
Commission, 1973.   55p.
D F I N   8375

961 JARRE, G.
The aeronautical and space industries of the Community compared with those of the United Kingdom and the United States (Les industries aéronautiques et spatiales de la Communauté, comparées à celles de la Grande-Bretagne et des États-Unis).
Commission, 1971.   5 vols.   Studies: industry series, 4.
D E F I N   8284

962 JARRE, G.
Les industries aéronautiques et spatiales de la Communauté, comparées à celles de la Grande-Bretagne et des États-Unis. Annexe au Rapport Général [The aeronautical and space industries of the Community compared with those of the United Kingdom and the United States. Appendix to General Report].
Commission, 1969.   10 vols.
F

963 JASAY, A. de
Report on the contribution of pension funds to the capital markets of the EEC (Étude sur les moyens d'améliorer l'apport des fonds de pension aux marchés des capitaux dans les pays de la CEE).
Commission, 1969.   70p.   Studies: economic and financial series, 7.
D E F I N   8249

964 JENARD, P.
Rapport sur la convention concernant la compétence judiciaire et l'exécution des décisions en matière civile et commerciale [Report on the convention on jurisdiction and the enforcement of judgments in civil and commercial matters].
Commission, 1967.   135p.
D F I N

965 JENARD, P.
Report on the Convention on jurisdiction and the enforcement of judgments in civil and commercial matters

(Rapport sur la Convention concernant la compétence judiciaire et l'exécution des décisions en matière civile et commerciale).
In Bulletin of the European Communities. Supplement, 12/1972. Council and Commission, 1972. 113p.
D E F I N   4001/S/12/72

966 JENKINS, R.
Address by Mr. Roy Jenkins, President of the Commission of the European Communities, to the European Parliament on 8 February 1977 [Discours prononcé par M. Roy Jenkins, Président de la Commission des Communautés européennes, devant le Parlement européen, 8 février 1977].
In Programme of the Commission for 1977.
Commission, 1977.   pp.5–20.
DK D E F I N   8809

967 JENSEN, C. H.
The law and practice relating to pollution control in Denmark [Loi et usage concernant le contrôle de la pollution au Danemark].
Commission, 1976.   208p.
E   0 86010 029 4

968 JENSEN, I. F.
Credit to agriculture. 4: Denmark [Crédits à l'agriculture. 4: Danemark].
Commission, 1975.   177p.   Internal information on agriculture, 146.
E   VI/1592/75

969 JENTZSCH, E. G.
L'aide alimentaire de la C.E.E. aux pays en voie de développement problèmes et possibilités réelles. 10: L'utilisation d'excédents agricoles en Arabie Séoudite [Food aid from the E.E.C. to the developing countries. Problems and possibilities. 10: The use of agricultural surpluses in Saudi Arabia].
Commission EEC, 1963.   10p.
F   7829

970 JENTZSCH, E. G.
L'aide alimentaire de la C.E.E. aux pays en voie de
développement problèmes et possibilités réelles. 12:
Élements d'un système d'évaluation des possibilités
d'utilisation des excédents agricoles dans les pays en voie
de développement [Food aid from the E.E.C. to the
developing countries. Problems and possibilities. 12:
Elements of an evaluation system of possibilities for the
use of agricultural surpluses in the developing countries].
Commission EEC, 1963.   16p.
F   7829

971 JENTZSCH, E. G.
L'aide alimentaire de la C.E.E. aux pays en voie de
développement problèmes et possibilités réelles. 13:
Organisation de l'utilisation des excédents agricoles aux
États-Unis [Food aid from the E.C.C. to the developing
countries. Problems and possibilities. 13: Organisation of
the use of agricultural surpluses in the United States].
Commission EEC, 1963.   15p.
F   7829

972 JENTZSCH, E. G.
L'aide alimentaire de la C.E.E. aux pays en voie de
développement problèmes posés et possibilités réelles. 6:
Etude régionale. Turquie [Food aid from the E.E.C. to
the developing countries. Problems and possibilities. 6:
Regional study. Turkey].
Commission EEC, 1963.   61p.
F   7829

973 JENTZSCH, E. G.
L'aide alimentaire de la C.E.E. aux pays en voie de
développement problèmes posés et possibilités réelles. 7:
Etude régionale. Inde [Food aid from the E.E.C. to the
developing countries. Problems and possibilities. 7:
Regional study. India].
Commission EEC, 1963.   63p.
F   7829

974 JENTZSCH, E. G.
L'aide alimentaire de la C.E.E. aux pays en voie de
développement problèmes posés et possibilités réelles. 8:
Étude régionale. Tanganyika [Food aid from the E.E.C.
to the developing countries. Problems and possibilities. 8:
Regional study. Tanganyika].
Commission EEC, 1963.   25p.
F   7829

975 JENTZSCH, E. G.
L'aide alimentaire de la C.E.E. aux pays en voie de
développement problèmes posés et possibilités réelles. 9:
Étude régionale. Afghanistan [Food aid from the E.E.C.
to the developing countries. Problems and possibilities. 9:
Regional study. Afghanistan].
Commission EEC, 1963.   25p.
F   7829

976 JONAS, C.
Kredite an die Landwirtschaft. 2: B.R. Deutschland
[Credit to agriculture. 2: F.R. Germany / Crédits à
l'agriculture. 2: R.F. Allemagne].
Commission, 1976   225p.   Information on
agriculture, 2.
D   8832

977 JONES, K.
The United Kingdom economy [L'économie britannique].
Commission, 1975.   155p.   Studies: economic and
financial series, 9.
E   8461

978 JONG, H. W. de
Studie betreffende de ontwikkeling van de concentratie in
enkele bedrijfstakken in de chemische industrie in
Nederland. Farmaceutische industrie (N.I.C.E. 313.1).
Fotochemische industrie (N.I.C.E. 313.2).
Onderhoudsmiddelen (N.I.C.E. 313.5) [A study of the
evolution of concentration in the sectors of the chemical
industry in the Netherlands. Pharmaceutical industry
(N.I.C.E. 313.1). Photographic industry (N.I.C.E. 313.2).

Maintenance products (N.I.C.E. 313.5) / Étude sur
l'évolution de la concentration dans les secteurs de
l'industrie chimique aux Pays-Bas. Industrie
pharmaceutique (N.I.C.E. 313.1). Industrie
photographique (N.I.C.E. 313.2). Produits d'entretien
(N.I.C.E. 313.5)].
Commission, 1973.   var. pag.
N   IV/350/73

979 JONG, H. W. de
Studie betreffende de ontwikkeling van de concentratie in
de rijwiel- en bromfietsenindustrie in Nederland
(N.I.C.E. 385.1) [A study of the evolution of concentration
in the cycles and motorcycles industry in the Netherlands
(N.I.C.E. 385.1) / Étude sur l'évolution de la
concentration dans l'industrie des cycles et motocycles aux
Pays-Bas (N.I.C.E. 385.1)].
Commission, 1973.   18p.
N   IV/351/73

980 JONG, H. W. de
A study of the evolution of concentration in the Dutch
beverages industry [Étude sur l'évolution de la
concentration dans l'industrie des boissons aux Pays-Bas].
Commission, 1977.   149p.
E   8764

981 JONG, H. W. de
A study of the evolution of concentration in the food
industry in the Netherlands [Étude sur l'évolution de la
concentration dans l'industrie alimentaire aux Pays-Bas].
Commission, 1974.   var. pag.
E   IV/209/74

982 JONG, H. W. de
A study of the evolution of concentration in the
pharmaceutical industry in the Netherlands [Étude sur
l'évolution de la concentration dans l'industrie
pharmaceutique aux Pays-Bas].
Commission, 1975.   115p.
E   8742

983 JØRGENSEN, N.
A study of the evolution of concentration in the Danish
food distribution industry. Part one: Concentration in the
Danish food distribution system. Part two: The first and the
second price surveys in Denmark [Étude sur l'évolution de
la concentration dans l'industrie de la distribution des
produits alimentaires au Danemark. Partie première: La
concentration dans le système de la distribution des
produits alimentaires au Danemark. Partie deuxième: Les
enquêtes des prix premières et deuxièmes au Danemark].
Commission, 1977.   292p.
E   8766

984 JØRGENSEN, N.
A study of the evolution of concentration in the Danish
pharmaceutical industry [Étude sur l'évolution de la
concentration dans l'industrie pharmaceutique au
Danemark].
Commission, 1974.   114p.
E   IV/457/74

985 JOSTARNDT, K.
Educational leave in Member States (Les congès culturels
dans les États membres).
Commission, 1977.   416p.   Studies: social policy
series, 26.
D E F I N   CH-SN-76-026-EN-C

986 JULIENNE, R.
Possibilités d'industrialisation des États africains et
malgache associés. Volume 1: Côte-d'Ivoire, Dahomey,
Haute-Volta, Mali, Mauritanie, Niger, Sénégal, Togo
[Possibilities for the industrialization of the Associated
African States and Madagascar. Volume 1: Ivory Coast,
Dahomey, Upper Volta, Mali, Mauritania, Niger,
Senegal, Togo].
Commission EEC, 1966.   3 vols.
F   13071/VIII/B/66, 13072/VIII/B/66, 13073/VIII/B/66

987 JURGENSEN, H.
The effects of national price controls in the European
Economic Community (Effets des réglementations

nationales des prix dans la Communauté économique
européenne).
Commission, 1971.   168p.   Studies:
competition–approximation of legislation series, 9.
D E F I N   8267

988 KALINKE, R. J.
Conditions de commercialisation et de formation des prix
des vins de consommation courante au niveau de la
première vente. France, Italie [Conditions for marketing
and price formation of ordinary wines at the first sale.
France, Italy].
Commission, 1969.   474p.   Internal information on
agriculture, 52.
D F   1789/VI/70

989 KALINKE, R. J.
Conditions de commercialisation et de formation des prix
des vins de consommation courante au niveau de la
première vente. Synthèse, R.F. d'Allemagne, G.D. de
Luxembourg [Conditions for marketing and price
formation of ordinary wines at the first sale. Summary,
F.R. of Germany, G.D. of Luxembourg].
Commission, 1973.   var. pag.   Internal information
on agriculture, 51.
D F   5305/VI/67

990 KAMMEL
Monographie du centre de médecine du travail des usines
sidérurgiques Hoesch AG, usine Westfalenhütte de
Dortmund (Allemagne) [Monograph of the Industrial
Medical Centre of the Hoesch AG iron and steel works,
Westfalenhütte factory of Dortmund (Germany)].
Commission, 1967.   92p.   Collected practical
information, 4.
D F I N   16150

991 KARSSEN, W.
A study of the evolution of concentration in the food
industry in the Netherlands [Étude sur l'évolution de la

concentration dans l'industrie alimentaire aux Pays-Bas].
Commission, 1974.   var. pag.
E   IV/209/74

992 KASCHIG, O.
Possibilités d'industrialisation des États africains et
malgache associés. Volume 1: Côte-d'Ivoire, Dahomey,
Haute-Volta, Mali, Mauritanie, Niger, Sénégal, Togo
[Possibilities for the industrialization of the Associated
African States and Madagascar. Volume 1: Ivory Coast,
Dahomey, Upper Volta, Mali, Mauritania, Niger,
Senegal, Togo].
Commission EEC, 1966.   3 vols.
F   13071/VIII/B/66, 13072/VIII/B/66, 13073/VIII/B/66

993 KASPERCZYCK, J.
Augmentation de la production de coke par régularisation
de la charge des fours. Rapport final 1970–1972/StBV
[Increasing coke production by regularising the furnace
load. Final report 1970–1972/StBV].
Commission, 1973.   48p.   Technical research: coal,
45. Coal valorisation,
D F   5873

994 KAUFFMANN, J. R.
Étude sur l'application de la taxe sur la valeur ajoutée aux
petites entreprises dans les six anciens États membres de
la Communauté [Study on the application of the
value-added tax to small firms in the six original Member
States of the Community].
Commission, 1974.   45p.   Studies:
competition–approximation of legislation series, 23.
D F I N   8435

995 KAYSER, A.
Le contrat de travail dans le droit des pays membres de la
CECA [The employment contract in the law of the
member countries of the ECSC].
ECSC HA, 1966.   727p.   Collection: labour law.
D F I N   3568

996 KAYSER, A.
Étude sur la physionomie actuelle de la sécurité sociale
dans les pays de la C.E.E. [Study on the current situation
of social security in the countries of the E.E.C.].
Commission EEC, 1962.   130p.   Studies: social
policy series, 3.
D F I N   8058

997 KAYSER, A.
Grève et lock-out [Strike and lock-out].
ECSC HA, 1961.   399p.   Collection: labour law. 2:
Labour law in the Community, 5.
D F I N   2367

998 KAYSER, A.
La juridiction du travail et la juridiction de la sécurité
sociale dans les pays de la Communauté européenne
[Employment and social security jurisdiction in the
countries of the European Community].
Commission, 1972.   615p.   Collection: labour law.
D F I N   8341

999 KAYSER, A.
La protection des travailleurs en cas de perte de l'emploi
[Protection of workers in the event of loss of employment].
ECSC HA, 1961.   489p.   Collection: labour law. 2:
Labour law in the Community, 11.
D F I N   2626

1000 KAYSER, A.
La représentation des travailleurs sur le plan de
l'entreprise dans le droit des pays membres de la
C.E.C.A. [Workers' representation at management level
in the law of the member countries of the E.C.S.C.].
ECSC HA, 1959.   348p.   Collection: labour law, 3.
D F I N   2104

1000A KAYSER, A.
Les sources du droit du travail [Sources of labour law].
ECSC HA, 1962   192p.   Collection: labour law.
2: Labour law in the Community, 1.
D F I N   2773

1001 KAYSER, A.
La stabilité de l'emploi dans le droit des pays membres de
la C.E.C.A. [Stability of employment in the law of the
member countries of the E.C.S.C.].
ECSC HA, 1958.   311p.   Collection: labour law, 2.
D F I N   1999

1002 KAYSER, W.
Crédits a l'agriculture. 2: R.F. d'Allemagne [Credit to
agriculture. 2: F.R. of Germany].
Commission, 1973.   187p.   Internal information on
agriculture, 104.
D F   VI/1508/73

1003 KEARNEY, B.
Forms of cooperation between farms for production and
marketing in the new Member States [Formes de
collaboration entre exploitations agricoles dans les
nouveaux États membres].
Commission, 1976.   340p.   Information on
agriculture, 20.
E   8876

1004 KEGEL, H.
Rapports sur les premières mesures proposées en vue
d'une coordination des politiques énergétiques [Reports
on the first measures proposed for a coordination of
energy policies].
ECSC CC, 1961.   var. pag.
D F I N   8013

1005 KEMMERS, W. H.
La structure du commerce des fruits et légumes dans les
pays de la C.E.E. Standardisation et système de contrôle
[The structure of the fruit and vegetable trade in the
countries of the E.E.C. Grading and inspection system].
Commission EEC, 1963.   45p.   Studies: agricultural
series, 12.
D F I N   8101

1006 KENDALL, W.
Les délégués d'ateliers au Royaume-Uni [Shop stewards
in the United Kingdom].
In Documentation européenne. Série syndicale et
ouvrière, 4/1973.   Pr Inf, 1973.   4p.
D F I N   S/73/4

1007 KENNEDY, K.A.
The Irish economy [L'économie irlandaise].
Commission, 1975.   168p.   Studies: economic and
financial series, 10.
E   8462

1008 KENNET, W., chairman
The Europe plus thirty report [Rapport sur l'Europe et le
trente].
Commission, 1975.   var. pag.
E   XII/694/75

1009 KENNET, W., chairman
The Europe plus thirty report. Summary [Rapport sur
l'Europe et le trente. Sommaire].
Commission, 1975.   29p.
E   XII/665/75

1010 KERBAOL, M.
Analyse régionale des structures socio-économiques
agricoles. Essai de typologie régionale pour la
Communauté des Six. Partie 1: Rapport [Regional
analysis of agricultural socio-economic structures.
Attempt at a regional classification for the Community of
the Six. Part 1: Report].
Commission, 1975.   225p.   Internal information on
agriculture, 139.
F   VI/1189/4/73

1011 KERBAOL, M.
Analyse régionale des structures socio-économiques
agricoles. Essai d'une typologie régionale pour la
Communauté des Six. Partie 2: Données de base par
circonscription [Regional analysis of agricultural

socio-economic structures. Attempt at a regional
classification for the Community of the Six. Part 2: Basic
data by area].
Commission, 1975.   513p.   Internal information on
agriculture, 168.
F   VI/4466/75

1012 KERSTEN, L.
Projektionen über Erzeugung und Verbrauch
landwirtschaftlicher Erzeugnisse—'1977'. 4: B.R.
Deutschland [Projections of production and consumption
of agricultural products—'1977'. 4: F.R. Germany /
Projections de la production et de la consommation de
produits agricoles—'1977'. 4: R.F. Allemagne].
Commission, 1974.   348p.   Internal information on
agriculture, 120.
D   VI/1383/72

1013 KIEL, H.
Les problèmes que pose l'établissement d'une statistique
CE comparative par pays des prix du matériel et des
tracteurs agricoles [The problems of the establishment of
comparative EC statistics by country for the prices of
agricultural equipment and tractors].
In Agricultural prices. Special number, S9.
Eurostat, 1975.   pp.6–19.
D/F   6776

1014 KIMMINICH, O.
The law and practice relating to pollution control in the
Federal Republic of Germany [Loi et usage concernant le
contrôle de la pollution en Allemagne].
Commission, 1976.   402p.
D E   0 86010 032 4

1015 KIMPE, de
Earnings in agriculture 1975 (Gains dans l'agriculture
1975).
Eurostat, 1977.   145p.
DK/D/E/F/I/N   CA-22-76-035-6A-C

1016 KIMPE, M. de
Enquête sur les budgets familiaux en Belgique [Survey on family budgets in Belgium].
In Budgets familiaux 1963/64. Belgique.
Eurostat, 1965.   pp.25–122.   Social statistics: special series, 2.
F

1017 KINDER, R. de
Incidences de l'implantation d'une aciérie sur la région de Gand-Zelzate [Effects of the construction of a steelworks on the Ghent-Zelzate region].
ECSC HA, 1967.   176p.   Collection: regional economy and policy. 2: Development and conversion programme, 8.
D F I N   3889

1018 KIPPER, M.
Social indicators for the European Community 1960–1975 (Indicateurs sociaux pour la Communauté européenne 1960–1975).
Eurostat, 1977.   486p.
DK/D/E/F/I/N   CA-22-77-766-6A-C

1019 KIRCHEN, C.
Education statistics 1970–1975 (Statistiques de l'enseignement 1970–1975).
Eurostat, 1977.   194p.
DK/D/E/F/I/N   CA-22-76-043-6A-C

1020 KIRCHEN, C.
Population and employment 1950–1976 (Population et emploi 1950–1976).
Eurostat, 1977.   201p.
E/F   CA-22-77-031-2A-C

1021 KIRCHEN, C.
Schematic presentation of the educational systems. Evolution of the number of pupils and students. EUR 9 1962–1973 (Présentation schématique des systèmes

d'enseignement. Évolution des effectifs scolaires et
universitaires. EUR 9 1962–1973).
In Social statistics, 5/1973.　　　Eurostat, 1975.　　　127p.
D/E/F/I/N　　6635

1022　KIRCHHOFF, H.
L'industrie de conservation et de transformation de fruits
et légumes dans la CEE [The fruit and vegetable
preservation and processing industry in the EEC].
Commission, 1969.　　314p.　　Internal information on
agriculture, 49.
D F　　7069/VI/69

1023　KIRKPATRICK, J.
Dispositions fiscales en matière de coopération et de fusion
d'exploitations agricoles. 1: Belgique, France, G.D. de
Luxembourg [Tax arrangements concerning cooperation
and amalgamation of farms. 1: Belgium, France, G.D. of
Luxembourg].
Commission, 1972.　　var. pag.　　Internal information
on agriculture, 83.
F　　VI/894/71

1024　KIRSCH, G.
Enseignements à tirer en agriculture d'expérience des
'Revolving funds' [Lessons to learn in agriculture from the
experience of 'Revolving funds'].
Commission, 1970.　　97p.　　Internal information on
agriculture, 62.
D F　　VI/11144/70

1025　KIRSCHEN
La taxe sur la valeur ajoutée (TVA). 1: Les données du
problème [The value-added tax (VAT). 1: The facts of the
problem].
In Documentation européenne. Série agricole; série
syndicale et ouvrière, 3.　　Pr Inf, 1969.　　4p.
D F I N

1026　KLANBERG, F.
Study on the possible part played by certain primary
non-employment incomes in the inflationary process in the

Federal Republic of Germany (Étude sur le rôle éventuel
de certains revenus primaires non-salariaux dans le
développement de l'inflation en Allemagne).
Commission, 1976.   101p.   Series: medium-term
economic policy, 5.
D E F I N   8860

1027 KLATZMANN, J.
Les grandes régions agricoles dans la C.E.E. [The main
agricultural regions in the E.E.C.].
Commission EEC, 1960.   57p.   Studies: agricultural
series, 1.
D F   VI/707

1028 KLATZMANN, J.
Tendances de la production et de la consommation en
denrées alimentaires dans la C.E.E. 1956–1965 [Trends in
food production and consumption in the E.E.C.
1956–1965].
Commission EEC, 1960.   266p.   Studies:
agricultural series, 2.
D F I N   8005

1029 KLEFFNER, F.
La conduite sur place des opérations de conversion
industrielle [On-the-spot direction of industrial conversion
operations].
ECSC HA, 1963.   352p.   Collection: regional
economy and policy. 1: Industrial conversion in Europe, 4.
D F I N   3324

1030 KLEINMANN
Possibilités de création d'industries exportatrices dans les
États africains et malgache associés. Produits de
l'élevage. Viandes, cuirs et peaux, chaussures, articles en
cuir [Possibilities for the establishment of exporting
industries in the Associated African States and
Madagascar. Products from rearing. Meat, hides and
skins, shoes, leather articles].
Commission, 1974.   5 vols.
F   VIII/223/74

1031 KLEINMANN

Possibilités de création d'industries exportatrices dans les États africains et malgache associés. Produits de l'élevage. Viandes, cuirs et peaux, chaussures, articles en cuir. Rapport de synthèse [Possibilities for the establishment of exporting industries in the Associated African States and Madagascar. Products from rearing. Meat, hides and skins, shoes, leather articles. Summary report].

Commission, 1975.   27p.

D E F I N   VIII/223/74

1032 KLEINSTEUBER, F.

Untersuchung zur Konzentrationsentwicklung in einem Untersektor des Fahrzeugbaues in Deutschland. Fahrräder (N.I.C.E. 385.1). Motorräder und Mopeds (N.I.C.E. 385.1) [A study of the evolution of concentration in one sub-sector of the manufacture of transport equipment in Germany. Cycles (N.I.C.E. 385.1). Motorcycles and power-assisted cycles (N.I.C.E. 385.1) / Étude sur l'évolution de la concentration dans un sous-secteur de la construction de matériel de transport en Allemagne. Cycles (N.I.C.E. 385.1). Motocycles et cyclomoteurs (N.I.C.E. 385.1)].

Commission, 1976.   79p.

D   8748

1033 KLEINSTEUBER, F.

Untersuchung zur Konzentrationsentwicklung in verschiedenen Untersektoren der Papier- und Pappeindustrie in Deutschland. Herstellung (N.I.C.E. 271). Verarbeitung (N.I.C.E. 272) [A study of the evolution of concentration in various sub-sectors of the paper and paperboard industry in Germany. Manufacture (N.I.C.E. 271). Processing (N.I.C.E. 272) / Étude sur l'évolution de la concentration dans quelques sous-secteurs de l'industrie du papier et du carton en Allemagne. Fabrication (N.I.C.E. 271). Transformation (N.I.C.E. 272)].

Commision, 1976.   88p.

D   7195

1034 KLEMM, H.
Possibilités de création d'industries exportatrices dans les
États africains et malgache associés. Produits de
l'élevage. Viandes, cuirs et peaux, chaussures, articles en
cuir [Possibilities for the establishment of exporting
industries in the Associated African States and
Madagascar. Products from rearing. Meat, hides and
skins, shoes, leather articles].
Commission, 1974.   5 vols.
F   VIII/223/74

1035 KLEMM, H.
Possibilités de création d'industries exportatrices dans les
États africains et malgache associés. Produits de
l'élevage. Viandes, cuirs et peaux, chaussures, articles en
cuir. Rapport de synthèse [Possibilities for the
establishment of exporting industries in the Associated
African States and Madagascar. Products from rearing.
Meat, hides and skins, shoes, leather articles. Summary
report].
Commission, 1975.   27p.
D E F I N   VIII/223/74

1036 KLEMM, H.
La production de produits animaux dans des entreprises à
grande capacité de la CEE. Partie 2: Position
concurrentielle [The production of animal products in
large scale enterprises in the EEC. Part 2: Competitive
position].
Commission, 1969.   70p.   Internal information on
agriculture, 37.
D F   769/VI/69

1037 KLEMMER, P.
Problèmes de la structure économique de la Sarre
[Problems of the economic structure of the Saar].
ECSC HA, 1967.   196p.   Collection: regional
economy and policy. 2: Development and conversion
programme, 9.
D F   4098

1038 KLOPPER, C.
A study of the evolution of concentration in the food
industry in the Netherlands [Étude sur l'évolution de la
concentration dans l'industrie alimentaire aux Pays-Bas].
Commission, 1974.   var. pag.
E   IV/209/74

1039 KLOSE, F.
Le boisement des terres marginales [The afforestation of
marginal lands].
Commission EEC, 1964.   var. pag.   Internal
information on agriculture, 1.
D F   VI/5221/64

1040 KLOTEN, N.
La région d'Amberg. Tendances et possibilités de
développement économique [The Amberg region. Trends
and possibilities for economic development].
ECSC HA, 1966.   184p.   Collection: regional
economy and policy. 2: Development and conversion
programme, 7.
D F   3898

1041 KNAGGS, J.
Population and employment 1950–1976 (Population et
emploi 1950–1976).
Eurostat, 1977.   201p.
E/F   CA-22-77-031-2A-C

1042 KNOP, P.
Les services de la main-d'œuvre des États membres de la
Communauté. Exposé de synthèse [Employment
exchanges in the Member States of the Community.
Summary].
Commission EEC, 1967.   131p.   Studies: social
policy series, 16.
D F I N   8193

1043 KOCK, W.
L'aide alimentaire de la C.E.E. aux pays en voie de
développement problèmes et possibilités réelles. 10:

L'utilisation d'excédents agricoles en Arabie Séoudite
[Food aid from the E.E.C. to the developing countries.
Problems and possibilities. 10: The use of agricultural
surpluses in Saudi Arabia].
Commission EEC, 1963.   10p.
F   7829

1044 KOCK, W.
L'aide alimentaire de la C.E.E. aux pays en voie de
développement problèmes et possibilités réelles. 12:
Élements d'un système d'évaluation des possibilités
d'utilisation des excédents agricoles dans les pays en voie
de développement [Food aid from the E.E.C. to the
developing countries. Problems and possibilities. 12:
Elements of an evaluation system of possibilities for the
use of agricultural surpluses in the developing countries].
Commission EEC, 1963.   16p.
F   7829

1045 KOCK, W.
L'aide alimentaire de la C.E.E. aux pays en voie de
développement problèmes et possibilités réelles. 13:
Organisation de l'utilisation des excédents agricoles aux
États-Unis [Food aid from the E.E.C. to the developing
countries. Problems and possibilities. 13: Organisation of
the use of agricultural surpluses in the United States].
Commission EEC, 1963.   15p.
F   7829

1046 KOCK, W.
L'aide alimentaire de la C.E.E. aux pays en voie de
développement problèmes posés et possibilités réelles. 6:
Étude régionale. Turquie [Food aid from the E.E.C. to
the developing countries. Problems and possibilities. 6:
Regional study. Turkey].
Commission EEC, 1963.   61p.
F   7829

1047 KOCK, W.
L'aide alimentaire de la C.E.E. aux pays en voie de
développement problèmes posés et possibilités réelles. 7:

Étude régionale. Inde [Food aid from the E.E.C. to the
developing countries. Problems and possibilities. 7:
Regional study. India].
Commission EEC, 1963.   63p.
F   7829

1048 KOCK, W.
L'aide alimentaire de la C.E.E. aux pays en voie de
développement problèmes posés et possibilités réelles. 8:
Étude régionale. Tanganyika [Food aid from the E.E.C.
to the developing countries. Problems and possibilities. 8:
Regional study. Tanganyika].
Commission EEC, 1963.   25p.
F   7829

1049 KOCK, W.
L'aide alimentaire de la C.E.E. aux pays en voie de
développement problèmes posés et possibilités réelles. 9:
Étude régionale. Afghanistan [Food aid from the E.E.C.
to the developing countries. Problems and possibilities. 9:
Regional study. Afghanistan].
Commission EEC, 1963.   25p.
F   7829

1050 KOHL, G.
La technique de mesure et de l'automation [Measurement
and automation technique].
ECSC HA, 1967.   204p.   New technical processes in
the iron and steel industry: a personal training manual, 1.
Studies: vocational training.
D F I N   13233

1051 KOHNKE, M.
Prévisions agricoles. 2: Possibilités d'utilisation de
certains modelès, méthodes et techniques dans la
Communauté [Agricultural forecasting. 2: Possibilities of
using certain models, methods and techniques in the
Community].
Commission, 1970.   249p.   Internal information on
agriculture, 63.
D F   8433/VI/69

1052 KOKTVEDGAARD, H.
Rapport sur le droit économique danois [Report on Danish economic law].
Commission, 1975.   136p.   Studies: competition–approximation of legislation series, 20/6.
F   8633

1053 KOLBENSCHLAG, H.
The situation of small and medium-sized undertakings in the European Community. Study (La situation des petites et moyennes entreprises dans la Communauté européenne. Étude).
ESC, 1976.   66p.
DK D E F I N   6688

1054 KOLNAAR, A. H. J.
Study on the possible part played by certain primary non-employment incomes in the inflationary process in the Netherlands (Étude sur le rôle éventuel de certains revenus primaires non-salariaux dans le développement de l'inflation aux Pays-Bas).
Commission, 1977.   85p.   Series: medium-term economic policy, 7.
DK D E F I N   8828

1055 KORMOSS, I. B. F.
Cartes des pentes moyennes. Italie [Maps of average slopes. Italy].
Commission, 1975.   var. pag.   Internal information on agriculture, 143.
F I   VI/1600/75

1056 KORMOSS, I. B. F.
Cartes des pentes moyennes. 2: France, Belgique, Grand-Duché de Luxembourg [Maps of average slopes. 2: France, Belgium, Grand Duchy of Luxembourg].
Commission, 1975.   var. pag.   Internal information on agriculture, 166.
F   VI/511/76

1057 KORMOSS, I. B. F.
The European Community in maps (La Communauté
européenne. Cartes).
Commission, 1974.   14 maps.
DK D E F I N   6574

1058 KORMOSS, I. B. F.
Les grandes régions agricoles dans la C.E.E. [The main
agricultural regions in the E.E.C.].
Commission EEC, 1960.   57p.   Studies: agricultural
series, 1.
D F   VI/707

1059 KORMOSS, I. B. F.
Les liaisons et les transports terrestres dans la
Communauté européenne [Links and land transport in the
European Community].
In Documentation européenne. Série pédagogique; série
agricole, 2/1974.   Pr Inf, 1974.   4p.
D F I N   U/A/74/2

1060 KORMOSS, I. B. F.
La population de l'Europe [Population of Europe].
In Documentation européenne. Série pédagogique; série
agricole; série syndicale et ouvrière, 3/1972.
Pr Inf, 1972.   4p.
D F I N   U/A/S/72/3

1061 KORMOSS, I. B. F.
Les ports d'Europe: évolution et mutations [The ports of
Europe: development and changes].
In Documentation européenne. Série pédagogique; série
agricole, 3/1972.   Pr Inf, 1972.   4p.
D F I N   U/A 72/3

1062 KOTOWSKI, N.
Glossaire des normes de l'acier. Normes d'essai, de qualité
et de dimensions établi sur la base des EURONORM et
des normes nationales [Glossary of steel standards.
Standards of testing, quality and dimensions established

on the basis of EURONORM and national standards].
Commission, n.d.   307p.
D/F/I/N

1063 KOTOWSKI, N.
Glossary new transport technologies (Glossaire nouvelles
techniques de transport).
Commission, 1976.   900p.
DK/D/E/F/I/N   IX/2061/74

1064 KÖTTER, H.
Les tendances d'évolution des structures des exploitations
agricoles. Causes et motifs d'abandon et de
restructuration [Trends of development in farm
structures. Causes and reasons for desertion and
reconstruction].
Commission, 1967.   386p.   Internal information on
agriculture, 20.
D F   8159/VI/67

1065 KRÄNTZER, K. R.
Coûts de construction de bâtiments d'exploitation
agricole. Étables pour vaches laitières, veaux et jeunes
bovins à l'engrais [Construction costs of farm buildings.
Stables for dairy cattle, calves and young fattening cattle].
Commission, 1973.   var. pag.   Internal information
on agriculture, 101.
D F   VI/4429/71

1066 KREMER, J.
Les aciéries [The steel-works].
Commission, 1971.   283p.   New technical processes
in the iron and steel industry: a personal training manual,
3.   Studies: vocational training.
D F I N   17433

1067 KREMER, J.
Les laminoirs [The rolling mills].
Commission, 1972.   240p.   New technical processes
in the iron and steel industry: a personal training manual,
4.   Studies: vocational training.
D F I N   8349

1068 KREMER, J.
Mécanisation, automatisation et techniques de mesure
dans les services des hauts fourneaux [Mechanisation,
automation and measurement techniques in blast-furnace
works].
Commission, 1969.   172p.   New technical processes
in the iron and steel industry: a personal training manual,
2.   Studies: vocational training.
D F I N   14722

1069 KREMER, J.
La technique de mesure et de l'automation [Measurement
and automation technique].
ECSC HA, 1967.   204p.   New technical processes in
the iron and steel industry: a personal training manual, 1.
Studies: vocational training.
D F I N   13233

1070 KRENGEL, R.
La productivité du capital de 21 branches industrielles
dans la république fédérale d'Allemagne de 1950 à 1975
[Capital productivity of 21 industrial branches in the
Federal Republic of Germany from 1950 to 1975].
Commission, 1968.   132p.   Studies: economic and
financial series, 6.
D F   8219

1071 KREYSSIG, G.
Rapport du Commissaire aux comptes relatif au deuxième
exercice financier qui a pris fin de 30 juin 1954 [Auditor's
report for the second financial year which ended in 30 June
1954].
ECSC CA, 1955.   var. pag.
D F I N   1594

1072 KREYSSIG, G.
Rapport du Commissaire aux comptes relatif au premier
exercice financier qui a pris fin de 30 juin 1953 [Auditor's
report for the first financial year which ended in 30 June
1953].
ECSC CA, 1954.   503p.
D F I N   1344

1073 KREYSSIG, G.
Révision du Traité instituant la Communauté Européenne
du Charbon et de l'Acier [Revision of the Treaty
establishing the European Coal and Steel Community].
ECSC, 1958.   57p.
F   2018

1074 KRIJNSE LOCKER, H.
Les exportations de biens d'équipement de la
Communauté. Essai et prévisions jusqu'en 1970 [Exports
of capital goods from the Community. Sample and
forecasts until 1970].
ECSC HA, 1967.   249p.   Collection: general
objectives for steel, 3A.
D F I N   12885

1075 KRIJNSE LOCKER, H.
Méthodologie communautaire des tableaux
Entrées-Sorties 1965 [Community input-output tables
1965 methodology].
Eurostat, 1970.   222p.   Special series: input-output
tables 1965, 1.
D F   4963

1076 KRISTENSEN, T.
A study of the evolution of concentration in the Danish
food distribution industry. Part one: Concentration in the
Danish food distribution system. Part two: The first and
the second price surveys in Denmark [Étude sur
l'évolution de la concentration dans l'industrie de la
distribution des produits alimentaires au Danemark.
Partie première: La concentration dans le système de la
distribution des produits alimentaires au Danemark.
Partie deuxième: Les enquêtes des prix premières et
deuxièmes au Danemark].
Commission, 1977.   292p.
E   8766

1077 KRISTENSEN, T.
A study of the evolution of concentration in the Danish
food processing industry [Étude sur l'évolution de la

concentration dans l'industrie de la transformation des produits alimentaires au Danemark].
Commission, 1977.   252p.
E   8761

1078 KROGSTRUP, E.
Credit to agriculture. 4: Denmark [Crédits à l'agriculture. 4: Danemark].
Commission, 1975.   177p.   Internal information on agriculture, 146.
E   VI/1592/75

1079 KROHN, H.-B.
Le marché commun des produits agricoles. Perspectives '1970' [The common market in agricultural products. Prospects '1970'].
Commission EEC, 1963.   198p.   Studies: agricultural series, 10.
D F I N   8077

1080 KROLL
Essai d'appréciation des conditions d'application et des résultats d'une politique de réforme en agriculture dans des régions agricoles difficiles. 1: Morvan [Attempt at estimating the conditions from the application and results of a reform policy in agriculture in difficult agricultural regions. 1: Morvan].
Commission, 1974.   183p.   Internal information on agriculture, 138.
F   VI/4572/74

1081 KRONSTEIN
La réparation des conséquences dommageables d'une violation des articles 85 et 86 du traité instituant la CEE [Compensation for damage suffered through infringement of Articles 85 and 86 of the Treaty establishing the EEC].
Commission EEC, 1966.   74p.   Studies: competition series, 1.
D F I N   8153

1082 KROTH, W.
Forstwirtschaftliche Probleme und deren Auswirkungen
auf die Umwelt in den Mitgliedstaaten der EG. 1:
Ergebnisse und Empfehlungen [Forestry problems and
their implications for the environment in the Member
States of the EC. 1: Results and recommendations / Les
problèmes forestiers et leurs incidences sur
l'environnement dans les États membres des CE. 1:
Résultats et recommandations].
Commission, 1977.   129p.   Information on
agriculture, 25.
D   8881

1083 KROTH, W.
Forstwirtschaftliche Probleme und deren Auswirkungen
auf die Umwelt in den Mitgliedstaaten der EG. 2: Öffnung
des Waldes für die Allgemeinheit und seine Nutzung als
Erholungsraum [Forestry problems and their implications
for the environment in the Member States of the EC. 2:
Access of the public to forests and their use for
recreational purposes / Les problèmes forestiers et leurs
incidences sur l'environnement dans les États membres
des CE. 2: Ouverture de la forêt au public à des fins
récréatives].
Commission, 1977.   222p.   Information on
agriculture, 31.
D   CH-SA-77-031-DE-C

1084 KROTH, W.
Forstwirtschaftliche Probleme und deren Auswirkungen
auf die Umwelt in den Mitgliedstaaten der EG. 3: Stand,
Entwicklung und Probleme der Mechanisierung bei der
Bestandsbegründung und Holzernte und deren
Auswirkungen auf die Umwelt [Forestry problems and
their implications for the environment in the Member
States of the EC. 3: Position, development and problems
of mechanization of stand establishment and timber
harvesting / Les problèmes forestiers et leurs incidences
sur l'environnement dans les États membres des CE. 3:
Problèmes de la mécanisation des travaux de boisement et
de récolte en forêt].

Commission, 1977.　　202p.　　Information on
agriculture, 32.
D　　CH-SA-77-032-DE-C

1085　KROTH, W.
Forstwirtschaftliche Probleme und deren Auswirkungen
auf die Umwelt in den Mitgliedstaaten der EG. 4:
Staatliche Beihilfen (Subventionen) zur Finanzierung
forstlicher Massnahmen im Nichtstaatswald [Forestry
problems and their implications for the environment in the
Member States of the EC. 4: State aid for the financing of
forestry measures in forests not owned by the State / Les
problèmes forestiers et leurs incidences sur
l'environnement dans les États membres des CE. 4: Aides
nationales propres à encourager des mesures en faveur de
la forêt privée].
Commission, 1977.　　160p.　　Information on
agriculture, 33.
D　　CH-SA-77-033-DE-C

1086　KROTH, W.
Forstwirtschaftliche Probleme und deren Auswirkungen
auf die Umwelt in den Mitgliedstaaten der EG. 5: Systeme
der Waldbesteuerung und die steuerliche Belastung
privater Forstbetriebe [Forestry problems and their
implications for the environment in the Member States of
the EC. 5: Systems of forest taxation and the tax liability
of private forest holdings / Les problèmes forestiers et
leurs incidences sur l'environnement dans les États
membres des CE. 5: Systèmes d'imposition et charges
fiscales supportées par la forêt privée].
Commission, 1977.　　233p.　　Information on
agriculture, 34.
D　　CH-SA-77-034-DE-C

1087　KRUPP, H.-J.
Study on the possible part played by certain primary
non-employment incomes in the inflationary process in the
Federal Republic of Germany (Étude sur le rôle éventuel
de certains revenus primaires non-salariaux dans le
développement de l'inflation en Allemagne).

Commission, 1976.   101p.   Series: medium-term
economic policy, 5.
D E F I N   8860

1088 KRUSE-RODENACKER, A.
Food aid from the EEC to developing countries. Problems
and possibilities (L'aide alimentaire de la C.E.E. aux
pays en voie de développement. Problèmes posés et
possibilités réelles).
Commission EEC, 1964.   233p.   Studies: agricultural
series, 14.
D E F I N   8102

1089 KRUSE-RODENACKER, A.
Organization of world markets for agricultural
commodities. A joint action programme for developed and
developing countries (L'organisation des marchés
agricoles mondiaux. Une action commune des pays
économiquement développés et des pays en voie de
développement).
Commission EEC, 1964.   52p.   Studies: agricultural
series, 15.
D E F I N   8117

1090 KRUST, M.-M.
Droit au travail et problèmes d'emploi des travailleurs
culturels du spectacle et de l'interprétation musicale dans
la Communauté économique européenne [Labour law and
employment problems of theatre and musical workers in
the European Economic Community].
Commission, 1977.   2 vols.
F

1091 KUHNER, R.
Le coût de la main-d'œuvre dans les industries de la
Communauté 1966 [The cost of labour in the industries of
the Community 1966].
In Social statistics, 4/1969.   Eurostat, 1969.   358p.
D/F, I/N   4755

1092 KUHNER, R.
Le coût de la main-d'œuvre dans les industries de la
Communauté 1969 [The cost of labour in the industries of
the Community 1969].
In Social statistics, 3/1971.   Eurostat, 1971.   533p.
D/F, I/N   5456

1093 KUHNER, R.
Le coût de la main-d'œuvre dans les transports routiers
1967 [The cost of labour in road transport 1967].
In Social statistics, 1/1970.   Eurostat, 1970.   83p.
D/F, I/N   4929

1094 KUHNER, R.
Les coûts de la main-d'œuvre dans les banques, les
assurances et le commerce de détail 1970 [Labour costs in
banks, insurance and the retail trade 1970].
In Social statistics, 4/1972.   Eurostat, 1973.   247p.
D/F/I/N   5785

1095 KUHNER, R.
Enquête sur les salaires dans les industries de la
Communauté économique européenne 1962 [Survey on
wages in the industries of the European Economic
Community 1962].
In Social statistics, 5/1964.   Eurostat, 1964.   519p.
D/F, I/N

1096 KUHNER, R.
Enquête sur les salaires dans les industries de la
Communauté économique européenne 1963 [Survey on
wages in the industries of the European Economic
Community 1963].
In Social statistics, 6/1965.   Eurostat, 1965.   365p.
D/F, I/N

1097 KUHNER, R.
Enquête sur les salaires dans les industries de la
Communauté économique européenne 1964 [Survey on
wages in the industries of the European Economic
Community 1964].
In Social statistics, 5/1966.   Eurostat, 1966.   445p.
D/F, I/N   3996

1098 KUIPERS, J. D., chairman
Enlarging the Community (Rapport d'information sur
l'élargissement de la Communauté).
ESC, 1970. 12p.
D E F I N 16682

1099 KUSTER, R.
Les industries de la confection dans la Communauté
économique européenne. Analyse et perspectives 1975
[The ready-to-wear industry in the European Economic
Community. Analysis and prospects 1975].
Commission, 1970. 2 vols.
D F 12734/III/70

1100 KUTSCHER, H.
Mémorandum sur les objectifs de 1965. Méthodes
d'élaboration et résultats détaillés [Memorandum on the
1965 objectives. Methods of elaboration and detailed
results].
ECSC HA, 1962. 540p. Collection: general
objectives for steel, 1.
D F I N 3017

1101 KUTSCHER, H.
La situation sur les marchés sidérurgiques dans les pays
tiers [State of the iron and steel market in non-member
countries].
ECSC HA, 1965. 239p. Collection: iron and steel
market, 1.
D F I N 11780

1102 KUTSCHER, H.
La situation sur les marchés sidérurgiques dans les pays
tiers. Plans d'investissement et possibilités de production
[State of the iron and steel market in non-member
countries. Investment plans and production possibilities].
ECSC HA, 1967. 145p. Collection: iron and steel
market, 2.
D F I N 13609

1103 LA BEAUMELLE, S. de
Science and European public opinion [La science et
l'opinion publique européenne].
Commission, 1977.   98p.
E   XII/922/77

1104 LA BELLA, M.
Évolution régionale de la population active agricole. 5:
Italie [Regional development of the working agricultural
population. 5: Italy].
Commission, 1969.   var. pag.   Internal information
on agriculture, 43.
D F   11445/VI/69

LA MOTHE, T. Quinthrie, *see* QUINTHRIE LA
MOTHE, T.

LA VALLEE POUSSIN, C. de, *see* POUSSIN, C. de la
Vallee

LA VINELLE, L. Duquesne de, *see* DUQUESNE DE
LA VINELLE, L.

LA VINELLE, M. Duquesne de, *see* DUQUESNE DE
LA VINELLE, M.

1105 LACCI
Les exportations de biens d'équipement de la
Communauté. Essai et prévisions jusqu'en 1970 [Exports
of capital goods from the Community. Sample and
forecasts until 1970].
ECSC HA, 1967.   249p.   Collection: general
objectives for steel, 3A.
D F I N   12885

1106 LAGASSE, A.
Étude sur la physionomie actuelle de la sécurité sociale
dans les pays de la C.E.E. [Study on the current situation
of social security in the countries of the E.E.C.].
Commission EEC, 1962.   130p.   Studies: social
policy series, 3.
D F I N   8058

1107 LAGROU, E.
Environmental problems of city centres [Les problèmes d'environnement des centres de cité].
Commission, 1976.   88p.
E

1108 LAHACHE, M.
Le rôle des ports de la Communauté pour le trafic de céréales et de farines. 1: Synthèse pour les principaux ports français et italiens [List of Community ports for the cereals and flour trade. 1: Summary for the chief French and Italian ports].
Commission, 1974.   var. pag.   Internal information on agriculture, 122.
F   VI/2941/73

1109 LAHACHE, M.
Le rôle des ports de la Communauté pour le trafic de céréales et de farines. 2: Monographies pour les principaux ports français de la Manche [List of Community ports for the cereals and flour trade. 2: Monographs for the chief French Channel ports].
Commission, 1974.   var. pag.   Internal information on agriculture, 123.
F   VI/1169/74

1110 LAHACHE, M.
Le rôle des ports de la Communauté pour le trafic de céréales et de farines. 3: Monographies pour les principaux ports français de l'Atlantique [List of Community ports for the cereals and flour trade. 3: Monographs for the chief French Atlantic ports].
Commission, 1974.   var. pag.   Internal information on agriculture, 124.
F   VI/1263/74

1111 LAHACHE, M.
Le rôle des ports de la Communauté pour le trafic de céréales et de farines. 4: Monographies pour les principaux ports français de la Méditerranée [List of Community

ports for the cereals and flour trade. 4: Monographs for the
chief French Mediterranean ports].
Commission, 1974.   var. pag.   Internal information
on agriculture, 125.
F   VI/1264/74

1112 LAHACHE, M.
Le rôle des ports de la Communauté pour le trafic de
céréales et de farines. 5: Monographies pour les principaux
ports italiens de la Côte Ouest [List of Community ports
for the cereals and flour trade. 5: Monographs for the chief
Italian West Coast ports].
Commission, 1974.   var. pag.   Internal information
on agriculture, 126.
F   VI/1265/74

1113 LAHACHE, M.
Le rôle des ports de la Communauté pour le trafic de
céréales et de farines. 6: Monographies pour les principaux
ports italiens de la Côte Est [List of Community ports for
the cereals and flour trade. 6: Monographs for the chief
Italian East Coast ports].
Commission, 1974.   var. pag.   Internal information
on agriculture, 127.
F   VI/1266/74

1114 LAIDLER, D. E. W.
Study on the possible part played by certain primary
non-employment incomes in the inflationary process in the
United Kingdom [Étude sur le rôle éventuel de certains
revenus primaires non-salariaux dans le développement
de l'inflation au Royaume-Uni].
Commission, 1976.   261p.   Series: medium-term
economic policy, 6.
E   8664

1115 LAMOUCHE, J. P.
Recherche scientifique et comptabilité nationale [Scientific
research and national accounts].
In Statistical studies and surveys, 1/1968.
Eurostat, 1968.   pp.117–211.
F   4407

1116 LAMOUR, P.
Le financement des investissements et les aspects sociaux
de la reconversion [Financing of investments and social
aspects of conversion].
ECSC HA, 1963.   255p.   Collection: regional
economy and policy. 1: Industrial conversion in Europe, 3.
D F I N   3323

1117 LANCKSWEIRT, F.
Possibilités de création d'industries exportatrices dans les
États africains et malgache associés. Transformation du
bois et fabrication d'articles en bois. Première
transformation: Sciages, déroulages, tranchages.
Deuxième transformation: Profilés, moulures,
contreplaqués, panneaux, produits finis: pour la
construction et l'ameublement. Rapport de synthèse
[Possibilities for the establishment of exporting industries
in the Associated African States and Madagascar. Wood
processing and manufacture of articles in wood. First
process: Sawing, wood-peeling, slicing. Second process:
Shapes, mouldings, plywood, panels, finished products:
for building and furniture. Summary report].
Commission, 1974.   445p.
F   VIII/227/74

1118 LANDAU, A.
Étude sur l'évolution de la concentration dans l'industrie
de la construction électrique en France. Construction
d'appareils électriques, radios, télévision,
électro-acoustique (N.I.C.E. 375). Fabrication d'appareils
électrodomestiques (N.I.C.E. 376) [A study of the
evolution of concentration in the electrical engineering
industry in France. Manufacture of electrical and audio
equipment, radio and television receivers (N.I.C.E. 375).
Manufacture of electrical domestic appliances (N.I.C.E.
376)].
Commission, 1974.   93p.
F   IV/25/74

1119 LANDGRAF, H.
L'automatisation d'agglomération à Forges de la
Providence, Marchienne-au-Pont, Belgique [Automated

sintering at Forges de la Providence,
Marchienne-au-Pont, Belgium].
ECSC HA, 1965.   8p.
D F   12009

1120 LANDGRAF, H.
Recherches sur l'automatisation de la bande
d'agglomération de l'usine de Marchienne de la Société des
Forges de la Providence (Belgique).
(Rapport final) [Researches on the automation of the
sinter strand at the Marchienne factory of the Forges de la
Providence company (Belgium). (Final report)].
ECSC HA, 1966.   35p.
D F

1121 LANDO, O.
The law of property in the European Community [Le droit
de la propriété dans la Communauté européenne].
Commission, 1977.   305p.   Studies:
competition–approximation of legislation series, 27.
E   8727

1122 LANGE, R. de
A study of the evolution of concentration in the food
industry in the Netherlands [Étude sur l'évolution de la
concentration dans l'industrie alimentaire aux Pays-Bas].
Commission, 1974.   var. pag.
F   IV/209/74

1123 LANGE, R. de
A study of the evolution of concentration in the
pharmaceutical industry in the Netherlands [Étude sur
l'évolution de la concentration dans l'industrie
pharmaceutique aux Pays-Bas].
Commission, 1975.   115p.
E   8742

1124 LANGEN, H.
Méthodes d'établissement des bilans fourragers dans les
Pays membres des Communautés Européennes [Methods
of estimating feed balance-sheets in the Member

Countries of the European Communities].
In Agricultural statistical studies, 11.
Eurostat, 1973.   var. pag.
D F   17801

1125 LANGENDONCK, E. van
Enquête sur les budgets familiaux en Belgique [Survey on
family budgets in Belgium].
In Budgets familiaux 1963/64. Belgique.
Eurostat, 1965.   pp. 25–122.   Social statistics: special
series, 2.
F

1126 LANGER, W., chairman
Objectifs et méthodes de la politique régionale dans la
Communauté européenne. 1: Rapport [Objectives and
methods of regional policy in the European Community.
1: Report].
Commission EEC, 1964.   113p.
F   II/720/5/64

1127 LANGER, W., chairman
Preliminary draft of the first medium-term economic
policy programme 1966–1970 (Avant-projet de premier
programme de politique économique à moyen terme
1966–1970).
MTEPC EEC, 1966.   3 vols.
E F   787/II/1966

1128 LANGER, W.
Rapport sur la capacité concurrentielle de la Communauté
européenne [Report on the competitive capacity of the
European Community].
Commission, 1972.   3 vols.
D F   II/481/72

1129 LANGER, W., chairman
Reports of Working Parties on Regional Policy in the
EEC (Rapports de groupes d'experts sur la politique
régionale dans la CEE).
Commission EEC, 1965.   404p.
D E F I N   8154

1130 LANGEVIN, M.
Intercomparison of measurement of carboxyhaemoglobin
in different European laboratories and establishment of
the methodology for the assessment of COH_B levels in
exposed populations [Inter-comparaison de la mesure du
carboxyle-hémoglobine dans les laboratoires divers
européens et l'établissement de la méthodologie pour
l'imposition des niveaux COH_B dans les populations
exposées].
Commission, 1977.   118p.
E   V/F/1315/77

1131 LANGLOIS
Management, organization and methods in the American
iron and steel industry. E.C.S.C. fact finding mission to
U.S.A. March–April 1957 [Direction, organisation et
méthodes dans la sidérurgie des États-Unis. C.E.C.A.
mission des faits-fournitures aux États-Unis mars–avril
1957].
ECSC HA, 1958.   364p.
E   4444

1132 LANGSTRAAT, D. J.
Formes de coopération dans le secteur de la pêche. 2:
France, Belgique, Pays-Bas [Forms of cooperation in the
fishing industry. 2: France, Belgium, the Netherlands].
Commission, 1970.   var. pag.   Internal information
on agriculture, 69.
D F   14715/VI/69

1133 LANNO, O.
Rapport sur le droit économique danois [Report on Danish
economic law].
Commission, 1975.   136p.   Studies:
competition–approximation of legislation series, 20/6.
F   8633

1134 LANZETTI, R.
Studio sull'evoluzione della concentrazione dell'industria
cartaria in Italia [A study of the evolution of concentration
of the paper industry in Italy / Étude sur l'évolution de la

concentration de l'industrie du papier en Italie].
Commission, 1977.   189p.
I   8753

1135 LANZETTI, R.
Studio sull'evoluzione della concentrazione nel settore
della costruzione di macchine per l'industria tessile in
Italia [A study of the evolution of concentration in the
sector of the manufacture of machines for the textile
industry in Italy / Étude sur l'évolution de la concentration
dans le secteur de la construction des machines pour
l'industrie textile en Italie].
Commission, 1977.   159p.
I   8755

1136 LANZETTI, R.
Studio sull'evoluzione della concentrazione nell'industria
della costruzione di macchine non elettriche in Italia.
Costruzione di materiale per sollevamento e trasporto.
Costruzione di ascensori [A study of the evolution of
concentration in the mechanical engineering industry in
Italy. Manufacture of hoisting and handling equipment.
Manufacture of lifts / Étude sur l'évolution de la
concentration dans le secteur de la construction de
machines non électriques en Italie. Construction de
matériel de levage et de manutention. Construction des
ascenseurs].
Commission, 1977.   152p.
I   8758

1137 LANZETTI, R.
Studio sull'evoluzione della concentrazione nell'industria
delle bevande in Italia [A study of the evolution of
concentration in the beverages industry in Italy / Étude
sur l'évolution de la concentration dans l'industrie des
boissons en Italie].
Commission, 1977.   143p.
I   8770

1138 LAPIE, P.-O.
Les institutions européennes et les problèmes
énergétiques de l'Europe. Communication faite aux 13e

Journées d'Études de l'Institut Économique de l'Énergie à
l'Université de Cologne des 25 et 26 mars 1965 [The
European institutions and Europe's energy problems.
Paper presented to the 13th study symposium of the
Energy Economy Institute at the University of Cologne
on 25 and 26 March 1965].
ECSC HA, 1965.   22p.
F   11456

1139 LAPIE, P.-O., chairman
Memorandum on energy policy (June 25 1962)
(Mémorandum sur la politique énergétique (25 juin 1962)).
ECSC HA, Commission EEC and Commission EAEC,
1962.   32p.
E F   5051

1140 LAPIE, P.-O., chairman
Study on the long-term energy outlook for the European
Community (Étude sur les perspectives énergétiques à
long terme de la Communauté européenne).
ECSC HA, Commission EEC and Commission EAEC,
1964.   199p.
D E F I N   3365

1141 LAPORTE, J. P.
Étude sur l'évolution de la concentration dans l'industrie
des spiritueux en France [A study of the evolution of
concentration in the spirits industry in France].
Commission, 1977.   163p.
F   8751

1142 LAPORTE, J. P.
Étude sur l'évolution de la concentration dans les
industries des boissons et des boissons non alcoolisées en
France [A study of the evolution of concentration in the
beverages and soft drinks industries in France].
Commission, 1977.   284p.
F   8768

1143 LAPORTE, J. P.
L'évolution de la concentration dans l'industrie de la
brasserie en France [The evolution of concentration in the
brewing industry in France].
Commission, 1976.   99p.
F   8705

1144 LAPORTE, J. P.
L'évolution de la concentration dans l'industrie des
champagnes et mousseux en France [The evolution of
concentration in the champagne and sparkling wines
industry in France].
Commission, 1977.   127p.
F   8752

1145 LAPPAS, A., chairman
European Union. Opinion (Union européenne. Avis).
ESC, 1975.   33p.
DK D E F I N   6937

1146 LARDINOIS, P.
The European Community's partnership with the United
States in the farm sector. Speech by Mr. Pierre Lardinois
to the National Soyabean Processors Association on
August 24, 1976 (La coopération entre la Communauté
européenne et les États-Unis dans le secteur agricole.
Discours prononcé par M. Pierre Lardinois devant la
National Soyabean Processors Association le 24 août
1976).
In Newsletter on the common agricultural policy,
7/1976.   Pr Inf, 1976.   5p.
D E F I N   X/505/76

1147 LARGER, F.
La balance des paiements des institutions
communautaires européennes [Balance of payments of the
European Communities' institutions].
In Statistical studies and surveys, 3/1970.
Eurostat, 1970.   pp.5–47.
F   5123

1148 LARSEN, H.
Apprenticeships in Denmark [L'apprentissage au
Danemark].
Commission, 1977.   54p.   Studies: social policy
series, 32.
DK E   CB-NN-77-032-EN-C

LATRIE, de Mas, *see* MAS LATRIE, de

1149 LAUCKNER, M. W.
Tableaux 'Entrées-Sorties' pour les pays de la
Communauté Économique Européenne ['Input-Output'
tables for the countries of the European Economic
Community].
Eurostat, 1964.   var. pag.
D F

1150 LAUCKNER, M. W.
Tableaux 'Entrées-Sorties' pour les pays de la
Communauté Économique Européenne. Seconde version
['Input-Output' tables for the countries of the European
Economic Community. Second version].
Eurostat, 1965.   var. pag.
D F

1151 LAUFFS, H. -W.
La reconversion des charbonnages dans les bassins
allemands. Ruhr [The conversion of coalmines in the
German basins. Ruhr].
Commission, 1973.   101p.   Pamphlets on industrial
conversion, 19.
D F I N   8391

1152 LAURENT, A.
Indicateurs de sécurité sociale [Social security indicators].
Commission, 1971.   122p.
D F I N   8292

1153 LAURISCH
La formation des formateurs. Problèmes, méthodes et
expériences dans les industries de la C.E.C.A. [Training

of the trainers. Problems, methods and experiments in the
industries of the E.C.S.C.].
ECSC HA, 1962.   127p.
F   8514

1154 LAUX, H.-G.
School and professional education of the children of Italian
workers in the Saar (Formation scolaire et professionnelle
des enfants des travailleurs italiens en Sarre).
Commission, 1975.   176p.
D E F   V/722/75

1155 LAVAL, A., chairman
Regional development problems of the Community during
the period 1975–1977 and establishment of a common
regional policy. Opinion (Problèmes de développement
régional de la Communauté au cours de la période
1975–1977 et établissement d'une politique régionale
communautaire. Avis).
ESC, 1976.   11p.
DK D E F I N   7253

1155A LAVENNE, F.
Aide-mémoire pour la pratique des épreuves d'exercice
en médecine du travail [Manual for the practice of
exercise tests in industrial medicine].
Commission, 1971.   49p.   Collection: industrial
health and medicine, 12.
D F I N   16741

1156 LE BIHAN, J.
Incidence du développement de l'intégration verticale et
horizontale sur les structures de production agricole.
Contributions monographiques [Effect of the development
of vertical and horizontal integration on the structures of
agricultural production. Monographic contributions].
Commission EEC, 1966.   var. pag.   Internal
information on agriculture, 11.
D F   6855/2/VI/64

1157 LE BIHAN, J.
Organisation de la production et de la commercialisation
d poulet de chair dans les pays de la CEE [Organisation
o. production and marketing of table chicken in the
countries of the EEC].
Commission EEC, 1965.   286p.   Internal
information on agriculture, 4.
D F   8310/2/VI/63

1158 LE BIHAN, J.
La production de produits animaux dans des entreprises à
grande capacité de la CEE. Nombre et formes dans le
secteur de l'engraissement de porcs, de veaux et de jeunes
bovins [The production of animal products in large scale
enterprises in the EEC. Number and types in the pig, calf
and store cattle fattening industry].
Commission, 1968.   158p.   Internal information on
agriculture, 23.
D F   11974/1/VI/67

1159 LE BIHAN, J.
La production et la commercialisation de parties de
volaille [The production and marketing of poultry cuts].
Commission, 1974.   var. pag.   Internal information
on agriculture, 136.
D F   VI/3723/74

1160 LE BIHAN, J.
La spéculation ovine [Sheep specialization].
Commission, 1972.   373p.   Internal information on
agriculture, 90.
D F   VI/1896/72

1161 LE BIHAN, J.
La spéculation ovine. 2: France, Belgique [Sheep
specialization. 2: France, Belgium].
Commission, 1973.   185p.   Internal information on
agriculture, 99.
D F   VI/734/73

1162 LE BRUN, O.
Possibilités d'industrialisation des États africains et
malgache associés. Volume 3: République démocratique
du Congo [Possibilities for the industrialization of the
Associated African States and Madagascar. Volume 3:
Democratic Republic of the Congo].
Commission EEC, 1966.   2 vols.
F   13077/VIII/B/66, 13078/VIII/B/66

1163 LE BRUN, O.
Possibilités d'industrialisation des États africains et
malgache associés. Volume 4: Burundi, Rwanda et région
Centre-orientale du Congo (Kinshasa) (région des Grands
Lacs) [Possibilities for the industrialization of the
Associated African States and Madagascar. Volume 4:
Burundi, Rwanda and Centre-eastern region of the Congo
(Kinshasa) (region of the Great Lakes)].
Commission EEC, 1966.   2 vols.
F   13079/VIII/B/66, 13080/VIII/B/66

1164 LE GALL
Les conditions d'installation d'entreprises industrielles
dans les États africains et malgache associés. Volume 3:
République du Mali [Conditions for the setting-up of
industrial undertakings in the Associated African States
and Madagascar. Volume 3: Republic of Mali].
Commission, 1972.   80p.
F   VIII/1313/72

1165 LE GALL
Les conditions d'installation d'entreprises industrielles
dans les États africains et malgache associés. Volume 4:
République du Niger [Conditions for the setting-up of
industrial undertakings in the Associated African States
and Madagascar. Volume 4: Republic of the Niger].
Commission, 1972.   80p.
F   VIII/1314/72

1166 LE GALL
Les conditions d'installation d'entreprises industrielles
dans les États africains et malgache associés. Volume 5:

République de Haute-Volta [Conditions for the setting-up of industrial undertakings in the Associated African States and Madagascar. Volume 5: Republic of Upper Volta].
Commission, 1972.   88p.
F   VIII/1315/72

1167 LE GALL
Les conditions d'installation d'entreprises industrielles dans les États africains et malgache associés. Volume 10: République du Tchad [Conditions for the setting-up of industrial undertakings in the Associated African States and Madagascar. Volume 10: Republic of Chad].
Commission, 1972.   86p.
F   VIII/1320/72

1168 LE GALL
Les conditions d'installation d'entreprises industrielles dans les États africains et malgache associés. Volume 16: République du Burundi [Conditions for the setting-up of industrial undertakings in the Associated African States and Madagascar. Volume 16: Republic of Burundi].
Commission, 1973.   80p.
F   VIII/1326/72

1169 LE GRONTEC, P.
Community input-output tables 1970–1975 methodology (Méthodologie des tableaux entrées-sorties communautaires 1970–1975).
Eurostat, 1977.   38p.   Special series, 1.
DK D E F I N   7197/1

1170 LE PETIT, L.
Report on the ECSC experimental programme of modernization of housing (Rapport sur le programme expérimental de construction de la CECA. Modernisation des logements).
Commission, 1977.   368p.
D E F I N   8451

1171 LEACH, T. M.
Review of pre-slaughter stunning in the E.C. [Examen de
l'étourdissement avant l'abattage pratique dans la C.E.].
Commission, 1977.   90p.   Information on
agriculture, 30.
D E   CH-SA-77-030-EN-C

1172 LECERF, J.
L'Europe judiciaire. La Cour de justice des Communautés
européennes au service de 185 millions d'Européens
[Legal Europe. The Court of Justice of the European
Communities at the service of 185 million Europeans].
Pr Inf, 1970.   95p.
F

1173 LECHI, F.
Projections de la production et de la consommation de
produits agricoles—'1977'. 3: Italie [Projections of
production and consumption of agricultural
products—'1977'. 3: Italy].
Commission, 1973.   186p.   Internal information on
agriculture, 117.
D F   VI/815/72

1174 LECLERCQ, J.
Conséquences écologiques de l'application des techniques
modernes de production en agriculture [Ecological results
from the application of modern production techniques in
agriculture].
Commission, 1974.   var. pag.   Internal information
on agriculture, 137.
D F   VI/3722/74

1175 LECLERCQ, J.
Surfaces agricoles pouvant être mobilisées pour une
réforme de structure [Agricultural areas that could be
mobilised for a structural reform].
Commission, 1973.   336p.   Internal information on
agriculture, 77.
D F   VI/14453/69

1176 LECOINTRE, A.
Possibilités d'industrialisation des États africains et
malgache associés. Volume 3: République démocratique
du Congo [Possibilities for the industrialization of the
Associated African States and Madagascar. Volume 3:
Democratic Republic of the Congo].
Commission EEC, 1966.   2 vols.
F   13077/VIII/B/66, 13078/VIII/B/66

1177 LECOINTRE, A.
Possibilités d'industrialisation des États africains et
malgache associés. Volume 4: Burundi, Rwanda et région
Centre-orientale du Congo (Kinshasa) (région des Grands
Lacs) [Possibilities for the industrialization of the
Associated African States and Madagascar. Volume 4:
Burundi, Rwanda and Centre-eastern region of the Congo
(Kinshasa) (region of the Great Lakes)].
Commission EEC, 1966.   2 vols.
F   13079/VIII/B/66, 13080/VIII/B/66

1178 LECOINTRE, A.
Possibilités d'industrialisation des États africains et
malgache associés. Volume 5: Madagascar [Possibilities
for the industrialization of the Associated African States
and Madagascar. Volume 5: Madagascar].
Commission EEC, 1966.   2 vols.
F   13081/VIII/B/66, 13082/VIII/B/66

1179 LECOINTRE, A.
Possibilités d'industrialisation des États africains et
malgache associés. Volume 6: Somalie [Possibilities for the
industrialization of the Associated African States and
Madagascar. Volume 6: Somalia].
Commission EEC, 1966.   2 vols.
F   13083/VIII/B/66, 13084/VIII/B/66

1180 LECOMTE, R.
Conséquences écologiques de l'application des techniques
modernes de production en agriculture [Ecological results
from the application of modern production techniques in
agriculture].

Commission, 1974.   var. pag.   Internal information
on agriculture, 137.
D F   VI/3722/74

1181 LECOURT, R.
The development of Community law [Le développement
du droit communautaire].
Inf Ser, 1968.   12p.   Current notes on the European
Community, 4.
E

1182 LEDEBOER, L. V.
Étude sur la physionomie actuelle de la sécurité sociale
dans les pays de la C.E.E. [Study on the current situation
of social security in the countries of the E.E.C.].
Commission EEC, 1962.   130p.   Studies: social
policy series, 3.
D F I N   8058

1183 LEDENT, A.
Évolution de la productivité de l'agriculture dans la CEE
[Development of agricultural productivity in the EEC].
Commission, 1969.   509p.   Internal information on
agriculture, 44.
D F   11774/VI/69

1184 LEE, N.
Environmental impact assessment of physical plans in the
European Communities [L'imposition d'impact de
l'environnement des plans physiques dans les
Communautés européennes].
Commission, 1977.   162p.
E   ENV/37/78

1185 LEEUW, A. de
Examen des possibilités de simplification et d'accélération
de certaines opérations administratives de remembrement
[Examining the possibilities for the simplification and
speeding up of certain administrative reparcelling
operations].

Commission, 1969.   173p.   Internal information on
agriculture, 38.
D F   6442/VI/69

1186 LEFEBRE, A.
Évolution de la demande en petrole [Development of the
demand in petrol].
Commission, 1970.   55p.
F   18457/XVII/70

1187 LEFEBVRE, A.
La reconversion des travailleurs qui quittent l'agriculture.
Les situations et les problèmes dans les six pays de la
CEE. Rapport de synthèse [The conversion of workers
who leave agriculture. The situation and problems in the
six countries of the EEC. Summary report].
Commission, 1974.   67p.
D F I N   8382

1188 LEGENDRE, P.
L'emploi agricole dans les pays de la C.E.E. Tome 1:
Structure [Agricultural employment in the countries of
the E.E.C. Volume 1: Structure].
Commission EEC, 1964.   61p.   Studies: social policy
series, 7.
D F I N   8108

1189 LEGENDRE, P.
L'emploi agricole dans les pays de la C.E.E. Tome 2:
Évolution et perspectives [Agricultural employment in
the countries of the E.E.C. Volume 2: Development and
prospects].
Commission EEC, 1964.   51p.   Studies: social policy
series, 8.
D F I N   8123

1190 LEGRIS, B.
General survey of the world situation regarding fats and
oils (Document synthétique sur l'économie mondiale des
matières grasses).

Commission EEC, 1964.   63p.   Studies: overseas
development series, 2.
D E F I N   8116

1191 LEHAYE, A.
Possibilités de création d'industries exportatrices dans les
États africains et malgache associés. Transformation du
bois et fabrication d'articles en bois. Première
transformation: Sciages, déroulages, tranchages.
Deuxième transformation: Profilés, moulures,
contreplaqués, panneaux, produits finis: pour la
construction et l'ameublement. Rapport de synthèse
[Possibilities for the establishment of exporting industries
in the Associated African States and Madagascar. Wood
processing and manufacture of articles in wood. First
process: Sawing, wood-peeling, slicing. Second process:
Shapes, mouldings, plywood, square panels, finished
products: for building and furniture. Summary report].
Commission, 1974.   445p.
F   VIII/227/74

1192 LEJEUNE, W.
Forschung im deutschen Eisenerzbergbau [Research in
the German iron mines / Recherche dans les mines de fer
allemandes].
Commission, 1968.   114p.   Collection: occupational
physiology and psychology, 3/5.
D   13749

1193 LEJEUNE, W.
Forschung in den deutschen Kohlenbergwerken
[Research in the German coalmines / Recherche dans les
charbonnages allemands].
Commission, 1968.   82p.   Collection: occupational
physiology and psychology, 3/1.
D   12427

1194 LEMAIGNEN, R.
Discours prononcé par M. Robert Lemaignen membre de
la Commission de la Communauté économique
européenne, à l'assemblée annuelle des comités nationaux

allemands de la Chambre de commerce internationale, à
Hambourg, le 17 septembre 1959 [Speech by Mr. Robert
Lemaignen, member of the Commission of the European
Economic Community, to the annual meeting of the
German national committees of the International
Chamber of Commerce, in Hamburg, September 17 1959].
Commission EEC, 1959.   19p.
D F   2301

1195 LEMAIGNEN, R.
EEC policy towards the developing countries. Bari
Symposium, 7–8 October 1961. Address by Mr. Robert
Lemaignen, member of the Commission of the European
Economic Community (La politique de la C.E.E. à l'égard
des pays en voie de développement. Colloque de Bari, 7–8
octobre 1961. Discours prononcé par M. Robert
Lemaignen, membre de la Commission de la Communauté
économique européenne).
Commission EEC, 1961.   10p.
D E F I N   8034

1196 LEMAÎTRE, M.
Modelès d'analyse d'entreprises de polyculture-élevage
bovin. Données technico-économiques de base. Région du
Bassin de Rennes (France) [Models for analysis of mixed
crop and cattle farms. Basic technico-economic data.
Bassin de Rennes region (France)].
Commission, 1977.   98p.   Information on
agriculture, 37.
F   CB-NA-77-037-FR-C

1197 LEMONNIER, C.
The tropical oils and oilseeds market in the Member States
of the EEC. Recent evolution and actual situation (Le
marché des oléagineux tropicaux dans les États membres
de la CEE. Évolution recente et situation actuelle).
Commission EEC, 1966.   201p.   Studies: overseas
development series, 4.
D E F I N   8177

1198 LENGELLE, M.
Use of substitute products in livestock feeding (Utilisation de produits de remplacement dans l'alimentation animale).
Commission, 1974.   var. pag.   Internal information on agriculture, 130.
E F   VI/3806/73

LENZI, E. Ratti-, *see* RATTI-LENZI, E.

1199 LEPLAT, J.
Recherche dans la sidérurgie française [Research in the French iron and steel industry].
Commission, 1967.   210p.   Collection: occupational physiology and psychology, 3/9.
F   13749

1200 LEPLAT, J.
Recherche dans les mines de fer françaises [Research in the French iron mines].
Commission, 1967.   97p.   Collection: occupational physiology and psychology, 3/6.
F   13749

1201 LEROY, R.
Le chômage et la main-d'œuvre sous-employée. Miss en œuvre d'une méthode de recherche. Belgique [Unemployment and underemployed manpower. Implementing of a research method. Belgium].
Commission EEC, 1965.   176p.   Studies: social policy series, 9.
D F I N   8135

1202 LEROY, R.
The dynamics of unemployment and employment. Belgium, 1947–1973 (La dynamique du chômage et de l'emploi. Belgique, 1947–1973).
Commission, 1977.   101p.   Studies: social policy series, 24.
E F N   8459

1203 LESAFFRE, H.
La conduite sur place des opérations de conversion
industrielle [On-the-spot direction of industrial conversion
operations].
ECSC HA, 1963.   352p.   Collection: regional
economy and policy. 1: Industrial conversion in Europe, 4.
D F I N   3324

1204 LETTENHOVE, K. de, chairman
Perspectives de développement économique dans la CEE
jusqu'en 1970 [Prospects of economic development in the
EEC until 1970].
Commission EEC, 1966.   2 vols.
F   COM (66) 170

1205 LEVENBACH, M. G.
Le contrat de travail dans le droit des pays membres de la
CECA [The employment contract in the law of the
member countries of the ECSC].
ECSC HA, 1966.   727p.   Collection: labour law.
D F I N   3568

1206 LEVENBACH, M. G.
Le régime juridique des organisations professionnelles
dans les pays membres de la C.E.C.A. [Legal
administration of professional organisations in the
member countries of the E.C.S.C.].
ECSC HA, 1968.   666p.   Collection: labour law.
D F I N   13879

1207 LEVESQUE, A.
Évolution régionale de la population active agricole. 4:
France [Regional development of the working agricultural
population. 4: France].
Commission, 1969.   403p.   Internal information on
agriculture, 42.
D F   9890/VI/69

1208 LEVESQUE, Q.
Évolution et prévisions de la population active agricole
[Development and estimates of the working agricultural
population].

Commission, 1970. var. pag. Internal information
on agriculture, 61.
D F   4131/VI/70

1209 LEVI, A.
L'Italia e il Mercato Comune oggi e domani [Italy and the
Common Market today and tomorrow / L'Italie et le
Marché Commun aujourd'hui et demain].
Uff St Inf, 1966. 61p.
I

1210 LEVI SANDRI, L.
Les aspects sociaux du Marché commun [Social aspects of
the Common Market].
Commission, 1967. 15p.
F   8212

1211 LEVI SANDRI, L.
Colloque sur la politique des logements sociaux. Besoins
[Conference on social housing policy. Requirements].
Commission EEC, 1964. 21p.
D F I N   8111

1212 LEVI SANDRI, L.
L'Italie dans l'âge du marché commun. Discours prononcé
par M. Lionello Levi Sandri vice-président de la
Commission de la CEE, le 14 octobre 1966 à Charleroi,
devant la 'Dante Alighieri' société [Italy in the age of the
Common Market. Speech delivered by Mr. Lionello Levi
Sandri Vice-President of the Commission of the EEC, to
the 'Dante Alighieri' Society in Charleroi, October 14,
1966].
Commission EEC, 1966. 20p.
F   8194

1213 LEVI SANDRI, L.
Labour market policy at the European level and the
functions of vocational training [La politique du marché du
travail au niveau européen et les fonctions de la formation
professionnelle].
Commission EEC, 1963. 12p.
E   9401

1214 LEVI SANDRI, L.
La politique sociale de la Communauté en 1968 [Social
policy of the Community in 1968].
Commission, 1969.   14p.
D F I N   8263

1215 LEVI SANDRI, L.
La politique sociale de la Communauté européenne au
début des années soixante-dix [Social policy of the
European Community at the beginning of the seventies].
Commission, 1970.   10p.
D F I N   8306

1216 LEVI SANDRI, L.
Pour une politique sociale moderne dans la Communauté
européenne [Towards a modern social policy in the
European Community].
Commission, 1968.   16p.
D F I N   8232

1217 LEVI SANDRI, L.
Réalisations et perspectives de la politique sociale de la
CEE. Discours prononcé par Prof. L. Levi Sandri,
Vice-président de la Commission de la Communauté
économique européenne et Président du groupe 'Affaires
sociales' devant le Parlement européen, à Strasbourg, 24
novembre 1965 [Achievements and prospects for the social
policy of the EEC. Address by Prof. L. Levi Sandri,
Vice-president of the Commission of the European
Economic Community and President of the 'Social Affairs'
Group, to the European Parliament, Strasbourg,
November 24, 1965].
Commission EEC, 1965.   20p.
D F I N   8714

1218 LEVI SANDRI, L.
Réalisations et perspectives de la politique sociale de la
Communauté européenne [Achievements and prospects
for the social policy of the European Community].
Commission, 1970.   20p.
D F I N   8312

1219 LEVI SANDRI, L.
La sécurité sociale dans la Communauté européenne.
Discours prononcés par Prof. Lionello Levi Sandri,
Président du groupe 'Affaires sociales', à la Conférence
européenne sur la sécurité sociale organisée par les trois
communautés européennes Bruxelles, 10–15 décembre
1962 [Social security in the European Community.
Addresses by Prof. Lionello Levi Sandri, President of the
'Social Affairs' Group, at the European Conference on
Social Security organized by the three European
Communities Brussels, December 10–15, 1962].
Commission EEC, 1963.   30p.
D F I N   8081

1220 LEVI SANDRI, L.
Social policy in the Common Market [La politique sociale
dans le Marché commun].
Inf Ser, 1966.   11p.   Community topics, 22.
E

1221 LEVINE, S. H.
Arrangements to facilitate the establishment of new
economic activities. Legal and financial arrangements in
force in the member states of the Community and the
United Kingdom (Dispositions pour faciliter la création
d'activités nouvelles. Dispositions juridiques et financières
en vigueur dans les États membres et le Royaume-Uni).
ECSC HA, 1962.   loose-leaf.
D E F I N   3019

1222 LEVINE, S. H.
Dispositions pour faciliter la création d'activités nouvelles.
Dispositions juridiques et financières en vigueur dans les
États membres et le Royaume-Uni [Arrangements to
facilitate the establishment of new activities. Legal and
financial arrangements in force in the Member States and
United Kingdom].
ECSC HA, 1959.   loose-leaf.
D F I N   2275

1223 LEVINE, S. H.
Le financement des investissements et les aspects sociaux
de la reconversion [Financing of investments and social
aspects of conversion].
ECSC HA, 1963.   255p.   Collection: regional
economy and policy. 1: Industrial conversion in Europe, 3.
D F I N   3323

1224 LEVINE, S. H.
The policy and practice of the British Government for
dealing with local unemployment [La politique et la
pratique du Gouvernement britannique pour faire face au
chômage local].
ECSC HA, 1960.   18p.   Intergovernmental
Conference on Industrial Redevelopment.
E   5128

1225 LEVINE, S. H.
Les politiques nationales de développement régional et de
conversion [National policies of regional development and
conversion].
ECSC HA, 1961.   195p.   Collection: regional
economy and policy. 1: Industrial conversion in Europe, 1.
F   2626

1226 LIBCHABER
Les conditions d'installation d'entreprises industrielles
dans les États africains et malgache associés. Volume 14:
République du Zaïre [Conditions for the setting-up of
industrial undertakings in the Associated African States
and Madagascar. Volume 14: Republic of Zaïre].
Commission, 1972.   116p.
F   VIII/1324/72

1227 LIBCHABER
Les conditions d'installation d'entreprises industrielles
dans les États africains et malgache associés. Volume 15:
République Rwandaise [Conditions for the setting-up of
industrial undertakings in the Associated African States
and Madagascar. Volume 15: Republic of Rwanda].
Commission, 1972.   72p.
F   VIII/1325/72

1228 LIBOUTON
Statistiques dans le domaine de la production de porcs
dans les États membres des Communautés européennes
1968–1971 [Statistics in the domain of pork production in
the Member States of the European Communities
1968–1971].
In Agricultural statistical studies, 14.
Eurostat, 1974.   2 vols.
D F   6654

1229 LICHABER
Possibilités de création d'industries exportatrices dans les
États africains et malgache associés. Produits de
l'élevage. Viandes, cuirs et peaux, chaussures, articles en
cuir [Possibilities for the establishment of exporting
industries in the Associated African States and
Madagascar. Products from rearing. Meat, hides and
skins, shoes, leather articles].
Commission, 1974.   5 vols.
F   VIII/223/74

1230 LICHABER
Possibilités de création d'industries exportatrices dans les
États africains et malgache associés. Produits de
l'élevage. Viandes, cuirs et peaux, chaussures, articles en
cuir. Rapport de synthèse [Possibilities for the
establishment of exporting industries in the Associated
African States and Madagascar. Products from rearing.
Meat, hides and skins, shoes, leather articles. Summary
report].
Commission, 1975.   27p.
D E F I N   VIII/223/74

1231 LILTI-HUGUET, N.
Schooling and professional training of children of Italian
and Portuguese workers in the Moselle region
(Scolarisation et formation professionnelle des enfants des
travailleurs italiens et portugais en Moselle).
Commission, 1975.   151p.
D E F   V/723/75

1232 LIMORTE, G.

Besoins de détente en tant que facteurs pour le développement régionale et agricole [Needs of detente in so far as the factors for regional and agricultural development].

Commission, 1973.   var. pag.   Internal information on agriculture, 116.

F   VI/3808/73

1233 LIMPENS

La réparation des conséquences dommageables d'une violation des articles 85 et 86 du traité instituant la CEE [Compensation for damage suffered through infringement of Articles 85 and 86 of the Treaty establishing the EEC].

Commission EEC, 1966.   74p.   Studies: competition series, 1.

D F I N   8153

1234 LINDA, R.

Methodology of concentration analysis applied to the study of industries and markets (Méthodologie de l'analyse de la concentration appliquée à l'étude des secteurs et des marchés).

Commission, 1977.   156p.

E F   8756

1235 LINDNER, R., chairman

Energy for Europe: research and development [L'énergie pour l'Europe: recherche et développement].

Commission, 1974.   65p.

E   SEC (74) 2592 final/Annex II

1236 LINK, D.

Possibilités d'un service de nouvelles de marchés pour les produits horticoles non comestibles dans la CEE [Possibilities for a new marketing service for inedible horticultural products in the EEC].

Commission, 1968.   66p.   Internal information on agriculture, 25.

D F   7280/VI/67

1237 LINK, D.
Production and marketing of bananas from the Associated
African States and Madagascar. Summary (La production
et l'écoulement des bananes originaires des États africains
et malgache associés. Synthèse).
Commission, 1972.   133p.   Studies: development aid
series, 4.
D E F I N   8346

1238 LINK, D.
Standardisation des produits horticoles non comestibles
[Standardization of inedible horticultural products].
Commission EEC, 1967.   215p.   Studies:
agricultural series, 23.
D F I N   8178

1239 LISMONT, R.
L'information relative aux revenus et aux patrimoines
dans les pays de la Communauté [Information relating to
incomes and inheritances in the countries of the
Community].
Commission, 1973.   43p.   Studies: social policy
series, 22.
D F I N   8377

1240 LIST, H.
Phraseological vocabulary compiled on the basis of the
Treaties establishing the European Communities
(Vocabulaire phraséologique établi sur la base des Traités
instituant les Communautés européennes); 2nd ed.
Commission, 1974.   var. pag.
DK/D/E/F/I/N   IX/1572/73

LOCKER, H. Krijnse, *see* KRIJNSE LOCKER, H.

1241 LOCKHART, J.
Agricultural co-operation in the EEC (La coopération
agricole dans la CEE).
Commission EEC, 1967.   247p.   Studies:
agricultural series, 21.
D E F I N   8148

1242 LÖFFLER, H. D.
Forstwirtschaftliche Probleme und deren Auswirkungen
auf die Umwelt in den Mitgliedstaaten der EG. 1:
Ergebnisse und Empfehlungen [Forestry problems and
their implications for the environment in the Member
States of the EC. 1: Results and recommendations / Les
problèmes forestiers et leurs incidences sur
l'environnement dans les États membres des CE. 1:
Résultats et recommandations].
Commission, 1977.   129p.   Information on
agriculture, 25.
D   8881

1243 LÖFFLER, H. D.
Forstwirtschaftliche Probleme und deren Auswirkungen
auf die Umwelt in den Mitgliedstaaten der EG. 2: Öffnung
des Waldes für die Allgemeinheit und seine Nutzung als
Erholungsraum [Forestry problems and their implications
for the environment in the Member States of the EC. 2:
Access of the public to forests and their use for
recreational purposes / Les problèmes forestiers et leurs
incidences sur l'environnement dans les États membres
des CE. 2: Ouverture de la forêt au public à des fins
récréatives].
Commission, 1977.   222p.   Information on
agriculture, 31.
D   CH-SA-77-031-DE-C

1244 LÖFFLER, H. D.
Forstwirtschaftliche Probleme und deren Auswirkungen
auf die Umwelt in den Mitgliedstaaten der EG. 3: Stand,
Entwicklung und Probleme der Mechanisierung bei der
Bestandsbegründung und Holzernte und deren
Auswirkungen auf die Umwelt [Forestry problems and
their implications for the environment in the Member
States of the EC. 3: Position, development and problems
of mechanization of stand establishment and timber
harvesting / Les problèmes forestiers et leurs incidences
sur l'environnement dans les États membres des CE. 3:
Problèmes de la mécanisation des travaux de boisement et
de récolte en forêt].

Commission, 1977.   202p.   Information on
agriculture, 32.

D   CH-SA-77-032-DE-C

1245 LÖFFLER, H. D.

Forstwirtschaftliche Probleme und deren Auswirkungen
auf die Umwelt in den Mitgliedstaaten der EG. 4:
Staatliche Beihilfen (Subventionen) zur Finanzierung
forstlicher Massnahmen im Nichtstaatswald [Forestry
problems and their implications for the environment in the
Member States of the EC. 4: State aid for the financing of
forestry measures in forests not owned by the State / Les
problèmes forestiers et leurs incidences sur
l'environnement dans les États membres des CE. 4: Aides
nationales propres à encourager des mesures en faveur de
la forêt privée].

Commission, 1977.   160p.   Information on
agriculture, 33.

D   CH-SA-77-033-DE-C

1246 LÖFFLER, H. D.

Forstwirtschaftliche Probleme und deren Auswirkungen
auf die Umwelt in den Mitgliedstaaten der EG. 5: Systeme
der Waldbesteuerung und die steuerliche Belastung
privater Forstbetriebe [Forestry problems and their
implications for the environment in the Member States of
the EC. 5: Systems of forest taxation and the tax liability
of private forest holdings / Les problèmes forestiers et
leurs incidences sur l'environnement dans les États
membres des CE. 5: Systèmes d'imposition et charges
fiscales supportées par la forêt privée].

Commission, 1977.   233p.   Information on
agriculture, 34.

D   CH-SA-77-034-DE-C

1247 LOGELAIN

La formation professionnelle dans les houillères des pays
de la Communauté [Vocational training in the coal mines
of the countries of the Community].

ECSC HA, 1956.   514p.

F   1669

LOMBARDI, L. Clevering-, *see* CLEVERING-
LOMBARDI, L.

1248 LOMMEZ, J. M. J.
Les organismes groupant les producteurs pour la vente
des fruits et légumes frais dans les États membres de la
CEE. Aspects juridiques. Importance. Rôle économique
[Growers' associations for the sale of fresh fruit and
vegetables in the Member States of the EEC. Legal
aspects. Importance. Economic role].
Commission EEC, 1965.   123p.   Studies:
agricultural series, 19.
D F I N   8139

1249 LOO, J. W. H. van de
La production et la commercialisation de parties de
volaille [The production and marketing of poultry cuts].
Commission, 1974.   var. pag.   Internal information
on agriculture, 136.
D F   VI/3723/74

1250 LOUWES, S. L., chairman
Statistiques de pêche. Bilans d'approvisionnement,
débarquements, captures, prix, membres, d'équipage,
flotte [Fishing statistics. Supply balance-sheets, landings,
catches, prices, crew-members, fishing fleet].
In Agricultural statistics, 12/1967.
Eurostat, 1967.   125p.
D/F   4302

1251 LUCHETTA, M.
Crédits à l'agriculture. 3: Italie [Credit to agriculture. 3:
Italy].
Commission, 1976.   155p.   Information on
agriculture, 3.
F I   8833

1252 LUCKE, F.
Essais de réduction des minerais de fer au four tournant.
Rapport intérimaire sur les essais effectués du 1.1.1960 au
31.3.1961 [Experiments by reduction of iron ore in the

rotary furnace. Provisional report of the experiments
carried out from 1.1.1960 to 31.3.1961].
ECSC HA, 1961.   20p.
F   7838

1253 LÜCKEMEYER, M.
Intégration verticale et contrats en agriculture. 1: R.F.
d'Allemagne [Vertical integration and contracts in
agriculture. 1: F.R. of Germany].
Commission, 1973.   136p.   Internal information on
agriculture, 106.
D F   VI/3359/73

1254 LUDWIG, P.
La production de produits animaux dans des entreprises à
grande capacité de la CEE. Nombre et formes dans le
secteur de l'engraissement de porcs, de veaux et de jeunes
bovins [The production of animal products in large scale
enterprises in the EEC. Number and types in the pig, calf
and store cattle fattening industry].
Commission, 1968.   158p.   Internal information on
agriculture, 23.
D F   11974/1/VI/67

1255 LULLING, A.
Les conditions de travail des femmes salariées dans les six
États membres de la Communauté européenne.
Grand-Duché de Luxembourg [The conditions of work for
wage-earning women in the six Member States of the
European Community. Grand Duchy of Luxembourg].
Commission, 1972.   87p.
F   V/168/73

1256 LUNS, J. M. A. H.
Gedenken an Robert Schuman Ehrenpräsident des
Europäischen Parlaments [In memory of Robert Schuman
honorary president of the European Parliament / En
souvenir de Robert Schuman président honoraire du
parlement européen].
EP, 1963.   23p.
D   3371

1257 LUTZ, B.
Les modifications dans la structure et la formation de la
main-d'œuvre de l'industrie sidérurgique [Modifications in
manpower structure and training in the iron and steel
industry].
Commission, 1968.   83p.
D F I N   4450

1258 LUTZ, B.
Niveau de mécanisation et mode de rémunération [Level
of mechanization and mode of payment].
ECSC HA, 1960.   149p.
F   2347

1259 LYON-CAEN, G.
Contribution à l'étude des modes de représentation des
intérêts des travailleurs dans le cadre des sociétés
anonymes européennes [Contribution to the study of ways
of representing workers' interests in the framework of
European joint-stock companies].
Commission, 1970.   64p.   Studies:
competition–approximation of legislation series, 10.
D F I N   8278

1260 MAAS, M. J.
L'organisation du marché du lait de consommation dans
les États membres de la CEE [The organization of the
drinking milk market in the Member States of the EEC].
Commission EEC, 1965.   50p.   Studies: agricultural
series, 20.
D F I N   8147

1261 MABBIT, L. A.
Objectivation of the bacteriological and organoleptic
quality of milk for consumption [Critères objectifs pour
l'appréciation de la qualité bactériologique et
organoleptique du lait de consommation].
Commission, 1977.   161p.   Information on
agriculture, 21.
E   8875

1262 MacCANNA, P.
Models for analysis mixed crop and cattle farms. Basic
techno-economic data. South-East Leinster (Ireland),
West Cambridgeshire (United Kingdom), Fünen
(Denmark) [Modèles d'analyse d'entreprises de
polyculture-élevage bovin. Données technico-économiques
de base. South-East Leinster (Irlande), West
Cambridgeshire (Royaume-Uni), Fünen (Danemark)].
Commission, 1976.   var. pag.   Information on
agriculture, 7.
E   8836

1263 MacCANNA, P.
Models for analysis mixed crop and cattle farms. 6:
Characteristics and possible applications. South-East
Leinster (Ireland), West Cambridgeshire (United
Kingdom), Fünen (Denmark), Schwäbisch-bayerisches
Hügelland (F.R. Germany) (Modèles d'analyse
d'entreprises de polyculture-élevage bovin. 6:
Caractéristiques et possibilités d'utilisation. South-East
Leinster (Irlande), West Cambridgeshire (Royaume-Uni),
Fünen (Danemark), Schwäbisch-bayerisches Hügelland
(R.F. d'Allemagne)).
Commission, 1976.   47p.   Internal information on
agriculture, 152.
E F   VI/3715/1/74

1264 McCARTHY, T.
Apprenticeships in Ireland [L'apprentissage en Irlande].
Commission, 1977.   82p.   Studies: social policy
series, 33.
E   CB-NN-77-033-EN-C

1265 McGEE, G.
A study of the evolution of concentration in the
pharmaceutical industry for the United Kingdom [Étude
sur l'évolution de la concentration dans l'industrie
pharmaceutique au Royaume-Uni].
Commission, 1977.   168p.
E   8707

1266 McGEE, J.
A study of the evolution of concentration in the mechanical
engineering sector for the United Kingdom [Étude sur
l'évolution de la concentration dans le secteur de la
construction de machines non électriques au
Royaume-Uni].
Commission, 1976.   264p.
E   8708

1267 McLOUGHLIN, J.
The law and practice relating to pollution control in the
Member States of the European Communities. A
comparative survey [Loi et usage concernant le contrôle
de la pollution aux États membres des Communautés
européennes. Une enquête comparative].
Commission, 1976.   545p.
E   0 86010 040 5

1268 McLOUGHLIN, J.
The law and practice relating to pollution control in the
United Kingdom [Loi et usage concernant le contrôle de la
pollution au Royaume-Uni].
Commission, 1976.   386p.
E   0 86010 037 5

1269 McMAHON, B. M. E.
Report on Irish economic law [Rapport sur le droit
économique irlandais].
Commission, 1977.   151p.   Studies:
competition–approximation of legislation series, 20/7.
D E   CG-SP-77-007-EN-C

1270 MacNEARY, A. J.
A study of the evolution of concentration in the beverages
industry for the United Kingdom. Part one: Industry
structure and concentration, 1969–1974 [Étude sur
l'évolution de la concentration dans l'industrie des
boissons au Royaume-Uni. Partie première: La structure
industrielle et la concentration, 1969–1974.].
Commission, 1977.   263p.
E   8942

1271 MacNEARY, A. J.
A study of the evolution of concentration in the food
distribution industry for the United Kingdom. Volume 2:
Price surveys [Étude sur l'évolution de la concentration
dans l'industrie de la distribution des produits
alimentaires au Royaume-Uni. Tome 2: Enquêtes de prix].
Commission, 1977.   152p.
E   8762

1272 MACONIO, M.
Il contributo delle 'Comunità montane' in Italia allo
sviluppo dell'agricoltura di montagna [The contribution of
'Comunità montane' to the development of hill farming in
Italy / La contribution des 'Comunità montane' au
développement de l'agriculture de montagne en Italie].
Commission, 1976.   209p.   Information on
agriculture, 11.
I   8861

1273 MACONIO, M.
Gli 'enti di sviluppo agricolo' in Italia nella riforma delle
strutture. Problemi e prospettive di adattamento [The
'enti di sviluppo agricolo' in structural reform in Italy.
Adjustment problems and prospects / Les 'enti di sviluppo
agricolo' en Italie et la réforme des structures. Problèmes
et perspectives d'adaptation].
Commission, 1976.   285p.   Information on
agriculture, 12.
I   8862

1274 MAESMANS, A.
Modèles d'analyse d'entreprises de polyculture-élevage
bovin. 2: Données technico-économiques de base.
Circonscription Nord-Picardie et région limoneuse du
Limbourg belge [Models for analysis of mixed crop and
cattle farms. 2: Basic technico-economic data.
Nord-Picardie area and the limoneuse region of Belgian
Limbourg].
Commission, 1973.   200p.   Internal information on
agriculture, 111.
D F   VI/1792/73

1275 MAGAUD, J. E.
La formation des formateurs. Problèmes, méthodes et
expériences dans les industries de la C.E.C.A. [Training
of the trainers. Problems, methods and experiments in the
industries of the E.C.S.C.].
ECSC HA, 1962.   127p.
F   8514

1276 MAHER, T. J.
Regional development problems of the Community during
the period 1975–1977 and establishment of a common
regional policy. Opinion (Problèmes de développement
régional de la Communauté au cours de la période
1975–1977 et établissement d'une politique régionale
communautaire. Avis).
ESC, 1976.   11p.
DK D E F I N   7253

1277 MAHON, P.
Models for analysis mixed crop and cattle farms. Basic
techno-economic data. South-East Leinster (Ireland),
West Cambridgeshire (United Kingdom), Fünen
(Denmark) [Modèles d'analyse d'entreprises de
polyculture-élevage bovin. Données technico-économiques
de base. South-East Leinster (Irlande), West
Cambridgeshire (Royaume-Uni), Fünen (Danemark)].
Commission, 1976.   var. pag.   Information on
agriculture, 7.
E   8836

MAHONY, D. o'. see O'MAHONY, D.

1278 MAILLET, P.
Fifteen years of Community policy (Quinze ans de
politique communautaire).
Commission, 1974.   69p.
DK D E F I N   8438

1279 MAILLET, P., chairman
Groupe 1985–2000. Premier Rapport [1985–2000 Group.
First report].
Commission, 1971.   60p.
F   XII/83/1/71

1280 MAILLET, P.
Mémorandum sur les objectifs de 1965. Méthodes
d'élaboration et résultats détaillés [Memorandum on the
1965 objectives. Methods of elaboration and detailed
results].
ECSC HA, 1962.   540p.   Collection: general
objectives for steel, 1.
D F I N   3017

1281 MAILLET, P., chairman
Travaux du Groupe 1985–2000 [Works of 1985–2000
Group].
Commission, 1971.   2 vols.
F   1073, 244

1282 MAJOR, R. L.
The United Kingdom economy [L'économie britannique].
Commission, 1975.   155p.   Studies: economic and
financial series, 9.
E   8461

1283 MALCOR, R.
Problèmes posés par l'application pratique d'une
tarification pour l'utilisation des infrastructures routières
[Problems posed by the practical application of a tariffing
for the use of road infrastructures].
Commission, 1970.   167p.   Studies: transport
series, 2.
D F I N   8255

1284 MALDAGUE, R., chairman
Report of the Study Group 'Problems of inflation'
(Rapport du groupe d'études 'Problèmes de l'inflation').
Commission, 1976.   3 vols.
D E F   II/198/76

1285 MALEZIEUX, R.
Accès à l'exploitation agricole. Dispositions et pratiques
existant dans les États membres de la CEE en vue de
l'obtention et de l'aménagement d'une exploitation
agricole [Access to the farm. Arrangements and practices

existing in the Member States of the EEC for obtaining
and managing a farm].
Commission, 1967.   var. pag.   Internal information
on agriculture, 21.
D F   8325/VI/66

1286 MALFATTI, F. M.
Address delivered on 6 December 1971 at the University
of Mogadishu [Discours prononcé le 6 décembre 1971 à
l'Université de Mogadishu].
Commission, 1972.   15p.
E I   8372

1287 MALFATTI, F. M.
Address delivered on 23 November 1971 to both Houses of
the Malagasy National Assembly in Tananarive (Discours
prononcé le 23 novembre 1971 devant les deux chambres
de l'Assemblée nationale malgache à Tananarive).
Commission, 1972.   17p.
D E F I N   8371

1288 MALFATTI, F. M.
The Commission's programme for 1971. Address given by
the President of the Commission, Franco Maria Malfatti,
before the European Parliament, Strasbourg, 10
February 1971 (Le programme de la Commission pour
l'année 1971. Discours prononcé devant le Parlement
européen, le 10 février 1971, par M. Franco Maria
Malfatti, président de la Commission des Communautés
européennes).
Commission, 1971.   29p.
D E F I N   8347

1289 MALFATTI, F. M.
The Commission's Programme for 1972 (Le programme de
la Commission pour l'année 1972).
Commission, 1972.   28p.
D E F I N   8376

1290 MALFATTI, F. M.
La funzione di una Comunità ampliata nel contesto
europeo. Discorso pronunciato dinanzi al Parlamento

europeo l'8 giugno 1971 [The function of a large
Community in a European context. Address to the
European Parliament 8 June 1971 / La fonction d'une
Communauté ample dans le contexte européen. Discours
prononcé devant le Parlement européen, le 8 juin 1971].
Commission, 1971.   10p.
I   8365

1291 MALFATTI, F. M.
Speech made by Mr Franco Maria Malfatti, President of
the Commission, at the signing of the Acts of Accession,
Brussels, 22 January 1972 [Discours prononcé par M.
Franco Maria Malfatti, président de la Commission, à la
passation des Actes de l'Adhésion, Bruxelles, le 22 janvier
1972].
In Bulletin of the European Communites. Supplement,
1/1972.   Commission, 1972.   pp.7–9.
D E F I N   4001/S/1/72

1292 MALFATTI, F. M.
Statement to the European Parliament, Strasbourg, 15
September 1970 (Déclaration prononcée devant le
Parlement européen, Strasbourg, 15 septembre 1970).
Commission, 1970.   22p.
D E F I N   8329

1293 MALFATTI, F. M.
W. Hallstein and J. Rey, Freemen of the City of Brussels.
Speeches given on 2 December 1971 at the conferring of
the Freedom of the City of Brussels on the former
Presidents of the Commission of the European Economic
Community and of the Commission of the European
Communities (W. Hallstein et J. Rey, citoyens de la ville
de Bruxelles. Discours prononcés le 2 décembre 1971 à
l'occasion de la remise du diplôme de citoyen d'honneur de
la ville de Bruxelles aux anciens présidents de la
Commission de la Communauté économique européene et
de la Commission des Communautés européennes).
Commission, 1972.   20p.
D E F I N   8368

1294 MALISSEN, M.
Le financement des investissements et les aspects sociaux
de la reconversion [Financing of investments and social
aspects of conversion].
ECSC HA, 1963.   255p.   Collection: regional
economy and policy. 1: Industrial conversion in Europe, 3.
D F I N   3323

1295 MALISSEN, M.
Société pour la conversion et le développement industriels
[Company for industrial conversion and development].
ECSC HA, 1960.   2p.   Intergovernmental
Conference on Industrial Redevelopment.
F   5437

1296 MALLET, J.
L'économie française dans le Marché Commun [The
French economy in the Common Market].
Bureau (P), 1968.   28p.   Les documents de
Communauté européenne, 46.
F

1297 MALVESTITI, P.
Address delivered by Mr. Piero Malvestiti President of
the High Authority of the European Coal and Steel
Community to the European Parliament at Strasbourg.
May 8, 1961 (Discours de M. Piero Malvestiti Président de
la Haute Autorité de la Communauté européenne du
charbon et de l'acier devant l'Assemblée parlementaire
européenne à Strasbourg. 8 Mai 1961).
ECSC HA, 1961.   34p.
D E F I N   2681

1298 MALVESTITI, P.
Address delivered by Piero Malvestiti President of the
High Authority of the European Coal and Steel
Community before the European Parliamentary
Assembly at Strasbourg. 1 April 1960 [Discours prononcé
par Piero Malvestiti Président de la Haute Autorité de la
Communauté européenne du charbon et de l'acier devant

l'Assemblée parlementaire européenne à Strasbourg. 1
avril 1960].
ECSC HA, 1960.   28p.
E   2424

1299 MALVESTITI, P.
Address delivered to The European Parliament by Mr.
Piero Malvestiti President of the High Authority at
Strasbourg. July 1960 [Discours prononcé par M. Piero
Malvestiti Président de la Haute Autorité devant le
Parlement européen à Strasbourg. Juillet 1960].
ECSC HA, 1960.   14p.
E   2498

1300 MALVESTITI, P.
Address delivered to The European Parliament by Mr.
Piero Malvestiti President of the High Authority of the
European Coal and Steel Community at Strasbourg. May
7, 1962 (Discours prononcé par M. Piero Malvestiti
Président de la Haute Autorité de la Communauté
européenne du charbon et de l'acier devant le Parlement
européen à Strasbourg. 7 mai 1962).
ECSC HA, 1962.   31p.
D E F I N   2976

1301 MALVESTITI, P.
'E pluribus unum'. Address delivered by the President of
the High Authority to the European Parliamentary
Assembly at Strasbourg. November 1960 ('E pluribus
unum'. Discours prononcé par le président de la Haute
Autorité devant l'Assemblée parlementaire européenne à
Strasbourg. Novembre 1960).
ECSC HA, 1960.   31p.
D E F I N   2568

1302 MALVESTITI, P.
Le rôle des institutions communautaires dans la
construction européenne [The role of Community
institutions in European integration].
Bureau (P), 1960.   12p.   Les documents de
Communauté européene, 6.
F

1303 MALVESTITI, P.
Sources of energy and industrial revolutions [Sources de l'énergie et les révolutions industrielles].
n.i., 1961.   50p.
E   2780/5/61/6

1304 MALVESTITI, P.
There is hope in Europe. Addresses delivered at the occasion of the setting-up of the High Authority of the European Coal and Steel Community. 16–23 September 1959 (Il y a un espoir en Europe. Discours prononcés à l'occasion de l'installation de la Haute Autorité de la Communauté Européenne du Charbon et de l'Acier. 16–23 septembre 1959).
ECSC, 1959.   58p.
D E F I N   2292

1305 MALVESTITI, P.
Towards an economic programme for Europe. An address delivered by the President of the High Authority to the European Parliament in Strasbourg. November 20, 1962 (Pour une programmation économique européenne. Discours prononcé par le président de la Haute Autorité devant le Parlement européen à Strasbourg. 20 Novembre 1962).
ECSC HA, 1962.   25p.
D E F I N   3202

1306 MANEGOLD, D.
Analyse des comptes de l'agriculture de l'EUROSTAT—1975 (Analysis of the EUROSTAT agricultural accounts for 1975).
In Agricultural accounts, 1976.
Eurostat, 1977.   pp.xxvii–lix.
D/F   7365

1307 MANEGOLD, D.
Projektionen über Erzeugung und Verbrauch landwirtschaftlicher Erzeugnisse—'1977'. 4: B.R. Deutschland [Projections of production and consumption of agricultural products—'1977'. 4: F.R. Germany /

Projections de la production et de la consommation de
produits agricoles—'1977'. 4: R.F. Allemagne].
Commission, 1974.   348p.   Internal information on
agriculture, 120.
D   VI/1383/72

1308 MANSHOLT, S. L.
Agriculture in the light of world events. Address by Dr.
S. L. Mansholt, Vice-President of the Commission of the
European Economic Community, on June 12, 1963, on the
occasion of the seventh centenary of the town of
Wageningen [L'agriculture dans la lumière des
événements mondiales. Discours par Dr. S. L. Mansholt,
vice-président de la Commission de la Communauté
économique européenne, sur l'occasion du centenaire
septième de la ville de Wageningen, le 12 juin 1963].
Commission EEC, 1963.   14p.
D E F I N   8100

1309 MANSHOLT, S. L.
Déclaration faite par Dr. S. L. Mansholt, Vice-Président
de la Commission de la Communauté économique
européenne, à l'assemblée du Comité des organisations
professionnelles agricoles (COPA), Milan, 6 avril 1962
[Speech delivered by Dr. S. L. Mansholt, Vice-President
of the Commission of the European Economic Community,
at the meeting of the Committee of Agricultural
Organizations (COPA), Milan, April 6 1962].
Commission EEC, 1962.   22p.
D F I N   8052

1310 MANSHOLT, S. L.
The future shape of agricultural policy (La forme future de
la politique agricole).
In Newsletter on the common agricultural policy,
1/1968.   Pr Inf, 1968.
D E F I N

1311 MANSHOLT, S. L.
Memorandum on the reform of agriculture in the
European Economic Community (Mémorandum sur la

réforme de l'agriculture dans la Communauté économique européenne).
In Bulletin of the European Communities. Supplement, 1/1969.   Commission, 1969.   85p.
D E F I N

1312 MANSHOLT, S. L.
Perspectives de la CEE pour l'ensemble de l'Europe.
Discours, Bonn, 23 avril 1968 [Prospects of the EEC for the whole of Europe. Address, Bonn, April 23 1968].
Commission, 1968.   19p.
D F I N   6140

1313 MANSHOLT, S. L.
Le plan Mansholt [The Mansholt Plan].
Pr Inf, 1969.   533p.
F

1314 MANSHOLT, S. L., chairman
Recueil des documents de la conférence agricole des États membres de la Communauté économique européenne à Stresa, du 3 au 12 juillet 1958 [Collected documents of the agricultural conference of the Member States of the European Economic Community in Stresa, July 3–12 1958].
Commission EEC, 1958.   250p.
D F I N   2116

1315 MARCHAL, A.
Kartelle und Zusammenschlüsse in Gemeinsamen Markt [Cartels and combinations in the Common Market / Ententes et associations dans le Marché commun].
Pr Inf, 1959.   24p.   Studienreihe.
D   4793

1316 MARCILLAC, de
Projections de la production et de la consommation de produits agricoles—'1977'. 8: France [Projections of production and consumption of agricultural products—'1977'. 8: France].

Commission, 1975.   173p.   Internal information on
agriculture, 164.
F   VI/1123/72

1317 MARIGNETTI, M. T.
Analyse de certains expériences d'aménagement et de
gestion de 'zones industrielles' dans les pays de la
Communauté économique européenne (Belgique, France,
république fédérale d'Allemagne, Italie, Pays-Bas)
[Analysis of some schemes for planning and administration
of 'industrial zones' in the countries of the European
Economic Community (Belgium, France, Federal
Republic of Germany, Italy, the Netherlands)].
Commission, 1972.   175p.   Collection: regional
economy and policy. 1: Industrial conversion in Europe, 9.
D F I N   8362

1318 MARINI, A., chairman
Deuxième programme de constructions expérimentales
[Second programme of experimental buildings].
ECSC, 1962.   390p.
F   2801

1319 MARINI, A., chairman
Premier programme de constructions expérimentales
[First programme of experimental buildings].
ECSC, 1958.   255p.
F   2006

1320 MARJOLIN, R.
The Common Market: inward or outward looking [Le
Marché commun: aspect intérieur ou extérieur].
Inf Ser, 1964.   11p.   Community topics, 12.
E

1321 MARJOLIN, R.
L'espansione economica nel mercato commune dal 1958 ad
oggi. Le prospettive per il 1966 [The economic expansion
of the Common Market from 1958 until today. Prospects
until 1966 / L'expansion économique du Marché Commun
de 1958 à aujourd'hui. Les perspectives jusqu'en 1966].

Uff St Inf, 1966.   21p.   Documenti di Comunità
europee, 18.
I

1322 MARJOLIN, R.
Les problèmes économiques du Marché Commun en 1964
[The economic problems of the Common Market in 1964].
Bureau (P), 1964.   15p.   Les documents de
Communauté européenne, 20.
F

1323 MARJOLIN, R., chairman
Report of the study group 'Economic and Monetary Union
1980' (Rapport du groupe de réflexion 'Union économique
et monétaire 1980').
Commission, 1975.   2 vols.
D E F   II/675/3/74

1324 MARLY, M.
La conduite sur place des opérations de conversion
industrielle [On-the-spot direction of industrial conversion
operations].
ECSC HA, 1963.   352p.   Collection: regional
economy and policy. 1: Industrial conversion in Europe, 4.
D F I N   3324

MARMOL, del, *see* DEL MARMOL

1325 MARSCHALL, D.
Temporary-employment business. Comparative study of
provisions laid down by law and regulation in force in the
Member States of the European Communities (Le travail
temporaire. Étude comparée des dispositions législatives
et réglementaires en vigueur dans les États membres des
Communautés européenes).
Commission, 1976.   69p.   Studies: social policy
series, 25.
D E F   8723

1326 MARTELLI, G.
Studio sull'evoluzione della concentrazione industriale in

Italia (1968–1974). Pneumatici. Candele. Accumulatori [A study of the evolution of industrial concentration in Italy (1968–1974). Tyres. Sparking plugs. Batteries / Étude sur l'évolution de la concentration industrielle en Italie (1968–1974). Pneumatiques. Bougies. Accumulateurs]. Commission, 1976.   341p.

I   8750

1327 MARTELLI, G.
Studio sull'evoluzione della concentrazione nell'industria della costruzione elettrica in Italia. Costruzione di apparecchiature elettroniche ed elettroacustiche e di apparecchi radio e televisivi (N.I.C.E. 375). Costruzione di apparecchi elettrodomestici (N.I.C.E. 376) [A study of the evolution of concentration in the electrical engineering industry in Italy. Manufacture of electronic and audio equipment and radio and television receivers (N.I.C.E. 375). Manufacture of electrical domestic appliances (N.I.C.E. 376) / Étude sur l'évolution de la concentration dans l'industrie de la construction électrique en Italie. Construction d'appareils électroniques, radios, télévision, électro-acoustique (N.I.C.E. 375). Fabrication d'appareils électrodomestiques (N.I.C.E. 376)].
Commission, 1974.   109p.

I   IV/189/74

1328 MARTELLI, G.
Studio sull'evoluzione della concentrazione nell'industria della costruzione elettrica in Italia (1970–1974).
Costruzione di apparecchi elettrodomestici (NICE 376).
Costruzione di apparecchiature elettroniche ed elettroacustiche e di apparecchi radio e televisivi (NICE 375) [A study of the evolution of concentration in the electrical engineering industry in Italy (1970–1974).
Manufacture of electrical domestic appliances (NICE 376). Manufacture of electronic and audio equipment and radio and television receivers (NICE 375) / Étude sur l'évolution de la concentration dans l'industrie de la construction électrique en Italie (1970–1974). Fabrication d'appareils électrodomestiques (NICE 376). Construction

d'appareils électroniques, radios, télévision,
électro-acoustique (NICE 375)].
Commission, 1975. 236p.
I 8746

1329 MARTELLI, G.
Studio sull'evoluzione della concentrazione nell'industria
di cicli, motocicli e ciclomotori in Italia 1970–1972 [A study
of the evolution of concentration in the cycles, motorcycles
and power-assisted cycles industry in Italy 1970–1972 /
Étude sur l'évolution de la concentration dans l'industrie
des cycles, motocycles et cyclomoteurs en Italie
1970–1972].
Commission, 1975. 87p.
I 8699

1330 MARTENS, L.
Nouvelles formes de collaboration dans le domaine de la
production agricole. 2: Benelux [New forms of cooperation
in the field of agricultural production. 2: Benelux].
Commission, 1972. 470p. Internal information on
agriculture, 94.
D F N VI/2514/72

1331 MARTENS, L.
Nouvelles formes de collaboration dans le domaine de la
production agricole. 4: Synthèse [New forms of
cooperation in the field of agricultural production. 4:
Summary].
Commission, 1973. 73p. Internal information on
agriculture, 110.
D F VI/1181/73

1332 MARTENS, P.
Conséquences écologiques de l'application des techniques
modernes de production en agriculture [Ecological results
from the application of modern production techniques in
agriculture].
Commission, 1974. var. pag. Internal information
on agriculture, 137.
D F VI/3722/74

1333 MARTINO, E.
La Comunidad Europea y América Latina [The European
Community and Latin America / La Communauté
européenne et l'Amérique latine].
Pr Inf. 1965.   34p.   Documentos de la Comunidad
Europea, 1.
S

1334 MARTINO, G.
Gedenken an Robert Schuman Ehrenpräsident des
Europäischen Parlaments [In memory of Robert Schuman
honorary president of the European Parliament / En
souvenir de Robert Schuman président honoraire du
Parlement européen].
EP, 1963.   23p.
D   3371

1335 MAS LATRIE, de, chairman
Report on the long and medium term development of the
shipbuilding market (Rapport sur l'évolution à moyen et à
long terme du marché de la construction navale).
Commission, 1972.   166p.
D E F I N   8302

1336 MASSA-ROLANDINO, F.
Review of studies carried out in the producer countries on
the forecast consumption of the alloying elements Ni, Cr,
Mo, V, W and Co for special steel production in the years
1980 and 1985 (Synthèse des études effectuées dans les
pays producteurs sur les prévisions de consommation des
éléments d'alliage Ni, Cr, Mo, V, W, Co pour la
production d'aciers spéciaux pour les années 1980 et 1985).
Commission, 1977.   33p.   Series: raw material
supply for the iron and steel industry, 1.
D E F I   8935

1337 MASSACESI, E.
La conduite sur place des opérations de conversion
industrielle [On-the-spot direction of industrial conversion
operations].

ECSC HA, 1963. 352p. Collection: regional
economy and policy. 1: Industrial conversion in Europe, 4.
D F I N 3324

1338 MASSACESI, E.
Localisation et aménagement de terrains industriels. 1re
partie: Expériences dans les pays de la Communauté
européenne, en Grande-Bretagne et aux États-Unis. 2e
partie: Complexes industriels planifiés aux États-Unis
[Selection and planning of industrial sites. Part 1:
Experiments in the countries of the European
Community, in Great Britain and in the United States.
Part 2: Planned industrial complexes in the United
States].
ECSC HA, 1966–1967. 2 vols. Collection: regional
economy and policy. 1: Industrial conversion in Europe, 7.
D F I N 3693

1339 MASSANTE, S.
Méthodes statistiques en vue de déterminer le potentiel de
production des vergers [Statistical methods used to
determine the potential of orchard production].
In Agricultural statistical studies, 2.
Eurostat, 1968. var. pag.
D F 14892

1340 MASSE
Les conditions d'installation d'entreprises industrielles
dans les États africains et malgache associés. Volume 3:
République malgache [Conditions for the setting-up of
industrial undertakings in the Associated African States
and Madagascar. Volume 3: Malagasy Republic]; 2nd ed.
Commission, 1975. 90p.
F VIII/1251/74

1341 MASSE
Conditions for the setting-up of industrial undertakings in
the Associated African States and Madagascar. Volume
12: Mauritius (Les conditions d'installation d'entreprises
industrielles dans les États africains et malgache associés.
Volume 12: Île Maurice); 2nd ed.
Commission, 1975. 74p.
E F VIII/1253/74

1342 MASSOTH, K.
Le progrès technique et l'organisation de l'entreprise dans
les industries de la C.E.C.A. [Technical progress and the
organization of the firm in the industries of the E.C.S.C.].
ECSC HA, 1963.   41p.
F   199

1343 MATHIEU, G.
French industry and the Common Market [L'industrie
française et le Marché Commun].
Inf Ser, 1962.   55p.   Community topics, 5.
E

1344 MAUGERI, S.
Les activités de la direction générale des affaires sociales
en matière de recherches de médecine et d'hygiène du
travail [The activities of the Directorate-General of Social
Affairs concerning research in medicine and
industrial health].
Commission, 1969.   19p.   Collection: industrial
health and medicine.
D F I N   15313

1345 MAUGINI, A.
L'aide alimentaire de la C.E.E. aux pays en voie de
développement problèmes posés et possibilités réelles. 2:
Étude régionale. Libye [Food aid from the E.E.C. to the
developing countries. Problems and possibilities. 2:
Regional study. Libya].
Commission EEC, 1963.   16p.
F   7829

1346 MAUGINI, A.
L'aide alimentaire de la C.E.E. aux pays en voie de
développement problèmes posés et possibilités réelles. 4:
Étude régionale. Somalie [Food aid from the E.E.C. to
the developing countries. Problems and possibilities. 4:
Regional study. Somalia].
Commission EEC, 1963.   17p.
F   7829

1347 MAUGINI, A.
L'aide alimentaire de la C.E.E. aux pays en voie de
développement problèmes posés et possibilités réelles. 5:
Étude régionale. Empire d'Ethiopie [Food aid from the
E.E.C. to the developing countries. Problems and
possibilities. 5: Regional study. Ethiopian Empire].
Commission EEC, 1963.   25p.
F   7829

1348 MAUGINI, A.
L'aide alimentaire de la C.E.E. aux pays en voie de
développement. Problèmes posés et possibilités réelles.
11: Étude régionale. Amérique latine [Food aid from the
E.E.C. to the developing countries. Problems and
possibilities. 11: Regional study. Latin America].
Commission EEC, 1963.   20p.
F   7829

1349 MAUGINI, A.
Food aid from the EEC to developing countries. Problems
and possibilities (L'aide alimentaire de la C.E.E. aux pays
en voie de développement. Problèmes posés et possibilités
réelles).
Commission EEC, 1964.   233p.   Studies:
agricultural series, 14.
D E F I N   8102

1350 MAYER, K. E.
Les aciéries [The steel-works].
Commission, 1971.   283p.   New technical processes
in the iron and steel industry: a personal training manual,
3.   Studies: vocational training.
D F I N   17433

1351 MAYER, K. E.
Les laminoirs [The rolling mills].
Commission, 1972.   240p.   New technical processes
in the iron and steel industry: a personal training manual,
4.   Studies: vocational training.
D F I N   8349

1352 MAYER, K. E.
Mécanisation, automatisation et techniques de mesure
dans les services des hauts fourneaux [Mechanisation,
automation and measurement techniques in blast-furnace
works].
Commission, 1969.   172p.   New technical processes
in the iron and steel industry: a personal training manual,
2.   Studies: vocational training.
D F I N   14722

1353 MAYER, K. E.
La technique de mesure et de l'automation [Measurement
and automation technique].
ECSC HA, 1967.   204p.   New technical processes in
the iron and steel industry: a personal training manual, 1.
Studies: vocational training.
D F I N   13233

1354 MAYER, R.
Address by M. René Mayer President of the High
Authority to the Common Assembly. Ordinary Session
1956–1957 Strasbourg. May 14, 1957 [Discours de M. René
Mayer Président de la Haute Autorité devant l'Assemblée
Commune. Session ordinaire 1956–1957 Strasbourg.
14 mai, 1957].
ECSC HA, 1957.   32p.
E   1899

1355 MAYER, R.
Allocution de Monsieur René Mayer Président de la Haute
Autorité devant l'Assemblée Commune. Première Session
extraordinaire 1955–1956 Strasbourg. 23 Novembre 1955
[Speech by Mr. René Mayer President of the High
Authority to the Common Assembly. First Extraordinary
Session 1955–1956 Strasbourg. 23 November 1955].
ECSC, 1955.   22p.
F   1661

1356 MAYER, R.
Discours de Monsieur René Mayer Président de la Haute
Autorité devant l'Assemblée Commune. Session ordinaire

1955 Strasbourg. 21 Juin 1955 [Address by Mr. René
Mayer President of the High Authority to the Common
Assembly. Ordinary Session 1955 Strasbourg. 21 June
1955].
ECSC, 1955.   20p.
F   1626

1357 MAYER, R.
Pour une politique européenne. Conférence faite par M.
René Mayer Président de la Haute Autorité de la
C.E.C.A. à Luxembourg, le 25 janvier 1956 sous les
auspices du Conseil Luxembourgeois du Mouvement
Européen [Towards a European policy. Lecture by Mr.
René Mayer President of the High Authority of the
E.C.S.C. in Luxembourg, 25 January 1956 under the
auspices of the Luxembourg Council of the European
Movement].
ECSC HA, 1956.   18p.
F   1715

1358 MAYER, R.
Speech by Monsieur René Mayer President of the High
Authority before the Common Assembly. Ordinary
Session 1955–1956. Strasbourg. 8 May 1956 [Allocution de
Monsieur René Mayer, Président de la Haute Autorité
devant l'Assemblée Commune. Session ordinaire
1955–1956. Strasbourg. 8 mai 1956].
ECSC, 1956.   50p.
E   1754

1359 MAZOYER, M.
Essai d'appréciation des conditions d'application et des
résultats d'une politique de réforme en agriculture dans
des régions agricoles difficiles. 1: Morvan [Attempt at
estimating the conditions from the application and results
of a reform policy in agriculture in difficult agricultural
regions. 1: Morvan].
Commission, 1974.   183p.   Internal information on
agriculture, 138.
F   VI/4572/74

1360 MAZOYER, M.
Essai d'appréciation des conditions d'application et des
résultats d'une politique de réforme en agriculture dans
des régions agricoles difficiles. 2: Queyras [Attempt at
estimating the conditions from the application and results
of a reform policy in agriculture in difficult agricultural
regions. 2: Queyras].
Commission, 1975.   var. pag.   Internal information
on agriculture, 150.
F   VI/1988/75

1361 MAZOYER, M.
Possibilités et conditions de développement des systèmes
de production agricole extensifs dans la CEE [Possibilities
and conditions of developing extensive agricultural
production systems in the EEC].
Commission, 1971.   174p.   Internal information on
agriculture, 72.
D F   VI/17410/70

1362 MEADOWS, P. C.
The United Kingdom economy [L'économie britannique].
Commission, 1975.   155p.   Studies: economic and
financial series, 9.
E   8461

1363 MEDERNACH, H.
Crédits à l'agriculture [Credit to agriculture].
Commission, 1973.   var. pag.   Internal information
on agriculture, 102.
D F   VI/18121/70

1364 MEDERNACH, H.
Crédits à l'agriculture. 1: France, Belgique, Grand-Duché
de Luxembourg [Credit to agriculture. 1: France,
Belgium, Grand-Duchy of Luxembourg].
Commission, 1976.   var. pag.   Information on
agriculture, 1.
F   8831

1365 MEEUSEN, W.

Comparaison entre le soutien accordé à l'agriculture aux États-Unis et dans la Communauté [Comparison between the support given to agriculture in the United States and in the Community].
Commission, 1971.   256p.   Internal information on agriculture, 70.
D F   5493/VI/70

1366 MEIER, E. F.

Mesures et problèmes relatifs à la suppression du morcellement de la propriété rurale dans les États membres de la CEE [Measures and problems relating to the abolition of the division of rural property in the Member States of the EEC].
Commission EEC, 1965.   77p.   Internal information on agriculture, 8.
D F   4690/VI/65

1367 MEISSNER, W.

Study of the characteristics of a Community programme on the environment and its effect on employment [Étude des traits d'un programme communautaire sur l'environnement et son effet sur l'emploi].
n.i., 1977.   225p.
D E   ENV/223/74

1368 MELIEZCK, H.

L'aide alimentaire de la C.E.E. aux pays en voie de développement problèmes et possibilités réelles. 10: L'utilisation d'excédents agricoles en Arabie Séoudite [Food aid from the E.E.C. to the developing countries. Problems and possibilities. 10: The use of agricultural surpluses in Saudi Arabia].
Commission EEC, 1963.   10p.
F   7829

1369 MELIEZCK, H.

L'aide alimentaire de la C.E.E. aux pays en voie de développement problèmes et possibilités réelles. 12: Élements d'un système d'évaluation des possibilités

d'utilisation des excédents agricoles dans les pays en voie
de développement [Food aid from the E.E.C. to the
developing countries. Problems and possibilities. 12:
Elements of an evaluation system of possibilities for the
use of agricultural surpluses in the developing countries].
Commission EEC, 1963.   16p.
F   7829

1370 MELIEZCK, H.
L'aide alimentaire de la C.E.E. aux pays en voie de
développement problèmes et possibilités réelles. 13;
Organisation de l'utilisation des excédents agricoles aux
État-Unis [Food aid from the E.E.C. to the developing
countries. Problems and possibilities. 13: Organisation of
the use of agricultural surpluses in the United States].
Commission EEC, 1963.   15p.
F   7829

1371 MELIEZCK, H.
L'aide alimentaire de la C.E.E. aux pays en voie de
développement problèmes posés et possibilités réelles. 6:
Étude régionale. Turquie [Food aid from the E.E.C. to the
developing countries. Problems and possibilities. 6:
Regional study. Turkey].
Commission EEC, 1963.   61p.
F   7829

1372 MELIEZCK, H.
L'aide alimentaire de la C.E.E. aux pays en voie de
développement problèmes posés et possibilités réelles. 7:
Étude régionale. Inde [Food aid from the E.E.C. to the
developing countries. Problems and possibilities. 7:
Regional study. India].
Commission EEC, 1963.   63p.
F   7829

1373 MELIEZCK, H.
L'aide alimentaire de la C.E.E. aux pays en voie de
développement problèmes posés et possibilités réelles. 8:
Étude régionale. Tanganyika [Food aid from the E.E.C.

to the developing countries. Problems and possibilities. 8:
Regional study. Tanganyika].
Commission EEC, 1963.   25p.
F   7829

1374 MELIEZCK, H.
L'aide alimentaire de la C.E.E. aux pays en voie de
développement problèmes posés et possibilités réelles. 9:
Étude régionale. Afghanistan [Food aid from the E.E.C.
to the developing countries. Problems and possibilities. 9:
Regional study. Afghanistan].
Commission EEC, 1963.   25p.
F   7829

1375 MENGONI, L.
Le contrat de travail dans le droit des pays membres de la
CECA [The employment contract in the law of the
member countries of the ECSC].
ECSC HA, 1966.   727p.   Collection: labour law.
D F I N   3568

1376 MENGONI, L.
Grève et lock-out [Strike and lock-out].
ECSC HA, 1961.   399p.   Collection: labour law. 2:
Labour law in the Community, 5.
D F I N   2367

1377 MENGONI, L.
La juridiction du travail et la juridiction de la sécurité
sociale dans les pays de la Communauté européenne
[Employment and social security jurisdiction in the
countries of the European Community].
Commission, 1972.   615p.   Collection: labour law.
D F I N   8341

1378 MENGONI, L.
La protection des travailleurs en cas de perte de l'emploi
[Protection of workers in the event of loss of employment].
ECSC HA, 1961.   489p.   Collection: labour law. 2:
Labour law in the Community, 11.
D F I N   2626

1379 MENGONI, L.
Le régime juridique des organisations professionnelles
dans les pays membres de la C.E.C.A. [Legal
administration of professional organisations in the
member countries of the E.C.S.C.].
ECSC HA, 1968.   666p.   Collection: labour law.
D F I N   13879

1380 MENGONI, L.
La représentation des travailleurs sur le plan de
l'entreprise dans le droit des pays membres de la
C.E.C.A. [Workers' representation at management level
in the law of the member countries of the E.C.S.C.].
ECSC HA, 1959.   348p.   Collection: labour law, 3.
D F I N   2104

1380A MENGONI, L.
Les sources du droit de travail [Sources of labour law].
ECSC HA, 1962.   192p.   Collection: labour law.
2: Labour law in the Community, 1.
D F I N   2773

1381 MENGONI, L.
La stabilité de l'emploi dans le droit des pays membres de
la C.E.C.A. [Stability of employment in the law of the
member countries of the E.C.S.C.].
ECSC HA, 1958.   311p.   Collection: labour law, 2.
D F I N   1999

1382 MERCKELBAGH, A.
Forms of cooperation in the fishing industry. Denmark,
Ireland, United Kingdom [Formes de coopération dans le
secteur de la pêche. Danemark, Irlande, Royaume-Uni].
Commission, 1976.   var. pag.   Information on
agriculture, 9.
E   8842

1383 MERCKELBAGH, A.
La pêche artisanale en méditerranée. Situation et revenus
[Small-scale fishing in the Mediterranean. Condition and
incomes].

Commission, 1974.   323p.   Internal information on
agriculture, 135.
F I   VI/3274/74

1384 MERTENS DE WILMARS, C.
Recherche dans la sidérurgie belge [Research in the
Belgian iron and steel industry].
Commission, 1967.   152p.   Collection: occupational
physiology and psychology, 3/8.
F   13749

1385 MESNAGE, M.
Élimination des variations saisonnières. La nouvelle
méthode de l'OSCE [Elimination of seasonal variations.
The S.O.E.C.'s new method].
In Statistical studies and surveys, 1/1968.
Eurostat, 1968.   pp. 7–78.
F   4407

1386 MESTRES, R.
The content of organo-halogen compounds detected
between 1968 and 1972 in water, air and foodstuffs and the
methods of analysis used in the nine member states of the
European Community [Le contenu des composés
organo-halogènes découverte entre 1968 et 1972 dans
l'eau, l'air et les produits alimentaires et les méthodes de
l'analyse utilisées dans les neuf États membres
de la Communauté européenne].
Commission, 1974.   70p.
E   V/F/1630/74

1387 METZGER, L.
Vers l'élection directe de l'Assemblée parlementaire
européenne [Towards the direct election of the European
Parliamentary Assembly].
EPA, 1960.   79p.
F   2516

1388 METZGER, M.
L'Association de la Communauté européenne et des États
africains [Association of the European Community and the
African States].

Bureau (P), 1968.   41p.   Les documents de
Communauté européenne, 50.
F

1389 MEYBLUM, J. L.
Possibilités de création d'industries exportatrices dans les
États africains et malgaches associés. Produits
électro-mécaniques. Produits électroniques [Possibilities
for the establishment of exporting industries in the
Associated African States and Madagascar.
Electro-mechanical products. Electronic products].
Commission, 1975.   3 vols.
F   VIII/224/74

1390 MEYBLUM, J. L.
Possibilités de création d'industries exportatrices dans les
États africains et malgache associés. Produits
électro-mécaniques. Produits électroniques. Rapport de
synthèse [Possibilities for the establishment of exporting
industries in the Associated African States and
Madagascar. Electro-mechanical products. Electronic
products. Summary report].
Commission, 1975.   23p.
D E F I N   VIII/224/74

1391 MEYER, G.
Essais de réduction des minerais de fer au four tournant.
Rapport intérimaire sur les essais effectués du 1.1.1960 au
31.3.1961 [Experiments by reduction of iron ore in the
rotary furnace. Provisional report of the experiments
carried out from 1.1.1960 to 31.3.1961].
ECSC HA, 1961.   20p.
F   7838

1392 MEYER, H.
Les laminoirs [The rolling mills].
Commission, 1972.   240p.   New technical processes
in the iron and steel industry: a personal training manual,
4.   Studies: vocational training.
D F I N   8349

1393 MEYER, K. J.

Le financement des investissements et les aspects sociaux de la reconversion [Financing of investments and social aspects of conversion].
ECSC HA, 1963.   255p.   Collection: regional economy and policy. 1: Industrial conversion in Europe, 3.
D F I N   3323

1394 MICHAELIS, H.

Rapport sur les résultats d'une enquête effectuée en janvier 1956 sur la situation des coûts et recettes des charbonnages de la Ruhr [Report on the results of a survey carried out in January 1956 on the situation of costs and returns of the Ruhr coalfields].
ECSC HA, 1956.   48p.
F   729

1395 MICHEL, F. W.

Constatation des cours des vins de table à la production. 1: France et RF d'Allemagne [Ascertaining the production prices of table wines. 1: France and FR of Germany].
Commission, 1970.   171p.   Internal information on agriculture, 59.
D F   2565/VI/70

1396 MICHEL, F. W.

Constatation des cours des vins de table à la production. 2: Italie, GD de Luxembourg [Ascertaining the production prices of table wines. 2: Italy, GD of Luxembourg].
Commission, 1971.   var. pag.   Internal information on agriculture, 75.
D F   VI/17662/69

1397 MICHEL, F. W.

L'emploi agricole dans les pays de la C.E.E. Tome 1: Structure [Agricultural employment in the countries of the E.E.C. Volume 1: Structure].
Commission EEC, 1964.   61p.   Studies: social policy series, 7.
D F I N   8108

1398 MICHEL, F. W.
L'emploi agricole dans les pays de la C.E.E. Tome 2:
Évolution et perspectives [Agricultural employment in
the countries of the E.E.C. Volume 2: Development and
prospects].
Commission EEC, 1964.   51p.   Studies: social policy
series, 8.
D F I N   8123

1399 MICKWITZ, G. von
Review of pre-slaughter stunning in the E.C. [Examen de
l'étourdissement avant l'abattage pratique dans la C.E.].
Commission, 1977.   90p.   Information on
agriculture, 30.
D E   CH-SA-77-030-EN-C

1400 MIERT, K. van
Structure institutionnelle et fonctionnement des
Communautés Européennes [Institutional structure and
working of the European Communities].
In Dossier mensuel du Bureau de Bruxelles. Numéro
spécial, 1973.
Bureau (B), 1973.   75p.
F N

1401 MIEULLE, de
Possibilités de création d'industries exportatrices dans les
États africains et malgache associés. Produits de
l'élevage. Viandes, cuirs et peaux, chaussures, articles en
cuir [Possibilities for the establishment of exporting
industries in the Associated African States and
Madagascar. Products from rearing. Meat, hides and
skins, shoes, leather articles].
Commission, 1974.   5 vols.
F   VIII/223/74

1402 MIEULLE, de
Possibilités de création d'industries exportatrices dans les
États africains et malgache associés. Produits de
l'élevage. Viandes, cuirs et peaux, chaussures, articles en
cuir. Rapport de synthèse [Possibilities for the

establishment of exporting industries in the Associated
African States and Madagascar. Products from rearing.
Meat, hides and skins, shoes, leather articles. Summary
report].
Commission, 1975.   27p.
D E F I N   VIII/223/74

1403 MILANI, T.
Analyse de certains expériences d'aménagement et de
gestion de 'zones industrielles' dans les pays de la
Communauté économique européenne (Belgique, France,
république fédérale d'Allemagne, Italie, Pays-Bas)
[Analysis of some schemes for planning and administration
of 'industrial zones' in the countries of the European
Economic Community (Belgium, France, Federal
Republic of Germany, Italy, the Netherlands)].
Commission, 1972.   175p.   Collection: regional
economy and policy. 1: Industrial conversion in Europe, 9.
D F I N   8362

1404 MILLER, W.G.N., chairman
Objectives and priorities for a common Research and
Development policy. Study (Objectifs et priorités d'une
politique commune de la recherche et du développement.
Étude).
ESC, 1977.   37p.
DK D E F I N   7331

1405 MILOCCHI
Labour force sample survey 1975 (Enquête par sondage
sur les forces de travail 1975).
Eurostat, 1977.   221p.
DK/D/E/F/I/N   7353

1406 MIONI, M.
Tobacco. Present situation and prospects (Le tabac.
Situation et perspectives).
In Newsletter on the common agricultural policy,
3/1976.   Pr Inf, 1976.   16p.
DK D E F I N   X/403/76

1407 MISSLIN, A.
La Confédération européenne des syndicats et l'extension de la coopération syndicale [The European Trade Union Confederation and the extension of trade union co-operation].
In Documentation européenne. Série syndicale et ouvrière, 3/1973.   Pr Inf, 1973.   4p.
D F I N   S 73/3

1408 MIXA, A.
Teneur en métaux lourds des jus de fruits et produits similaires [Heavy metal content of fruit juices and similar products].
Commission, 1975.   215p.   Internal information on agriculture, 148.
D F   VI/1594/75

1409 MOCKERS, J. P.
Study on the possible part played by certain primary non-employment incomes in the inflationary process in France (Étude sur le rôle éventuel de certains revenus primaires non-salariaux dans le développement de l'inflation en France).
Commission, 1975.   243p.   Series: medium-term economic policy, 3.
DK D E F I N   8455

1410 MOERKERK, G. H. J. M.
La collaboration entre l'enseignement et les industries de la C.E.C.A. [Co-operation between education and the industries of the E.C.S.C.].
ECSC HA, 1959.   134p.
F   4704

1411 MOL, J.
Modèles d'exploitations agricoles. Méthodes, applications et possibilités d'utilisation dans le cadre de la C.E.E. [Models of farms. Methods, applications and possibilities of use in the framework of the E.E.C.].
Commission EEC, 1964.   75p.   Studies: agricultural series, 13.
D F   8099

1412 MOLENAAR, A. N.
Grève et lock-out [Strike and lock-out].
ECSC HA, 1961. 399p. Collection: labour law. 2:
Labour law in the Community, 5.
D F I N 2367

1413 MOLENAAR, A. N.
La protection des travailleurs en cas de perte de l'emploi
[Protection of workers in the event of loss of employment].
ECSC HA, 1961. 489p. Collection: labour law. 2:
Labour law in the Community, 11.
D F I N 2626

1414 MOLENAAR, A. N.
La représentation des travailleurs sur le plan de
l'entreprise dans le droit des pays membres de la
C.E.C.A. [Workers' representation at management level
in the law of the member countries of the E.C.S.C.].
ECSC HA, 1959. 348p. Collection: labour law, 3.
D F I N 2104

1414A MOLENAAR, A. N.
Les sources du droit du travail [Sources of labour law].
ECSC HA, 1962. 192p. Collection: labour law.
2: Labour law in the Community, 1.
D F I N 2773

1415 MOLENAAR, A. N.
La stabilité de l'emploi dans le droit des pays membres de
la C.E.C.A. [Stability of employment in the law of the
member countries of the E.C.S.C.].
ECSC HA, 1958. 311p. Collection: labour law, 2.
D F I N 1999

1416 MÖLLER
La politique économique régionale, condition du succès de
la politique agricole [Regional economic policy,
prerequisite for a successful agricultural policy].
Commission EEC, 1961. 20p. Studies: agricultural
series, 4.
D F I N 8020

1417 MONNET, J.
Address delivered by Mr. Jean Monnet President of the
High Authority before the Common Assembly at the
opening of the extraordinary session of Janury 1954.
Strasbourg 14 January 1954 [Discours prononcé par M.
Jean Monnet, Président de la Haute Autorité devant
l'Assemblée Commune à la première session de la session
extraordinaire de janvier 1954. Strasbourg, le 14 janvier
1954].
ECSC HA, 1954.   18p.
E   1272

1418 MONNET, J.
Allocution de Monsieur Jean Monnet Président de la
Haute Autorité devant l'Assemblée Commune. Session
ordinaire mai 1955 Strasbourg [Speech by Mr. Jean
Monnet President of the High Authority before the
Common Assembly. Ordinary session May 1955
Strasbourg].
ECSC HA, 1955.   16p.
F   1603

1419 MONNET, J.
Allocution prononcée par Monsieur Jean Monnet Président
de la Haute Autorité devant l'Assemblée Commune au
cours de la session extraordinaire de janvier 1954 [Speech
delivered by Mr. Jean Monnet President of the High
Authority before the Common Assembly during the
extraordinary session of Janury 1954].
ECSC HA, 1954.   18p.
F   1279

1420 MONNET, J.
Allocutions prononcées par Monsieur Jean Monnet
Président de la Haute Autorité à la première séance de la
Haute Autorité le 10 Août 1952 à Luxembourg; à la
première session de l'Assemblée le 11 Septembre 1952 à
Strasbourg [Speeches delivered by Mr. Jean Monnet
President of the High Authority at the first meeting of the
High Authority, 10th August 1952 at Luxembourg; at the

first session of the Assembly, 11th September 1952 at
Strasbourg].
ECSC, 1952.   30p.
F

1421 MONNET, J.
Allocutions prononcées par Monsieur Jean Monnet
Président de la Haute Autorité au cours de la session
ordinaire 1953 de l'Assemblée Commune [Speeches
delivered by Mr. Jean Monnet President of the High
Authority to the Common Assembly during the 1953
ordinary session].
ECSC HA, 1953.   55p.
F   1147

1422 MONNET, J.
Allocutions prononcées par Monsieur Jean Monnet
Président de la Haute Autorité devant l'Assemblée
Commune au cours de sa session de Janvier 1953 à
Strasbourg [Speeches delivered by Mr. Jean Monnet
President of the High Authority to the Common Assembly
during its session of January 1953 at Strasbourg].
ECSC, 1953.   30p.
F

1423 MONNET, J.
L'Europe se fait. Exposé de M. Jean Monnet Président de
la Haute Autorité de la Communauté Européenne du
Charbon et de l'Acier devant la Société d'Économie
Politique de Belgique à Bruxelles, le 30 juin 1953 [Europe
comes into being. Report by Mr. Jean Monnet President of
the High Authority of the European Coal and Steel
Community to the Society of Political Economy of Belgium
at Brussels, 30th June 1953].
ECSC, 1953.   23p.
F

1424 MONTJOIE
Management, organization and methods in the American
iron and steel industry. E.C.S.C. fact finding mission to
U.S.A. March–April 1957 [Direction, organisation et

méthodes dans la sidérurgie des États-Unis. C.E.C.A.
mission des faits-fournitures aux États-Unis mars–avril
1957].
ECSC HA, 1958.　　364p.
E　　4444

1425 MORANO, N.
Le marché foncier et les baux ruraux. Effets des mesures
de réforme des structures agricoles. 1: Italie [The land
market and rural leases. Effects of reform measures of
agricultural structures. 1: Italy].
Commission, 1972.　　var. pag.　　Internal information
on agriculture, 81.
D F　　VI/10832/70

1426 MORANO, N.
Surfaces agricoles pouvant être mobilisées pour une
réforme de structure [Agricultural areas that could be
mobilised for a structural reform].
Commission, 1973.　　336p.　　Internal information on
agriculture, 77.
D F　　VI/14453/69

1427 MORDREL, L.
Formes de coopération dans le secteur de la pêche. 1:
Synthèse, R.F. d'Allemagne, Italie [Forms of cooperation
in the fishing industry. 1: Summary, F.R. of Germany,
Italy].
Commission, 1970.　　var. pag.　　Internal information
on agriculture, 68.
D F　　14715/VI/69

1428 MORDREL, L.
Formes de coopération dans le secteur de la pêche. 2:
France, Belgique, Pays-Bas [Forms of cooperation in the
fishing industry. 2: France, Belgium, the Netherlands].
Commission, 1970.　　var. pag.　　Internal information
on agriculture, 69.
D F　　14715/VI/69

1429 MORDREL, L.
La pêche artisanale en méditerranée. Situation et revenus [Small-scale fishing in the Mediterranean. Condition and incomes].
Commission, 1974.   323p.   Internal information on agriculture, 135.
F I   VI/3274/74

1430 MORERE
Essai d'appréciation des conditions d'application et des résultats d'une politique de réforme en agriculture dans des régions agricoles difficiles. 2: Queyras [Attempt at estimating the conditions from the application and results of a reform policy in agriculture in difficult agricultural regions. 2: Queyras].
Commission, 1975.   var. pag.   Internal information on agriculture, 150.
F   VI/1988/75

1431 MORGAN, A. D.
The United Kingdom economy [L'économie britannique].
Commission, 1975.   155p.   Studies: economic and financial series, 9.
E   8461

1432 MORI-UBALDINI, L.
Possibilités de création d'industries exportatrices dans les États africains et malgache associés. Production sidérurgique [Possibilities for the establishment of exporting industries in the Associated African States and Madagascar. Iron and steel production].
Commission, 1975.   3 vols.
F   VIII/228/74

1433 MORI-UBALDINI, L.
Possibilités de création d'industries exportatrices dans les États africains et malgache associés. La production sidérurgique. Pelletisation du minerai de fer et électro-sidérurgie. Ferro-alliages (ferro-silicium, -manganèse et -nickel). Rapport de synthèse [Possibilities for the establishment of exporting industries in the

Associated African States and Madagascar. Iron and steel
production. Pelletisation of iron ore and electro-siderurgy.
Ferro-alloys (ferro-silicon, -manganese and -nickel).
Summary report].
Commission, 1975.   40p.
D E F I N   VIII/228/74

1434 MORITZ, E.
Les laminoirs [The rolling mills].
Commission, 1972.   240p.   New technical processes
in the iron and steel industry: a personal training manual,
4.   Studies: vocational training.
D F I N   8349

1435 MORSIANI, G. S.
Rapport sur le droit économique italien [Report on Italian
economic law].
Commission, 1974.   154p.   Studies:
competition–approximation of legislation series, 20/3.
D F I   8427

1436 MOSINI, F.
Studio sull'evoluzione della concentrazione nel settore
della costruzione di macchine per ufficio in Italia [A study
of the evolution of concentration in the sector of the
manufacture of office machinery in Italy / Étude sur
l'évolution de la concentration dans le secteur de la
construction des machines de bureau en Italie].
Commission, 1977.   149p.
I   8754

1437 MOSINI, F.
Studio sull'evoluzione della concentrazione nell'industria
cotoniera italiana (N.I.C.E. 233) [A study of the evolution
of concentration in the Italian cotton industry (N.I.C.E.
233) / Étude sur l'évolution de la concentration dans
l'industrie de coton en Italie (N.I.C.E. 233)].
Commission, 1975.   149p.
I   8743

1438 MOT, M. de
Possibilités de création d'industries exportatrices dans les
États africains et malgache associés. Transformation du
bois et fabrication d'articles en bois. Première
transformation: Sciages, déroulages, tranchages.
Deuxième transformation: Profilés, moulures,
contreplaqués, panneaux, produits finis: pour la
construction et l'ameublement. Rapport de synthèse
[Possibilities for the establishment of exporting industries
in the Associated African States and Madagascar. Wood
processing and manufacture of articles in wood. First
process: Sawing, wood-peeling, slicing. Second process:
Shapes, mouldings, plywood, panels, finished products:
for building and furniture. Summary report].
Commission, 1974.   445p.
F   VIII/227/74

MOTHE, T. Quinthrie la, *see* QUINTHRIE LA
MOTHE, T.

1439 MOTTERSHEAD, P.
The United Kingdom economy [L'économie britannique].
Commission, 1975.   155p.   Studies: economic and
financial series, 9.
E   8461

1440 MOULLE, N.
Le rôle des ports de la Communauté pour le trafic de
céréales et de farines. 1: Synthèse pour les principaux
ports français et italiens [List of Community ports for the
cereals and flour trade. 1: Summary for the chief French
and Italian ports].
Commission, 1974.   var. pag.   Internal information
on agriculture, 122.
F   VI/2941/73

1441 MOULLE, N.
Le rôle des ports de la Communauté pour le trafic de
céréales et de farines. 2: Monographies pour les principaux
ports français de la Manche [List of Community ports for
the cereals and flour trade. 2: Monographs for the chief
French Channel ports].

Commission, 1974.   var. pag.   Internal information
on agriculture, 123.
F   VI/1169/74

1442 MOULLE, N.
Le rôle des ports de la Communauté pour le trafic de
céréales et de farines. 3: Monographies pour les principaux
ports français de l'Atlantique [List of Community ports for
the cereals and flour trade. 3: Monographs for the chief
French Atlantic ports].
Commission, 1974.   var. pag.   Internal information
on agriculture, 124.
F   VI/1263/74

1443 MOULLE, N.
Le rôle des ports de la Communauté pour le trafic de
céréales et de farines. 4: Monographies pour les principaux
ports français de la Méditerranée [List of Community
ports for the cereals and flour trade. 4: Monographs for the
chief French Mediterranean ports].
Commission, 1974.   var. pag.   Internal information
on agriculture, 125.
F   VI/1264/74

1444 MOULLE, N.
Le rôle des ports de la Communauté pour le trafic de
céréales et de farines. 5: Monographies pour les principaux
ports italiens de la Côte Ouest [List of Community ports
for the cereals and flour trade. 5: Monographs for the chief
Italian West Coast ports].
Commission, 1974.   var. pag.   Internal information
on agriculture, 126.
F   VI/1265/74

1445 MOULLE, N.
Le rôle des ports de la Communauté pour le trafic de
céréales et de farines. 6: Monographies pour les principaux
ports italiens de la Côte Est [List of Community ports for
the cereals and flour trade. 6: Monographs for the chief
Italian East Coast ports].

Commission, 1974.   var. pag.   Internal information
on agriculture, 127.
F   VI/1266/74

1446 MOULLE, N.
Le rôle des ports de la Communauté pour le trafic de
céréales et de farines. 7: Synthèse pour les principaux
ports de la R.F. d'Allemagne, du Royaume-Uni, des
Pays-Bas, de la Belgique, de l'Irlande et du Danemark
[List of Community ports for the cereals and flour trade. 7:
Summary for the chief ports of F.R. of Germany, United
Kingdom, the Netherlands, Belgium, Ireland and
Denmark].
Commission, 1975.   var. pag.   Internal information
on agriculture, 155.
F   VI/3170/75

1447 MOULLE, N.
Le rôle des ports de la Communauté pour le trafic de
céréales et de farines. 8: Monographies pour les principaux
ports de la R.F. d'Allemagne [List of Community ports for
the cereals and flour trade. 8: Monographs for the chief
ports of the F.R. of Germany].
Commission, 1975.   var. pag.   Internal information
on agriculture, 156.
F   VI/3171/75

1448 MOULLE, N.
Le rôle des ports de la Communauté pour le trafic de
céréales et de farines. 9: Monographies pour les principaux
ports du Royaume-Uni [List of Community ports for the
cereals and flour trade. 9: Monographs for the chief ports
of the United Kingdom].
Commission, 1975.   var. pag.   Internal information
on agriculture, 157.
F   VI/3172/75

1449 MOULLE, N.
Le rôle des ports de la Communauté pour le trafic de
céréales et de farines. 10: Monographies pour les
principaux ports des Pays-Bas [List of Community ports
for the cereals and flour trade. 10: Monographs for the
chief ports of the Netherlands].

Commission, 1975.   var. pag.   Internal information
on agriculture, 158.
F   VI/3173/75

1450 MOULLE, N.
Le rôle des ports de la Communauté pour le trafic de
céréales et de farines. 11: Monographies pour les
principaux ports de la Belgique [List of Community ports
for the cereals and flour trade. 11: Monographs for the
chief ports of Belgium].
Commission, 1975.   var. pag.   Internal information
on agriculture, 159.
F   VI/3174/75

1451 MOULLE, N.
Le rôle des ports de la Communauté pour le trafic de
céréales et de farines. 12: Monographies pour les
principaux ports de l'Irlande et du Danemark [List of
Community ports for the cereals and flour trade. 12:
Monographs for the chief ports of Ireland and Denmark].
Commission, 1975.   var. pag.   Internal information
on agriculture, 160.
F   VI/3175/75

1452 MOULLE, N.
Le rôle des ports de la Communauté pour le trafic de
céréales et de farines. 13: Résumé et conclusions [List of
Community ports for the cereals and flour trade. 13:
Summary and conclusions].
Commission, 1975.   var. pag.   Internal information
on agriculture, 161.
F   VI/3791/75

1453 MOURIER, G. L.
Forms of cooperation in the fishing industry. Denmark,
Ireland, United Kingdom [Formes de coopération dans le
secteur de la pêche. Danemark, Irlande, Royaume-Uni].
Commission, 1976.   var. pag.   Information on
agriculture, 9.
E   8842

1454 MOUTON, C.

Le marché commun des produits agricoles. Perspectives
'1970' [The common market in agricultural products.
Prospects '1970'].
Commission EEC, 1963.   198p.   Studies:
agricultural series, 10.
D F I N   8077

1455 MROHS

Le marché foncier et les baux ruraux. Effets des mesures
de réforme des structures agricoles. 2: R.F. d'Allemagne,
France [The land market and rural leases. Effects of
reform measures of agricultural structures. 2: F.R. of
Germany, France].
Commission, 1972.   var. pag.   Internal information
on agriculture, 82.
F   VI/537/72

1456 MÜCKE, G.

Amélioration du climat dans les chantiers d'abbatage des
mines de houille. Rapport de synthèse 1967–1971/StBV
[Improvement of the surroundings in the blasting sites of
coal mines. Summary report 1967–1971/StBV].
Commission, 1973.   66p.   Technical research:
coal, 43. Mining technique.
D F   5845

1457 MÜCKE, G.

Gisement et dégagement de grisou. 2: Rapport de
synthèse 1968–1971/StBV [Discovering and clearing of
firedamp. 2: Summary report 1968–1971/StBV].
Commission, 1973.   330p.   Technical research: coal,
47. Mining technique.
D F   6031

MUGNOZZA, C. Scarascia, *see* SCARASCIA
MUGNOZZA, C.

1458 MÜLLER, J.

Untersuchung zur Konzentrationsentwicklung in der
Ernährungsindustrie in Deutschland.

Ernährungsindustrie (ohne Getränkeindustrie) insegesamt
(N.I.C.E. 20 B). Herstellung von Fleischkonserven
(N.I.C.E. 201). Herstellung von Obst- und
Gemüsekonserven (N.I.C.E. 203). Herstellung von
Fischkonserven (N.I.C.E. 204) [A study of the evolution
of concentration in the food industry in Germany. The food
industry as a whole (without the beverages industry)
(N.I.C.E. 20 B). Manufacture of canned meat (N.I.C.E.
201). Manufacture of canned fruit and vegetables
(N.I.C.E. 203). Manufacture of canned fish (N.I.C.E. 204)
/ Étude sur l'évolution de la concentration dans l'industrie
alimentaire en Allemagne. L'industrie alimentaire
entièrement (sans l'industrie des boissons) (N.I.C.E. 20
B). Fabrication des conserves de viande (N.I.C.E. 201).
Fabrication des conserves de fruit et légumes (N.I.C.E.
203). Fabrication des conserves de poissons (N.I.C.E.
204)].
Commission, 1973.   190p.
D

1459 MÜLLER, J.
Untersuchung zur Konzentrationsentwicklung in
verschiedenen Untersektoren der Maschinenbauindustrie
in Deutschland. Landwirtschaftliche Maschinen und
Ackerschlepper (N.I.C.E. 361). Büromaschinen
(N.I.C.E. 362). Textilmaschinen und Zubehör (N.I.C.E.
364.1). Bau- und Baustoffmaschinen (N.I.C.E. 366.4).
Hebezeuge und Fördermittel (N.I.C.E. 366.5) [A study of
the evolution of concentration in various sub-sectors of the
mechanical engineering industry in Germany.
Agricultural machinery and tractors (N.I.C.E. 361).
Office machinery (N.I.C.E. 362). Textile machinery and
accessories (N.I.C.E. 364.1). Machinery for the
preparation of building materials (N.I.C.E. 366.4).
Mechanical lifting and handling equipment (N.I.C.E.
366.5) / Étude sur l'évolution de la concentration dans
quelques sous-secteurs de l'industrie de la construction de
machines non électriques en Allemagne. Machines et
tracteurs agricoles (N.I.C.E. 361). Machines de bureau
(N.I.C.E. 362). Machines textiles et accessoires (N.I.C.E.
364.1). Machines pour la préparation mécanique des

matériaux de construction (N.I.C.E. 366.4). Matériel de
levage et de manutention (N.I.C.E. 366.5)].
Commission, 1973.   var. pag.
D   IV/343/73

1460 MÜLLER, J.
Untersuchung zur Konzentrationsentwicklung in
verschiedenen Untersektoren der Maschinenbauindustrie
in Deutschland. 1: Landwirtschaftliche Maschinen und
Ackerschlepper (N.I.C.E. 361). 2: Büromaschinen
(N.I.C.E. 362). 3: Textilmaschinen und Zubehör
(N.I.C.E. 364.1). 4: Bau- und Baustoffmaschinen
(N.I.C.E. 366.4). 5: Hebezeuge und Fördermittel
(N.I.C.E. 366.5) [A study of the evolution of concentration
in various sub-sectors of the mechanical engineering
industry in Germany. 1: Agricultural machinery and
tractors (N.I.C.E. 361). 2: Office machinery (N.I.C.E.
362). 3: Textile machinery and accessories (N.I.C.E.
364.1). 4: Machinery for the preparation of building
materials (N.I.C.E. 366.4). 5: Mechanical lifting and
handling equipment (N.I.C.E. 366.5) / Étude sur
l'évolution de la concentration dans quelques
sous-secteurs de l'industrie de la construction de machines
non électriques en Allemagne. 1: Machines et tracteurs
agricoles (N.I.C.E. 361). 2: Machines de bureau (N.I.C.E.
362). 3: Machines textiles et accessoires (N.I.C.E. 364.1).
4: Machines pour la préparation mécanique des matériaux
de construction (N.I.C.E. 366.4). 5: Matériel de levage et
de manutention (N.I.C.E. 366.5)].
Commission, 1976.   var. pag.
D   8744

1461 MÜLLER, J. H.
Problèmes de la structure économique de la Sarre
[Problems of the economic structure of the Saar].
ECSC HA, 1967.   196p.   Collection: regional
economy and policy. 2: Development and conversion
programme, 9.
D F   4098

1462 MULLEY, L.
Labour force sample survey (Enquête par sondage sur les forces de travail).
In Social statistics, 1/1975.   Eurostat, 1975.   233p.
DK/D/E/F/I/N   6936/1

1463 MURCIER, A.
French industry and the Common Market [L'industrie française et le Marché Commun].
Inf Ser, 1962.   55p.   Community topics, 5.
E

1464 MURPHY, F. P.
Study on the possible part played by certain primary non-employment incomes in the inflationary process in Ireland (Étude sur le rôle éventuel de certains revenus primaires non-salariaux dans le développement de l'inflation en Irlande).
Commission, 1977.   110p.   Series: medium-term economic policy, 9.
E F   CD-ST-77-001-EN-C

1464A MUYSERS, K.
Aide-mémoire pour la pratique des épreuves d'exercice en médecine du travail [Manual for the practice of exercise tests in industrial medicine].
Commission, 1971.   49p.   Collection: industrial health and medicine, 12.
D F I N   16741

1465 MYLENBUSCH, H.
Untersuchung der Konzentrationsentwicklung in der Reifenindustrie sowie ein Branchenbild der Kraftfahrzeug-Elektrikindustrie in Deutschland [A study of the evolution of concentration in the tyre industry, as well as a survey of electrical equipment for the motor vehicle industry in Germany / Étude sur l'évolution de la concentration dans l'industrie des pneumatiques, aussi que un examen des appareils électriques pour l'industrie des véhicules à moteur en Allemagne].
Commission, 1977.   190p.
D   8757

1466 MYLENBUSCH, H.
Untersuchung zur Konzentrationsentwicklung in
verschiedenen Untersektoren der Papier- und
Pappeindustrie in Deutschland. Herstellung (N.I.C.E.
271). Verarbeitung (N.I.C.E. 272) [A study of the
evolution of concentration in various sub-sectors of the
paper and paperboard industry in Germany. Manufacture
(N.I.C.E. 271). Processing (N.I.C.E. 272) / Étude sur
l'évolution de la concentration dans quelques
sous-secteurs de l'industrie du papier et du carton en
Allemagne. Fabrication (N.I.C.E. 271). Transformation
(N.I.C.E. 272)].
Commission, 1976.   88p.
D   7195

1467 NABOKOFF, N.
L'expérience belge de reconversion industrielle dans le
Borinage (1959–1960) [The Belgian experience of
industrial conversion in the Borinage (1959–1960)].
ECSC HA, 1960.   26p.   Intergovernmental
Conference on Industrial Redevelopment: Belgian
national report.
F   5660

1468 NABOKOFF, N.
Les politiques nationales de développement régional et de
conversion [National policies of regional development and
conversion].
ECSC HA, 1961.   195p.   Collection: regional
economy and policy. 1: Industrial conversion in Europe, 1.
F   2626

1469 NACAMULI, S.
Nouvelles formes de collaboration dans le domaine de la
production agricole. 1: Italie [New forms of cooperation in
the field of agricultural production. 1: Italy].
Commission, 1972.   266p.   Internal information on
agriculture, 93.
D F I   VI/2513/72

1470 NANNINGA, H. G. C.
Problèmes et méthodes de mesure de la productivité dans
les industries de la Communauté [Problems and methods
of measuring productivity in the industries of the
Community].
ECSC HA, 1964.   81p.   Collection: industrial
economics, 2.
D F I N   3535

NARDI, G. di, *see* DI NARDI, G.

NATERS, J. van der Goes van, *see* GOES VAN
NATERS, J. van der

1471 NEGRE, M.
Constatation des cours des vins de table à la production. 1:
France et RF d'Allemagne [Ascertaining the production
prices of table wines. 1: France and FR of Germany].
Commission, 1970.   171p.   Internal information on
agriculture, 59.
D F   2565/VI/70

1472 NEGRE, M.
Constatation des cours des vins de table à la production. 2:
Italie, GD de Luxembourg [Ascertaining the production
prices of table wines. 2: Italy, GD of Luxembourg].
Commission, 1971.   var. pag.   Internal information on
agriculture, 75.
D F   VI/17662/69

1473 NELTNER ALTARELLI, A.
La collaboration entre l'enseignement et les industries de
la C.E.C.A. [Cooperation between education and the
industries of the E.C.S.C.].
ECSC HA, 1959.   134p.
F   4704

1474 NETTER
L'évolution financière de la sécurité sociale dans les États
membres de la Communauté. 1965–1970–1975. 1ère
Partie: Rapport de synthèse [Financial development of
social security in the Member States of the Community.

1965–1970–1975. First Part: Summary report].
Commission, 1973.   55p.
D F I N   8375

1475 NEUMARK, F.
Rapport du Comité fiscal et financier [Report of the Fiscal
and Financial Committee].
Commission EEC, 1962.   150p.
D F I N   8070

1476 NEURAY, G.
Méthodes statistiques en vue de déterminer le potentiel de
production des vergers [Statistical methods used to
determine the potential of orchard production].
In Agricultural statistical studies, 2.
Eurostat, 1968.   var. pag.
D F   14892

NIELSEN, T. Herborg-, *see* HERBORG-NIELSEN, T.

1477 NIEMANN
Monographie du centre de médecine du travail des usines
sidérurgiques Hoesch AG, usine Westfalenhütte de
Dortmund (Allemagne) [Monograph of the Industrial
Medical Centre of the Hoesch AG iron and steel works,
Westfalenhütte factory of Dortmund (Germany)].
Commission, 1967.   92p.   Collected practical
information, 4.
D F I N   16150

1478 NIOLLET, P.
Possibilités d'industrialisation des États africains et
malgache associés. Volume 2: Cameroun,
Congo-Brazzaville, Gabon, République centrafricaine,
Tchad (Union douanière et économique de l'Afrique
centrale) [Possibilities for the industrialization of the
Associated African States and Madagascar. Volume 2:
Cameroon, Congo-Brazzaville, Gabon, Central African
Republic, Chad (Customs and economic union of Central
Africa)].
Commission EEC, 1966.   4 vols.
F   13074/VIII/B/66, 13075/VIII/B/66, 13076/VIII/B/66,
13085/VIII/B/66

1478A NISSARDI, G.
Aide-mémoire pour la pratique des épreuves d'exercice
en médecine du travail [Manual for the practice of
exercise tests in industrial medicine].
Commission, 1971.   49p.   Collection: industrial
health and medicine, 12.
D F I N   16741

1479 NOËL, E.
Comment fonctionnent les institutions de la Communauté
européenne [How the European Community's institutions
work]; rev. ed.
Pr Inf, 1972.   28p.
DK D F I N S G   5777

1480 NOËL, E.
How the European Community's Institutions work
[Comment fonctionnent les institutions de la Communauté
européenne]; rev. ed.
Inf Ser, 1969.   Community topics, 32.
E

1481 NOËL, E.
How the European Community's institutions work
[Comment fonctionnent les institutions de la Communauté
européenne]; rev. ed.
Inf Ser, 1973.   12p.   Community topics, 39.
E

1482 NOËL, E.
How the European Economic Community's institutions
work [Comment fonctionnent les institutions de la
Communauté économique européenne].
Inf Ser, 1963.   8p.   Community topics, 11.
E

1483 NOËL, E.
How the European Economic Community's Institutions
work [Comment fonctionnent les institutions de la
Communauté économique européenne]; rev. ed.
Inf Ser, 1966.   12p.   Community topics, 27.
E

1484 NOIRFALISE, A.
Conséquences écologiques de l'application des techniques
modernes de production en agriculture [Ecological results
from the application of modern production techniques in
agriculture].
Commission, 1974.   var. pag.   Internal information
on agriculture, 137.
D F   VI/3722/74

1485 NOLS, J.
Les accidents du travail dans l'industrie sidérurgique 1960
[Work accidents in the iron and steel industry 1960].
In Social statistics, 2/1962.   Eurostat, 1962.   53p.
D/F, I/N   3006

1486 NOLS, J.
Les comptes sociaux des Pays Membres de la
Communauté Économique Européenne 1962–1963 [Social
accounts of the Member Countries of the European
Economic Community 1962–1963].
In Social statistics, 5/1967.   Eurostat, 1967.   184p.
D/F, I/N   4145

1487 NOLS, J.
Les coûts de la main-d'œuvre dans les banques, les
assurances et le commerce de détail 1970 [Labour costs in
banks, insurance and the retail trade 1970].
In Social statistics, 4/1972.   Eurostat, 1973.   247p.
D/F/I/N   5785

1488 NOLS, J., chairman
Structure of earnings in wholesale and retail distribution,
banking and insurance in 1974. Methods and definitions
(Structure des salaires dans le commerce, les banques et
les assurances en 1974. Méthodes et définitions).
Eurostat, 1977.   223p.   Special series, B1.
DK/D/E/F/I/N   7330/1

1489 NOOIJ, A. T. J.
Les tendances d'évolution des structures des exploitations
agricoles. Causes et motifs d'abandon et de

restructuration [Trends of development in farm
structures. Causes and reasons for desertion and
reconstruction].
Commission, 1967.   386p.   Internal information on
agriculture, 20.
D F   8159/VI/67

1490 NOORDWAL, P. H.
Objectives and priorities for a common Research and
Development policy. Study (Objectifs et priorités d'une
politique commune de la recherche et du développement.
Étude).
ESC, 1977.   37p.
DK D E F I N   7331

1491 NOOTEBOOM, L.
Tableaux 'Entrées-Sorties' pour les pays de la
Communauté Économique Européene ['Input-Output'
tables for the countries of the European Economic
Community].
Eurostat, 1964.   var. pag.
D F

1492 NOOTEBOOM, L.
Tableaux 'Entrées-Sorties' pour les pays de la
Communauté Économique Européenne. Seconde version
['Input-Output' tables for the countries of the European
Economic Community. Second version].
Eurostat, 1965.   var. pag.
D F

1493 NORA, S.
Mémorandum sur les objectifs de 1965. Méthodes
d'élaboration et résultats détaillés [Memorandum on the
1965 objectives. Methods of elaboration and detailed
results].
ECSC HA, 1962.   540p.   Collection: general
objectives for steel, 1.
D F I N   3017

1494 NORA, S.
Toward a single energy policy. Individual national policies
vs. a concerted European policy [Vers une politique
énergétique seule. Les politiques nationales individuelles
contre une politique concertée européenne].
n.i., 1962.   61p.
E   8379

1495 NOUVIAIRE
La formation professionnelle dans les mines de fer des
pays de la Communauté [Vocational training in the iron
mines of the countries of the Community].
ECSC HA, 1959.   182p.
F   8149

1496 NOWICKI
Les exportations de biens d'équipment de la
Communauté. Essai et prévisions jusqu'en 1970 [Exports
of capital goods from the Community. Sample and
forecasts until 1970].
ECSC HA, 1967.   249p.   Collection: general
objectives for steel, 3A.
D F I N   12885

1497 NYS, A.
Genèse et croissance de la Communauté européenne
[Origin and growth of the European Community].
In Documentation européenne. Série pédagogique; série
agricole, 1/1974.   Pr Inf, 1974.   4p.
D F I N   U/A/74/1

1498 O'MAHONY, D.
Le mouvement syndical irlandais [The Irish trade union
movement].
In Documentation européenne. Série syndicale et
ouvrière, 1/1973.   Pr Inf, 1973.   4p.
D F I N   S 73/1

1499 ODIJK, J. L. van
Credit to agriculture. 4: The Netherlands [Crédits à
l'agriculture. 4: Pays-Bas].

Commission, 1976.   116p.   Information on
agriculture, 4.
E N   8834

1500 OLIVER
Possibilités de création d'industries exportatrices dans les
États africains et malgache associés. Produits de
l'élevage. Viandes, cuirs et peaux, chaussures, articles en
cuir [Possibilities for the establishment of exporting
industries in the Associated African States and
Madagascar. Products from rearing. Meat, hides and
skins, shoes, leather articles].
Commission, 1974.   5 vols.
F   VIII/223/74

1501 OLIVER
Possibilités de création d'industries exportatrices dans les
États africains et malgache associés. Produits de
l'élevage. Viandes, cuirs et peaux, chaussures, articles en
cuir. Rapport de synthèse [Possibilities for the
establishment of exporting industries in the Associated
African States and Madagascar. Products from rearing.
Meat, hides and skins, shoes, leather articles. Summary
report].
Commission, 1975.   27p.
D E F I N   VIII/223/74

1502 OLSEN, K. H.
Les grandes régions agricoles dans la C.E.E. [The main
agricultural regions in the E.E.C.].
Commission EEC, 1960.   57p.   Studies: agricultural
series, 1.
D F   VI/707

1503 OORT, C. J.
Conséquences budgétaires, économiques et sociales de
l'harmonisation des taux de la TVA dans la CEE avec une
analyse quantitative pour les Pays-Bas [Budgetary,
economic and social results of the harmonisation of VAT
rates in the EEC with a quantitative analysis for the
Netherlands].

Commission, 1970.   92p.   Studies:
competition–approximation of legislation series, 16.
D F I N   8316

1504 OORT, C. J.
Options in transport tariff policy (Options de la politique
tarifaire dans les transports).
Commission EEC, 1966.   189p.   Studies: transport
series, 1.
D E F I N   8146

1505 OPPEN, M. von
Les établissements de stockage de céréales dans la CEE.
Partie 1 [The establishment of cereal storage in the EEC.
Part 1].
Commission, 1968.   281p.   Internal information on
agriculture, 28.
D F   12751/VI/68

1506 OPPENLÄNDER
Les exportations de biens d'équipement de la
Communauté. Essai et prévisions jusqu'en 1970 [Exports
of capital goods from the Community. Sample and
forecasts until 1970].
ECSC HA, 1967.   249p.   Collection: general
objectives for steel, 3A.
D F I N   12885

1507 ORIE, N. G. M., chairman
Symposium Bronchite-Emphysème [Bronchitis with
Emphysema Symposium].
ECSC HA, 1967.   266p.   Collection: industrial
health and medicine, 5.
D F I N   3978

1508 ORJOLLET
La Communauté Européenne. Son agriculture [The
European Community and its agriculture].
Pr Inf, 1968.   99p.
F

1509 ORLANDO, G.
Tendances de la production et de la consommation en
denrées alimentaires dans la C.E.E. 1956–1965 [Trends in
food production and consumption in the E.E.C.
1956–1965].
Commission EEC, 1960.   266p.   Studies:
agricultural series, 2.
D F I N   8005

1510 ORLANDO, O.
Les grandes régions agricoles dans la C.E.E. [The main
agricultural regions in the E.E.C.].
Commission EEC, 1960.   57p.   Studies: agricultural
series, 1.
D F   VI/707

1511 ORT, W.
Évolution régionale de la population active agricole. 2:
R.F. d'Allemagne [Regional development of the working
agricultural population. 2: F.R. of Germany].
Commission, 1969.   170p.   Internal information on
agriculture, 40.
D F   6718/VI/69

1512 ORTOLI, F.-X.
Address by Mr. François-Xavier Ortoli, President of the
Commission of the European Communities, to the
European Parliament. Presentation of the General Report
for 1972 and programme of the Commission for 1973
Luxembourg, 13 February 1973 (Discours prononcé
devant le Parlement européen par M. François-Xavier
Ortoli, président de la Commission. Présentation du
Rapport général 1972 et programme de la Commission
pour l'année 1973 Luxembourg, 13 février 1973).
Commission, 1973.   24p.
D E F I N   8399

1513 ORTOLI, F.-X.
Address by Mr. François-Xavier Ortoli, President of the
Commission of the European Communities, to the
European Parliament. Presentation of the General Report

for 1974 and programme of the Commission for 1975
[Discours prononcé devant le Parlement européen par M.
François-Xavier Ortoli, président de la Commission des
Communautés européennes. Présentation du Rapport
général 1974 et programme de la Commission pour l'année
1975].
Commission, 1975.   46p.
E   SEC (74) 4000

1514 ORTOLI, F.-X.
Address by the President of the Commission. Programme
of the Commission for 1976 (Discours du président de la
Commission. Programme de la Commission pour l'année
1976).
Commission, 1976.   60p.
DK D E F I N   Disc. Pres./76

1515 ORTOLI, F.-X.
The construction of Europe: balance-sheet and outlook.
Address given in Mainz on 13 September 1974 by Mr.
François-Xavier Ortoli, President of the Commission, to
the Twelfth Annual Congress of the Association of
European Journalists (Bilan et perspectives de la
construction européenne. Allocution prononcée le 13
septembre 1974 à Mayence par M. François-Xavier Ortoli,
président de la Commission, devant le douzième congrès
annuel de l'Association des journalistes européens).
Commission, 1974.   9p.
DK D E F I N   6467

1516 ORTOLI, F.-X.
Declaration on the state of the Community (Déclaration
sur l'état de la Communauté).
In Information: political affairs, 53/1974.
Pr Inf, 1974.   7p.
D E F I N   59/X/74

1517 OS, F. J. J. H. M. van
Analyse comparative des structures socio-économiques
des régions minières et sidérurgiques de la Communauté.
Fascicule 1: Analyse des différentes régions de

l'Allemagne, de la Belgique, de la France, de l'Italie, des
Pays-Bas. Fascicule 2: Cartes établies sur la base des
renseignements fournis et graphiques comparatifs
[Comparative analysis of socio-economic structures in the
mining and iron and steel regions of the Community. Part
1: Analysis of different regions of Germany, Belgium,
France, Italy, the Netherlands. Part 2: Maps drawn up on
the basis of information supplied and comparative graphs].
Commission, 1968.   2 vols.   Collection: regional
economy and policy. 1: Industrial conversion in Europe, 8.
D F I N   4118

1518 OS, F. J. J. H. M. van
Arrangements to facilitate the establishment of new
economic activities. Legal and financial arrangements in
force in the member states of the Community and the
United Kingdom (Dispositions pour faciliter la création
d'activités nouvelles. Dispositions juridiques et financières
en vigueur dans les États membres et le Royaume-Uni).
ECSC HA, 1962.   loose-leaf.
D E F I N   3019

1519 OS, F. J. J. H. M. van
La politique d'industrialisation régionale poursuivie aux
Pays-Bas [Regional industrialization policy pursued in the
Netherlands].
ECSC HA, 1960.   4p.   Intergovernmental
Conference on Industrial Redevelopment: Dutch national
report.
F   5248

1520 OS, F. J. J. H. M. van
Les politiques nationales de développement régional et de
conversion [National policies of regional development and
conversion].
ECSC HA, 1961.   195p.   Collection: regional
economy and policy. 1: Industrial conversion in Europe, 1.
F   2626

1521 OSTINELLI, G.
Population and employment in the countries of the
Community 1970–1973 (Population et emploi dans les pays
de la Communauté 1970–1973).
Eurostat, 1974.   31p.   Social statistics.
E/F   7091

1522 OSTINELLI, G.
Population and employment 1968–1972 (Population et
emploi 1968–1972).
In Social statistics, 2/1973.   Eurostat, 1974.   168p.
D/E/F   6310

1523 OTTMANN, O.
Intégration verticale et contrats en agriculture. 1: R.F.
d'Allemagne [Vertical integration and contracts in
agriculture. 1: F.R. of Germany].
Commission, 1973.   136p.   Internal information on
agriculture, 106.
D F   VI/3359/73

1524 OURSIN, T.
Possibilités d'industrialisation des États africains et
malgache associés. Volume 2: Cameroun,
Congo-Brazzaville, Gabon, République centrafricaine,
Tchad (Union douanière et économique de l'Afrique
centrale) [Possibilities for the industrialization of the
Associated African States and Madagascar. Volume 2:
Cameroon, Congo-Brazzaville, Gabon, Central African
Republic, Chad (Customs and economic union of Central
Africa)].
Commission EEC, 1966.   4 vols.
F   13074/VIII/B/66, 13075/VIII/B/66, 13076/VIII/B/66,
13085/VIII/B/66

1525 OVERGAAUW, J. G. A.
Credit to agriculture. 4: The Netherlands [Crédits à
l'agriculture. 4: Pays-Bas].
Commission, 1976.   116p.   Information on
agriculture, 4.
E N   8834

1526 OWEN, N.
A study of the evolution of concentration in the mechanical engineering sector for the United Kingdom [Étude sur l'évolution de la concentration dans le secteur de la construction de machines non électriques au Royaume-Uni].
Commission, 1976.   264p.
E   8708

1527 OWEN, N.
A study of the evolution of concentration in the pharmaceutical industry for the United Kingdom [Étude sur l'évolution de la concentration dans l'industrie pharmaceutique au Royaume-Uni].
Commission, 1977.   168p.
E   8707

1528 PAASCH, F.
Kredite an die Landwirtschaft. 2: B.R. Deutschland [Credit to agriculture. 2: F.R. Germany / Crédits à l'agriculture. 2: R.F. d'Allemagne].
Commission, 1976.   225p.   Information on agriculture, 2.
D   8832

1529 PAGANINI, G. P.
Schematic presentation of the educational systems. Evolution of the number of pupils and students. EUR 9 1962–1973 (Présentation schématique des systèmes d'enseignement. Évolution des effectifs scolaires et universitaires. EUR 9 1962–1973).
In Social statistics, 5/1973.   Eurostat, 1975.   127p.
D/E/F/I/N   6635

1530 PAGANINI, G. P.
Statistiques de l'enseignement. Effectifs scolaires et quelques aspects financiers des systèmes d'enseignement dans les pays de la Communauté 1960–1971 [Education statistics. Pupil numbers and some financial aspects of educational systems in the countries of the Community 1960–1971].

In Social statistics, 6/1972.   Eurostat, 1973.   189p.
D/F/I/N   5874

1531 PALAZZI
Recherche sur la réduction directe des minerais de fer
dans le four à cuve [Research on direct reduction of iron
ore in a shaft furnace].
ECSC HA, 1964.   70p.
D F   10991

PALIANO, G. Colonna di, *see* COLONNA DI
PALIANO, G.

1532 PALUMBO
Recherche sur la réduction directe des minerais de fer dans
le four à cuve [Research on direct reduction of iron ore in a
shaft furnace].
ECSC HA, 1964.   70p.
D F   10991

1533 PANNIER, M.
Mémorandum sur les objectifs de 1965. Méthodes
d'élaboration et résultats détaillés [Memorandum on the
1965 objectives. Methods of elaboration and detailed
results].
ECSC HA, 1962.   540p.   Collection: general
objectives for steel, 1.
D F I N   3017

1534 PANUNZIO, V.
La conduite sur place des opérations de conversion
industrielle [On-the-spot direction of industrial conversion
operations].
ECSC HA, 1963.   352p.   Collection: regional
economy and policy. 1: Industrial conversion in Europe, 4.
D F I N   3324

1535 PAQUIER, B.
Les conditions d'installation d'entreprises industrielles
dans les États africains et malgache associés. Volume 1:
République islamique de Mauritanie [Conditions for the
setting-up of industrial undertakings in the Associated

African States and Madagascar. Volume 1: Islamic
Republic of Mauritania].
Commission, 1972.   92p.
F   VIII/1311/72

1536 PAQUIER, B.
Les conditions d'installation d'entreprises industrielles
dans les États africains et malgache associés. Volume 2:
République du Sénégal [Conditions for the setting-up of
industrial undertakings in the Associated African States
and Madagascar. Volume 2: Republic of Senegal].
Commission, 1972.   100p.
F   VIII/1312/72

1537 PAQUIER, B.
Les conditions d'installation d'entreprises industrielles
dans les États africains et malgache associés. Volume 3:
République du Mali [Conditions for the setting-up of
industrial undertakings in the Associated African States
and Madagascar. Volume 3: Republic of Mali].
Commission, 1972.   80p.
F   VIII/1313/72

1538 PAQUIER, B.
Les conditions d'installation d'entreprises industrielles
dans les États africains et malgache associés. Volume 4:
République du Niger [Conditions for the setting-up of
industrial undertakings in the Associated African States
and Madagascar. Volume 4: Republic of the Niger].
Commission, 1972.   80p.
F   VIII/1314/72

1539 PAQUIER, B.
Les conditions d'installation d'entreprises industrielles
dans les États africains et malgache associés. Volume 5:
République de Haute-Volta [Conditions for the setting-up
of industrial undertakings in the Associated African
States and Madagascar. Volume 5: Republic of Upper
Volta].
Commission, 1972.   88p.
F   VIII/1315/72

1540 PAQUIER, B.
Les conditions d'installation d'entreprises industrielles
dans les États africains et malgache associés. Volume 6:
République de Côte-d'Ivoire [Conditions for the
setting-up of industrial undertakings in the Associated
African States and Madagascar. Volume 6: Republic of
Ivory Coast].
Commission, 1972.   100p.
F   VIII/1316/72

1541 PAQUIER, B.
Les conditions d'installation d'entreprises industrielles
dans les États africains et malgache associés. Volume 7:
République togolaise [Conditions for the setting-up of
industrial undertakings in the Associated African States
and Madagascar. Volume 7: Republic of Togo].
Commission, 1972.   100p.
F   VIII/1317/72

1542 PAQUIER, B.
Les conditions d'installation d'entreprises industrielles
dans les États africains et malgache associés. Volume 8:
République du Dahomey [Conditions for the setting-up of
industrial undertakings in the Associated African States
and Madagascar. Volume 8: Republic of Dahomey].
Commission, 1972.   88p.
F   VIII/1318/72

1543 PAQUIER, B.
Les conditions d'installation d'entreprises industrielles
dans les États africains et malgache associés. Volume 9:
République unie du Cameroun [Conditions for the
setting-up of industrial undertakings in the Associated
African States and Madagascar. Volume 9: United
Republic of Cameroon].
Commission, 1972.   94p.
F   VIII/1319/72

1544 PAQUIER, B.
Les conditions d'installation d'entreprises industrielles
dans les États africains et malgache associés. Volume 10:

République du Tchad [Conditions for the setting-up of
industrial undertakings in the Associated African States
and Madagascar. Volume 10: Republic of Chad].
Commission, 1972.   86p.
F   VIII/1320/72

1545 PAQUIER, B.
Les conditions d'installation d'entreprises industrielles
dans les États africains et malgache associés. Volume 11:
République Centrafricaine [Conditions for the setting-up
of industrial undertakings in the Associated African
States and Madagascar. Volume 11: Central African
Republic].
Commission, 1972.   68p.
F   VIII/1321/72

1546 PAQUIER, B.
Les conditions d'installation d'entreprises industrielles
dans les États africains et malgache associés. Volume 12:
République gabonaise [Conditions for the setting-up of
industrial undertakings in the Associated African States
and Madagascar. Volume 12: Republic of Gabon].
Commission, 1972.   84p.
F   VIII/1322/72

1547 PAQUIER, B.
Les conditions d'installation d'entreprises industrielles
dans les États africains et malgache associés. Volume 13:
République populaire du Congo [Conditions for the
setting-up of industrial undertakings in the Associated
African States and Madagascar. Volume 13: Popular
Republic of the Congo].
Commission, 1972.   80p.
F   VIII/1323/72

1548 PAQUIER, B.
Les conditions d'installation d'entreprises industrielles
dans les États africains et malgache associés. Volume 14:
République du Zaïre [Conditions for the setting-up of
industrial undertakings in the Associated African States
and Madagascar. Volume 14: Republic of Zaïre].

Commission, 1972.   116p.
F   VIII/1324/72

1549 PAQUIER, B.
Les conditions d'installation d'entreprises industrielles
dans les États africains et malgache associés. Volume 15:
République Rwandaise [Conditions for the setting-up of
industrial undertakings in the Associated African States
and Madagascar. Volume 15: Republic of Rwanda].
Commission, 1972.   72p.
F   VIII/1325/72

1550 PAQUIER, B.
Les conditions d'installation d'entreprises industrielles
dans les États africains et malgache associés. Volume 16:
République du Burundi [Conditions for the setting-up of
industrial undertakings in the Associated African States
and Madagascar. Volume 16: Republic of Burundi].
Commission, 1973.   80p.
F   VIII/1326/72

1551 PAQUIER, B.
Les conditions d'installation d'entreprises industrielles
dans les États africains et malgache associés. Volume 17:
République démocratique de Somalie [Conditions for the
setting-up of industrial undertakings in the Associated
African States and Madagascar. Volume 17: Democratic
Republic of Somalia].
Commission, 1972.   52p.
F   VIII/1327/72

1552 PAQUIER, B.
Les conditions d'installation d'entreprises industrielles
dans les États africains et malgache associés. Volume 18:
République Malgache [Conditions for the setting-up of
industrial undertakings in the Associated African States
and Madagascar. Volume 18: Malagasy Republic].
Commission, 1973.   96p.
F   VIII/1328/72

1553 PAQUIER, B.
Les conditions d'installation d'entreprises industrielles
dans les États africains et malgache associés. Volume 1:
République du Dahomey [Conditions for the setting-up of
industrial undertakings in the Associated African States
and Madagascar. Volume 1: Republic of Dahomey]; 2nd
ed.
Commission, 1975.   78p.
F   VIII/1248/74

1554 PAQUIER, B.
Les conditions d'installation d'entreprises industrielles
dans les États africains et malgache associés. Volume 2:
République de Haute Volta [Conditions for the setting-up
of industrial undertakings in the Associated African
States and Madagascar. Volume 2: Republic of Upper
Volta]; 2nd ed.
Commission, 1975.   82p.
F   VIII/1250/74

1555 PAQUIER, B.
Les conditions d'installation d'entreprises industrielles
dans les États africains et malgache associés. Volume 3:
République malgache [Conditions for the setting-up of
industrial undertakings in the Associated African States
and Madagascar. Volume 3: Malagasy Republic]; 2nd ed.
Commission, 1975.   90p.
F   VIII/1251/74

1556 PAQUIER, B.
Les conditions d'installation d'entreprises industrielles
dans les États africains et malgache associés. Volume 4:
République du Mali [Conditions for the setting-up of
industrial undertakings in the Associated African States
and Madagascar. Volume 4: Republic of Mali]; 2nd ed.
Commission, 1975.   97p.
F   VIII/1252/74

1557 PAQUIER, B.
Les conditions d'installation d'entreprises industrielles
dans les États africains et malgache associés. Volume 5:

République islamique de Mauritanie [Conditions for the
setting-up of industrial undertakings in the Associated
African States and Madagascar. Volume 5: Islamic
Republic of Mauritania]; 2nd ed.
Commission, 1975. 112p.
F   VIII/1254/74

1558 PAQUIER, B.
Les conditions d'installation d'entreprises industrielles
dans les États africains et malgache associés. Volume 6:
République du Niger [Conditions for the setting-up of
industrial undertakings in the Associated African States
and Madagascar. Volume 6: Republic of the Niger]; 2nd
ed.
Commission, 1975. 69p.
F   VIII/1255/74

1559 PAQUIER, B.
Les conditions d'installation d'entreprises industrielles
dans les États africains et malgache associés. Volume 7:
République du Tchad [Conditions for the setting-up of
industrial undertakings in the Associated African States
and Madagascar. Volume 7: Republic of Chad]; 2nd ed.
Commission, 1975. 83p.
F   VIII/1259/74

1560 PAQUIER, B.
Les conditions d'installation d'entreprises industrielles
dans les États africains et malgache associés. Volume 8:
République togolaise [Conditions for the setting-up of
industrial undertakings in the Associated African States
and Madagascar. Volume 8: Republic of Togo]; 2nd ed.
Commission, 1975. 86p.
F   VIII/1260/74

1561 PAQUIER, B.
Les conditions d'installation d'entreprises industrielles
dans les États africains et malgache associés. Volume 9:
République du Burundi [Conditions for the setting-up of
industrial undertakings in the Associated African States
and Madagascar. Volume 9: Republic of Burundi]; 2nd ed.
Commission, 1975. 79p.
F   VIII/1243/74

1562 PAQUIER, B.
Les conditions d'installation d'entreprises industrielles
dans les États africains et malgache associés. Volume 10:
République du Rwanda [Conditions for the setting-up of
industrial undertakings in the Associated African States
and Madagascar. Volume 10: Republic of Rwanda];
2nd ed.
Commission, 1975.   72p.
F   VIII/1256/74

1563 PAQUIER, B.
Les conditions d'installation d'entreprises industrielles
dans les États africains et malgache associés. Volume 11:
République du Zaïre [Conditions for the setting-up of
industrial undertakings in the Associated African States
and Madagascar. Volume 11: Republic of Zaïre]; 2nd ed.
Commission, 1975.   104p.
F   VIII/1261/74

1564 PAQUIER, B.
Les conditions d'installation d'entreprises industrielles
dans les États africains et malgache associés. Volume 15:
République centrafricaine [Conditions for the setting-up
of industrial undertakings in the Associated African
States and Madagascar. Volume 15: Central African
Republic]; 2nd ed.
Commission, 1975.   67p.
F   VIII/1245/74

1565 PAQUIER, B.
Les conditions d'installation d'entreprises industrielles
dans les États africaines et malgache associés. Volume 16:
République populaire du Congo [Conditions for the
setting-up of industrial undertakings in the Associated
African States and Madagascar. Volume 16: Popular
Republic of the Congo]; 2nd ed.
Commission, 1975.   89p.
F   VIII/1246/74

1566 PAQUIER, B.
Les conditions d'installation d'entreprises industrielles
dans les États africains et malgache associés. Volume 17:

République gabonaise [Conditions for the setting-up of industrial undertakings in the Associated African States and Madagascar. Volume 17: Republic of Gabon]; 2nd ed. Commission, 1975.   87p.

F   VIII/1249/74

1567 PAQUIER, B.
Les conditions d'installation d'entreprises industrielles dans les États africains et malgache associés. Volume 18: République de Sénégal [Conditions for the setting-up of industrial undertakings in the Associated African States and Madagascar. Volume 18: Republic of Senegal]; 2nd ed. Commission, 1975.   111p.

F   VIII/1257/74

1568 PAQUIER, B.
Les conditions d'installation d'entreprises industrielles dans les États africains et malgache associés. Volume 19: République de Côte-d'Ivoire [Conditions for the setting-up of industrial undertakings in the Associated African States and Madagascar. Volume 19: Republic of Ivory Coast]; 2nd ed.
Commission, 1975.   80p.

F   VIII/1247/74

1569 PAQUIER, B.
Conditions for the setting-up of industrial undertakings in the Associated African States and Madagascar. Volume 12: Mauritius (Les conditions d'installation d'entreprises industrielles dans les États africains et malgache associés. Volume 12: Île Maurice); 2nd ed.
Commission, 1975.   74p.

E F   VIII/1253/74

1570 PAQUIER, B.
Conditions for the setting-up of industrial undertakings in the Associated African States and Madagascar. Volume 13: Democratic Republic of Somalia (Les conditions d'installation d'entreprises industrielles dans les États

africains et malgache associés. Volume 13: République démocratique de Somalie); 2nd ed.
Commission, 1975.   71p.
E F I   VIII/1258/74

1571 PAQUIER, B.
Conditions for the setting-up of industrial undertakings in the Associated African States and Madagascar. Volume 14: United Republic of Cameroon (Les conditions d'installation d'entreprises industrielles dans les États africains et malgache associés. Volume 14: République unie du Cameroun); 2nd ed.
Commission, 1975.   87p.
E F   VIII/1244/74

1572 PAQUIER, B.
Possibilités de création d'industries exportatrices dans les États africains et malgache associés. Produits de l'élevage. Viandes, cuirs et peaux, chaussures, articles en cuir [Possibilities for the establishment of exporting industries in the Associated African States and Madagascar. Products from rearing. Meat, hides and skins, shoes, leather articles].
Commission, 1974.   5 vols.
F   VIII/223/74

1573 PAQUIER, B.
Possibilités de création d'industries exportatrices dans les États africains et malgache associés. Produits de l'élevage. Viandes, cuirs et peaux, chaussures, articles en cuir. Rapport de synthèse [Possibilities for the establishment of exporting industries in the Associated African States and Madagascar. Products from rearing. Meat, hides and skins, shoes, leather articles. Summary report].
Commission, 1975.   27p.
D E F I N   VIII/223/74

1574 PARÉ
L'industrie électronique des pays de la Communauté et les investissements américains [The electronics industry of

the countries of the Community and American investments].

Commission, 1969.   168p.   Studies: industry series, 1.

D F I N   8240

1575 PARETTI, V.

Méthodologie communautaire des tableaux Entrées-Sorties 1965 [Community input-output tables 1965 methodology].

Eurostat, 1970.   222p.   Special series: input-output tables 1965, 1.

D F   4963

1576 PARODI, M.

Arrangements to facilitate the establishment of new economic activities. Legal and financial arrangements in force in the member states of the Community and the United Kingdom (Dispositions pour faciliter la création d'activités nouvelles. Dispositions juridiques et financières en vigueur dans les États membres et le Royaume-Uni].

ECSC HA, 1962.   loose-leaf.

D E F I N   3019

1577 PARODI, M.

Le bâtiment industriel dans la politique de développement régional [Industrial building in regional development policy].

ECSC HA, 1966.   215p.   Collection: regional economy and policy. 1: Industrial conversion in Europe, 5.

D F I N   3847

1578 PARODI, M.

Bâtiments industriels en Frise [Industrial buildings in Friesland].

ECSC HA, 1964.   68p.   Pamphlets on industrial conversion, 2.

D/F/I/N   11008

1579 PARODI, M.

La conversion des entreprises industrielles (l'expérience française) [Conversion of industrial undertakings (the French experience)].

ECSC HA, 1960.   23p.   Intergovernmental
Conference on Industrial Redevelopment: French national
report.
F   3873

1580 PARODI, M., chairman
Le financement de la reconversion industrielle. Formes
particulières de financement [Financing of industrial
conversion. Particular forms of financing].
ECSC HA, 1965.   107p.   Collection: regional
economy and policy. 1: Industrial conversion in Europe,
10.
D F I N   3708

1581 PARODI, M.
Les politiques nationales de développement régional et de
conversion [National policies of regional development and
conversion].
ECSC HA, 1961.   195p.   Collection: regional
economy and policy. 1: Industrial conversion in Europe, 1.
F   2626

1582 PASCAUD
Earnings in agriculture 1975 (Gains dans l'agriculture
1975).
Eurostat, 1977.   145p.
DK/D/E/F/I/N   CA-22-76-035-6A-C

1583 PASDELOUP
La Communauté Européenne. Son agriculture [The
European Community and its agriculture].
Pr Inf, 1968.   99p.
F

1584 PASSE
La formation professionnelle dans l'industrie sidérurgique
des pays de la Communauté [Vocational training in the
iron and steel industry of the countries of the
Community].
ECSC HA, 1954.   264p.
F

1585 PASSE, G.
Les aciéries [The steel-works].
Commission, 1971.   283p.   New technical processes
in the iron and steel industry: a personal training manual,
3.   Studies: vocational training.
D F I N   17433

1586 PASSE, G.
Les laminoirs [The rolling mills].
Commission, 1972.   240p.   New technical processes
in the iron and steel industry: a personal training manual,
4.   Studies: vocational training.
D F I N   8349

1587 PASSE, G.
Mécanisation, automatisation et techniques de mesure
dans les services des hauts fourneaux [Mechanisation,
automation and measurement techniques in blast-furnace
works].
Commission, 1969.   172p.   New technical processes
in the iron and steel industry: a personal training manual,
2.   Studies: vocational training.
D F I N   14722

1588 PASSE, G.
La technique de mesure et de l'automation [Measurement
and automation technique].
ECSC HA, 1967.   204p.   New technical processes in
the iron and steel industry: a personal training manual, 1.
Studies: vocational training.
D F I N   13233

1589 PATTERSON, B.
Direct elections [Les élections directes].
In European studies. Teachers' series, 20.
Commission (L), 1975.   4p.
E   U/74/20

1590 PAUL, K.
Gisement et dégagement de grisou. 2: Rapport de
synthèse 1968–1971/StBV [Discovering and clearing of

firedamp. 2: Summary report 1968–1971/StBV].
Commission, 1973.   330p.   Technical research: coal,
47. Mining technique.
D F   6031

1591 PAUL, L.
Évolution régionale de la population active agricole. 2:
R.F. d'Allemagne [Regional development of the working
agricultural population. 2: F.R. of Germany].
Commission, 1969.   170p.   Internal information on
agriculture, 40.
D F   6718/VI/69

PAYEN, M. L. Deveaux-, *see* DEVEAUX-PAYEN,
M. L.

1592 PEAL, J. A.
Intercomparison of measurement of carboxyhaemoglobin
in different European laboratories and establishment of
the methodology for the assessment of COH_B levels in
exposed populations [Inter-comparaison de la mesure du
carboxyle-hémoglobine dans les laboratoires divers
européens et l'établissement de la méthodologie pour
l'imposition des niveaux COH_B dans les populations
exposées].
Commission, 1977.   118p.
E   V/F/1315/77

1593 PECO, F.
La situation sur les marchés sidérurgiques dans les pays
tiers [State of the iron and steel market in non-member
countries].
ECSC HA, 1965.   239p.   Collection: iron and steel
market, 1.
D F I N   11780

1594 PECO, F.
La situation sur les marchés sidérurgiques dans les pays
tiers. Plans d'investissement et possibilités de production
[State of the iron and steel market in non-member
countries. Investment plans and production possibilities].

ECSC HA, 1967.   145p.   Collection: iron and steel market, 2.

D F I N   13609

1595 PEDERSEN, O. K.
Ermittlung des Muskelfleischanteils an Schlachttierkörpen von Schweinen mit dem dänischen KSA-Gerät [Determination of the proportion of lean meat on pig carcasses using the Danish KSA-equipment / Détermination de la teneur en viande maigre des carcasses de porc à l'aide de l'appareil danois KSA]. Commission, 1977.   29p.   Information on agriculture, 38.

D   CB-NA-77-038-DE-C

1596 PEDRINI, E.
Nouvelles formes de collaboration dans le domaine de la production agricole. 1: Italie [New forms of cooperation in the field of agricultural production. 1: Italy]. Commission, 1972.   266p.   Internal information on agriculture, 93.

D F I   VI/2513/72

1597 PEEMANS, J. P.
Possibilités d'industrialisation des États africains et malgache associés. Volume 3: République démocratique du Congo [Possibilities for the industrialization of the Associated African States and Madagascar. Volume 3: Democratic Republic of the Congo]. Commission EEC, 1966.   2 vols.

F   13077/VIII/B/66, 13078/VIII/B/66

1598 PEEMANS, J. P.
Possibilités d'industrialisation des États africains et malgache associés. Volume 4: Burundi, Rwanda et région Centre-orientale du Congo (Kinshasa) (région des Grands Lacs) [Possibilities for the industrialization of the Associated African States and Madagascar. Volume 4: Burundi, Rwanda and Centre-eastern region of the Congo (Kinshasa) (region of the Great Lakes)]. Commission EEC, 1966   2 vols.

F   13079/VIII/B/66, 13080/VIII/B/66

1599 PEEMANS, J. P.
Possibilités d'industrialisation des États africains et
malgache associés. Volume 5: Madagascar [Possibilities
for the industrialization of the Associated African States
and Madagascar. Volume 5: Madagascar].
Commission EEC, 1966.   2 vols.
F   13081/VIII/B/66, 13082/VIII/B/66

1600 PEEMANS, J. P.
Possibilités d'industrialisation des États africains et
malgache associés. Volume 6: Somalie [Possibilities for the
industrialization of the Associated African States and
Madagascar. Volume 6: Somalia].
Commission EEC, 1966.   2 vols.
F   13083/VIII/B/66, 13084/VIII/B/66

1601 PEETERS, P.
Application du modèle gravitationnel à la structure des
échanges internationaux de biens d'équipement
[Application of a gravitational model to the structure of
international trade in capital goods].
In Statistical studies and surveys, 1/1970.
Eurostat, 1970.   pp.63–94.
F   16543

1602 PEETERS, P.
Les exportations de biens d'équipment de la
Communauté. Essai et prévisions jusqu'en 1970 [Exports
of capital goods from the Community. Sample and
forecasts·until 1970].
ECSA HA, 1967.   249p.   Collection: general
objectives for steel, 3A.
D F I N   12885

1603 PEHL, G.
Perspectives du salaire d'investissement en Allemagne
[Prospects for investment reward in Germany].
In Documentation européene. Série syndicale et
ouvrière, 14.   Pr Inf, 1971.   4p.
D F I N

1604 PEHL, G.
Le salaire d'investissement en R.F.A. [The reward for
investment in F.R.G.].
In Dossiers pédagogiques, 42.
Bureau (P), 1971.   4p.
F

1605 PELSHENKE, P. F.
Possibilités d'introduire un système de gradation pour le
blé et l'orge produits dans la CEE [Possibilities for
introducing a grading system for wheat and barley
products in the EEC].
Commission, 1968.   193p.   Internal information on
agriculture, 35.
D F   21863/VI/68

1606 PELSHENKE, P. F.
Problèmes relatifs à la qualité du blé, de la farine et du
pain dans les pays de la C.E.E. [Problems relating to the
quality of wheat, flour and bread in the countries of the
E.E.C.].
Commission EEC, 1962.   36p.   Studies: agricultural
series, 7.
D F I N   8043

1607 PELSHENKE, P. F.
Problèmes relatifs à la qualité du blé tendre, de la farine et
du pain dans les pays de la CEE. Deuxième partie
[Problems relating to the quality of common wheat, flour
and bread in the countries of the EEC. Second part].
Commission EEC, 1965.   38p.   Studies: agricultural
series, 16.
D F I N   8124

1608 PELT, A. J. van
Pesticide residues in tobacco and tobacco products. 3:
Appendix. Pesticide residues found in tobacco.
Toxicological aspects of residues in tobacco (Les résidus
de pesticides dans le tabac et les produits de tabac. 3:
Annexe. Résidues de pesticides trouvés dans le tabac.
Aspects toxicologiques des résidus dans le tabac).

Commission, 1977.   var. pag.   Information on
agriculture, 26.
E F   8882

1609 PELZER, K. H.
Cantemus. Collection of European Schools songs
(Cantemus. Recueil de chants des écoles européenes).
ES, 1963.   296p.
D/E/F/I/N

1610 PENNINGTON, R. R.
Report on take over and other bids [Rapport sur les offres
de rachat et autres].
Commission, 1974.   123p.
E   XI/56/74

PERL, B. Weber-, *see* WEBER-PERL, B.

1611 PERSOONS, F., chairman
L'adaptation des régions d'ancienne industrialisation.
Volume 1: Rapport [The adaptation of old industrialized
regions. Volume 1: Report].
Commission EEC, 1964.   97p.
F   II/1045/4/64

1612 PESCE, U.
Il contributo delle 'Comunità montane' in Italia allo
sviluppo dell'agricoltura di montagna [The contribution of
'Comunità montane' to the development of hill farming in
Italy/La contribution des 'Comunità montane' au
développement de l'agriculture de montagne en Italie].
Commission, 1976.   209p.   Information on
agriculture, 11.
I   8861

1613 PESCE, U.
Gli 'enti di sviluppo agricolo' in Italia nella riforma delle
strutture. Problemi e prospettive di adattamento [The
'enti di sviluppo agricolo' in structural reform in Italy.
Adjustment problems and prospects/Les 'enti di sviluppo

agricolo' en Italie et la réforme des structures. Problèmes
et perspectives d'adaptation].
Commission, 1976.   285p.   Information on
agriculture, 12.
I   8862

1614 PESCIA, L.
The preparation of young people for work and for
transition from education to working life [La préparation
des jeunes à l'activité professionnelle et pour le passage de
l'éducation à la vie active].
In Bulletin of the European Communities. Supplement,
12/1976.   Commission, 1977.   pp.13–63.
DK D E F I N   4001/S/76/13

1615 PETER, H.
Le financement des investissements et les aspects sociaux
de la reconversion [Financing of investments and social
aspects of conversion].
ECSC HA, 1963.   255p.   Collection: regional
economy and policy. 1: Industrial conversion in Europe, 3.
D F I N   3323

1616 PETER, R.
School and professional education of the children of Italian
workers in the Saar (Formation scolaire et professionnelle
des enfants des travailleurs italiens en Sarre).
Commission, 1975.   176p.
D E F   V/722/75

PETIT, L. le, *see* LE PETIT, L.

1617 PETITJEAN, R.
Introduction à quelques problèmes posés par
l'automatisation des bloomings [Introduction to several
problems posed by the automation of bloomings].
ECSC HA, 1968.   136p.
F   14431

1618 PETITJEAN, R.
Quelques problèmes posés par l'automatisation des bandes
d'agglomération Dwight-Lloyd [Several problems posed

by the automation of the Dwight-Lloyd sinter strand].
ECSC HA, 1965.
F

1619 PETRE, M.
Les comptes sociaux des Pays Membres de la
Communauté Économique Européenne 1962–1963 [Social
accounts of the Member Countries of the European
Economic Community 1962–1963].
In Social statistics, 5/1967.   Eurostat, 1967.   184p.
D/F, I/N   4145

1620 PETRICCIONE, S.
Coordination of investments in transport infrastructures.
Analysis. Recommendations. Procedures (Coordination
des investissements en infrastructure de transport.
Analyse. Recommandations. Procédures).
Commission, 1974.   85p.   Studies: transport
series, 3.
D E F I N   8423

1621 PETRY, M.
Méthodes statistiques en vue de déterminer le potentiel de
production des vergers [Statistical methods used to
determine the potential of orchard production].
In Agricultural statistical studies, 2.
Eurostat, 1968.   var. pag.
D F   14892

1622 PFEIFFER, A.
Report on the economic situation in the Community
[Rapport sur la situation économique dans la
Communauté].
ESC, 1977.   2 vols.   Dossier: ECO/21/short-term
economic policy.
E   CES 363/77

1623 PHILIBERT, P.
Gestion économique des bateaux pour la pêche à la
sardine. Recherche des conditions optimales Italie, Côte
méditerranéenne française. 1: Synthèse [Economic

administration of sardine fishing boats. Research into the optimum conditions, Italy, French Mediterranean Coast. 1: Summary].
Commission, 1971.   178p.   Internal information on agriculture, 79.
F I   VI/3012/71

1624 PHILIBERT, P.
Gestion économique des bateaux pour la pêche à la sardine. Recherche des conditions optimales Italie, Côte méditerranéenne française. 2: Résultats des enquêtes dans les zones de pêche [Economic administration of sardine fishing boats. Research into the optimum conditions, Italy, French Mediterranean Coast. 2: Results of the fishing zone surveys].
Commission, 1971.   334p.   Internal information on agriculture, 80.
F I   VI/3012/71

1625 PHILIBERT, P.
La pêche artisanale en méditerranée. Situation et revenus [Small-scale fishing in the Mediterranean. Condition and incomes].
Commission, 1974.   323p.   Internal information on agriculture, 135.
F I   VI/3274/74

1626 PHLIPS, L.
The measurement of industrial concentration. A reassessment based on European data (Mesures de la concentration industrielle. Un réexamen à partir de données européennes).
In Statistical studies and surveys, 3/1975.
Eurostat, 1976.   43p.
E/F   6916/3

1627 PHLIPS, L.
Spatial pricing and competition (Les systèmes de prix géographiques et la concurrence).
Commission, 1977.   61p.   Studies: competition–approximation of legislation series, 29.
D E F   8868

1628 PIEREZZA, D.
Studio sull'evoluzione della concentrazione nel settore dei
detersivi per uso domestico in Italia dal 1968 al 1975 [A
study of the evolution of concentration in the sector of
detergents for domestic use from 1968 to 1975 in
Italy / Étude sur l'évolution de la concentration dans le
secteur des détergents pour la maison de 1968 à 1975 en
Italie].
Commission, 1977. 249p.
I CB-NL-77-012-IT-C

1629 PIERINI, M.
Non-governmental organizations for the protection of the
environment in the European Community [Les
organisations non-gouvernementales sur la protection de
l'environnement dans la Communauté européenne].
Commission, 1975. 16p.
E X/280/75

1630 PIESCH, W.
Détermination des erreurs lors des recensements du bétail
au moyen de sondages [Determination of errors in
sample livestock censuses].
Commission, 1967. 62p. Internal information on
agriculture, 16.
F

1631 PIJNAPPEL, T.
A study of the evolution of concentration in the Dutch
beverages industry [Étude sur l'évolution de la
concentration dans l'industrie des boissons aux Pays-Bas].
Commission, 1977. 149p.
E 8764

1632 PINELLI, A.
Le condizioni di lavoro delle donne salariate nei sei stati
membri della Comunità europea. Italia [The conditions of
work for wage-earning women in the six Member States of
the European Community. Italy/Les conditions de travail

des femmes salariées dans les six États membres de la
Communauté européenne. Italie].
Commission, 1972.   186p.
I   V/167/73

PINNA, V. Cao-, *see* CAO-PINNA, V.

1633 PIOGE
Possibilités de création d'industries exportatrices dans les
États africains et malgache associés. Produits de
l'élevage. Viandes, cuirs et peaux, chaussures, articles en
cuir [Possibilities for the establishment of exporting
industries in the Associated African States and
Madagascar. Products from rearing. Meat, hides and
skins, shoes, leather articles].
Commission, 1974.   5 vols.
F   VIII/223/74

1634 PIOGE
Possibilités de création d'industries exportatrices dans les
États africains et malgache associés. Produits de
l'élevage. Viandes, cuirs et peaux, chaussures, articles en
cuir. Rapport de synthèse [Possibilities for the
establishment of exporting industries in the Associated
African States and Madagascar. Products from rearing.
Meat, hides and skins, shoes, leather articles. Summary
report].
Commission, 1975.   27p.
D E F I N   VIII/223/74

1635 PIRET, B.
Possibilités d'industrialisation des États africains et
malgache associés. Volume 5: Madagascar [Possibilities
for the industrialization of the Associated African States
and Madagascar. Volume 5: Madagascar].
Commission EEC, 1966.   2 vols.
F   13081/VIII/B/66, 13082/VIII/B/66

1636 PIRET, B.
Possibilités d'industrialisation des États africains et
malgache associés. Volume 6: Somalie [Possibilities for the

industrialization of the Associated African States and
Madagascar. Volume 6: Somalia].
Commission EEC, 1966.   2 vols.
F   13083/VIII/B/66, 13084/VIII/B/66

1637 PLATE, R.
Répercussions à court terme d'un alignement du prix des
céréales dans la CEE en ce qui concerne l'évolution de la
production de viande de porc, d'œufs et de viande de
volaille [Short-term results of an alignment of cereal
prices in the EEC relating to the development of pork,
eggs and poultry meat production].
Commission EEC, 1964.   41p.   Internal information
on agriculture, 2.
D F   398/VI/1/64

1638 PLATZER, F.
Incidences économiques de certains types
d'investissements structurels en agriculture.
Remembrement, irrigation [Economic effects of certain
types of structural investments in agriculture.
Reparcelling, irrigation].
Commission, 1969.   136p.   Internal information on
agriculture, 53.
D F   13527/VI/69

1639 PLATZER, F.
Le marché foncier et les baux ruraux. Effets des mesures
de réforme des structures agricoles. 1: Italie [The land
market and rural leases. Effects of reform measures of
agricultural structures. 1: Italy].
Commission, 1972.   var. pag.   Internal information
on agriculture, 81.
D F   VI/10832/70

1640 PLATZER, F.
Surfaces agricoles pouvant être mobilisées pour une
réforme de structure [Agricultural areas that could be
mobilised for a structural reform].
Commission, 1973.   336p.   Internal information on
agriculture, 77.
D F   VI/14453/69

1641 PLEBANI, N.
Problèmes des huileries d'olive. Contribution à l'étude de
leur rationalisation [Problems of olive oil refineries.
Contribution to the study of their rationalization].
Commission, 1971.   132p.   Internal information on
agriculture, 78.
F I   VI/1633/71

1642 PLOCHMANN, R.
Forstwirtschaftliche Probleme und deren Auswirkungen
auf die Umwelt in den Mitgliedstaaten der EG. 1:
Ergebnisse und Empfehlungen [Forestry problems and
their implications for the environment in the Member
States of the EC. 1: Results and recommendations / Les
problèmes forestiers et leurs incidences sur
l'environnement dans les États membres des CE. 1:
Résultats et recommandations].
Commission, 1977.   129p.   Information on
agriculture, 25.
D   8881

1643 PLOCHMANN, R.
Forstwirtschaftliche Probleme und deren Auswirkungen
auf die Umwelt in den Mitgliedstaaten der EG. 2: Öffnung
des Waldes für die Allgemeinheit und seine Nutzung als
Erholungsraum [Forestry problems and their implications
for the environment in the Member States of the EC. 2:
Access of the public to forests and their use for
recreational purposes / Les problèmes forestiers et leurs
incidences sur l'environnement dans les États membres
des CE. 2: Ouverture de la forêt au public à des fins
récréatives].
Commission, 1977.   222p.   Information on
agriculture, 31.
D   CH-SA-77-031-DE-C

1644 PLOCHMANN, R.
Forstwirtschaftliche Probleme und deren Auswirkungen
auf die Umwelt in den Mitgliedstaaten der EG. 3: Stand,
Entwicklung und Probleme der Mechanisierung bei der
Bestandsbegründung und Holzernte und deren
Auswirkungen auf die Umwelt [Forestry problems and

their implications for the environment in the Member
States of the EC. 3: Position, development and problems
of mechanization of stand establishment and timber
harvesting / Les problèmes forestiers et leurs incidences
sur l'environnement dans les États membres des CE. 3:
Problèmes de la mécanisation des travaux de boisement et
de récolte en forêt].
Commission, 1977.   202p.   Information on
agriculture, 32.
D   CH-SA-77-032-DE-C

1645 PLOCHMANN, R.
Forstwirtschaftliche Probleme und deren Auswirkungen
auf die Umwelt in den Mitgliedstaaten der EG. 4:
Staatliche Beihilfen (Subventionen) zur Finanzierung
forstlicher Massnahmen im Nichtstaatswald [Forestry
problems and their implications for the environment in the
Member States of the EC. 4: State aid for the financing of
forestry measures in forests not owned by the State / Les
problèmes forestiers et leurs incidences sur
l'environnement dans les États membres des CE. 4: Aides
nationales propres à encourager des mesures en faveur de
la forêt privée].
Commission, 1977.   160p.   Information on
agriculture, 33.
D   CH-SA-77-033-DE-C

1646 PLOCHMANN, R.
Forstwirtschaftliche Probleme und deren Auswirkungen
auf die Umwelt in den Mitgliedstaaten der EG. 5: Systeme
der Waldbesteuerung und die steuerliche Belastung
privater Forstbetriebe [Forestry problems and their
implications for the environment in the Member States of
the EC. 5: Systems of forest taxation and the tax liability
of private forest holdings / Les problèmes forestiers et
leurs incidences sur l'environnnement dans les États
membres des CE. 5: Systèmes d'imposition et charges
fiscales supportées par la forêt privée].
Commission, 1977.   233p.   Information on
agriculture, 34.
D   CH-SA-77-034-DE-C

1647 PLUVINAGE, J.

Essai d'appréciation des conditions d'application et des résultats d'une politique de réforme en agriculture dans des régions agricoles difficiles. 2: Queyras [Attempt at estimating the conditions from the application and results of a reform policy in agriculture in difficult agricultural regions. 2: Queyras].
Commission, 1975.   var. pag.   Internal information on agriculture, 150.
F   VI/1988/75

1648 POHER, A.

Gedenken an Robert Schuman Ehrenpräsident des Europäischen Parlaments [In memory of Robert Schuman honorary president of the European Parliament / En souvenir de Robert Schuman président honoraire du Parlement européen].
EP, 1963.   23p.
D   3371

1648A POISVERT, M.

Aide-mémoire pour la pratique des épreuves d'exercice en médecine du travail [Manual for the practice of exercise tests in industrial medicine].
Commission, 1971.   49p.   Collection: industrial health and medicine, 12.
D F I N   16741

1649 POLAK, J. M.

Étude de droit comparé sur les rapports entre bailleur et preneur à ferme dans les pays de la C.E.E. [Legal study comparing the relations between the landlord and lessee of farmland in the countries of the E.E.C.].
Commission EEC, 1961.   48p.   Studies: agricultural series, 6.
D F I N   8025

1650 POLAK, J. M.

The law and practice relating to pollution control in the Netherlands [Loi et usage concernant le contrôle de la pollution aux Pays-Bas].

Commission, 1976.   184p.

E   0 86010 030 8

POLSKY, E. Vogel-, *see* VOGEL-POLSKY, E.

1651 POOK, W.

Le marché foncier et les baux ruraux. Effets des mesures
de réforme des structures agricoles. 2: R.F. d'Allemagne,
France [The land market and rural leases. Effects of
reform measures of agricultural structures. 2: F.R. of
Germany, France].

Commission, 1972.   var. pag.   Internal information
on agriculture, 82.

F   VI/537/72

1652 POPELIN

Essai d'appréciation des conditions d'application et des
résultats d'une politique de réforme en agriculture dans
des régions agricoles difficiles. 1: Morvan [Attempt at
estimating the conditions from the application and results
of a reform policy in agriculture in difficult agricultural
regions. 1: Morvan].

Commission, 1974.   183p.   Internal information on
agriculture, 138.

F   VI/4572/74

1653 PORNSCHLEGEL, H.

L'analyse des tâches et la qualification du travail.
Principes de base, méthodes et applications dans les
industries de la Communauté européenne du charbon et de
l'acier [Job analysis and work description. Basic
principles, methods and applications in the industries of
the European Coal and Steel Community].

ECSC HA, 1968.   149p.   Studies: industrial
economics, 3.

D F I N   4254

1654 POUS, J. W. de

Rapport sur la capacité concurrentielle de la Communauté
européenne [Report on the competitive capacity of the
European Community].

Commission, 1972.   3 vols.

D F   II/481/72

1655 POUSSIN, C. de la Vallee
Rapports sur les premières mesures proposées en vue
d'une coordination des politiques énergétiques [Reports
on the first measures proposed for a coordination of
energy policies].
ECSC CC, 1961.   var. pag.
D F I N   8013

1656 PRADO, R.
Education statistics 1970–1975 (Statistiques de
l'enseignement 1970–1975).
Eurostat, 1977.   194p.
DK/D/E/F/I/N   CA-22-76-043-6A-C

1657 PRADO, R.
General and vocational training 1973 (Formation générale
et professionnelle 1973).
In Social statistics, 4/1975.   Eurostat, 1976.   126p.
D/E/F/I/N   6936/4

1658 PRAIS, S. J.
A study of the evolution of concentration in the beverages
industry for the United Kingdom. Part one: Industry
structure and concentration, 1969–1974 [Étude sur
l'évolution de la concentration dans l'industrie des
boissons au Royaume-Uni. Partie première: La structure
industrielle et la concentration, 1969–1974].
Commission, 1977.   263p.
E   8942

1659 PRAIS, S. J.
A study of the evolution of concentration in the food
distribution industry for the United Kingdom. Volume 2:
Price surveys [Étude sur l'évolution de la concentration
dans l'industrie de la distribution des produits
alimentaires au Royaume-Uni. Tome 2: Enquêtes de prix].
Commission, 1977.   152p.
E   8762

1660 PRAIS, S. J.
A study of the evolution of concentration in the food
industry for the United Kingdom. Product market

structure [Étude sur l'évolution de la concentration dans l'industrie alimentaire au Royaume-Uni. Structure des marchés de produit].
Commission, 1976.   2 vols.
E   8827, 8709

1661 PRESTON
Dispositions pour faciliter la création d'activités nouvelles. Dispositions juridiques et financières en vigueur dans les États membres et le Royaume-Uni [Arrangements to facilitate the establishment of new activities. Legal and financial arrangements in force in the Member States and United Kingdom].
ECSC HA, 1959.   loose-leaf.
D F I N   2275

1662 PRIEBE, H.
L'emploi agricole dans les pays de la C.E.E. Tome 1: Structure [Agricultural employment in the countries of the E.E.C. Volume 1: Structure].
Commission EEC, 1964.   61p.   Studies: social policy series, 7.
D F I N   8108

1663 PRIEBE, H.
L'emploi agricole dans les pays de la C.E.E. Tome 2: Évolution et perspectives [Agricultural employment in the countries of the E.E.C. Volume 2: Development and prospects].
Commission EEC, 1964.   51p.   Studies: social policy series, 8.
D F I N   8123

1664 PRIEBE, H.
La politique économique régionale, condition du succès de la politique agricole [Regional economic policy, prerequisite for a successful agricultural policy].
Commission EEC, 1961.   20p.   Studies: agricultural series, 4.
D F I N   8020

1665 PRILLEVITZ, F. C.
Le marché foncier et les baux ruraux. Effets des mesures
de réforme des structures agricoles. 3: Pays-Bas [The land
market and rural leases. Effects of reform measures of
agricultural structures. 3: The Netherlands].
Commission, 1972.   2 vols.   Internal information on
agriculture, 88.
D F   VI/6362/70

1666 PROMPERS, L.
Surfaces agricoles pouvant être mobilisées pour une
réforme de structure [Agricultural areas that could be
mobilised for a structural reform].
Commission, 1973.   336p.   Internal information on
agriculture, 77.
D F   VI/14453/69

1667 PROSS, H.
Die Arbeitsbedingungen der erwerbstätigen Frauen der
sechs Mitgliedstaaten der Europäischen Gemeinschaft.
Deutschland [The conditions of work for wage-earning
women in the six Member States of the European
Community. Germany / Les conditions de travail des
femmes salariées dans les six États membres de la
Communauté européenne. Allemagne].
Commission, 1972.   99p.
D   V/164/73

1668 PUGET
Dispositions pour faciliter la création d'activités nouvelles.
Dispositions juridiques et financières en vigueur dans les
États membres et le Royaume-Uni [Arrangements to
facilitate the establishment of new activities. Legal and
financial arrangements in force in the Member States and
United Kingdom].
ECSC HA, 1959.   loose-leaf.
D F I N   2275

1669 PUJOL
Essai d'appréciation des conditions d'application et des
résultats d'une politique de réforme en agriculture dans

des régions agricoles difficiles. 1: Morvan [Attempt at
estimating the conditions from the application and results
of a reform policy in agriculture in difficult agricultural
regions. 1: Morvan].
Commission, 1974.   183p.   Internal information on
agriculture, 138.
F   VI/4572/74

1670 PUPAT, B.
Les organismes groupant les producteurs pour la vente
des fruits et légumes frais dans les États membres de la
CEE. Aspects juridiques. Importance. Rôle économique
[Growers' associations for the sale of fresh fruit and
vegetables in the Member States of the EEC. Legal
aspects. Importance. Economic role].
Commission EEC, 1965.   123p.   Studies:
agricultural series, 19.
D F I N   8139

1671 PUTTE, R. van de
Le financement des investissements et les aspects sociaux
de la reconversion [Financing of investments and social
aspects of conversion].
ECSC HA, 1963.   255p.   Collection: regional
economy and policy. 1: Industrial conversion in Europe, 3.
D F I N   3323

1672 QUENCEZ, G.
Die Länder der Europäischen Gemeinschaft [A geography
of the European Community / La géographie de la
Communauté européenne].
ES, 1966.   245p.
D   3617

1673 QUENCEZ, G.
Les pays de la Communauté européenne et les États ou
territoires qui leur sont associés [The countries of the
European Community and the States or territories which
are associated with them].
ES, 1959.   196p.
F

1674 QUENCEZ, G.
Les pays de la Communauté européenne et leurs
dépendances [The countries of the European Community
and their dependencies].
ES, 1958.   190p.
F   9574

1675 QUENTIN, J.-P.
La C.E.E. L'Europe de l'est [The E.E.C. East Europe].
Bureau (P), 1975.   loose-leaf.   Les documents de
Communauté européenne informations.   L'Europe
par les textes.
F

1676 QUENTIN, J.-P.
Les droits des travailleurs migrants dans la C.E.E. [The
rights of migrant workers in the E.E.C.].
Bureau (P), 1976.   loose-leaf.   Les documents de
Communauté européenne informations.   L'Europe
par les textes.
F

1677 QUERCY, C.
Le consommateur européen: ses préoccupations, ses
aspirations, son information [The interests, aspirations
and knowledge of the European consumer].
Commission, 1976.   175p.
F   X/309/76

1678 QUIEVRIEUX
Essai d'appréciation des conditions d'application et des
résultats d'une politique de réforme en agriculture dans
des régions agricoles difficiles. 1: Morvan [Attempt at
estimating the conditions from the application and results
of a reform policy in agriculture in difficult agricultural
regions. 1: Morvan].
Commission, 1974.   183p.   Internal information on
agriculture, 138.
F   VI/4572/74

1679 QUINN, G.
A study of the evolution of concentration in the Irish food
industry 1968–1973 [Étude sur l'évolution de la
concentration dans l'industrie alimentaire en Irlande
1968–1973].
Commission, 1975.   107p.
E   8696

1680 QUINTHRIE LA MOTHE, T.
Besoins de détente en tant que facteurs pour le
développement régional et agricole [Needs of detente in so
far as the factors for regional and agricultural
development].
Commission, 1973.   var. pag.   Internal information
on agriculture, 116.
F   VI/3808/73

1681 QVISTGAARD, B.
Vocabulary of the staff regulations of officials of the
European Communities and the conditions of employment
of other servants, plus other relevant Community
documents (Vocabulaire du statut des fonctionnaires des
Communautés européennes et du régime applicable aux
autres agents ainsi que de documents administratifs s'y
rapportant).
Commission, 1975.   var. pag.
DK/D/E/F/I/N   IX/1435/1975

1682 RABIER, J.-R.
Le consommateur européen: ses préoccupations, ses
aspirations, son information [The interests, aspirations
and knowledge of the European consumer].
Commission, 1976.   175p.
F   X/309/76

1683 RABIER, J.-R.
The perception of poverty in Europe [La découverte de la
pauvreté en Europe].
Commission, 1977.   123p.
E   V/171/77

1684 RÄDER-ROITZSCH, J. E.
Forstwirtschaftliche Probleme und deren Auswirkungen
auf die Umwelt in den Mitgliedstaaten der EG. 1:
Ergebnisse und Empfehlungen [Forestry problems and
their implications for the environment in the Member
States of the EC. 1: Results and recommendations / Les
problèmes forestiers et leurs incidences sur
l'environnement dans les États membres des CE. 1:
Résultats et recommandations].
Commission, 1977.   129p.   Information on
agriculture, 25.
D   8881

1685 RÄDER-ROITZSCH, J. E.
Forstwirtschaftliche Probleme und deren Auswirkungen
auf die Umwelt in den Mitgliedstaaten der EG. 2: Öffnung
des Waldes für die Allgemeinheit und seine Nutzung als
Erholungsraum [Forestry problems and their implications
for the environment in the Member States of the EC. 2:
Access of the public to forests and their use for
recreational purposes / Les problèmes forestiers et leurs
incidences sur l'environnement dans les États membres
des CE. 2: Ouverture de la forêt au public à des fins
récréatives].
Commission, 1977.   222p.   Information on
agriculture, 31.
D   CH-SA-77-031-DE-C

1686 RÄDER-ROITZSCH, J. E.
Forstwirtschaftliche Probleme und deren Auswirkungen
auf die Umwelt in den Mitgliedstaaten der EG. 3: Stand,
Entwicklung und Probleme der Mechanisierung bei der
Bestandsbegründung und Holzernte und deren
Auswirkungen auf die Umwelt [Forestry problems and
their implications for the environment in the Member
States of the EC. 3: Position, development and problems
of mechanization of stand establishment and timber
harvesting / Les problèmes forestiers et leurs incidences
sur l'environnement dans les États membres des CE. 3:
Problèmes de la mécanisation des travaux de boisement et
de récolte en forêt].

Commission, 1977.   202p.   Information on
agriculture, 32.
D   CH-SA-77-032-DE-C

1687 RÄDER-ROITZSCH, J. E.
Forstwirtschaftliche Probleme und deren Auswirkungen
auf die Umwelt in den Mitgliedstaaten der EG. 4:
Staatliche Beihilfen (Subventionen) zur Finanzierung
forstlicher Massnahmen im Nichtstaatswald [Forestry
problems and their implications for the environment in the
Member States of the EC. 4: State aid for the financing of
forestry measures in forests not owned by the State / Les
problèmes forestiers et leurs incidences sur
l'environnement dans les États membres des CE. 4: Aides
nationales propres à encourager des mesures en faveur de
la forêt privée].
Commission, 1977.   160p.   Information on
agriculture, 33.
D   CH-SA-77-033-DE-C

1688 RÄDER-ROITZSCH, J. E.
Forstwirtschaftliche Probleme und deren Auswirkungen
auf die Umwelt in den Mitgliedstaaten der EG. 5: Systeme
der Waldbesteuerung und die steuerliche Belastung
privater Forstbetriebe [Forestry problems and their
implications for the environment in the Member States of
the EC. 5: Systems of forest taxation and the tax liability
of private forest holdings / Les problèmes forestiers et
leurs incidences sur l'environnement dans les États
membres des CE. 5: Systèmes d'imposition et charges
fiscales supportées par la forêt privée].
Commission, 1977.   233p.   Information on
agriculture, 34.
D   CH-SA-77-034-DE-C

1689 RAINELLI, P.
Analyse régionale des structures socio-économiques
agricoles. Essai de typologie régionale pour la
Communauté des Six. Partie 1: Rapport [Regional
analysis of agricultural socio-economic structures.

Attempt at a regional classification for the Community of
the Six. Part 1: Report].
Commission, 1975.   225p.   Internal information on
agriculture, 139.
F   VI/1189/4/73

1690 RAINELLI, P.
Analyse régionale des structures socio-économiques
agricoles. Essai d'une typologie régionale pour la
Communauté des Six. Partie 2: Données de base par
circonscription [Regional analysis of agricultural
socio-economic structures. Attempt at a regional
classification for the Community of the Six. Part 2: Basic
data by area].
Commission, 1975.   513p.   Internal information on
agriculture, 168.
F   VI/4466/75

RANDACCIO, F. Sanna-, *see* SANNA-RANDACCIO,
F.

1691 RANSOM, C.
East-West relations [Les relations entre l'Est et l'Ouest].
In European studies. Teachers' series, 19.
Commission (L), 1975.   3p.
E   U/74/19

1692 RANSOM, C.
East-West relations in Europe. 2 [Les relations entre
l'Est et l'Ouest en Europe. 2].
In European studies. Teachers' series, 20.
Commission (L), 1975.   4p.
E   U/74/20

1693 RASMUSSEN, W.
L'enseignement au Danemark [Teaching in Denmark].
In Documentation européene. Série pédagogique; série
agricole, 2/1974.   Pr Inf, 1974.   4p.
D F I N   U/A/74/2

1694 RASTOIN, F.
Projections de la production et de la consommation de
produits agricoles—'1977'. 8: France [Projections of
production and consumption of agricultural
products—'1977'. 8: France].
Commission, 1975.   173p.   Internal information on
agriculture, 164.
F   VI/1123/72

1695 RASTOIN, J.-L.
Étude sur l'évolution de la concentration dans la
distribution des produits alimentaires en France [A study
of the evolution of concentration in food distribution in
France].
Commission, 1976.   213p.
F   8763

1696 RASTOIN, J.-L.
Étude sur l'évolution de la concentration dans l'industrie
alimentaire en France [A study of the evolution of
concentration in the food industry in France].
Commission, 1975.   238p.
F   6912

1697 RASTOIN, J.-L.
Étude sur l'évolution de la concentration dans l'industrie
alimentaire en France. Tableaux de concentration [A
study of the evolution of concentration in the food industry
in France. Concentration tables].
Commission, 1975.   307p.
F   8706

1698 RASTOIN, J.-L.
L'évolution de la concentration dans l'industrie de la
brasserie en France [The evolution of concentration in the
brewing industry in France].
Commission, 1976.   99p.
F   8705

1699 RASTOIN, J.-L.
L'évolution de la concentration dans l'industrie des
champagnes et mousseux en France [The evolution of

concentration in the champagne and sparkling wines
industry in France].
Commission, 1977.   127p.
F   8752

1700 RATTI-LENZI, E.
L'enseignement dans les pays de la Communauté
européenne [Teaching in the countries of the European
Community].
Pr Inf, 1970.   223p.   Références bibliographiques.
F   21368/X/70

1701 RAY, P.
Pesticide residues in tobacco and tobacco products. 1:
General report (Les résidus de pesticides dans le tabac et
les produits de tabac. 1: Rapport général).
Commission, 1976.   145p.   Information on
agriculture, 14.
E F   8864

1702 RAY, P.
Les résidus de pesticides dans le tabac et les produits de
tabac. 2: Substances phytosanitaires employées.
Législations. Méthodes d'analyse [Pesticide residues in
tobacco and tobacco products. 2: Plant health substances
employed. Legislation. Methods of analysis].
Commission, 1977.   157p.   Information on
agriculture, 23.
F   8877

1703 RAYMOND, C.
Les conditions d'installation d'entreprises industrielles
dans les États africains et malgache associés. Volume 15:
République centrafricaine [Conditions for the setting-up
of industrial undertakings in the Associated African
States and Madagascar. Volume 15: Central African
Republic]; 2nd ed.
Commission, 1975.   67p.
F   VIII/1245/74

1704 RAYMOND, C.
Les conditions d'installation d'entreprises industrielles
dans les États africains et malgache associés. Volume 16:
République populaire du Congo [Conditions for the
setting-up of industrial undertakings in the Associated
African States and Madagascar. Volume 16: Popular
Republic of the Congo]; 2nd ed.
Commission, 1975.   89p.
F   VIII/1246/74

1705 RAYMOND, C.
Les conditions d'installation d'entreprises industrielles
dans les États africains et malgache associés. Volume 17:
République gabonaise [Conditions for the setting-up of
industrial undertakings in the Associated African States
and Madagascar. Volume 17: Republic of Gabon]; 2nd ed.
Commission, 1975.   87p.
F   VIII/1249/74

1706 RAYMOND, C.
Conditions for the setting-up of industrial undertakings in
the associated African states and Madagascar. Volume 14:
United Republic of Cameroon (Les conditions
d'installation d'entreprises industrielles dans les États
africains et malgache associés. Volume 14: République
unie du Cameroun); 2nd ed.
Commission, 1975.   87p.
E F   VIII/1244/74

1707 REGUL, R.
Les distorsions globales de la concurrence et leurs
répercussions sur le Marché commun [Overall distortions
to competition and its effects on the Common Market].
Commission, 1971.   64p.   Studies:
competition–approximation of legislation series, 11.
D F I N   8280

1708 REGUL, R., chairman
Étude sur la structure et les tendances de l'économie
énergétique dans les pays de la Communauté [Study on

the structure and trends of the energy economy in the
countries of the Community].
ECSC, 1957.   113p.   Studies and documents.
D F I N   1944

1709 REGUL, R.
Mémorandum sur les objectifs de 1965. Méthodes
d'élaboration et résultats détaillés [Memorandum on the
1965 objectives. Methods of elaboration and detailed
results].
ECSC HA, 1962.   540p.   Collection: general
objectives for steel, 1.
D F I N   3017

1710 REGUL, R., chairman
Rapport de la Commission 'Modes de fixation et structure
des prix de l'énergie' [Report of the Commission 'Ways of
fixing and structure of prices for energy'].
ECSC HA, 1959.   43p.
F   3215/59

1711 REGUL, R., chairman
Rapport de la Commission 'Réglementations fiscales et
douanières applicables aux différents produits
énergétiques' [Report of the Commission 'Fiscal and
customs regulations applicable to different energy
products'].
ECSC HA, 1959.   20p.
F   3216/59

1712 REGUL, R., chairman
Study on the structure and trends of the energy economy
in the Community countries [Étude sur la structure et les
tendances de l'économie énergétique dans les pays de la
Communauté].
ECSC HA, 1956.   104p.
E   5880

1713 REGUZZONI, M.
La politique de l'éducation dans la Communauté
européenne. 1: La réforme des systèmes d'enseignement.

2: La formation récurrente [Education policy in the European Community. 1: Reform of teaching systems. 2: Continuing training].
In Documentation européenne. Série pédagogique; série agricole; série syndicale et ouvrière, 1/1974.
Pr Inf, 1974.   8p.
D F I N   U/A/S/74/1

1714 REGUZZONI, M.
Le recyclage des enseignants dans la Communauté européenne [The retraining of teachers in the European Community].
In Documentation européenne. Série pédagogique; série agricole, 3/1974.   Pr Inf, 1974.   4p.
D F I N   U/A/74/3

1715 REGUZZONI, M.
Teacher training in the European Community (La formation des enseignants dans la Communauté européenne).
In European documentation. School series, 2/1976.
Commission, 1976.   23p.
D E F I N   DOC/EUR/76/2

1715A REICHEL, G.
Aide-mémoire pour la pratique des épreuves d'exercice en médecine du travail [Manual for the practice of exercise tests in industrial medicine].
Commission, 1971.   49p.   Collection: industrial health and medicine, 12.
D F I N   16741

1716 REID, I. G.
Forms of cooperation between farms for production and marketing in the new Member States [Formes de collaboration entre exploitations agricoles dans les nouveaux États membres].
Commission, 1976.   340p.   Information on agriculture, 20.
E   8876

1717 REIDENBACH, J.
Possibilités d'industrialisation des États africains et malgache associés. Volume 1: Côte-d'Ivoire, Dahomey, Haute-Volta, Mali, Mauritanie, Niger, Sénégal, Togo [Possibilities for the industrialization of the Associated African States and Madagascar. Volume 1: Ivory Coast, Dahomey, Upper Volta, Mali, Mauritania, Niger, Senegal, Togo].
Commission EEC, 1966.   3 vols.
F   13071/VIII/B/66, 13072/VIII/B/66, 13073/VIII/B/66

1718 REINHARDT, H.
Agriculture de montagne dans la région alpine de la Communauté. 1: Bases et suggestions d'une politique de développement [Hill farming in the alpine region of the Community. 1: Bases and suggestions for a development policy].
Commission, 1973.   78p.   Internal information on agriculture, 100.
D F I   VI/1013/73

1719 REINHARDT, H.
Agriculture de montagne dans la région alpine de la Communauté. 3: R.F. d'Allemagne [Hill farming in the alpine region of the Community. 3: F.R. of Germany].
Commission, 1973.   196p.   Internal information on agriculture, 107.
D F   VI/2316/73

1720 REITHINGER, A.
Possibilités d'industrialisation des États africains et malgache associés. Volume 2: Cameroun, Congo-Brazzaville, Gabon, République centrafricaine, Tchad (Union douanière et économique de l'Afrique centrale) [Possibilities for the industrialization of the Associated African States and Madagascar. Volume 2: Cameroon, Congo-Brazzaville, Gabon, Central African Republic, Chad (Customs and economic union of Central Africa)].
Commission EEC, 1966.   4 vols.
F   13074/VIII/B/66, 13075/VIII/B/66, 13076/VIII/B/66, 13085/VIII/B/66

1721 REMPP, J.-M.
Enquêtes sur les budgets familiaux en France [Surveys on
family budgets in France].
In Budgets familiaux 1963/64. France.
Eurostat, 1966.   pp.27–183.   Social statistics:
special series, 6.
F   3979

1722 RENCKI, G.
The European Community and hill farming (and farming
in certain other less-favoured areas) (La Communauté
européenne et l'agriculture de montagne (et de certaines
autres zones défavorisées)).
In Newsletter on the common agricultural policy,
3/1974.   Pr Inf, 1974.   7p.
D E F I N   X/109/74

1723 REY, J.
Address by M. Jean Rey, member of the Commission of
the European Economic Community, to the Assembly of
Western European Union in Paris on 15 November 1965
(Discours prononcé par Monsieur Jean Rey, membre de la
Commission de la Communauté économique européenne,
le 15 novembre 1965 à Paris, devant l'Assemblée de
l'Union de l'Europe occidentale).
Commission EEC, 1965.   19p.
D E F I N   8173

1724 REY, J.
Address by M. Jean Rey, President of the Commission of
the European Communities, to the Assembly of Western
European Union, Paris, 15 October 1968 [Discours de M.
Jean Rey, Président de la Commission des Communautés
européennes, devant l'Assemblée de l'Union de l'Europe
occidentale, Paris, le 15 octobre 1968].
Commission, 1968.   11p.
E   8250

1725 REY, J.
Discours de M. Jean Rey, Président de la Commission des
Communautés Européennes devant le Parlement

Européen. Strasbourg, 15 mai 1968 [Address by Mr. Jean
Rey, President of the Commission of the European
Communities to the European Parliament. Strasbourg,
May 15 1968].
Commission, 1968.   13p.
F

1726 REY, J.
Discours de M. le président Rey devant le Parlement
européen. Exposé du programme de la Commission pour
l'année 1970 (Strasbourg, 4 février 1970). Exposé sur le
Rapport général de la Commission (Strasbourg, 10 mars
1970) [Address by President Rey to the European
Parliament. Outline of the Commission's programme for
the year 1970 (Strasbourg, February 4 1970). Statement
on the General Report of the Commission (Strasbourg,
March 10 1970)].
Commission, 1970.   32p.
D F I N   8311

1727 REY, J.
Discours prononcé par M. Jean Rey, membre de la
Commission de la Communauté économique européenne,
le 23 juin 1964 à Rome, devant l'Assemblée de l'Union de
l'Europe occidentale [Speech by Mr. Jean Rey, member of
the Commission of the European Economic Community,
to the Assembly of the Western European Union in Rome
on June 23 1964].
Commission EEC, 1964.   16p.
F   8127

1728 REY, J.
Economic union: the second phase of European integration
[L'union économique: la phase deuxième de la construction
européenne].
Inf Ser, 1968.   Community topics, 31.
E

1729 REY, J.
Exposé devant le Parlement européen, le 12 mars 1969, à
l'occasion de la présentation du 2e Rapport général sur

l'activité des Communautés en 1969 [Report to the
European Parliament, March 12th 1969 on the occasion of
the presentation of the Second General Report on the
activity of the Communities in 1969].
Commission, 1969.   10p.
F

1730 REY, J.
Outlook on the development of the economic union.
Address by M. Jean Rey, President of the Commission of
the European Communities to the European Parliament
at Strasbourg, 15 May 1968 (Perspectives de
développement de l'union économique. Discours de M.
Jean Rey, président de la Commission des Communautés
européennes, prononcé devant le Parlement européen à
Strasbourg, le 15 mai 1968).
Commission, 1968.   24p.
D E F I N   8238

1731 REY, J.
W. Hallstein and J. Rey, Freemen of the City of Brussels.
Speeches given on 2 December 1971 at the conferring of
the Freedom of the City of Brussels on the former
Presidents of the Commission of the European Economic
Community and of the Commission of the European
Communities (W. Hallstein et J. Rey, citoyens de la ville
de Bruxelles. Discours prononcés le 2 décembre 1971 à
l'occasion de la remise du diplôme de citoyen d'honneur de
la ville de Bruxelles aux anciens présidents de la
Commission de la Communauté économique européenne et
de la Commission des Communautés européennes).
Commission, 1972.   20p.
D E F I N   8368

1732 REYNAUD, R.
Rapport d'introduction [Introductory report].
ECSC, 1960.   16p.   Intergovernmental Conference
on Industrial Redevelopment: introductory report.
F   5458

1733 RIBAS, J.-J., chairman
L'évolution financière de la sécurité sociale dans les États
membres de la Communauté. 1965–1970–1975. lère Partie:
Rapport de synthèse [Financial development of social
security in the Member States of the Community.
1965–1970–1975. First Part: Summary report].
Commission, 1973.   55p.
D F I N   8375

1734 RIBAS, J.-J., chairman
Le financement de la sécurité sociale dans l'agriculture
[The financing of social security in agriculture].
Commission, 1970.   83p.   Studies: social policy
series, 20.
D F I N   8274

1735 RIBAS, J.-J.
Social security in the European Community [La sécurité
sociale dans la Communauté européenne].
Inf Ser, 1965.   15p.   Community topics, 18.
E

1736 RICCI, C.
Mémorandum sur les objectifs de 1965. Méthodes
d'élaboration et résultats détaillés [Memorandum on the
1965 objectives. Methods of elaboration and detailed
results].
ECSC HA, 1962.   540p.   Collection: general
objectives for steel, 1.
D F I N   3017

1737 RICHARDS, J.
Europe's architectural heritage [L'héritage architectural
de l'Europe].
In European studies. Teachers' series, 21.
Commission (L), 1975.   4p.
E   U/75/21

1738 RIEDEL, J.
Possibilités de création d'industries exportatrices dans les
États africains et malgache associés. Produits

électro-mécaniques. Produits électroniques [Possibilities for the establishment of exporting industries in the Associated African States and Madagascar. Electro-mechanical products. Electronic products].
Commission, 1975.   3 vols.
F   VIII/224/74

1739 RIEDEL, J.
Possibilités de création d'industries exportatrices dans les États africains et malgache associés. Produits électro-mécaniques. Produits électroniques. Rapport de synthèse [Possibilities for the establishment of exporting industries in the Associated African States and Madagascar. Electro-mechanical products. Electronic products. Summary report].
Commission, 1975   23p.
D E F I N   VIII/224/74

1740 RIEMANN, F.
Surfaces agricoles pouvant être mobilisées pour une réforme de structure [Agricultural areas that could be mobilised for a structural reform].
Commission, 1973.   336p.   Internal information on agriculture, 77.
D F   VI/14453/69

1741 RIFFAULT, H.
Le consommateur européen: ses préoccupations, ses aspirations, son information [The interests, aspirations and knowledge of the European consumer].
Commission, 1976.   175p.
F   X/309/76

1742 RIFFAULT, H.
The perception of poverty in Europe [La découverte de la pauvreté en Europe].
Commission, 1977.   123p.
E   V/171/77

1743 RIFFAULT, H.
Science and European public opinion [La science et
l'opinion publique européenne].
Commission, 1977.   98p.
E   XII/922/77

1744 RIJKEBDER, R. C.
La consommation d'énergie des moyens de transport.
Étude comparative [Energy consumption of various
means of transport. Comparative study].
Commission, 1974.   120p.
F   VII/76/74

1745 RINTELEN, P.
Agriculture de montagne dans la région alpine de la
Communauté. 1: Bases et suggestions d'une politique de
développement [Hill farming in the alpine region of the
Community. 1: Bases and suggestions for a development
policy].
Commission, 1973.   78p.   Internal information on
agriculture, 100.
D F I   VI/1013/73

1746 RINTELEN, P.
Agriculture de montagne dans la région alpine de la
Communauté. 3: R.F. d'Allemagne [Hill farming in the
alpine region of the Community. 3: F.R. of Germany].
Commission, 1973.   196p.   Internal information on
agriculture, 107.
D F   VI/2316/73

1747 RIPE
La formation professionnelle dans les houillères des pays
de la Communauté [Vocational training in the coal mines
of the countries of the Community].
ECSC HA, 1956.   514p.
F   1669

1748 RITTENBRUCH, K.
Problèmes de la structure économique de la Sarre
[Problems of the economic structure of the Saar].

ECSC HA, 1967.   196p.   Collection: regional
economy and policy. 2: Development and conversion
programme, 9.
D F   4098

1749 RIXHON, L.
Conséquences écologiques de l'application des techniques
modernes de production en agriculture [Ecological results
from the application of modern production techniques in
agriculture].
Commission, 1974.   var. pag.   Internal information
on agriculture, 137.
D F   VI/3722/74

1750 ROBERTS, E.
Consumers in the Common Market [Les consommateurs
dans le Marché commun].
In European studies. Teachers' series, 22.
Commission (L), 1975.   4p.
E   U/75/22

1751 ROBINET, A.
La promotion commerciale des cuirs et peaux originaires
des États africains associés de la zone soudano-sahelienne
sur le marché de la CEE [Commercial promotion of hides
and skins originating from the Sudan-Sahara area of the
Associated African States on the EEC market].
Commission, 1968.   3 vols.
F   14455/VIII/B/66

1752 ROBINET, A.
La promotion commerciale des cuirs et peaux originaires
des États africains associés de la zone soudano-sahelienne
sur le marché de la CEE. Résumé [Commercial promotion
of hides and skins originating from the Sudan-Sahara area
of the Associated African States on the EEC market.
Summary].
Commission, 1968.   18p.
D E F I   14455/VIII/B/68

1753 ROBYN, G.
Possibilités d'industrialisation des États africains et malgache associés. Volume 3: République démocratique du Congo [Possibilities for the industrialization of the Associated African States and Madagascar. Volume 3: Democratic Republic of the Congo].
Commission EEC, 1966.   2 vols.
F   13077/VIII/B/66, 13078/VIII/B/66

1754 ROBYN, G.
Possibilités d'industrialisation des États africains et malgache associés. Volume 4: Burundi, Rwanda et région Centre-orientale du Congo (Kinshasa) (région des Grands Lacs) [Possibilities for the industrialization of the Associated African States and Madagascar. Volume 4: Burundi, Rwanda and Centre-eastern region of the Congo (Kinshasa) (region of the Great Lakes)].
Commission EEC, 1966.   2 vols.
F   13079/VIII/B/66, 13080/VIII/B/66

1755 ROBYN, G.
Possibilités d'industrialisation des États africains et malgache associés. Volume 6: Somalie [Possibilities for the industrialization of the Associated African States and Madagascar. Volume 6: Somalia].
Commission EEC, 1966.   2 vols
F   13083/VIII/B/66, 13084/VIII/B/66

1756 ROCHE, B.
Le consommateur européen: ses préoccupations, ses aspirations, son information [The interests, aspirations and knowledge of the European consumer].
Commission, 1976.   175p.
F   X/309/76

1757 ROCHEREAU, H.
Relations between the African States and Madagascar and the EEC. Address by M. Henri Rochereau, Member of the Commission of the European Economic Community, chairman of the 'Overseas Development' Group to the symposium on Africa organized by the Afrika Instituut,

The Hague, 29 October 1962 (Les problèmes souléves par
les relations entre les états Africains et malgache et la
C.E.E. Discours prononcé par M. Henri Rochereau,
membre de la Commission de la Communauté Économique
Européenne, à l'occasion de la journée de l'Afrique,
organisée par l'Africa Instituut, La Haye, 29 octobre
1962).
Commission EEC, 1963.   19p.
E F   8073

RODENACKER, A. Kruse-, *see*
KRUSE-RODENACKER, A.

1758 RODIÈRE, R.
Le droit des sociétés dans ses rapports avec la
concentration [The right of firms in their relations with
concentration].
Commission, 1967.   99p.   Studies: competition
series, 5.
D F I N   8217

1759 ROEMEN, H. C. W.
La conduite sur place des opérations de conversion
industrielle [On-the-spot direction of industrial conversion
operations].
ECSC HA, 1963.   352p.   Collection: regional
economy and policy. 1: Industrial conversion in Europe, 4.
D F I N   3324

1760 ROIDER
Les conditions d'installation d'entreprises industrielles
dans les États africains et malgache associés. Volume 3:
République du Mali [Conditions for the setting-up of
industrial undertakings in the Associated African States
and Madagascar. Volume 3: Republic of Mali].
Commission, 1972.   80p.
F   VIII/1313/72

1761 ROIDER
Les conditions d'installation d'entreprises industrielles
dans les États africains et malgache associés. Volume 4:

République du Niger [Conditions for the setting-up of industrial undertakings in the Associated African States and Madagascar. Volume 4: Republic of the Niger].
Commission, 1972.   80p.
F   VIII/1314/72

1762 ROIDER
Les conditions d'installation d'entreprises industrielles dans les États africains et malgache associés. Volume 5: République de Haute-Volta [Conditions for the setting-up of industrial undertakings in the Associated African States and Madagascar. Volume 5: Republic of Upper Volta].
Commission, 1972.   88p.
F   VIII/1315/72

1763 ROIDER
Les conditions d'installation d'entreprises industrielles dans les États africains et malgache associés. Volume 10: République du Tchad [Conditions for the setting-up of industrial undertakings in the Associated African States and Madagascar. Volume 10: Republic of Chad].
Commission, 1972.   86p.
F   VIII/1320/72

ROITZSCH, J. E. Räder-, *see* RÄDER-ROITZSCH, J. E.

ROLANDINO, F. Massa-, *see* MASSA-ROLANDINO, F.

1764 ROLIN
La réparation des conséquences dommageables d'une violation des articles 85 et 86 du traité instituant la CEE [Compensation for damage suffered through infringement of Articles 85 and 86 of the Treaty establishing the EEC].
Commission EEC, 1966.   74p.   Studies: competition series, 1.
D F I N   8153

1765 ROMAGNOLI, E.
Accès à l'exploitation agricole. Dispositions et pratiques existant dans les États membres de la CEE en vue de

l'obtention et de l'aménagement d'une exploitation
agricole [Access to the farm. Arrangements and practices
existing in the Member States of the EEC for obtaining
and managing a farm].
Commission, 1967.   var. pag.   Internal information
on agriculture, 21.
D F   8325/VI/66

1766 ROMPUY, V. van
Concepts et méthodes de comparaison du revenu de la
population agricole avec celui d'autres groupes de
professions comparables [Concepts and methods of
comparison of the income of the agricultural population
with that of other groups of comparable occupations].
Commission, 1968.   302p.   Internal information on
agriculture, 33.
D F   16788/VI/68

1767 ROMUS, P.
Économie régionale des États de la Communauté
européenne [Regional economy of the States of the
European Community].
Pr Inf, 1975.   24p.
F   8467

1768 RONCHETTI, S.
Enquête sur les salaires dans les industries de la
Communauté économique européenne. Année 1959
[Survey on wages in the industries of the European
Economic Community. 1959].
In Social statistics, 3/1961.   Eurostat, 1961.   170p.
D F I N

1769 RONCHETTI, S.
Enquête sur les salaires dans les industries de la
Communauté économique européenne. Année 1959. Étude
sur les revenus des ouvriers [Survey on wages in the
industries of the European Economic Community. 1959.
Study on the incomes of workers].
In Social statistics, 3/1962.   Eurostat, 1962.   144p.
D/F, I/N

1770 RONCHETTI, S.
Enquête sur les salaires dans les industries de la
Communauté économique européenne. Année 1960
[Survey on wages in the industries of the European
Economic Community. 1960].
In Social statistics, 1/1963.   Eurostat, 1963.   383p.
D/F, I/N   3285

1771 RONCHETTI, S.
Enquête sur les salaires dans les industries de la
Communauté économique européenne 1961 [Survey on
wages in the industries of the European Economic
Community 1961].
In Social statistics, 2/1964.   Eurostat, 1964.   495p.
D/F, I/N   3484

1772 RONCHETTI, S.
Enquête sur les salaires dans les industries de la
Communauté économique européenne 1962 [Survey on
wages in the industries of the European Economic
Community 1962].
In Social statistics, 5/1964.   Eurostat, 1964.   519p.
D/F, I/N

1773 RONCHETTI, S.
Enquête sur les salaires dans les industries de la
Communauté économique européenne 1963 [Survey on
wages in the industries of the European Economic
Community 1963].
In Social statistics, 6/1965.   Eurostat, 1965.   365p.
D/F, I/N

1774 RONCHETTI, S.
Enquête sur les salaires dans les industries de la
Communauté économique européenne 1964 [Survey on
wages in the industries of the European Economic
Community 1964].
In Social statistics, 5/1966.   Eurostat, 1966.   445p.
D/F, I/N   3996

1775 RONCHETTI, S.
Harmonized statistics of average hourly gross wages in
the industries of the European Communities April 1964
(Statistiques harmonisées des gains horaires moyens
bruts dans les industries des Communautés européennes
Avril 1964).
In Social statistics, 3/1965.　　Eurostat, 1965.　　105p.
D E F I N

1776 RONCHETTI, S.
Prix, taux d'équivalence de pouvoir d'achat à la
consommation et revenus réels dans les pays de la
C.E.C.A. 1954–1958 [Prices, equivalent rates of
purchasing power from consumption and real incomes
in the countries of the E.C.S.C. 1954–1958].
In Social statistics, 2/1960.　　Eurostat, 1960.　　219p.
D F I N　　2500

1777 RONCHETTI, S.
Salaires CECA 1964. Les coûts de la main-d'œuvre et les
revenus des ouvriers dans les industries de la CECA.
Année 1964 et évolution 1954–1964 [ECSC wages 1964.
Labour costs and the incomes of workers in the industries
of the ECSC. 1964 and development 1954–1964].
In Social statistics, 2/1966.　　Eurostat, 1966.　　227p.
D/F, I/N

1778 RONCHI, L.
Les accidents du travail dans l'industrie sidérurgique
1960–1966 [Work accidents in the iron and steel industry
1960–1966].
In Statistical studies and surveys, 3/1968.
Eurostat, 1968.　　pp.67–173.
D/F/I/N　　4515

1779 RONCHI, L.
Les accidents du travail dans l'industrie sidérurgique
1960–1967 [Work accidents in the iron and steel industry
1960–1967].
In Social statistics, 3/1969.　　Eurostat, 1969.
pp. 167–287.
D/F/I/N　　4691

1780 RONCHI, L.
Les accidents du travail dans l'industrie sidérurgique
1960–1970 [Work accidents in the iron and steel industry
1960–1970].
In Social statistics, 5–6/1971.
Eurostat, 1972.   pp.1–139.
D/F/I/N   5547

1781 RONCHI, L.
Les accidents du travail dans l'industrie sidérurgique
1960–1971 [Work accidents in the iron and steel industry
1960–1971].
In Social statistics, 6 bis/1972.
Eurostat, 1973.   147p.
D/F/I/N   5874-A

1782 RONCHI, L.
Enquête sur le siège et la nature des lésions provoquées
par les accidents du travail (Industrie sidérurgique) 1970
[Survey on the centre and nature of injuries caused by
work accidents (Iron and Steel Industry) 1970].
In Social statistics, 5–6/1971.
Eurostat, 1972.   pp.141–277.
D/F/I/N   5547

1783 ROOSE, W. van
Volume et degré de l'emploi dans la pêche maritime
[Volume and extent of employment in sea fishing].
Commission, 1968.   var. pag.   Internal information
on agriculture, 32.
D F   6993/VI/68

1784 ROSA, L. de
Le financement des investissements et les aspects sociaux
de la reconversion [Financing of investments and social
aspects of conversion].
ECSC HA, 1963.   255p.   Collection: regional
economy and policy. 1: Industrial conversion in Europe, 3.
D F I N   3323

1785 ROSKAM, J.
Modèles d'analyse d'entreprises de polyculture-élevage
bovin. Données technico-économiques de base. Région
Volvestre (France) [Models for analysis of mixed crop and
cattle farms. Basic technico-economic data. Volvestre
region (France)].
Commission, 1977.   102p.   Information on
agriculture, 39.
F   CB-NA-77-039-FR-C

1786 ROSSI, A.
La dynamique du Marché Commun [The dynamics of the
Common Market].
Bureau (P), 1964.   Les documents de Communauté
européenne, 26.
F

ROSSI, G. di, *see* DI ROSSI, G.

1787 ROTONDI
La réparation des conséquences dommageables d'une
violation des articles 85 et 86 du traité instituant la CEE
[Compensation for damage suffered through infringement
of Articles 85 and 86 of the Treaty establishing the EEC].
Commission EEC, 1966.   74p.   Studies: competition
series, 1.
D F I N   8153

1788 ROTTIER, G.
Tendances de la production et de la consommation en
denrées alimentaires dans la C.E.E. 1956–1965 [Trends in
food production and consumption in the E.E.C.
1956–1965].
Commission EEC, 1960.   266p.   Studies:
agricultural series, 2.
D F I N   8005

1789 ROUCHY
Les conditions d'installation d'entreprises industrielles
dans les États africains et malgache associés. Volume 9:
République unie du Cameroun [Conditions for the

setting-up of industrial undertakings in the Associated
African States and Madagascar. Volume 9: United
Republic of Cameroon].
Commission, 1972.   94p.
F   VIII/1319/72

1790 ROUCHY
Les conditions d'installation d'entreprises industrielles
dans les États africains et malgache associés. Volume 11:
République Centrafricaine [Conditions for the setting-up
of industrial undertakings in the Associated African
States and Madagascar. Volume 11: Central African
Republic].
Commission, 1972.   68p.
F   VIII/1321/72

1791 ROUCHY
Les conditions d'installation d'entreprises industrielles
dans les États africains et malgache associés. Volume 12:
République gabonaise [Conditions for the setting-up of
industrial undertakings in the Associated African States
and Madagascar. Volume 12: Republic of Gabon].
Commission, 1972.   84p.
F   VIII/1322/72

1792 ROUCHY
Les conditions d'installation d'entreprises industrielles
dans les États africains et malgache associés. Volume 13:
République populaire du Congo [Conditions for the
setting-up of industrial undertakings in the Associated
African States and Madagascar. Volume 13: Popular
Republic of the Congo].
Commission, 1972.   80p.
F   VIII/1323/72

1793 ROUCHY
Les conditions d'installation d'entreprises industrielles
dans les États africains et malgache associés. Volume 1:
République du Dahomey [Conditions for the setting-up of
industrial undertakings in the Associated African States

and Madagascar. Volume 1: Republic of Dahomey]; 2nd
ed.
Commission, 1975.   78p.
F   VIII/1248/74

1794 ROUCHY
Les conditions d'installation d'entreprises industrielles
dans les États africains et malgache associés. Volume 6:
République du Niger [Conditions for the setting-up of
industrial undertakings in the Associated African States
and Madagascar. Volume 6: Republic of the Niger]; 2nd
ed.
Commission, 1975.   69p.
F   VIII/1255/74

1795 ROUY, chairman
L'augmentation de la production de viande bovine dans les
pays de la C.E.E. Étude sur les possibilités techniques et
les conditions économiques [Increasing beef production in
the countries of the E.E.C. Study on the technical
possibilities and economic conditions].
Commission EEC, 1961.   215p.   Studies:
agricultural series, 5.
D F   8022

1796 ROY, G.
Possibilités d'industrialisation des États africains et
malgache associés. Volume 1: Côte-d'Ivoire, Dahomey,
Haute-Volta, Mali, Mauritanie, Niger, Sénégal, Togo
[Possibilities for the industrialization of the Associated
African States and Madagascar. Volume 1: Ivory Coast,
Dahomey, Upper Volta, Mali, Mauritania, Niger,
Senegal, Togo].
Commission EEC, 1966.   3 vols.
F   13071/VIII/B/66, 13072/VIII/B/66,
      13073/VIII/B/66

1797 ROY, G.
Pré-sélection des industries d'exportation susceptibles
d'être implantées dans les États africains et malgache
associés. Rapport [Short-listing of exporting industries

capable of being established in the Associated African
States and Madagascar. Report].
Commission, 1971.   179p.
D F I N   847/VIII/71

1798 RUAULT, J. P.
L'information relative aux revenus et aux patrimoines
dans les pays de la Communauté [Information relating to
incomes and inheritances in the countries of the
Community].
Commission, 1973.   43p.   Studies: social policy
series, 22.
D F I N   8377

1799 RUITER, T. de
Surface agricoles pouvant être mobilisées pour une
réforme de structure [Agricultural areas that could be
mobilised for a structural reform].
Commission, 1973.   336p.   Internal information on
agriculture, 77.
D F   VI/14453/69

1800 RUNCI, M.
Tableaux 'Entrees-Sorties' pour les pays de la
Communauté Économique Européenne ['Input-Output'
tables for the countries of the European Economic
Community].
Eurostat, 1964.   var. pag.
D F

1801 RUNCI, M.
Tableaux 'Entrées-Sorties' pour les pays de la
Communauté Économique Européenne. Seconde version
['Input-Output' tables for the countries of the European
Economic Community. Second version].
Eurostat, 1965.   var. pag.
D F

1802 RUOZI, R.
Vertical integration and the use of contracts in
agriculture. 2: Italy (Intégration verticale et contrats en
agriculture. 2: Italie).

Commission, 1973.   103p.   Internal information on agriculture, 119.
E F I   VI/450/74

1803 RUSSO, V.
Étude sur les qualités des carcasses de bovins en Italy [Study on the qualities of beef carcasses in Italy].
In Agricultural statistical studies, 7.
Eurostat, 1970.   52p.
D F I   16843

1804 RUTTEN, F. J. T.
Onderzoek in de Nederlandse kolenmijnen [Research in the Dutch coalmines / Recherche dans les charbonnages néerlandais].
Commission, 1967.   162p.   Collection: occupational physiology and psychology, 3/4.
N   13749

1805 RÜTTIGER, K.
Les aciéries [The steel-works].
Commission, 1971.   283p.   New technical processes in the iron and steel industry: a personal training manual, 3.   Studies: vocational training.
D F I N   17433

1806 SACCHETTO, A.
La scuola e l'unità europea [Education and European unity / L'enseignement et l'unité européenne].
Uff ESCC, 1957.   103p.
I

1807 SADLER-FORSTER, A.
La conduite sur place des opérations de conversion industrielle [On-the-spot direction of industrial conversion operations].
ECSC HA, 1963.   352p.   Collection: regional economy and policy. 1: Industrial conversion in Europe, 4.
D F I N   3324

1808 SADLER-FORSTER, A.
Location of industry policy in Britain (La politique
d'implantation industrielle en Grande-Bretagne).
ECSC HA, 1965.   64p.   Pamphlets on industrial
conversion, 6.
D E F   11456

1808A SADOUL, P.
Aide-mémoire pour la pratique des épreuves d'exercice
en médecine du travail [Manual for the practice of
exercise tests in industrial medicine].
Commission, 1971.   49p.   Collection: industrial
health and medicine, 12.
D F I N   16741

1809 SADOUL, P.
Physiopathologie cardio-respiratoire. Étude synthétique
sur la base des travaux menés au cours du 2ᵉ programme
de médecine du travail [Cardio-respiratory
physiopathology. Summary study on the basis of work
carried out in the course of the second programme of
industrial medicine].
Commission, 1968.   88p.   Collection: industrial
health and medicine, 8.
D F I N   14662

1810 SAHNER, W.
Étude sur la structure sociale et économique de la région
Sieg-Lahn-Dill [Study on the social and economic
structure of the Sieg-Lahn-Dill region].
Commission, 1968.   160p.   Collection: regional
economy and policy. 2: Development and conversion
programme, 10,
D F   4252

1811 SAINT-GEOURS, J.
Le financement des investissements et les aspects sociaux
de la reconversion [Financing of investments and social
aspects of conversion].
ECSC HA, 1963.   255p.   Collection: regional
economy and policy. 1: Industrial conversion in Europe, 3.
D F I N   3323

1812 SAIVE, R.
Conséquences écologiques de l'application des techniques modernes de production en agriculture [Ecological results from the application of modern production techniques in agriculture].
Commission, 1974.   var. pag.   Internal information on agriculture, 137.
D F   VI/3722/74

1813 SALVATORE, A.
Studio sull'evoluzione della concentrazione nel settore dei detersivi per uso domestico in Italia dal 1968 al 1975 [A study of the evolution of concentration in the sector of detergents for domestic use from 1968 to 1975 in Italy / Étude sur l'évolution de la concentration dans le secteur des détergents pour la maison de 1968 à 1975 en Italie].
Commission, 1977.   249p.
I   CB-NL-77-012-IT-C

1814 SAMKALDEN, I.
La réparation des conséquences dommageables d'une violation des articles 85 et 86 du traité instituant la CEE [Compensation for damage suffered through infringement of Articles 85 and 86 of the Treaty establishing the EEC].
Commission EEC, 1966.   74p.   Studies: competition series, 1.
D F I N   8153

1815 SAMKOW, N.
L'édition dans la CEE [Publishing in the EEC].
In Documentation européenne. Série pédagogique; série agricole; série syndicale et ouvrière, 3/1973.
Pr Inf, 1973.   4p.
D F I N   U/A/S 73/3

1816 SANDERS, P.
Projet d'un statut des sociétés anonymes européennes [Plan for a statute for a European joint-stock company].
Commission, 1967.   132p.   Studies: competition series, 6.
D F I N   8213

1817 SANDERS, P.
Société anonyme européenne. Projet d'un Statut d'une
société anonyme européenne. Commentaires [European
joint-stock company. Plan for a Statute for a European
joint-stock company. Commentaries].
Commission EEC, 1967.   422p.
F   1100/IV/67

1818 SANDERS, P.
Société anonyme européenne. Projet d'un Statut d'une
société anonyme européenne. Textes [European
joint-stock company. Plan for a Statute for a European
joint-stock company. Texts].
Commission EEC, 1966.   206p.
F   16205/IV/66

1819 SANDMANN, G.
Temporary-employment business. Comparative study of
provisions laid down by law and regulation in force in the
Member States of the European Communities (Le travail
temporaire. Étude comparée des dispositions législatives
et réglementaires en vigueur dans les États membres des
Communautés européennes).
Commission, 1976.   69p.   Studies: social policy
series, 25.
D E F   8723

SANDRI, L. Levi, *see* LEVI SANDRI, L.

1819A SANNA-RANDACCIO, F.
Aide-mémoire pour la pratique des épreuves d'exercice
en médecine du travail [Manual for the practice of
exercise tests in industrial medicine].
Commission, 1971.   49p.   Collection: industrial
health and medicine, 12.
D F I N   16741

1820 SANTMAN
Management, organization and methods in the American
iron and steel industry. E.C.S.C. fact finding mission to
U.S.A. March–April 1957 [Direction, organisation et

méthodes dans la sidérurgie des États-Unis. C.E.C.A.
mission des faits-fournitures aux États-Unis mars–avril
1957].
ECSC HA, 1958.   364p.
E   4444

1821 SARNIGUET
Possibilités de création d'industries exportatrices dans les
États africains et malgache associés. Produits de
l'élevage. Viandes, cuirs et peaux, chaussures, articles en
cuir [Possibilities for the establishment of exporting
industries in the Associated African States and
Madagascar. Products from rearing. Meat, hides and
skins, shoes, leather articles].
Commission, 1974.   5 vols.
F   VIII/223/74

1822 SARNIGUET
Possibilités de création d'industries exportatrices dans les
États africains et malgache associés. Produits de
l'élevage. Viandes, cuirs et peaux, chaussures, articles en
cuir. Rapport de synthèse [Possibilities for the
establishment of exporting industries in the Associated
African States and Madagascar. Products from rearing.
Meat, hides and skins, shoes, leather articles. Summary
report].
Commission, 1975.   27p.
D E F I N   VIII/223/74

1823 SAROLEA, R.
Phraseological vocabulary compiled on the basis of the
Treaties establishing the European Communities
(Vocabulaire phraséologique établi sur la base des Traités
instituant les Communautés européennes); 2nd ed.
Commission, 1974.   var. pag.
DK/D/E/F/I/N   IX/1572/73

1824 SAROLEA, R.
Vocabulary of the staff regulations of officials of the
European Communities and the conditions of employment
of other servants, plus other relevant Community

documents (Vocabulaire du statut des fonctionnaires des Communautés européennes et du régime applicable aux autre agents ainsi que de documents administratifs s'y rapportant).
Commission, 1975.   var. pag.
DK/D/E/F/I/N   IX/1435/1975

1825 SASSEN, E. M. J. A.
Ensuring fair competition in the European Community [Assurant la concurrence équitable dans la Communauté européenne].
Inf Ser, 1970.   8p.   Community topics, 35.
E

1826 SAUVEUR, B.
Water content of frozen or deep-frozen poultry.
Examination of methods of determination (Teneur en eau de volailles congelées ou surgelées. Examen de méthodes de dosage).
Commission, 1976.   196p.   Information on agriculture, 15.
E F   8865

1827 SAVARY, A.
Fabrications nouvelles [New manufactures].
ECSC HA, 1965.   182p.   Collection: regional economy and policy. 1: Industrial conversion in Europe, 11.
D F I N   3709

1828 SAVIGNON, F.
Rapport général sur le Second Avant-projet de Convention relative au brevet européen pour le Marché commun [General report on the Second Preliminary Draft of a Convention for the European Patent for the Common Market].
In Second avant-projet de convention relative au brevet européen pour le Marché commun et documents annexes.   Council, 1971.   pp.165–170.
D/F/I/N   17360

1829 SCANNELL, Y.
The law and practice relating to pollution control in
Ireland [Loi et usage concernant le contrôle de la pollution
en Irlande].
Commission, 1976.   223p.
E   0 86010 031 6

1830 SCARASCIA MUGNOZZA, C.
Address by Mr. Carlo Scarascia Mugnozza,
Vice-President of the Commission of the European
Communities, to the European Parliament on 12 February
1974. Presentation of the General Report for 1973 and
Programme of the Commission for 1974. Strasbourg. 12
February 1974 (Discours prononcé le 12 février 1974
devant le Parlement européen par M. Carlo Scarascia
Mugnozza, vice-président de la Commission des
Communautés européennes. Présentation du Rapport
général 1973 et programme de la Commission pour l'année
1974. Strasbourg, 12 février 1974).
Commission, 1974.   14p.
DK D E F I N   8441

1831 SCARASCIA MUGNOZZA, C.
Bilans 1974 and perspectives 1975 (Bilan 1974 et
perspectives 1975).
In Information: transport, 83/1975.
Pr Inf, 1975.   8p.
D E F I N   44/X/75

1832 SCARASCIA MUGNOZZA, C.
Speech by Mr. Scarascia-Mugnozza, Vice-President of the
Commission, presenting to the European Parliament the
7th Report of the Activities of the European Communities
(Discours de M. Scarascia Mugnozza, vice-président de la
Commission, présentant au Parlement européen le 7e
Rapport annuel d'activité de la Communauté européenne).
In Information: political affairs, 54/1974.
Pr Inf, 1974.   12p.
D E F I N   91/X/74

1833 SCELBA, M.
Celebration of the fiftieth anniversary of the international labour organisation [Commémoration de l'anniversaire cinquantième de l'organisation internationale du travail].
EP, 1969.   32p.
E

1834 SCELBA, M.
The European Community and the development of its institutions. Speech delivered in Florence on 26 April 1970 (La Communauté européenne et ses développements institutionnels. Discours prononcé à Florence, le 26 avril 1970).
EP, 1970.   16p.
D E F I N

1835 SCHÄDLER
Possibilités de création d'industries exportatrices dans les États africains et malgache associés. Produits de l'élevage. Viandes, cuirs et peaux, chaussures, articles en cuir [Possibilities for the establishment of exporting industries in the Associated African States and Madagascar. Products from rearing. Meat, hides and skins, shoes, leather articles].
Commission, 1974.   5 vols.
F   VIII/223/74

1836 SCHÄDLER
Possibilités de création d'industries exportatrices dans les États africains et malgache associés. Produits de l'élevage. Viandes, cuirs et peaux, chaussures, articles en cuir. Rapport de synthèse [Possibilities for the establishment of exporting industries in the Associated African States and Madagascar. Products from rearing. Meat, hides and skins, shoes, leather articles. Summary report].
Commission, 1975.   27p.
D E F I N   VIII/223/74

1837 SCHÄFFER, K.-A.
Klassifizierung landwirtschaftlicher Betriebe mit Hilfe multivarianter statistischer Verfahren [Classification of

farms with the help of multivariable statistical methods /
Classification des exploitations agricoles à l'aide des
méthodes multivariables statistiques].
In Agricultural statistical studies, 10.
Eurostat, 1972.   48p.
D   17516

1838 SCHAUS, L.
Intervention et modération des pouvoirs publics dans le
domaine des transports. Exposé fait par Lambert Schaus,
membre de la Commission de la Communauté économique
européenne, à l'Institut des sciences des transports de
l'Université de Cologne, le 26 mars 1965 [Intervention and
restraint of public authorities in the field of transport.
Report made by Lambert Schaus, member of the
Commission of the European Economic Community, at
the Transport Institute of Cologne University, March 26
1965].
Commission EEC, 1965.   18p.
D F I N   8165

1839 SCHAUS, L.
Pensées sur le rôle du Benelux dans la Communauté
économique européenne. Discours prononcé par M.
Lambert Schaus, membre de la Commission de la
Communauté économique européenne, à la session finale
du 17ème congrès économique du Benelux, à Nemur, 18 mai
1963 [Thoughts on the role of Benelux in the European
Economic Community. Address by Mr. Lambert Schaus,
member of the Commission of the European Economic
Community, at the closing session of the 17th Benelux
Economic Congress at Namur, 18 May 1963].
Commission EEC, 1963.   18p.
F   8092

1840 SCHEDA, P.
Possibilités de création d'industries exportatrices dans les
États africains et malgache associés. Production
sidérurgique [Possibilities for the establishment of
exporting industries in the Associated African States and
Madagascar. Iron and steel production].

Commission, 1975.   3 vols.

F   VIII/228/74

1841 SCHEDA, P.
Possibilités de création d'industries exportatrices dans les
États africains et malgache associés. La production
sidérurgique. Pelletisation du minerai de fer et
électro-sidérurgie. Ferro-alliages (ferro-silicium,
-manganèse et -nickel). Rapport de synthèse [Possibilities
for the establishment of exporting industries in the
Associated African States and Madagascar. Iron and steel
production. Pellestisation of iron ore and electro-siderurgy.
Ferro-alloys (ferro-silicon, -manganese and -nickel).
Summary report].
Commission, 1975.   40p.
D E F I N   VIII/228/74

1842 SCHEDL, H.
Untersuchung zur Konzentrationsentwicklung in
verschiedenen Untersektoren der elektrotechnischen
Industrie in Deutschland. Rundfunk-, Fernseh- und
Phonogeräte (N.I.C.E. 375). Elektrohaushaltsgeräte
(N.I.C.E. 376) [A study of the evolution of concentration
in various sub-sectors of the electrical engineering
industry in Germany. Radios, televisions and record
players (N.I.C.E. 375). Electrical domestic appliances
(N.I.C.E. 376) / Étude sur l'évolution de la concentration
dans quelques sous-secteurs de l'industrie de la
construction électrique en Allemagne. Radios, télévisions
et tourne-disques (N.I.C.E. 375). Appareils
électrodomestiques (N.I.C.E. 376)].
Commission, 1973.   43p.
D   IV/446/73

1843 SCHEDL, H.
Untersuchung zur Konzentrationsentwicklung in
verschiedenen Untersektoren der elektrotechnischen
Industrie in Deutschland. 1: Rundfunk-, Fernseh- und
Phonogeräte (N.I.C.E. 375). 2: Elektrohaushaltsgeräte
(N.I.C.E. 376) [A study of the evolution of concentration
in various sub-sectors of the electrical engineering

industry in Germany. 1: Radios, televisions and record
players (N.I.C.E. 375). 2: Electrical domestic appliances
(N.I.C.E. 376) / Étude sur l'évolution de la concentration
dans quelques sous-secteurs de l'industrie de la
construction électrique en Allemagne. 1: Radios,
télévisions et tourne-disques (N.I.C.E. 375). 2: Appareils
électrodomestiques (N.I.C.E. 376)].
Commission, 1976.   var. pag.
D   8745

1844 SCHEEL, P.
Forms of cooperation between farms for production and
marketing in the new Member States [Formes de
collaboration entre exploitations agricoles dans les
nouveaux États membres].
Commission, 1976.   340p.   Information on
agriculture, 20.
E   8876

1845 SCHIFANI, C.
Incidence du rapport des prix de l'huile de graines et de
l'huile d'olive sur la consommation de ces huiles [The effect
of the report of linseed and olive oil prices on their
consumption].
Commission, 1968.   139p.   Internal information on
agriculture, 30.
D F   4785/VI/67

1846 SCHIFFMANN, C.
The developing countries and the enlargement of the
European Economic Community [Les pays en voie de
développement et l'élargissement de la Communauté
économique européenne].
Commission EEC, 1972.   63p.
E   513

1847 SCHIRMER, H.
Les aciéries [The steel-works].
Commission, 1971.   283p.   New technical processes
in the iron and steel industry: a personal training manual,
3. Studies: vocational training.
D F I N   17433

1848 SCHLECHTER, G.
Enquête sur les budgets familiaux au Luxembourg
[Survey on family budgets in Luxembourg].
In Budgets familiaux 1963/64.
Luxembourg.   Eurostat, 1965.   pp.25–124.
Social statistics: special series, 1.
F

1849 SCHLEIMER
La collaboration entre l'enseignement et les industries de
la C.E.C.A. [Cooperation between education and the
industries of the E.C.S.C.].
ECSC HA, 1959.   134p.
F   4704

1850 SCHLOCHAUER
La réparation des conséquences dommageables d'une
violation des articles 85 et 86 du traité instituant la CEE
[Compensation for damage suffered through infringement
of Articles 85 and 86 of the Treaty establishing the EEC].
Commission EEC, 1966.   74p.   Studies: competition
series, 1.
D F I N   8153

1851 SCHMID, W.
Modelle zur Analyse von
Ackerbau-Rindviehhaltungsbetrieben.
Technisch-wirtschaftliche Grundangaben.
Schwäbisch-Bayerisches Hügelland (B.R. Deutschland)
[Models for analysis of mixed crop and cattle farms. Basic
technico-economic data. Schwäbisch-bayerisches
Hügelland (F.R. Germany) / Modèles d'analyse
d'entreprises de polyculture-élevage bovin. Données
technico-économiques de base. Schwäbisch-bayerisches
Hügelland (R.F. Allemagne)].
Commission, 1976.   86p.   Information on
agriculture, 6.
D   8835

1852 SCHMIDT, E.
Projektionen über Erzeugung und Verbrauch
landwirtschaftlicher Erzeugnisse—'1977'. 4: B.R.
Deutschland [Projections of production and consumption
of agricultural products—'1977'. 4: F.R. Germany /
Projections de la production et de la consommation de
produits agricoles—'1977'. 4: R.F. Allemagne].
Commission, 1974.   348p.   Internal information on
agriculture, 120.
D   VI/1383/72

1853 SCHMIDT, H.
Évolution de la productivité de l'agriculture dans la CEE
[Development of agricultural productivity in the EEC].
Commission, 1969.   509p.   Internal information on
agriculture, 44.
D F   11774/VI/69

1854 SCHMIDT, H.
La production de produits animaux dans des entreprises à
grande capacité de la CEE. Nombre et formes dans le
secteur de l'engraissement de porcs, de veaux et de jeunes
bovins [The production of animal products in large scale
enterprises in the EEC. Number and types in the pig, calf
and store cattle fattening industry].
Commission, 1968.   158p.   Internal information on
agriculture, 23.
D F   11974/1/VI/67

1855 SCHMIDT, H.
La production de produits animaux dans des entreprises à
grande capacité de la CEE. Partie 2: Position
concurrentielle [The production of animal products in
large scale enterprises in the EEC. Part 2: Competitive
position].
Commission, 1969.   70p.   Internal information on
agriculture, 37.
D F   769/VI/69

1856 SCHMIDT, N.
Conditions de commercialisation et de formation des prix
des vins de consommation courante au niveau de la

première vente. Synthèse, R.F. d'Allemagne, G.D. de
Luxembourg [Conditions for marketing and price
formation of ordinary wines at the first sale. Summary,
F.R. of Germany, G.D. of Luxembourg].
Commission, 1973.   var. pag.   Internal information
on agriculture, 51.
D F   5305/VI/67

1857 SCHMIDT, R.
Agriculture et politique agricole de quelques pays de
l'Europe occidentale. 5: Royaume-Uni [Agriculture and
agricultural policy of several Western European
countries. 5: United Kingdom].
Commission, 1970.   308p.   Internal information on
agriculture, 66.
D F   VI/4808/69

1858 SCHMIDT, R.
Agriculture et politique agricole de quelques pays de
l'Europe occidentale. 8: Irlande [Agriculture and
agricultural policy of several Western European
countries, 8: Ireland].
Commission, 1971.   400p.   Internal information on
agriculture, 73.
D F   VI/1898/72

1859 SCHMIDT, R.
Agriculture et politique agricole de quelques pays de
l'Europe occidentale. 10: Aperçu synoptique [Agriculture
and agricultural policy of several Western European
countries. 10: Synoptic summary].
Commission, 1972.   196p.   Internal information on
agriculture, 89.
D F   VI/3168/72

1860 SCHMIDT, R.
Projection of production and consumption of agricultural
products—'1977'. 2: Denmark, Ireland (Projections de la
production et de la consommation de produits
agricoles—'1977'. 2: Danemark, Irlande).

Commission, 1973.   137p.   Internal information on
agriculture, 109.
D E F   VI/2942/72

1861 SCHMIDT, R.
Die voraussichtliche Entwicklung der internationalen
Versorgung mit landwirtschaftlichen Erzeugnissen und
ihre Folgen für die Gemeinschaft. 1: Weizen,
Futtergetreide, Zucker, Gesamtzusammenfassung [The
foreseeable trend in world availabilities of agricultural
products and the consequences for the Community. 1:
Wheat, feed grain, sugar, summary / L'évolution
prévisible de l'approvisionnement international en
produits agricoles et ses conséquences pour la
Communauté. 1: Blé, céréales fourragères, sucre,
résumé].
Commission, 1977.   244p.   Information on
agriculture, 18.
D   8874

1862 SCHMIDT, R.
Die voraussichtliche Entwicklung der internationalen
Versorgung mit landwirtschaftlichen Erzeugnissen und
ihre Folgen für die Gemeinschaft. 3: Öle und Fette,
Eiweissfuttermittel [The foreseeable trend in world
availabilities of agricultural products and the
consequences for the Community. 3: Oils and fats, protein
products / L'évolution prévisible de l'approvisionnement
international en produits agricoles et ses conséquences
pour la Communauté. 3: Huiles et graisses, aliments
azotés pour animaux].
Commission, 1977.   200p.   Information on
agriculture, 36.
D   CB-NA-77-036-DE-C

1863 SCHMIT, R.
Projection of production and consumption of agricultural
products—'1977'. 1: United Kingdom (Projections de la
production et de la consommation de produits
agricoles—'1977'. 1: Royaume-Uni).

Commission, 1973. 253p. Internal information on agriculture, 108.

D E F   VI/3709/74

1864 SCHMITT, G.
La limitation de l'offre des produits agricoles au moyen des mesures administratives [Limitation of the supply of agricultural products by administrative measures].
Commission EEC, 1966. 278p. Internal information on agriculture, 9.

D F   2083/VI/64

1865 SCHMITT, G.
Méthodes et possibilités d'établissement des projections à long terme pour la production agricole [Methods and possibilities of drawing up long term projections for agricultural production].
Commission EEC, 1961. 80p. Studies: agricultural series, 3.

D F   8080

1866 SCHMITT, H. R.
La consommation du vin et les facteurs qui la déterminent. RF d'Allemagne [Wine consumption and the factors which determine it. FR of Germany].
Commission, 1969. 117p. Internal information on agriculture, 46.

D F   13859/VI/69

1867 SCHNEIDER
Statistiques dans le domaine de la production de porcs dans les États membres des Communautés européennes 1968–1971 [Statistics in the domain of pork production in the Member States of the European Communities 1968–1971].
In Agricultural statistical studies, 14. Eurostat, 1974. 2 vols.

D F   6654

1868 SCHOLZ, L.
Possibilités de création d'industries exportatrices dans les États africains et malgache associés. Produits

électro-mécaniques. Produits électroniques [Possibilities for the establishment of exporting industries in the Associated African States and Madagascar. Electro-mechanical products. Electronic products]. Commission, 1975.   3 vols.
F   VIII/224/74

1869 SCHOLZ, L.
Possibilités de création d'industries exportatrices dans les États africains et malgache associés. Produits électro-mécaniques. Produits électroniques. Rapport de synthèse [Possibilities for the establishment of exporting industries in the Associated African States and Madagascar. Electro-mechanical products. Electronic products. Summary report].
Commission, 1975.   23p.
D E F I N   VIII/224/74

1870 SCHON
Les exportations de biens d'équipement de la Communauté. Essai et prévisions jusqu'en 1970 [Exports of capital goods from the Community. Sample and forecasts until 1970].
ECSC HA, 1967.   249p.   Collection: general objectives for steel, 3A.
D F I N   12885

1871 SCHÖN, L.
Données objectives concernant la composition des carcasses de porcs en vue de l'élaboration de coefficients de valeur [Given objectives concerning the composition of pork carcasses for working out coefficients of value].
Commission, 1968.   51p.   Internal information on agriculture, 26.
D F   21322/VI/68

1872 SCHÖN, L.
Ermittling des Muskelfleischanteils an Schlachttierkörpen von Schweinen mit dem dänischen KSA-Gerät [Determination of the proportion of lean meat on pig carcasses using the Danish KSA-equipment /

Détermination de la teneur en viande maigre des
carcasses de porc à l'aide de l'appareil danois KSA].
Commission, 1977.   29p.   Information on
agriculture, 38.
D   CB-NA-77-038-DE-C

1873 SCHÖNDUBE, C.
Deux études sur les problèmes de jeunesse. Les chances
de coopération entre la jeunesse allemande et la jeunesse
autrichienne. La jeune génération dans l'Europe de l'Est
et du Sud-Est [Two studies on the problems of youth. The
chances of cooperation between German and Austrian
youth. The young generation in East and South-East
Europe].
Pr Inf, 1967.   63p.
F

1874 SCHOPEN, W.
Les établissements de stockage de céréales dans le CEE.
Partie 1 [The establishment of cereal storage in the EEC.
Part 1].
Commission, 1968.   281p.   Internal information on
agriculture, 28.
D F   12751/VI/68

1875 SCHOUTEN, D. B. J.
Critères à la base de la fixation des salaires et problèmes
qui y sont liés pour une politique des salaires et des
revenus [Criteria at the basis for the fixing of wages and
problems connected for a wages and incomes policy].
Commission, 1967.   98p.   Studies: social policy
series, 19.
D F I N   8227

1876 SCHREIBER
Les exportations de biens d'équipement de la
Communauté. Essai et prévisions jusqu'en 1970 [Exports
of capital goods from the Community. Sample and
forecasts until 1970].
ECSC HA, 1967.   249p.   Collection: general
objectives for steel, 3A.
D F I N   12885

1877 SCHUDDEBOOM, L. J.
Pesticide residues in tobacco and tobacco products. 1:
General report (Les résidus de pesticides dans le tabac et
les produits de tabac. 1: Rapport général).
Commission, 1976.   145p.   Information on
agriculture, 14.
E F   8864

1878 SCHUDDEBOOM, L. J.
Pesticide residues in tobacco and tobacco products. 3:
Appendix. Pesticide residues found in tobacco.
Toxicological aspects of residues in tobacco (Les résidus
de pesticides dans le tabac et les produits de tabac. 3:
Annexe. Résidus de pesticides trouvés dans le tabac.
Aspects toxicologiques des résidus dans le tabac).
Commission, 1977.   var. pag.   Information on
agriculture, 26.
E F   8882

1879 SCHUDDEBOOM, L. J.
Les résidus de pesticides dans le tabac et les produits de
tabac. 2: Substances phytosanitaires employées.
Législation. Méthodes d'analyse [Pesticide residues in
tobacco and tobacco products. 2: Plant health substances
employed. Legislation. Methods of analysis].
Commission, 1977.   157p.   Information on
agriculture, 23.
F   8877

1880 SCHUIJT, W. J.
Vers l'élection directe de l'Assemblée parlementaire
européenne [Towards the direct election of the European
Parliamentary Assembly].
EPA, 1960.   79p.
F   2516

1881 SCHULER
La formation professionnelle dans l'industrie
sidérurgiques des pays de la Communauté [Vocational
training in the iron and steel industry of the countries of
the Community].
ECSC HA, 1954.   264p.
F

1882 SCHÜLER, J.
Agriculture et politique agricole de quelques pays de
l'Europe occidentale. 2: Danemark [Agriculture and
agricultural policy of several Western European
countries. 2: Denmark].
Commission, 1970.   var. pag.   Internal information
on agriculture, 57.
D F   VI/12396/69

1883 SCHÜLER, J.
Agriculture et politique agricole de quelques pays de
l'Europe occidentale. 3: Norvège [Agriculture and
agricultural policy of several Western European
countries. 3: Norway].
Commission, 1970.   246p.   Internal information on
agriculture, 58.
D F   7308/VI/70

1884 SCHÜLER, J.
Agriculture et politique agricole de quelques pays de
l'Europe occidentale. 4: Suède [Agriculture and
agricultural policy of several Western European
countries. 4: Sweden].
Commission, 1970.   var. pag.   Internal information
on agriculture, 64.
D F   23003/VI/69

1885 SCHÜLER, J.
Agriculture et politique agricole de quelques pays de
l'Europe occidentale. 10: Aperçu synoptique [Agriculture
and agricultural policy of several Western European
countries. 10: Synoptic summary].
Commission, 1972.   196p.   Internal information on
agriculture, 89.
D F   VI/3168/72

1886 SCHULZ, R.
Les manipulations usuelles dans le commerce de gros et de
détail du point de vue allemand [Habitual handling in the
wholesale and retail trade from the German point of view].
In Marché interieur, 1/1966.   Eurostat, 1966.   17p.
D F

1887 SCHUMAN, R.
Declaration of May 9, 1950 by French Foreign Minister
Robert Schuman (La déclaration de Robert Schuman, 9
mai 1950).
Commission EEC, 1967.   6p.
E F

1888 SEBEL, H.
Untersuchung der Konzentrationsentwicklung in der
Reifenindustrie sowie ein Branchenbild der
Kraftfahrzeug-Elektrikindustrie in Deutschland [A study
of the evolution of concentration in the tyre industry, as
well as a survey of electrical equipment for the motor
vehicle industry in Germany / Étude sur l'évolution de la
concentration dans l'industrie des pneumatiques, aussi
que un examen des appareils électriques pour l'industrie
des véhicules à moteur en Allemagne].
Commission, 1977.   190p.
D   8757

1889 SEEMANN, J.
Carte de la durée de la période de végétation dans les
États membres des Communautés européennes [Map of
the duration of the vegetation period in the Member
States of the European Communities].
Commission, 1976.   17p.   Information on
agriculture, 5.
D F   8839

1890 SEGGER, V.
Vorausschätzungen für den Agrarsektor-Prognose der
Entwicklung der Agrarstruktor und des Faktoreinsatzes
in der Landwirtschaft der EG. 1: Theoretische
Grundlagen und Analyse vorliegender Untersuchungen
[Projections for the agricultural sector-Forecasts of the
trends in farm structures and factor input in agriculture in
the EC. 1: Theoretical basis and analysis of existing
studies / Prévisions concernant le secteur
agricole-Prévisions de l'évolution des structures agricoles
et des facteurs de production dans l'agriculture dans les
CE. 1: Bases théoriques et analyse des enquêtes
réalisées].

Commission, 1977.   167p.   Information on
agriculture, 35.
D   CB-NA-77-035-DE-C

1891 SEGRÉ, C., chairman
The development of a European capital market (Le
développement d'un marché européen des capitaux).
Commission EEC, 1967.   382p.
D E F I N   8181

1892 SEIFERT, G.
Agriculture et politique agricole de quelques pays de
l'Europe occidentale. 1: Autriche [Agriculture and
agricultural policy of several Western European
countries. 1: Austria].
Commission, 1970.   var. pag.   Internal information
on agriculture, 56.
D F   12396/VI/69

1893 SEIFERT, G.
Agriculture et politique agricole de quelques pays de
l'Europe occidentale. 4: Suède [Agriculture and
agricultural policy of several Western European
countries. 4: Sweden].
Commission, 1970.   var. pag.   Internal information
on agriculture, 64.
D F   23003/VI/69

1894 SEIFERT, G.
Agriculture et politique agricole de quelques pays de
l'Europe occidentale. 6: Suisse [Agriculture and
agricultural policy of several Western European
countries. 6: Switzerland].
Commission, 1970.   var. pag.   Internal information
on agriculture, 67.
D F   VI/21229/69

1895 SEIFERT, G.
Agriculture et politique agricole de quelques pays de
l'Europe occidentale. 7: Portugal [Agriculture and
agricultural policy of several Western European
countries. 7: Portugal].

Commission, 1971.   var. pag.   Internal information
on agriculture, 71.
D F   VI/705/71

1896 SEIFERT, G.
Agriculture et politique agricole de quelques pays de
l'Europe occidentale. 10: Aperçu synoptique [Agriculture
and agricultural policy of several Western European
countries. 10: Synoptic summary].
Commission, 1972.   196p.   Internal information on
agriculture, 89.
D F   VI/3168/72

1897 SELLIER
Critères à la base de la fixation des salaires et problèmes
qui y sont liés pour une politique des salaires et des
revenus [Criteria at the basis for the fixing of wages and
problems connected for a wages and incomes policy].
Commission, 1967.   98p.   Studies: social policy
series, 19.
D F I N   8227

1898 SERBENT, H.
Essais de réduction des minerais de fer au four tournant.
Rapport intérimaire sur les essais effectués du 1.1.1960 au
31.3.1961 [Experiments by reduction of iron ore in the
rotary furnace. Provisional report of the experiments
carried out from 1.1.1960 to 31.3.1961].
ECSC HA, 1961.   364p.
F   7838

1899 SERMON, L.
Comment l'entreprise privée s'intéresse-t-elle aux
conversions industrielles [How private enterprise
interests itself in industrial conversions].
ECSC HA, 1960.   9p.   Intergovernmental
Conference on Industrial Redevelopment.
F   5500

1900 SERMON, L.
La conduite sur place des opérations de conversion
industrielle [On-the-spot direction of industrial conversion
operations].

ECSC HA, 1963.   352p.   Collection: regional
economy and policy. 1: Industrial conversion in Europe, 4.
D F I N   3324

1901 SERMON, L.
Le financement des investissements et les aspects sociaux
de la reconversion [Financing of investments and social
aspects of conversion].
ECSC HA, 1963.   255p.   Collection: regional
economy and policy. 1: Industrial conversion in Europe, 3.
D F I N   3323

1902 SEVERAC, G.
Les tendances d'évolution des structures des exploitations
agricoles. Causes et motifs d'abandon et de
restructuration [Trends of development in farm
structures. Causes and reasons for desertion and
reconstruction].
Commission, 1967.   386p.   Internal information on
agriculture, 20.
D F   8159/VI/67

1903 SEVILLIA, M.
Essai d'appréciation des conditions d'application et des
résultats d'une politique de réforme en agriculture dans
des régions agricoles difficiles. 2: Queyras [Attempt at
estimating the conditions from the application and results
of a reform policy in agriculture in difficult agricultural
regions. 2: Queyras].
Commission, 1975.   var. pag.   Internal information
on agriculture, 150.
F   VI/1988/75

1904 SEYLER, A.
La reconversion des charbonnages dans les bassins de la
république fédérale d'Allemagne. Sarre [The conversion of
coalmines in the basins of the Federal Republic of
Germany. Saar].
Commission, 1974.   69p.   Pamphlets on industrial
conversion, 23.
D F I N   8389

1905 SIBILLE, P.
Régime fiscal des exploitations agricoles et imposition de l'exploitant agricole dans les pays de la CEE [Tax arrangements for farms and taxation of the farmer in the countries of the EEC].
Commission, 1968.   148p.   Internal information on agriculture, 27.
D F   10092/VI/68

1906 SIEMER
Dispositions pour faciliter la création d'activités nouvelles. Dispositions juridiques et financières en vigueur dans les États membres et le Royaume-Uni [Arrangements to facilitate the establishment of new activities. Legal and financial arrangements in force in the Member States and United Kingdom].
ECSC HA, 1959.   loose-leaf.
D F I N   2275

1907 SIMEONI, C.
Enquête sur les salaires dans les industries de la Communauté économique européenne 1962 [Survey on wages in the industries of the European Economic Community 1962].
In Social statistics, 5/1964.   Eurostat, 1964.   519p.
D/F, I/N

1908 SIMEONI, C.
Enquête sur la structure et la réparation des salaires 1966 [Survey on the structure and distribution of wages 1966].
Eurostat, 1969–1970.   8 vols.   Social statistics: special series.
D/F/I/N   4730, 4795, 4928, 4964, 5032, 5033, 5034, 5188

1909 SIMEONI, C.
Harmonized statistics of average hourly gross wages in the industries of the European Communities April 1964 (Statistiques harmonisées des gains horaires moyens bruts dans les industries des Communautés européennes Avril 1964).
In Social statistics, 3/1965.   Eurostat, 1965.   105p.
D E F I N

1910 SIMEONI, C.
Salaires C.E.C.A. 1961. Les coûts de la main-d'œuvre et
les revenus des ouvriers dans les industries de la
C.E.C.A. Année 1961 et évolution 1954–1961 [E.C.S.C.
wages 1961. Labour costs and the incomes of workers in
the industries of the E.C.S.C. 1961 and development
1954–1961].
In Social statistics, 2/1963.   Eurostat, 1963.   201p.
D/F, I/N

1911 SIMEONI, C.
Salaires CECA 1964. Les coûts de la main-d'œuvre et les
revenus des ouvriers dans les industries de la CECA.
Année 1964 et évolution 1954–1964 [ECSC wages 1964.
Labour costs and the incomes of workers in the industries
of the ECSC. 1964 and development 1954–1964].
In Social statistics, 2/1966.   Eurostat, 1966.   227p.
D/F, I/N

1912 SIMEONI, C.
Statistiques harmonisées des gains horaires bruts, de la
durée hebdomadaire du travail offerte et de l'emploi
salarié dans l'industrie Avril 1967 [Harmonized statistics
of gross hourly wages, weekly hours of work and
employees in industry April 1967].
In Statistical studies and surveys, 2/1968.
Eurostat, 1968.   222p.
D/F/I/N   4411

1913 SIMEONI, C.
Structure of earnings in industry 1972 (Structure des
salaires dans l'industrie 1972).
Eurostat, 1975–1977.   13 vols.   Social statistics:
special series.
DK/D/E/F/I/N   6817 (v.1), 6887 (v.2), 6949 (v.3), 7043
(v.4), 7118 (v.5), 7159 (v.6), 7289 (v.7)

1914 SIMEONI, C., chairman
Structure of earnings in wholesale and retail distribution,
banking and insurance in 1974. Methods and definitions

(Structure des salaires dans le commerce, les banques et les assurances en 1974. Méthodes et définitions).
Eurostat, 1977. 223p. Special series, B1.
DK/D/E/F/I/N 7330/1

1915 SIMONNET, M.
Les services de la main-d'œuvre des États membres de la Communauté. Exposé de synthèse [Employment exchanges in the Member States of the Community. Summary].
Commission EEC, 1967. 131p. Studies: social policy series, 16.
D F I N 8193

1916 SINE, L.
Conséquences écologiques de l'application des techniques modernes de production en agriculture [Ecological results from the application of modern production techniques in agriculture].
Commission, 1974. var. pag. Internal information on agriculture, 137.
D F VI/3722/74

1917 SINGER, R.
General Report on the First Preliminary Draft of the Implementing Regulations to the Convention (Rapport général concernant le premier Avant-projet de Règlement d'exécution de la Convention).
In Reports on the Second preliminary draft of a convention establishing a European system for the grant of patents. Council, 1971. pp.83–90.
D/E/F 17275-B

1918 SINGER, R.
Rapport général sur les Premiers Avant-projets de règlement d'exécution et de règlement relatif aux taxes [General report on the First preliminary drafts of the implementing regulations and the rules relating to fees].
In Second avant-projet de convention relative au brevet européen pour le Marché commun et documents annexes. Council, 1971. pp.171–175.
D/F/I/N 17360

1919 SINKWITZ, P.
Premier séminaire pour cadres dirigeants de la formation
dans l'agriculture et en milieu rural. Rapport final [First
seminar for executive officials about training in
agriculture and the rural environment. Final report].
Commission, 1970.   var. pag.
F

1920 SLATTER, S.
A study of the evolution of concentration in the
pharmaceutical industry for the United Kingdom [Étude
sur l'évolution de la concentration dans l'industrie
pharmaceutique au Royaume-Uni].
Commission, 1977.   168p.
E   8707

1921 SLOTEN, P. van
La consommation d'énergie des moyens de transport.
Étude comparative [Energy consumption of various
means of transport. Comparative study].
Commission, 1974.   120p.
F   VII/76/74

1922 SMITH, J.-L.
Europe's frontier regions [Les régions frontières de
l'Europe].
In European studies. Teachers' series, 18.
Commission (L), 1974.   5p.
E   U/74/18

1923 SMITH, L. P. F.
A study of the evolution of concentration in the Irish food
industry 1968–1973 [Étude sur l'évolution de la
concentration dans l'industrie alimentaire en Irlande
1968–1973].
Commission, 1975.   107p.
E   8696

1924 SMOLDERS, A. H.
Studie betreffende de ontwikkeling van de concentratie in
enkele bedrijfstakken in de chemische industrie in

Nederland. Farmaceutische industrie (N.I.C.E. 313.1).
Fotochemische industrie (N.I.C.E. 313.2).
Onderhoudsmiddelen (N.I.C.E. 315.5) [A study of the
evolution of concentration in the sectors of the chemical
industry in the Netherlands. Pharmaceutical industry
(N.I.C.E. 313.1). Photographic industry (N.I.C.E. 313.2).
Maintenance products (N.I.C.E. 313.5) / Étude sur
l'évolution de la concentration dans les secteurs de
l'industrie chimique aux Pays-Bas. Industrie
pharmaceutique (N.I.C.E. 313.1). Industrie
photographique (N.I.C.E. 313.2). Produits d'entretien
(N.I.C.E. 313.5)].
Commission, 1973.   var. pag.
N   IV/350/73

1925 SMOLDERS, A. H.
Studie betreffende de ontwikkeling van de concentratie in
de rijwiel- en bromfietsenindustrie in Nederland
(N.I.C.E. 385.1) [A study of the evolution of concentration
in the cycles and motorcycles industry in the Netherlands
(N.I.C.E. 385.1) / Étude sur l'évolution de la
concentration dans l'industrie des cycles et motocycles aux
Pays-Bas (N.I.C.E. 385.1)].
Commission, 1973.   18p.
N   IV/351/73

1926 SMOLDERS, A. H.
A study of the evolution of concentration in the food
industry in the Netherlands [Étude sur l'évolution de la
concentration dans l'industrie alimentaire aux Pays-Bas].
Commission, 1974.   var. pag.
E   IV/209/74

1927 SNICK, G. van
Dispositions en matière de zootechnie bovine [Provisions
concerning bovine husbandry].
Commission, 1976.   138p.   Information on
agriculture, 8.
F   8840

1928 SOBOTSCHINSKI, A.
Enquête sur les budgets familiaux en Allemagne fédérale
[Survey on family budgets in Federal Germany].
In Budgets familiaux 1962/63. Deutschland (BR).
Eurostat, 1966.   pp.25–129.   Social statistics:
special series, 5.
F   3953

1929 SOENEN, M.
Problèmes relatifs à la qualité de blé, de la farine et du
pain dans les pays de la C.E.E. [Problems relating to the
quality of wheat, flour and bread in the countries of the
E.E.C.].
Commission EEC, 1962.   36p.   Studies: agricultural
series, 7.
D F I N   8043

1930 SOENEN, M.
Problèmes relatifs à la qualité de blé tendre, de la farine et
du pain dans les pays de la CEE. Deuxième partie
[Problems relating to the quality of common wheat, flour
and bread in the countries of the EEC. Second part].
Commission EEC, 1965.   38p.   Studies: agricultural
series, 16.
D F I N   8124

1931 SOMMER, H.
Les laminoirs [The rolling mills].
Commission, 1972.   240p.   New technical processes
in the iron and steel industry: a personal training manual,
4.   Studies: vocational training.
D F I N   8349

1932 SOMMERVILLE, J. G.
Comparative study on the rehabilitation of handicapped
persons in the countries of the Community. Legal,
administrative and technical aspects. Volume 3: Denmark.
Republic of Ireland. United Kingdom [Étude comparative
sur la réhabilitation des personnes handicapées dans les
pays de la Communauté. Aspects juridiques,
administratifs et techniques. Volume 3: Danemark.

République de l'Irlande, Royaume-Uni].
Commission, 1975.   104p.
E   3128/75

1933 SØRENSEN, J. B.
Forms of cooperation between farms for production and
marketing in the new Member States [Formes de
collaboration entre exploitations agricoles dans les
nouveaux États membres].
Commission, 1976.   340p.   Information on
agriculture, 20.
E   8876

1934 SØRENSEN, P.
La Fédération des syndicats danois [The Danish
Federation of Trade Unions].
In Documentation européenne. Série syndicale et
ouvrière, 4/1972.   Pr Inf, 1972.   4p.
D F I N   S 72/4

1935 SPERL, H.
Recueil de textes. Organisation, compétences et
procédure de la Cour [Collected texts. Organization,
jurisdiction and procedure of the Court].
Court, 1963.   332p.
D F I N   3306

1936 SPIERENBURG, D. P.
Address by Mr. D. P. Spierenburg Member of the High
Authority before the Swedish Iron and Steel Federation.
Stockholm, 6 October 1955 [Discours de M. D. P.
Spierenburg, membre de la Haute autorité devant la
fédération de la sidérurgie suèdoise. Stockholm, 6 octobre
1955].
ECSC, 1955.   49p.
E

1937 SPIERENBURG, D. P.
The European Coal and Steel Community—past
experience and future prospects [La Communauté

européenne du charbon et de l'acier—l'expérience
dernière et les perspectives futures].
ECSC, 1958.   45p.
E   2046

1938 SPIERENBURG, D. P.
Gegenwart und Zukunft. Rede des Mitglieds der Hohen
Behörde der Europäischen Gemeinschaft für Kohle und
Stahl Herrn D. P. Spierenburg vor der Bundeskammer
der Gewerblichen Wirtschaft in Wien am 23. April 1954
[Present and future. Speech of Mr. D. P. Spierenburg,
Member of the High Authority of the European Coal and
Steel Community to the Federal Chamber of Industry in
Vienna on 23 April 1954 / Présent et futur. Discours de M.
D. P. Spierenburg, membre de la Haute autorité de la
Communauté européenne du charbon et de l'acier, devant
la chambre fédérale de l'industrie, à Vienne 23 avril 1954].
ECSC, 1954.   50p.
D

1939 SPINDLER, J. P., chairman
Le financement public de la recherche et du
développement dans les pays de la Communauté. Analyse
par objectifs 1968–1972 [Public expenditure on Research
and Development in the countries of the Community.
Analysis by objectives 1968–1972].
In Statistical studies and surveys, 1/1972.
Eurostat, 1972.   var. pag.
D/F   5840

1940 SPINEUX, A.
Le Comité économique et social et la consultation des
partenaires sociaux [The Economic and Social Committee
and consultation with social partners].
In Documentation européenne. Série pédagogique; série
agricole; série syndicale et ouvrière, 2/1973.
Pr Inf, 1973.   4p.
D F I N   U/A/S 73/2

1941 SPITZER
Management, organisation and methods in the American
iron and steel industry. E.C.S.C. fact finding mission to

U.S.A. March–April 1957 [Direction, organisation et
méthodes dans la sidérurgie des États-Unis. C.E.C.A.
mission des faits-fournitures aux États-Unis mars–avril
1957].
ECSC HA, 1958.   364p.
E   4444

1942 STABENOW, W.
European regional policy [La politique régionale
européenne].
Commission, 1973.   6p.
E   X/86/73

1943 STADLBAUER, J.
Consumer price indexes in the European Community.
Comparison of existing indexes and approaches to their
harmonization (Indices des prix à la consommation dans
les pays des Communautés européennes. Comparaison des
indices et proposition pour leur harmonisation).
Eurostat, 1977.   87p.
D E F   7336

1944 STAERCKE, J. de
Rapport du Commissaire aux Comptes de la Communauté
européenne du charbon et de l'acier relatif à la période
comprise entre le 1er juillet et le 31 décembre 1967 [Report
of the Auditor of the European Coal and Steel Community
for the period between 1st of July and 31st of December
1967].
ECSC, 1968.   69p.
D F I N   14765

1945 STAERCKE, J. de
Rapport du Commissaire aux Comptes pour l'exercice
1968 [Auditor's report for the year 1968].
ECSC, 1969.   91p.
D F I N   15569

1946 STAMMERS, A. J.
Le rôle des ports de la Communauté pour le trafic de
céréales et de farines. 7: Synthèse pour les principaux

ports de la R.F. d'Allemagne, du Royaume-Uni, des
Pays-Bas, de la Belgique, de l'Irlande et du Danemark
[List of Community ports for the cereals and flour trade.
7: Summary for the chief ports of F.R. of Germany,
United Kingdom, the Netherlands, Belgium, Ireland and
Denmark].
Commission, 1975.   var. pag.   Internal information
on agriculture, 155.
F   VI/3170/75

1947 STAMMERS, A. J.
Le rôle des ports de la Communauté pour le trafic de
céréales et de farines. 8: Monographies pour les principaux
ports de la R.F. d'Allemagne [List of Community ports for
the cereals and flour trade. 8: Monographs for the chief
ports of the F.R. of Germany].
Commission, 1975.   var. pag.   Internal information
on agriculture, 156.
F   VI/3171/75

1948 STAMMERS, A. J.
Le rôle des ports de la Communauté pour le trafic de
céréales et de farines. 9: Monographies pour les principaux
ports du Royaune-Uni [List of Community ports for the
cereals and flour trade. 9: Monographs for the chief ports
of the United Kingdom].
Commission, 1975.   var. pag.   Internal information
on agriculture, 157.
F   VI/3172/75

1949 STAMMERS, A. J.
Le rôle des ports de la Communauté pour le trafic de
céréales et de farines. 10: Monographies pour les
principaux ports des Pays-Bas [List of Community ports
for the cereals and flour trade. 10: Monographs for the
chief ports of the Netherlands].
Commission, 1975.   var. pag.   Internal information
on agriculture, 158.
F   VI/3173/75

1950 STAMMERS, A. J.
Le rôle des ports de la Communauté pour le trafic de
céréales et de farines. 11: Monographies pour les
principaux ports de la Belgique [List of Community ports
for the cereals and flour trade. 11: Monographs for the
chief ports of Belgium].
Commission, 1975.　　var. pag.　　Internal information
on agriculture, 159.
F　　VI/3174/75

1951 STAMMERS, A. J.
Le rôle des ports de la Communauté pour le trafic de
céréales et de farines. 12: Monographies pour les
principaux ports de l'Irlande et du Danemark [List of
Community ports for the cereals and flour trade. 12:
Monographs for the chief ports of Ireland and Denmark].
Commission, 1975.　　var. pag.　　Internal information
on agriculture, 160.
F　　VI/3715/75

1952 STAMMERS, A. J.
Le rôle des ports de la Communauté pour le trafic de
céréales et de farines. 13: Résumé et conclusions [List of
Community ports for the cereals and flour trade. 13:
Summary and conclusions].
Commission, 1975.　　var. pag.　　Internal information
on agriculture, 161.
F　　VI/3791/75

1953 STAMPA, L.
Enquête sur la situation des petites et moyennes
entreprises industrielles dans les pays de la CEE [Survey
on the situation of small and medium-sized industrial
undertakings in the countries of the EEC].
Commission EEC, 1966.　　108p.　　Studies:
competition series, 4.
D F I N　　8183

1954 STANTON, H.
The methodology of the United Kingdom balance of
payments (La méthodologie de la balance des paiements
du Royaume-Uni).

Eurostat, 1976.   114p.
E/F   7366

1955 STEEN, J. van de
Possibilités de création d'industries exportatrices dans les
États africains et malgache associés. Transformation du
bois et fabrication d'articles en bois. Première
transformation: Sciages, déroulages, tranchages.
Deuxième transformation: Profilés, moulures,
contreplaqués, panneaux, produits finis: pour la
construction et l'ameublement. Rapport de synthèse
[Possibilities for the establishment of exporting industries
in the Associated African States and Madagascar. Wood
processing and manufacture of articles in wood. First
process: Sawing, wood-peeling, slicing. Second process:
Shapes, mouldings, plywood, panels, finished products:
for building and furniture. Summary report].
Commission, 1974.   445p.
F   VIII/227/74

1956 STEENE, de
Management, organization and methods in the American
iron and steel industry. E.C.S.C. fact finding mission to
U.S.A. March–April 1957 [Direction, organisation et
méthodes dans la sidérurgie des États-Unis. C.E.C.A.
mission des faits-fournitures aux États-Unis mars–avril
1957].
ECSC HA, 1958.   364p.
E   4444

1957 STEIGER, H.
The law and practice relating to pollution control in the
Federal Republic of Germany [Loi et usage concernant le
contrôle de la pollution en Allemagne].
Commission, 1976.   420p.
D E   0 86010 032 4

1958 STEIJN, T. N.
A study of the evolution of concentration in the Dutch
paper products industry [Étude sur l'évolution de la

concentration dans l'industrie des articles en papier aux Pays-Bas].
Commission, 1977.   89p.
E   8765

1959 STEVENS, P.
Water content of frozen or deep-frozen poultry.
Examination of methods of determination (Teneur en eau de volailles congelées ou surgelées. Examen de méthodes de dosage).
Commission, 1976.   196p.   Information on agriculture, 15.
E F   8865

1960 STEYLAERTS, R.
Détermination des erreurs lors des recensements du bétail au moyen de sondages [Determination of errors in sample livestock censuses].
Commission, 1967.   62p.   Internal information on agriculture, 16.
F

1961 STEYLAERTS, R.
Méthode d'échantillonnage appliquée en vue de l'établissement de la statistique belge de la main-d'œuvre agricole [Sampling method used for the establishment of Belgian statistics of agricultural manpower].
Commission EEC, 1965.   89p.   Internal information on agriculture, 6.
F   VI/10670/65

1962 STOEL
La formation professionnelle dans l'industrie sidérurgique des pays de la Communauté [Vocational training in the iron and steel industry of the countries of the Community].
ECSC HA, 1954.   264p.
F

1963 STOEL, A.
Les aciéries [The steel-works].
Commission, 1971.   283p.   New technical processes

in the iron and steel industry: a personal training manual,
3.   Studies: vocational training.
D F I N   17433

1964 STOEL, A.
Les laminoirs [The rolling mills].
Commission, 1972.   240p.   New technical processes
in the iron and steel industry: a personal training manual,
4.   Studies: vocational training.
D F I N   8349

1965 STOEL, A.
Mécanisation, automatisation et techniques de mesure
dans les services des hauts fourneaux [Mechanisation,
automation and measurement techniques in blast-furnace
works].
Commission, 1969.   172p.   New technical processes
in the iron and steel industry: a personal training manual,
2.   Studies: vocational training.
D F I N   14722

1966 STOEL, A.
La technique de mesure et de l'automation [Measurement
and automation technique].
ECSC HA, 1967.   204p.   New technical processes in
the iron and steel industry: a personal training manual, 1.
Studies: vocational training.
D F I N   13233

1967 STORCK, H.
Méthodologie d'une enquête sur la structure des
exploitations horticoles professionnelles [Methodology of a
survey on the structure of professional horticultural
enterprises].
In Agricultural statistical studies, 3.
Eurostat, 1968.   148p.
D F   15200

1968 STRAATEN, C. van der
Enquête sur les budgets familiaux aux Pays-Bas [Survey
on family budgets in the Netherlands].

In Budgets familiaux 1963/64. Nederland.
Eurostat, 1966.   pp.25–173.   Social statistics special
series, 3.
F

1969 STRASSER, J.
Budgets familiaux des ouvriers de la Communauté
européenne du charbon et de l'acier 1956/57 [Family
budgets of workers of the European Coal and Steel
Community 1956/57].
In Social statistics series, 1/1960.
Eurostat, 1960.   436p.
D F I N   2333

1970 STRASSERT, G.
Problèmes de la structure économique de la Sarre
[Problems of the economic structure of the Saar].
ECSC HA, 1967.   196p.   Collection: regional
economy and policy. 2: Development and conversion
programme, 9.
D F   4098

1971 STRECKER, H.
Detérmination des erreurs lors des recensements du bétail
au moyen de sondages [Determination of errors in sample
livestock censuses].
Commission, 1967.   62p.   Internal information on
agriculture, 16.
F

1972 STRECKER, H.
Méthode d'échantillonage appliquée en vue de
l'établissement de la statistique belge de la main-d'œuvre
agricole [Sampling method used for the establishment of
Belgian statistics of agricultural manpower].
Commission EEC, 1965.   89p.   Internal information
on agriculture, 6.
F   VI/10670/65

1973 STRECKER, O.
Analyse du marché du porcelet dans l'optique d'une
stabilisation du marché du porc [Analysis of the piglet

market in the perspective of a stabilization of the pork market].
Commission, 1973.   143p.   Internal information on agriculture, 115.
D F   VI/3423/73

1974 STRECKER, O.
La consommation du vin et les facteurs qui la déterminent. RF d'Allemagne [Wine consumption and the factors which determine it. FR of Germany].
Commission, 1969.   117p.   Internal information on agriculture, 46.
D F   13859/VI/69

1975 STRECKER, O.
Les établissements de stockage de céréales dans la CEE. Partie 1 [The establishment of cereal storage in the EEC. Part 1].
Commission, 1968.   281p.   Internal information on agriculture, 28.
D F   12751/VI/68

1976 STRECKER, O.
La statistique des prix des œufs dans les États membres de la CEE [Egg price statistics in the Member States of the EEC].
In Agricultural statistical studies, 6.
Eurostat, 1969.   80p.
D F   15852

1977 STRUWE, K.
L'enseignement au Danemark [Teaching in Denmark].
In Documentation européenne. Série pédagogique: série agricole, 2/1974.   Pr Inf, 1974.   4p.
D F I N   U/A/74/2

1978 STRYG, P. E.
Models for analysis mixed crop and cattle farms. Basic techno-economic data. South-East Leinster (Ireland), West Cambridgeshire (United Kingdom), Fünen (Denmark) [Modèles d'analyse d'entreprises de

polyculture-élevage bovin. Données technico-économiques de base. South-East Leinster (Irlande), West Cambridgeshire (Royaume-Uni), Fünen (Danemark)].
Commission, 1976.   var. pag.   Information on agriculture, 7.
E   8836

1979 STRYG, P. E.
Models for analysis mixed crop and cattle farms. 6: Characteristics and possible applications. South-East Leinster (Ireland), West Cambridgeshire (United Kingdom), Fünen (Denmark), Schwäbisch-bayerisches Hügelland (F.R. Germany) (Modèles d'analyse d'entreprises de polyculture-élevage bovin. 6: Caractéristiques et possibilités d'utilisation. South-East Leinster (Irlande), West Cambridgeshire (Royaume-Uni), Fünen (Danemark), Schwäbisch-bayerisches Hügelland (R.F. d'Allemagne)).
Commission, 1976.   47p.   Internal information on agriculture, 152.
E F   VI/3715/1/74

1980 STUHLER, E.
Steuervorschriften für die überbetriebliche Zusammenarbeit oder Fusion landwirtschaftliche Betriebe. 2: BR Deutschland [Tax arrangements concerning cooperation and amalgamation of farms. 2: FR Germany / Dispositions fiscales en matière de coopération et de fusion d'exploitations agricoles. 2: RF Allemagne].
Commission, 1972.   269p.   Internal information on agriculture, 84.
D   VI/4053/71

1981 STUMPF, W. D., chairman
Report on the ECSC experimental programme of modernization of housing (Rapport sur le programme expérimental de construction de la CECA. Modernisation des logements).
Commission, 1977.   368p.
D E F I N   8451

1982 SUHREN, W.
Production and marketing of bananas from the Associated
African States and Madagascar. Summary (La production
et l'écoulement des bananes originaires des États africains
et malgache associés. Synthèse).
Commission, 1972.   133p.   Studies: development aid
series, 4.
D E F I N   8346

1983 SULLEROT, E.
Les conditions de travail des femmes salariées dans les six
États membres de la Communauté européenne. France
[The conditions of work for wage-earning women in the six
Member States of the European Community. France].
Commission, 1972.   184p.
F   V/166/73

1984 SULLEROT, E.
L'emploi des femmes [The employment of women].
In Documentation européenne. Série pédagogique; série
agricole; série syndicale et ouvrière, 4/1972.
Pr Inf, 1972.   4p.
D F I N   U/A/S/72/4

1985 SULLEROT, E.
L'emploi des femmes et ses problèmes dans les États
membres de la Communauté européenne [The
employment of women and the problems it raises in the
Member States of the European Community].
Commission, 1972.   237p.
D F I N   8333

1986 SULLEROT, E.
The employment of women and the problems it raises in
the Member States of the European Community (abridged
version) (L'emploi des femmes et ses problèmes dans les
États membres de la Communauté européenne (abrégé)).
Commission, 1972.   50p.
D E F I N   8334

1987 SUNNEN, R.
Mémorandum sur les objectifs de 1965. Méthodes
d'élaboration et résultats détaillés [Memorandum on the
1965 objectives. Methods of elaboration and detailed
results].
ECSC HA, 1962.   540p.   Collection: general
objectives for steel, 1.
D F I N   3017

1988 SUSSAMS, J. E.
A study of the evolution of concentration in the electrical
appliances industry for the United Kingdom. Electrical
appliances primarily for domestic use. Broadcast receiving
and sound reproducing equipment [Étude sur l'évolution
de la concentration dans l'industrie des appareils
électriques au Royaume-Uni. Appareils
électrodomestiques. Appareils électriques radios,
télévision et électro-acoustique].
Commission, 1977.   366p.
E   CH-SL-77-002-EN-C

1989 SUTTER, R. de
Crédits à l'agriculture. 1: France, Belgique, Grand-Duché
de Luxembourg [Credit to agriculture. 1: France,
Belgium, Grand Duchy of Luxembourg].
Commission, 1976.   var. pag.   Information on
agriculture, 1.
F   8831

1990 SYMANSKI, H.
Le travail de la soudure. Monographie des aspects
technologiques et pathologiques [Suture work.
Monograph of technological and pathological aspects].
Commission, 1969.   88p.   Collection: industrial
health and medicine, 9.
D F I N   4613

1991 SYS, H.
La production et la commercialisation de parties de
volaille [The production and marketing of poultry cuts].
Commission, 1974.   var. pag.   Internal information
on agriculture, 136.
D F   VI/3723/74

1992 TAFURI, F.
Méthodes pour la détermination du taux d'humidité du
tabac [Methods for the determination of the rate of
moisture in tobacco].
Commission, 1972.   var. pag.   Internal information
on agriculture, 91.
D F   VI/31/73/72

1993 TAHON, J.
Conséquences écologiques de l'application des techniques
modernes de production en agriculture [Ecological results
from the application of modern production techniques in
agriculture].
Commission, 1974.   var. pag.   Internal information
on agriculture, 137.
D F   VI/3722/74

1994 TALAMO, M.
Étude sur la zone de Carbonia. Les conséquences sociales
de la crise minière dans le bassin de Sulcis (Sardaigne)
[Study on the Carbonia area. Social consequences of the
coal crisis in the Sulcis coalfield (Sardinia)].
ECSC HA, 1966.   255p.   Collection: regional
economy and policy. 2: Development and conversion
programme, 6.
D F I N   3710

1995 TASSINARI, S.
Constatation des cours des vins de table à la production. 1:
France et RF d'Allemagne [Ascertaining the production
prices of table wines. 1: France and FR of Germany].
Commission, 1970.   171p.   Internal information on
agriculture, 59.
D F   2565/VI/70

1996 TASSINARI, S.
Constatation des cours des vins de table à la production. 2:
Italie, GD de Luxembourg [Ascertaining the production
prices of table wines. 2: Italy, GD of Luxembourg].
Commission, 1971.   var. pag.   Internal information
on agriculture, 75.
D F   VI/17662/69

1997 TEMPEL, A. J. van den
Corporation tax and individual income tax in the
European Communities [Impôt sur les sociétés et impôt
sur le revenu dans les Communautés européennes].
Commission, 1969.   80p.
E   14138/XIV/69

1998 TEMPEL, A. J. van den
Corporation tax and individual income tax in the
European Communities (Impôt sur les sociétés et impôt
sur le revenu dans les Communautés européennes).
Commission, 1971.   41p.   Studies:
competition–approximation of legislation series, 15.
D E F I N   8305

1999 TERPSTRA, G. H.
Les relations entre les employeurs et les travailleurs aux
Pays-Bas [The relations between the employers and the
workers in the Netherlands].
In Documentation européenne. Série syndicale et
ouvrière, 2/1973.   Pr Inf, 1973.   4p.
D F I N   S 73/2

2000 TEWES, T.
Projection of production and consumption of agricultural
products—'1977'. 2: Denmark, Ireland (Projections de la
production et de la consommation de produits
agricoles—'1977'. 2: Danemark, Irlande).
Commission, 1973.   137p.   Internal information on
agriculture, 109.
D E F   VI/2942/72

2001 TEWES, T.
Die voraussichtliche Entwicklung der internationalen
Versorgung mit landwirtschaftlichen Erzeugnissen und
ihre Folgen für die Gemeinschaft. 1: Weizen,
Futtergetreide, Zucker, Gesamtzusammenfassung [The
foreseeable trend in world availabilities of agricultural
products and the consequences for the Community. 1:
Wheat, feed grain, sugar, summary / L'évolution
prévisible de l'approvisionnement international en

produits agricoles et ses conséquences pour la
Communauté. 1: Blé, céréales fourragères, sucre, résumé].
Commission, 1977.   244p.   Information on
agriculture, 18.
D   8874

2002 TEWES, T.
Die voraussichtliche Entwicklung der internationalen
Versorgung mit landwirtschaftlichen Erzeugnissen und
ihre Folgen für die Gemeinschaft. 3: Öle und Fette,
Eiweissfuttermittel [The foreseeable trend in world
availabilities of agricultural products and consequences for
the Community. 3: Oils and fats, protein products /
L'évolution prévisible de l'approvisionnement
international en produits agricoles et ses conséquences
pour la Communauté. 3: Huiles et graisses, aliments
azotés pour animaux].
Commission, 1977.   200p.   Information on
agriculture, 36.
D   CB-NA-77-036-DE-C

THEMAAT, P. Verloren van, *see* VERLOREN VAN
THEMAAT, P.

2003 THEVENET
Possibilités de création d'industries exportatrices dans les
États africains et malgache associés. Fabrication de
cigares et cigarillos [Possibilities for the establishment of
exporting industries in the Associated African States and
Madagascar. Manufacture of cigars and cigarillos].
Commission, 1974.   158p.
F   VIII/226/74

2004 THEVENET
Possibilités de création d'industries exportatrices dans les
États africains et malgache associés. Fabrication de
cigares et cigarillos. Rapport de synthèse [Possibilities for
the establishment of exporting industries in the
Associated African States and Madagascar. Manufacture
of cigars and cigarillos. Summary report].
Commission, 1975.   19p.
D E F I N   VIII/226/74

2005 THIAULT, J.
The production of fruits and vegetables meeting
taste-quality standards [La production des fruits et des
légumes recontrée les normes de la qualité du goût].
Commission, 1975.　　300p.　　Internal information on
agriculture, 169.
E　　VI/520/76

2006 THOMAS
La formation professionnelle dans les houillères des pays
de la Communauté [Vocational training in the coal mines
of the countries of the Community].
ECSC HA, 1956.　　514p.
F　　1669

2007 THOMAS, J.
The dynamics of unemployment and employment.
Belgium, 1947–1973 (La dynamique du chômage et de
l'emploi. Belgique, 1947–1973).
Commission, 1977.　　101p.　　Studies: social policy
series, 24.
E F N　　8459

2008 THOMSEN, C.
Forms of cooperation between farms for production and
marketing in the new Member States [Formes de
collaboration entre exploitations agricoles dans les
nouveaux États membres].
Commission, 1976.　　340p.　　Information on
agriculture, 20.
E　　8876

2009 THOMSON, G., chairman
Report on the regional problems in the enlarged
Community (Rapport sur les problèmes régionaux dans la
Communauté élargie).
Commission, 1973.　　317p.
D E F I N　　COM (73) 550 final

2010 THOMSON, G., chairman
Report on the regional problems in the enlarged
Community (Rapport sur les problèmes régionaux dans la
Communauté élargie).
In Bulletin of the European Communities. Supplement,
8/1973.   Commission, 1973.   14p.
D E F I N   4001/S/8/73

2011 THUMM, U.
Problèmes de la structure économique de la Sarre
[Problems of the economic structure of the Saar].
ECSC HA, 1967.   196p.   Collection: regional
economy and policy. 2: Development and conversion
programme, 9.
D F   4098

2012 TINBERGEN, J., chairman
Report on the problems raised by the different turnover
tax systems applied within the Common Market (Rapport
sur les problèmes posés par les taxes sur le chiffre
d'affaires dans le Marché Commun).
ECSC HA, 1953.   48p.
D E F I N   1059

2013 TINDEMANS, L.
European Union. Report by Mr. Leo Tindemans to the
European Council (L'Union européenne. Rapport de M.
Leo Tindemans, premier ministre de Belgique, au Conseil
européen).
In Bulletin of the European Communities. Supplement,
1/1976.   Commission, 1976.   36p.
DK D E F I N   4001/S/76/1

2014 TOBERT, H.
Social policy—introduction [Introduction à la politique
sociale].
In European Community studies, 24.
Commission (L), 1976.   pp.1–3.
E

2015 TOLLE, A.
Dispositions législatives et administratives concernant les
résidus dans le lait, les produits laitiers et les aliments
pour le cheptel laitier [Legislative and administrative
provisions concerning residues in milk, dairy produce and
food for the dairy herd].
Commission, 1973.   198p.   Internal information on
agriculture, 114.
D F   VI/3359/73

2016 TOLLE, A.
Objectivation of the bacteriological and organoleptic
quality of milk for consumption [Critères objectifs pour
l'appréciation de la qualité bactériologique et
organoleptique du lait de consommation].
Commission, 1977.   161p.   Information on
agriculture, 21.
E   8875

2017 TRAPPEN, W. van
Intégration verticale et contrats en agriculture, 3:
Belgique [Vertical integration and contracts in
agriculture. 3: Belgium].
Commission, 1975.   121p.   Internal information on
agriculture, 144.
F N   VI/1590/75

2018 TREPTOW, H.
Teneur en métaux lourds des jus de fruits et produits
similaires [Heavy metal content of fruit juices and similar
products].
Commission, 1975.   215p.   Internal information on
agriculture, 148.
D F   VI/1594/75

2019 TRIEBEL, W.
Coûts de construction de bâtiments d'exploitation
agricole. Étables pour vaches laitières, veaux et jeunes
bovins à l'engrais [Construction costs of farm buildings.
Stables for dairy cattle, calves and young fattening cattle].

Commission, 1973.   var. pag.   Internal information
on agriculture, 101.
D F   VI/4429/71

2020 TRIFFIN, R.
Universalisme et régionalism sur le plan économique
[Universalism and regionalism of the economic plan].
Pr Inf, 1959.   var. pag.   Documents d'Information.
D/F

2021 TUININGA, E. J.
La consommation d'énergie des moyens de transport.
Étude comparative [Energy consumption of various
means of transport. Comparative study].
Commission, 1974.   120p.
F   VII/76/74

2022 TUPPEN, J.
Canals and waterways in the EEC [Les canaux et les voies
navigables dans la CEE].
In European studies. Teachers' series, 21.
Commission (L), 1975.   4p.
E   U/75/21

2023 TURVEY, R.
The analysis of economic costs and expenses in road and
rail transport (Analyse des coûts économiques et des
dépenses en matière de transports par rail et par route).
Commission, 1976.   36p.   Studies: transport
series, 4.
D E F   8725

2024 TWITCHETT, K.
A study guide to British books on the Common Market
[Un guide d'étude aux livres britanniques sur le Marché
commun].
In European studies. Teachers' series, 22.
Commission (L), 1975.   4p.
E   U/75/22

2025 TYC

Possibilités de création d'industries exportatrices dans les
États africains et malgache associés. Produits de
l'élevage. Viandes, cuirs et peaux, chaussures, articles en
cuir [Possibilities for the establishment of exporting
industries in the Associated African States and
Madagascar. Products from rearing. Meat, hides and
skins, shoes, leather articles].
Commission, 1974.   5 vols.
F   VIII/223/74

2026 TYC

Possibilités de création d'industries exportatrices dans les
États africains et malgache associés. Produits de
l'élevage. Viandes, cuirs et peaux, chaussures, articles en
cuir. Rapport de synthèse [Possibilities for the
establishment of exporting industries in the Associated
African States and Madagascar. Products from rearing.
Meat, hides and skins, shoes, leather articles. Summary
report].
Commission, 1975.   27p.
D E F I N   VIII/223/74

UBALDINI, L. Mori-, *see* MORI-UBALDINI, L.

2027 UHLMANN, F.

Étude de l'harmonisation des statistiques bovines des
États membres de la Communauté. Étude 2: Description
de la situation en Allemagne, aux Pays-Bas et en Belgique
[Study of the harmonization of beef statistics in the
Member States of the Community. Study 2: Description of
the situation in Germany, the Netherlands and Belgium].
In Agricultural statistical studies, 13.
Eurostat, 1974.   137p.
D F   18027

2028 ULLRICH

La formation des formateurs. Problèmes, méthodes et
expériences dans les industries de la C.E.C.A. [Training
of the trainers. Problems, methods and experiments in the
industries of the E.C.S.C.].
ECSC HA, 1962.   127p.
F   8514

2029 ULLRICH
La formation professionnelle dans les houillères des pays
de la Communauté [Vocational training in the coal mines
of the countries of the Community].
ECSC HA, 1956.   514p.
F   1669

2030 UMLAUF, J.
Le financement des investissements et les aspects sociaux
de la reconversion [Financing of investments and social
aspects of conversion].
ECSC HA, 1963.   255p.   Collection: regional
economy and policy. 1: Industrial conversion in Europe, 3.
D F I N   3323

2031 UNGER, H.
Problèmes d'une statistique CE des prix des engrais
[Problems of EC statistics for fertilizer prices].
In Agricultural prices. Special number, S6.
Eurostat, 1974.   pp.17–45.
D/F   6193

2032 URFF, W. von
Évolution régionale de la population active agricole. 2:
R.F. d'Allemagne [Regional development of the working
agricultural population. 2: F.R. of Germany].
Commission, 1969.   170p.   Internal information on
agriculture, 40.
D F   6718/VI/69

2033 URI, P., chairman
Economic development prospects in the EEC from 1960 to
1970 (Les perspectives de développement économique
dans la C.E.E. de 1960 à 1970).
Commission EEC, 1962.   85p.
D E F I N   8071

2034 URI, P., chairman
Rapport sur la capacité concurrentielle de la Communauté
européenne [Report on the competitive capacity of the
European Community].
Commission, 1972.   3 vols.
D F   II/481/72

2035 URI, P., chairman
Report on the economic situation in the countries of the
Community (Rapport sur la situation économique dans les
pays de la Communauté).
Commission EEC, 1958.   608p.
D E F I N   2079

2036 URI, P., chairman
Study on the structure and trends of the energy economy
in the Community countries [Étude sur la structure et les
tendances de l'économie énergétique dans les pays de la
Communauté].
ECSC HA, 1956.   104p.
E   5880

2037 UTTON, M. A.
The United Kingdom economy [L'économie britannique].
Commission, 1975.   155p.   Studies: economic and
financial series, 9.
E   8461

2038 VACCA, M.
Tableaux 'Entrées-Sorties' pour les pays de la
Communauté Économique Européenne ['Input-output'
tables for the countries of the European Economic
Community].
Eurostat, 1964.   var. pag.
D F

2039 VACCA, M.
Tableaux 'Entrées-Sorties' pour les pays de la
Communauté Économique Européenne. Seconde version
['Input-Output' tables for the countries of the European
Economic Community. Second version].
Eurostat, 1965.   var. pag.
D F

2040 VACHEL, J.-P.
Use of substitute products in livestock feeding (Utilisation
de produits de remplacement dans l'alimentation animale).

Commission, 1974.   var. pag.   Internal information
on agriculture, 130.
E F   VI/3806/73

2041 VAEREN, C. van der
Evolution of financial and technical cooperation between
the EEC and associated developing countries [Évolution
de la coopération financière et technique entre la CEE et
les pays en voie de développement associés].
Commission, 1970.   22p.
E   18443

2042 VAES, U. J.
Rapport du Commissaire aux Comptes de la Communauté
européenne du charbon et de l'acier Urbain J. Vaes relatif
au dixième exercice financier de la C.E.C.A. (1er juillet
1961 au 30 juin 1962) et à l'exercice 1961 (1er janvier au 31
décembre 1961) [Report of the Auditor of the European
Coal and Steel Community Urbain J. Vaes for the tenth
financial year of the E.C.S.C. (1st July 1961 to 30 June
1962) and the financial year 1961 (1st January to 31
December 1961)].
ECSC, 1962.   2 vols.
D F I N

2043 VAES, U. J.
Rapport du Commissaire aux Comptes de la Communauté
européenne du charbon et de l'acier Urbain J. Vaes relatif
au douzième exercice financier de la C.E.C.A. (1er juillet
1963 au 30 juin 1964) et à l'exercice 1963 (1er janvier au 31
décembre 1963) des institutions communes [Report of the
Auditor of the European Coal and Steel Community
Urbain J. Vaes for the twelfth financial year of the
E.C.S.C. (1st July 1963 to 30 June 1964) and the financial
year 1963 (1st January to 31 December 1963) of the
common institutions].
ECSC, 1964.   152p.
D F I N   11251

2044 VAES, U. J.
Rapport du Commissaire aux Comptes de la Communauté
européenne du charbon et de l'acier Urbain J. Vaes relatif

au huitième exercice financier de la C.E.C.A. (1er juillet
1959 au 30 juin 1960) et à l'exercice 1959 (1er janvier au 31
décembre 1959) des institutions communes [Report of the
Auditor of the European Coal and Steel Community
Urbain J. Vaes for the eighth financial year of the
E.C.S.C. (1st July 1959 to 30 June 1960) and the financial
year 1959 (1st January to 31 December 1959) of the
common institutions].
ECSC, 1960–1961.   3 vols.
D F I N   7169

2045 VAES, U. J.
Rapport du Commissaire aux Comptes de la Communauté
européenne du charbon et de l'acier Urbain J. Vaes relatif
au neuvième exercice financier de la C.E.C.A. (1er juillet
1960 au 30 juin 1961) et à l'exercice 1960 (1er janvier au 31
décembre 1960) des institutions communes [Report of the
Auditor of the European Coal and Steel Community
Urbain J. Vaes for the ninth financial year of the E.C.S.C.
(1st July 1960 to 30 June 1961) and the financial year 1960
(1st January to 31 December 1960) of the common
institutions].
ECSC, 1961.   3 vols.
D F I N   8050

2046 VAES, U. J.
Rapport du Commissaire aux Comptes de la Communauté
européenne du charbon et de l'acier Urbain J. Vaes relatif
au onzième exercice financier de la C.E.C.A. (1er juillet
1962 au 30 juin 1963) et à l'exercice 1962 (1er janvier au 31
décembre 1962) des institutions communes [Report of the
Auditor of the European Coal and Steel Community
Urbain J. Vaes for the eleventh financial year of the
E.C.S.C. (1st July 1962 to 30 June 1963) and the financial
year 1962 (1st January to 31 December 1962) of the
common institutions].
ECSC, 1963.   2 vols.
D F I N   10162

2047 VAES, U. J.
Rapport du Commissaire aux Comptes de la Communauté
européenne du charbon et de l'acier Urbain J. Vaes relatif

au quatorzième exercice financier de la C.E.C.A. (1er juillet 1965 au 30 juin 1966) et à l'exercice 1965 (1er janvier au 31 décembre 1965) des institutions communes [Report of the Auditor of the European Coal and Steel Community Urbain J. Vaes for the fourteenth financial year of the E.C.S.C. (1st July 1965 to 30 June 1966) and the financial year 1965 (1st January to 31 December 1965) of the common institutions].
ECSC HA, 1966.   131p.
D F I N   13102

2048 VAES, U. J.
Rapport du Commissaire aux Comptes de la Communauté européenne du charbon et de l'acier Urbain J. Vaes relatif au septième exercice financier de la C.E.C.A. (1er juillet 1958 au 30 juin 1959) et à l'exercice 1958 des Institutions Communes [Report of the Auditor of the European Coal and Steel Community Urbain J. Vaes for the seventh financial year of the E.C.S.C. (1st July 1958 to 30 June 1959) and the financial year 1958 of the Common Institutions].
ECSC, 1959–1960.   4 vols.
D F I N   6100

2049 VAES, U. J.
Rapport du Commissaire aux Comptes de la Communauté européenne du charbon et de l'acier Urbain J. Vaes relatif au treizième exercice financier de la C.E.C.A. (1er juillet 1964 au 30 juin 1965) et à l'exercice 1964 (1er janvier au 31 décembre 1964) des institutions communes [Report of the Auditor of the European Coal and Steel Community Urbain J. Vaes for the thirteenth financial year of the E.C.S.C. (1st July 1964 to 30 June 1965) and the financial year 1964 (1st January to 31 December 1964) of the common institutions].
ECSC, 1965.   143p.
D F I N   12169

2050 VAES, U. J.
Rapport du Commissaire aux Comptes Urbain J. Vaes relatif au cinquième exercice financier (1 juillet 1956 au 30

juin 1957) [Report of the Auditor Urbain J. Vaes for the fifth financial year (1 July 1956 to 30 June 1957)].
ECSC, 1957–1958.   2 vols.
D F I N

2051 VAES, U. J.
Rapport du Commissaire aux Comptes Urbain J. Vaes relatif au quatrième exercice financier (1 juillet 1955 au 30 juin 1956) [Report of the Auditor Urbain J. Vaes for the fourth financial year (1 July 1955 to 30 June 1956)].
ECSC, 1956–1957.   2 vols.
D F I N   9526

2052 VAES, U. J.
Rapport du Commissaire aux Comptes Urbain J. Vaes relatif au sixième exercice financier (1 juillet 1957 au 30 juin 1958) [Report of the Auditor Urbain J. Vaes for the sixth financial year (1 July 1957 to 30 June 1958)].
ECSC, 1958–1959.   2 vols.
D F I N   9586–7

2053 VALKENGOED, C. J. M. van
Credit to agriculture. 4: The Netherlands [Crédits à l'agriculture. 4: Pays-Bas].
Commission, 1976.   116p.   Information on agriculture, 4.
E N   8834

VALLEE POUSSIN, C. de la, *see* POUSSIN, C. de la Vallee

VAN ALMELO, *see* ALMELO, van

VAN ANDEL, G., *see* ANDEL, G. van

VAN BENTHEM, J. B., *see* BENTHEM, J. B. van

VAN BRAAM, A., *see* BRAAM, A van

VAN DE LOO, J. W. H., *see* LOO, J. W. H. van de

VAN DE PUTTE, R., *see* PUTTE, R. van de

VAN DE STEEN, J., *see* STEEN, J. van de

VAN DE VEN, A. C. M., *see* VEN, A. C. M. van de

VAN DEENEN, B., *see* DEENEN, B. van

VAN DEN BEMPT, P., *see* BEMPT, P. van den

VAN DEN TEMPEL, A. J., *see* TEMPEL, A. J. van den

VAN DER GIESSEN, H. B., *see* GIESSEN, H. B. van der

VAN DER GOES VAN NATERS, J., *see* GOES VAN NATERS, J. van der

VAN DER HEYDE, M., *see* HEYDE, M. van der

VAN DER STRAATEN, C., *see* STRAATEN, C. van der

VAN DER VAEREN, C., *see* VAEREN, C. van der

VAN DER WEERDEN, W., *see* WEERDEN, W. van der

VAN EIJCK, *see* EIJCK, van

VAN GHELUWE, G., *see* GHELUWE, G. van

VAN HOOF, J., *see* HOOF, J. van

VAN HOUT, T. J. G., *see* HOUT, T. J. G. van

VAN HOUTTE, A., *see* HOUTTE, A. van

VAN LANGENDONCK, E., *see* LANGENDONCK, E. van

VAN MIERT, K., *see* MIERT, K. van

VAN NATERS, J. van der Goes, *see* GOES VAN NATERS, J. van der

VAN ODIJK, J. L., *see* ODIJK, J. L. van

VAN OS, F. J. J. H. M., *see* OS, F. J. J. H. M. van

VAN PELT, A. J., *see* PELT, A. J. van

VAN ROMPUY, V., *see* ROMPUY, V. van

VAN ROOSE, W., *see* ROOSE, W. van

VAN SLOTEN, P., *see* SLOTEN, P. van

VAN SNICK, G., *see* SNICK, G. van

VAN THEMAAT, P. Verloren, *see* VERLOREN VAN THEMAAT, P.

VAN TRAPPEN, W., *see* TRAPPEN, W. van

VAN VALKENGOED, C. J. M., *see* VALKENGOED, C. J. M. van

VAN WINCKEL, V., *see* WINCKEL, V. van

VAN ZUILEN, D., *see* ZUILEN, D. van

2054 VANDENPLAS
Les exportations de biens d'équipement de la
Communauté. Essai et prévisions jusqu'en 1970 [Exports
of capital goods from the Community. Sample and
forecasts until 1970].
ECSC HA, 1967.   249p.   Collection: general
objectives for steel, 3A.
D F I N   12885

2055 VANDERMEEREN, J.-C.
Organisations syndicales et contrôle ouvrier en Belgique
[Trade union organisations and worker control in
Belgium].
In Documentation européenne. Série syndicale et ouvrière,
2/1972.   Pr Inf, 1972.   4p.
D F I N   S 72/2

2056 VANDERMOTTEN, C.
Déséquilibres régionaux et réseaux urbains [Regional
imbalances and urban networks].
Pr Inf, 1975.   21p.   La Communauté européenne.
F   X/647/74

2057 VANDEWALLE, G.
Comparaison entre le soutien accordé à l'agriculture aux
États-Unis et dans la Communauté [Comparison between
the support given to agriculture in the United States and
in the Community].

Commission, 1971.   256p.   Internal information on
agriculture, 70.
D F   5493/VI/70

2058 VANDEWALLE, G.
Study on the possible part played by certain primary
non-employment incomes in the inflationary process in
Belgium (Étude sur le rôle éventuel de certains revenus
primaires non-salariaux dans le développement de
l'inflation en Belgique).
Commission, 1976.   177p.   Series: medium-term
economic policy, 4.
DK D E F I N   8455

2059 VANHOVE, N.
The development of Flemish economy in the international
perspective. Synthesis and options of policy (L'évolution
de l'économie flamande considérée dans une perspective
internationale. Synthèse et options politiques).
Commission, 1974.   83p.   Studies: regional policy
series, 1.
DK D E F I N   8419

2060 VANNUTELLI, C.
Problèmes et méthodes de mesure de la productivité dans
les industries de la Communauté [Problems and methods
of measuring productivity in the industries of the
Community].
ECSC HA, 1964.   81p.   Collection: industrial
economics, 2.
D F I N   3535

2061 VARGA, J.
Deux études sur les problèmes de jeunesse. Les chances
de coopération entre la jeunesse allemande et la jeunesse
autrichienne. La jeune génération dans l'Europe de l'Est
et du Sud-Est [Two studies on the problems of youth. The
chances of cooperation between German and Austrian
youth. The young generation in East and South-East
Europe].
Pr Inf, 1967.   63p.
F

2062 VARKEVISSER, J.
Educational leave in Member States (Les congés culturels
dans les États membres).
Commission, 1977.   416p.   Studies: social policy
series, 26.
D E F I N   CH-SN-76-026-EN-C

2063 VAURIE
Les conditions d'installation d'entreprises industrielles
dans les États africains et malgaches associés. Volume 1:
République islamique de Mauritanie [Conditions for the
setting-up of industrial undertakings in the Associated
African States and Madagascar. Volume 1: Islamic
Republic of Mauritania].
Commission, 1972.   92p.
F   VIII/1311/72

2064 VAURIE
Les conditions d'installation d'entreprises industrielles
dans les États africains et malgache associés. Volume 2:
République du Sénégal [Conditions for the setting-up of
industrial undertakings in the Associated African States
and Madagascar. Volume 2: Republic of Senegal].
Commission, 1972.   100p.
F   VIII/1312/72

2065 VAURIE
Les conditions d'installation d'entreprises industrielles
dans les États africains et malgaches associés. Volume 6:
République de Côte-d'Ivoire [Conditions for the
setting-up of industrial undertakings in the Associated
African States and Madagascar. Volume 6: Republic of
Ivory Coast].
Commission, 1972.   100p.
F   VIII/1316/72

2066 VAURIE
Les conditions d'installation d'entreprises industrielles
dans les États africains et malgache associés. Volume 7:
République togolaise [Conditions for the setting-up of

industrial undertakings in the Associated African States
and Madagascar. Volume 7: Republic of Togo].
Commission, 1972.   100p.
F   VIII/1317/72

2067 VAURIE
Les conditions d'installation d'entreprises industrielles
dans les États africains et malgache associés. Volume 8:
République du Dahomey [Conditions for the setting-up of
industrial undertakings in the Associated African States
and Madagascar. Volume 8: Republic of Dahomey].
Commission, 1972.   88p.
F   VIII/1318/72

2068 VAYLET, J. L.
Le marché foncier et les baux ruraux. Effets des mesures
de réforme des structures agricoles. 2: R.F. d'Allemagne,
France [The land market and rural leases. Effects of
reform measures of agricultural structures. 2: F.R. of
Germany, France].
Commission, 1972.   var. pag.   Internal information
on agriculture, 82.
F   VI/537/72

2069 VEDEL, G., chairman
Report of the Working Party examining the problem of
the enlargement of the powers of the European
Parliament. 'Report Vedel' (Rapport du groupe ad hoc
pour l'examen du problème de l'accroissement des
compétences du Parlement européen. 'Rapport Vedel').
In Bulletin of the European Communities. Supplement,
4/1972.   Commission, 1972.   89p.
D E F I N   4001/S/4/72

2070 VEER, J. de
Évolution de la productivité de l'agriculture dans la CEE
[Development of agricultural productivity in the EEC].
Commission, 1969.   509p.   Internal information on
agriculture, 44.
D F   11774/VI/69

2071 VEER, J. de
Modèles d'analyse d'entreprises de polyculture-élevage
bovin. 3: Données technico-économiques de base. Région
Noordelijke Bouwstreek (Pays-Bas) [Models for analysis
of mixed crop and cattle farms. 3: Basic technico-economic
data. Noordelijke Bouwstreek region (Netherlands)].
Commission, 1975.   90p.   Internal information on
agriculture, 140.
F N   VI/17751/70

2072 VEER, J. de
Production laitière dans les exploitations ne disposant pas
de ressources fourragères propres suffisantes [Milk
production in the farms without its own sufficient fodder
resources].
Commission, 1974.   117p.   Internal information on
agriculture, 121.
D F N   VI/634/74

2073 VELAY, L.
Le boisement des terres marginales [The afforestation of
marginal lands].
Commission EEC, 1964.   var. pag.   Internal
information on agriculture, 1.
D F   VI/5221/64

2074 VEN, A. C. M. van de
Étude sur la physionomie actuelle de la sécurité sociale
dans les pays de la C.E.E. [Study on the current situation
of social security in the countries of the E.E.C.].
Commission EEC, 1962.   130p.   Studies: social
policy series, 3.
D F I N   8058

2075 VENNIER
Essai d'appréciation des conditions d'application et des
résultats d'une politique de réforme en agriculture dans
des régions agricoles difficiles. 1: Morvan [Attempt at
estimating the conditions from the application and results
of a reform policy in agriculture in difficult agricultural
regions. 1: Morvan].

Commission, 1974.   183p.   Internal information on
agriculture, 138.
F   VI/4572/74

2076 VENTEJOL, G.
Enlarging the Community (Rapport d'information sur
l'élargissement de la Communauté).
ESC, 1970.   12p.
D E F I N   16682

2077 VENTRIGLIA, F.
Les politiques nationales de développement régional et de
conversion [National policies of regional development and
conversion].
ECSC HA, 1961.   195p.   Collection: regional
economy and policy. 1: Industrial conversion in Europe, 1.
F   2626

2078 VERCHERAND
Essai d'appréciation des conditions d'application et des
résultats d'une politique de réforme en agriculture dans
des régions agricoles difficiles. 2: Queyras [Attempt at
estimating the conditions from the application and results
of a reform policy in agriculture in difficult agricultural
regions. 2: Queyras].
Commission, 1975.   var. pag.   Internal information
on agriculture, 150.
F   VI/1988/75

2079 VERDIANI, D., chairman
Proceedings of the European motor vehicles symposium
and the seminar on accident statistics (Actes du
symposium automobile européen et du séminaire sur les
statistiques des accidents).
Commission, 1977.   2 vols.
DK/D/E/F/I/N   CD-22-77-047-EN-C,
               CD-22-77-055-EN-C

2080 VERFAILLE, C.
Crédits à l'agriculture [Credit to agriculture].
Commission, 1973.   var. pag.   Internal information
on agriculture, 102.
D F   VI/18121/70

2081 VERHEIRSTRAETEN, A.
Concepts et méthodes de comparaison du revenu de la
population agricole avec celui d'autres groupes de
professions comparables [Concepts and methods of
comparison of the income of the agricultural population
with that of other groups of comparable occupations].
Commission, 1968.   302p.   Internal information on
agriculture, 33.
D F   16788/VI/68

2082 VERHEYDEN, J.
Possibilités d'industrialisation des États africains et
malgache associés. Volume 6: Somalie [Possibilities for the
industrialization of the Associated African States and
Madagascar. Volume 6: Somalia].
Commission EEC, 1966.   2 vols.
F   13083/VIII/B/66, 13084/VIII/B/66

2083 VERKINDEREN, A.
La spéculation ovine. 2: France, Belgique [Sheep
specialization. 2: France, Belgium].
Commission, 1973.   185p.   Internal information on
agriculture, 99.
D F   VI/734/73

2084 VERKOREN, J.
Incidences économiques de certains types
d'investissements structurels en agriculture.
Remembrement, irrigation [Economic effects of certain
types of structural investments in agriculture.
Reparcelling, irrigation].
Commission, 1969.   136p.   Internal information on
agriculture, 53.
D F   13527/VI/69

2085 VERLOREN VAN THEMAAT, P.
Cinq principes de la politique européenne dans le domaine
de la concurrence [Five principles of European policy in
the field of competition].
Pr Inf, 1959.   12p.   Documents d'Information.
D/F   705

2086 VERLOREN VAN THEMAAT, P.
Conséquences budgétaires, économiques et sociales de
l'harmonisation des taux de la TVA dans la CEE avec une
analyse quantitative pour les Bays-Pas [Budgetary,
economic and social results of the harmonisation of VAT
rates in the EEC with a quantitative analysis for the
Netherlands].
Commission, 1970.   92p.   Studies:
competition–approximation of legislation series, 16.
D F I N   8316

2087 VERLOREN VAN THEMAAT, P.
Economic law of the Member States of the European
Communities in an economic and monetary union (Le droit
économique des États membres des Communautés
européennes dans le cadre d'une Union économique et
monétaire).
Commission, 1976.   75p.   Studies:
competition–approximation of legislation series, 20.
D E F I N   8408

2088 VERLOREN VAN THEMAAT, P.
Rapport sur le droit économique néerlandais [Report on
Dutch economic law].
Commission, 1974.   190p.   Studies:
competition–approximation of legislation series, 20/4.
D F N   8428

2089 VERMAND, P.
Étude des problèmes particuliers posés par l'application
de la taxe sur la valeur ajoutée au secteur agricole des
pays de la Communauté européenne [Study of the
particular problems set by the application of the
value-added tax to the agricultural industry in the
countries of the European Community].
Commission, 1974.   72p.   Studies:
competition–approximation of legislation series, 24.
D F I N   8436

2090 VERNIER, J. N.
Le rôle des ports de la Communauté pour le trafic de
céréales et de farines. 7: Synthèse pour les principaux

ports de la R.F. d'Allemagne, du Royaume-Uni, des
Pays-Bas, de la Belgique, de l'Irlande et du Danemark
[List of Community ports for the cereals and flour trade.
7: Summary for the chief ports of F.R. of Germany,
United Kingdom, the Netherlands, Belgium, Ireland and
Denmark].
Commission, 1975.   var. pag.   Internal information
on agriculture, 155.
F   VI/3170/75

2091 VERNIER, J. N.
Le rôle des ports de la Communauté pour le trafic de
céréales et de farines. 8: Monographies pour les principaux
ports de la R.F. d'Allemagne [List of Community ports for
the cereals and flour trade. 8: Monographs for the chief
ports of the F.R. of Germany].
Commission, 1975.   var. pag.   Internal information
on agriculture, 156.
F   VI/3171/75

2092 VERNIER, J. N.
Le rôle des ports de la Communauté pour le trafic de
céréales et de farines. 9: Monographies pour les principaux
ports du Royaume-Uni [List of Community ports for the
cereals and flour trade. 9: Monographs for the chief ports
of the United Kingdom].
Commission, 1975.   var. pag.   Internal information
on agriculture, 157.
F   VI/3172/75

2093 VERNIER, J. N.
Le rôle des ports de la Communauté pour le trafic de
céréales et de farines. 10: Monographies pour les
principaux ports des Pays-Bas [List of Community ports
for the cereals and flour trade. 10: Monographs for the
chief ports of the Netherlands].
Commission, 1975.   var. pag.   Internal information
on agriculture, 158.
F   VI/3173/75

2094 VERNIER, J. N.
Le rôle des ports de la Communauté pour le trafic de
céréales et de farines. 11: Monographies pour les
principaux ports de la Belgique [List of Community ports
for the cereals and flour trade. 11: Monographs for the
chief ports of Belgium].
Commission, 1975.   var. pag.   Internal information
on agriculture, 159.
F   VI/3174/75

2095 VERNIER, J. N.
Le rôle des ports de la Communauté pour le trafic de
céréales et de farines. 12: Monographies pour les
principaux ports de l'Irlande et du Danemark [List of
Community ports for the cereals and flour trade. 12:
Monographs for the chief ports of Ireland and Denmark].
Commission, 1975.   var. pag.   Internal information
on agriculture, 160.
F   VI/3175/75

2096 VERNIER, J. N.
Le rôle des ports de la Communauté pour le trafic de
céréales et de farines. 13: Résumé et conclusions [List of
Community ports for the cereals and flour trade. 13:
Summary and conclusions].
Commission, 1975.   var. pag.   Internal information
on agriculture, 161.
F   VI/3791/75

2097 VERPRAET, G.
L'Europe judiciaire. La Cour de justice des Communautés
européennes au service de 185 millions d'Européens
[Legal Europe. The Court of Justice of the European
Communities at the service of 185 million Europeans].
Pr Inf, 1970.   95p.
F

2098 VERTESSEN, J.
Projections de la production et de la consommation de
produits agricoles—'1977'. 7: Belgique, Grand-Duché de
Luxembourg [Projections of production and consumption

of agricultural products—'1977'. 7: Belgium, Grand Duchy
of Luxembourg].
Commission, 1974.   199p.   Internal information on
agriculture, 134.
D F   VI/4822/71

2099 VESTERGÅRD, J.
A study of the evolution of concentration in the Danish
electrical appliances industry. Radio, television and
electro-acoustic industry. Electrical household appliances
industry [Étude sur l'évolution de la concentration dans
l'industrie des appareils électriques au Danemark.
Industrie de radio, télévision et électro-acoustique.
Industrie d'appareils électrodomestiques].
Commission, 1974.   var. pag.
E   IV/458/74

2100 VESTERGÅRD, J.
A study of the evolution of concentration in the Danish
food distribution industry. Part one: Concentration in the
Danish food distribution system. Part two: The first and
the second price surveys in Denmark [Étude sur
l'évolution de la concentration dans l'industrie de la
distribution des produits alimentaires au Danemark.
Partie première: La concentration dans le système de la
distribution des produits alimentaires au Danemark.
Partie deuxième: Les enquêtes des prix premières et
deuxièmes au Danemark].
Commission, 1977.   292p.
E   8766

2101 VESTERGÅRD, J.
A study of the evolution of concentration in the Danish
food processing industry [Étude sur l'évolution de la
concentration dans l'industrie de la transformation des
produits alimentaires au Danemark].
Commission, 1977.   252p.
E   8761

2102 VEYRET, P.
Agriculture de montagne dans la région alpine de la
Communauté. 2: France [Hill farming in the alpine region
of the Community. 2: France].

Commission, 1973.   92p.   Internal information on
agriculture, 105.
D F   VI/1184/73

2103 VIAENE, J.
La spéculation ovine. 2: France, Belgique [Sheep
specialization. 2: France, Belgium].
Commission, 1973.   185p.   Internal information on
agriculture, 99.
D F   VI/734/73

2104 VINCK, F.
L'action de la Haute Autorité pour le réemploi des
travailleurs [The action of the High Authority for the
re-employment of workers].
ECSC HA, 1960.   11p.   Intergovernmental
Conference on Industrial Redevelopment: report of the
High Authority.
F   5142

2105 VINCK, F.
Le financement des investissements et les aspects sociaux
de la reconversion [Financing of investments and social
aspects of conversion].
ECSC HA, 1963.   255p.   Collection: regional
economy and policy. 1: Industrial conversion in Europe, 3.
D F I N   3323

2106 VINCK, F.
Incidences de l'implantation d'une aciérie sur la région de
Gand–Zelzate [Effects of the construction of a steelworks
on the Ghent–Zelzate region].
ECSC HA, 1967.   176p.   Collection: regional
economy and policy. 2: Development and conversion
programme, 8.
D F I N   3889

VINELLE, L. Duquesne de la, *see* DUQUESNE DE LA
VINELLE, L.

VINELLE, M. Duquesne de la, *see* DUQUESNE DE LA
VINELLE, M.

2107 VIOT
Étude sur la physionomie actuelle de la sécurité sociale
dans les pays de la C.E.E. [Study on the current situation
of social security in the countries of the E.E.C.].
Commission EEC, 1962.   130p.   Studies: social
policy series, 3.
D F I N   8058

2108 VIROLE, J.
L'entreprise publique dans la Communauté [Public
undertaking in the Community].
In Dossiers pédagogiques, 44.
Bureau (P), 1971.   4p.
F

VISCOVO, M. del, *see* DEL VISCOVO, M.

2109 VISSCHER, G. de
La production de produits animaux dans des entreprises à
grande capacité de la CEE. Nombre et formes dans le
secteur de l'engraissement de porcs, de veaux et de jeunes
bovins [The production of animal products in large scale
enterprises in the EEC. Number and types in the pig, calf
and store cattle fattening industry].
Commission, 1968.   158p.   Internal information on
agriculture, 23.
D F   11974/1/VI/67

2109A VISSER, B.
Aide-mémoire pour la pratique des épreuves d'exercice en
médecine du travail [Manual for the practice of exercise
tests in industrial medicine].
Commission, 1971.   49p.   Collection: industrial
health and medicine, 12.
D F I N   16741

2110 VIZIANO
Le bruit [Noise].
Commission, 1969.   50p.
D F I N   4487

2111 VLAK, G. J. M.
Credit to agriculture in the E.C. Member States. A
comparative analysis (Crédits à l'agriculture dans les
États membres de la C.E. Une analyse comparative).
Commission, 1977.   104p.   Information on
agriculture, 28.
E F   8974

2112 VOGEL-POLSKY, E.
Les conditions de travail des femmes salariées dans les six
États membres de la Communauté européenne. Belgique
[The conditions of work for wage-earning women in the six
Member States of the European Community. Belgium].
Commission, 1972.   284p.
F   V/165/73

2113 VOGHEL, F. de
Policy on the bond markets in the countries of the EEC.
Current instruments and the use made of them from 1966
to 1969 (La politique du marché obligataire dans les pays
de la CEE. Instruments existants et leurs applications de
1966 à 1969).
Mon Com, 1970.   197p.
D E F I N   8320

2114 VOIGT, F.
Coordination of investments in transport infrastructures.
Analysis. Recommendations. Procedures (Coordination
des investissements en infrastructure de transport.
Analyse. Recommandations. Procédures).
Commission, 1974.   85p.   Studies: transport series,
3.
D E F I N   8423

VON ALVENSLEBEN, R., *see* ALVENSLEBEN, R.
von

VON AUENMÜLLER, H., *see* AUENMÜLLER, H.
von

VON BETHMANN, M., *see* BETHMANN, M. von

VON DER GROEBEN, H., *see* GROEBEN, H. von der

VON MICKWITZ, G., *see* MICKWITZ, G. von

VON OPPEN, M., *see* OPPEN, M. von

VON URFF, W., *see* URFF, W. von

2115 VOS, I. de
Glossary new transport technologies (Glossaire nouvelles
techniques de transport).
Commission, 1976.   900p.
DK/D/E/F/I/N   IX/2061/74

2116 VOSZ, J.
Amélioration du climat dans les chantiers d'abbatage des
mines de houille. Rapport de synthèse 1967–1971/StBV
[Improvement of the surroundings in the blasting sites of
coal mines. Summary report 1967–1971/StBV].
Commission, 1973.   66p.   Technical research: coal,
43. Mining technique.
D F   5845

2117 WÄCHTER, H.-H.
La politique des prix pour les produits agricoles dans la
C.E.E. [Pricing policy for agricultural products in the
E.E.C.].
n.i., 1968.   82p.
F   1001/VI/68

2118 WAGENFÜHR, R.
C.E.C.A. 1952–1962. Résultats. Limites. Perspectives
[E.C.S.C. 1952–1962. Achievements. Limits. Prospects].
ECSC HA, 1963.   645p.
D F I N   3352

2119 WAGENFÜHR, R.
Comparaison des revenus réels des travailleurs des
industries de la Communauté. Analyse statistique
[Comparison of real incomes of workers of the industries
of the Community. Statistical analysis].
ECSC, 1956.   151p.   Studies and documents.
F   1812

2119A WAGENFÜHR, R.
La production industrielle sovietique depassera-t-elle la
production americaine? [Will Soviet industrial production
overtake American?].
ECSC HA, 1959.   197p.
F   6020

2120 WAGNER, H. M.
The effect of nitrogen oxides on man and the environment
[L'effet des oxydes nitreux sur l'homme et
l'environnement].
Commission, 1974.   145p.
E

2121 WAGNER, M.
Educational leave in Member States (Les congés culturels
dans les États membres).
Commission, 1977.   416p.   Studies: social policy
series, 26.
D E F I N   CH-SN-76-026-EN-C

2122 WALTER, B.
Environmental problems of city centres [Les problèmes
d'environnement des centres de cité].
Commission, 1976.   88p.
E

2123 WALTER, H.
Les laminoirs [The rolling mills].
Commission, 1972.   240p.   New technical processes
in the iron and steel industry: a personal training manual,
4. Studies: vocational training.
D F I N   8349

2124 WANDELEER, R. de
Possibilités de création d'industries exportatrices dans les
États africains et malgache associés. Transformation du
bois et fabrication d'articles en bois. Première
transformation: Sciages, déroulages, tranchages.
Deuxième transformation: Profilés, moulures,
contreplaqués, panneaux, produits finis: pour la

construction et l'ameublement. Rapport de synthèse
[Possibilities for the establishment of exporting industries
in the Associated African States and Madagascar. Wood
processing and manufacture of articles in wood. First
process: Sawing, wood-peeling, slicing. Second process:
Shapes, mouldings, plywood, panels, finished products:
for building and furniture. Summary report].
Commission, 1974.   445p.
F   VIII/227/74

2125 WARNOD, A.
Possibilités de création d'industries exportatrices dans les
États africains et malgache associés. Produits de
l'élevage. Viandes, cuirs et peaux, chaussures, articles en
cuir [Possibilities for the establishment of exporting
industries in the Associated African States and
Madagascar. Products from rearing. Meat, hides and
skins, shoes, leather articles].
Commission, 1974.   5 vols.
F   VIII/223/74

2126 WARNOD, A.
Possibilités de création d'industries exportatrices dans les
États africains et malgache associés. Produits de
l'élevage. Viandes, cuirs et peaux, chaussures, articles en
cuir. Rapport de synthèse [Possibilities for the
establishment of exporting industries in the Associated
African States and Madagascar. Products from rearing.
Meat, hides and skins, shoes, leather articles. Summary
report].
Commission, 1975.   27p.
D E F I N   VIII/223/74

2127 WEBER
La réparation des conséquences dommageables d'une
violation des articles 85 et 86 du traité instituant la CEE
[Compensation for damage suffered through infringement
of Article 85 and 86 of the Treaty establishing the EEC].
Commission EEC, 1966.   74p.   Studies: competition
series, 1.
D F I N   8153

2128 WEBER, K. H.
Pesticide residues in tobacco and tobacco products. 1:
General report (Les résidus de pesticides dans le tabac et
les produits de tabac. 1: Rapport général).
Commission, 1976.   145p.   Information on
agriculture, 14.
E F   8864

2129 WEBER, K. H.
Pesticide residues in tobacco and tobacco products. 3:
Appendix. Pesticide residues found in tobacco.
Toxicological aspects of residues in tobacco (Les résidus
de pesticides dans le tabac et les produits de tabac. 3:
Annexe. Résidus de pesticides trouvés dans le tabac.
Aspects toxicologiques des résidus dans le tabac).
Commission, 1977.   var. pag.   Information on
agriculture, 26.
E F   8882

2130 WEBER, K. H.
Les résidus de pesticides dans le tabac et les produits de
tabac. 2: Substances phytosanitaires employées.
Législations. Méthodes d'analyse [Pesticide residues in
tobacco and tobacco products. 2: Plant health substances
employed. Legislation. Methods of analysis].
Commission, 1977.   157p.   Information on
agriculture, 23.
F   8877

2131 WEBER, M.
Étude du Comité économique et social sur les systèmes de
formation et de formation professionnelle dans les six pays
des Communautés européennes [Study of the Economic
and Social Committee on the systems of education and
vocational training in the six countries of the European
Communities].
ESC, 1973.   90p.
F   CES 926/73

2132 WEBER, M.
Systems of education and vocational training in the
member countries of the European Community. Study

(Systèmes de formation et de formation professionnelle dans les pays de la Communauté européenne. Étude).
ESC, 1976.   114p.
DK D E F I N   6967

2133 WEBER, P.
Le régime juridique des organisations professionnelles dans les pays membres de la C.E.C.A. [Legal administration of professional organisations in the member countries of the E.C.S.C.].
ECSC HA, 1968.   666p.   Collection: labour law.
D F I N   13879

2134 WEBER-PERL, B.
Labour costs in industry 1972–1975. Results of the surveys of 1972 and 1973. Updating of the costs to 1975 (Coût de la main-d'œuvre dans l'industrie 1972–1975. Résultats des enquêtes de 1972–1973. Actualisation des coûts jusqu'en 1975).
In Social statistics, 6/1975.   Eurostat, 1976.   456p.
DK/D/E/F/I/N   6936/6

2135 WEDEL, J., chairman
Social indicators for the European Community 1960–1975 (Indicateurs sociaux pour la Communauté européenne 1960–1975).
Eurostat, 1977.   486p.
DK/D/E/F/I/N   CA-22-77-766-6A-C

2136 WEERDEN, W. van der
Budgets familiaux des ouvriers de la Communauté européenne du charbon et de l'acier 1956/57 [Family budgets of workers of the European Coal and Steel Community 1956/57].
In Social statistics series, 1/1960.
Eurostat, 1960.   436p.
D F I N   2333

2137 WEERDEN, W. van der
Budgets familiaux 1963/64 [Family budgets 1963/64].
Eurostat, 1965–1966.   6 vols.   Social statistics: special series.
D/F/I/N   3953 (v.5), 3979 (v.6)

2138 WEERDEN, W. van der
Population and employment 1950–1976 (Population et
emploi 1950–1976).
Eurostat, 1977.   201p.
E/F   CA-22-77-031-2A-C

2139 WEHRER, A.
Exposé sur les travaux de Conseil d'Association entre la
Grande-Bretagne et la Communauté fait à la réunion du
Conseil de Ministres du 3 mai 1956 [Statement on the work
of the Association Council between Great Britain and the
Community at the meeting of the Council of Ministers of
3 May 1956].
Council, 1956.   14p.
F   3961

2140 WEHRER, A.
Les fusions et concentrations d'entreprises dans les pays
de la Communauté européenne du charbon et de l'acier.
Conférence faite à Longwy le 12 novembre 1955 [Mergers
and combinations of firms in the countries of the European
Coal and Steel Community. Conference held at Longwy,
12th November 1955].
ECSC HA, 1955.   22p.
F

2141 WEHRER, A.
Le principe supranational dans le traité C.E.C.A.
Discours prononcé par M. Albert Wehrer Membre de la
Haute Autorité de la Communauté Européenne du
Charbon et de l'Acier à la seance inaugurale du
Programme d'Études sur les Communautés Européennes
de l'Université Internationale de Droit Comparé le 20
juillet 1959 à Luxembourg [The supranational principle in
the E.C.S.C. treaty. Address delivered by Mr. Albert
Wehrer, Member of the High Authority of the European
Coal and Steel Community, at the inaugural meeting of
the Study Programme on the European Communities of
the International University of Comparative Law,
20th July 1959 at Luxembourg].
ECSC, 1959.   44p.
F   5666

2142 WEINDLMAIER, J.
Vorausschätzungen für den Agrarsektor—Prognose der
Entwicklung der Agrarstruktor und des Faktoreinsatzes
in der Landwirtschaft der EG. 1: Theoretische
Grundlagen und Analyse vorliegender Untersuchungen
[Projections for the agricultural sector—Forecasts of the
trends in farm structures and factor input in agriculture in
the EC. 1: Theoretical basis and analysis of existing
studies / Prévisions concernant le secteur
agricole—Prévisions de l'évolution des structures agricoles
et des facteurs de production dans l'agriculture dans les
CE. 1: Bases théoriques et analyse des enquêtes
realisées].
Commission, 1977.   167p.   Information on
agriculture, 35.
D   CB-NA-77-035-DE-C

2143 WEINSCHENCK, G.
La limitation de l'offre des produits agricoles au moyen
des mesures administratives [Limitation of the supply of
agricultural products by administrative measures].
Commission EEC, 1966.   278p.   Internal
information on agriculture, 9.
D F   2083/VI/64

2144 WEINSCHENCK, G.
Tendances de la production et de la consommation en
denrées alimentaires dans la C.E.E. 1956–1965 [Trends in
food production and consumption in the E.E.C.
1956–1965].
Commission EEC, 1960.   266p.   Studies:
agricultural series, 2.
D F I N   8005

2145 WEINSCHENCK, G.
Vorausschätzungen für den Agrarsektor—Prognose der
Entwicklung der Agrarstruktor und des Faktoreinsatzes
in der Landwirtschaft der EG. 1: Theoretische
Grundlagen und Analyse vorliegender Untersuchungen
[Projections for the agricultural sector—Forecasts of the
trends in farm structures and factor input in agriculture in

the EC. 1: Theoretical basis and analysis of existing
studies / Prévisions concernant le secteur
agricole—Prévisions de l'évolution des structures agricoles
et des facteurs de production dans l'agriculture dans les
CE. 1: Bases théoriques et analyse des enquêtes
realisées].
Commission, 1977.   167p.   Information on
agriculture, 35.
D   CB-NA-77-035-DE-C

2146 WEINSTOCK, U.
L'emploi agricole dans les pays de la C.E.E. Tome 1:
Structure [Agricultural employment in the countries of
the E.E.C. Volume 1: Structure].
Commission EEC, 1964.   61p.   Studies: social policy
series, 7.
D F I N   8108

2147 WEINSTOCK, U.
L'emploi agricole dans les pays de la C.E.E. Tome 2:
Évolution et perspectives [Agricultural employment in
the countries of the E.E.C. Volume 2: Development and
prospects].
Commission EEC, 1964.   51p.   Studies: social policy
series, 8.
D F I N   8123

2148 WEISS, G.
The decision-making process for agriculture in the
European Community (La procédure de décision dans le
domaine de l'agriculture dans la Communauté
européenne).
In Newsletter on the common agricultural policy,
5/1973.   Pr Inf, 1973.   8p.
D E F I N   X/597/73

2149 WELBERS, G.
The preparation of young people for work and for
transition from education to working life [La préparation
des jeunes à l'activité professionnelle et pour le passage de
l'éducation à la vie active].

In Bulletin of the European Communities. Supplement,
12/1976.
Commission, 1977.   pp.13–63.
DK D E F I N   4001/S/76/13

2150 WELLS, J. D.
Comparaison des bilans d'énergie du Royaume-Uni et de
la Communauté [Comparison of energy balances between
the United Kingdom and the Community].
In Bulletin de la Communauté européenne du charbon et
de l'acier, 12–3/1967.   ECSC HA, 1967.   pp.38–52.
F   4125

2151 WENIGER, J. H.
Étude sur les qualités des carcasses de bovins et porcins
dans les pays de la Communauté Économique Européenne
[Study on the qualities of beef and pork carcasses in the
countries of the European Economic Community].
Eurostat, 1966.   80p.   Agricultural statistics.
D/F   3944

2152 WERNER, P., chairman
Interim report on the establishment by stages of economic
and monetary union. 'Werner Report' (Rapport
intérimaire concernant la réalisation par étapes de l'union
économique et monétaire. 'Rapport Werner').
In Bulletin of the European Communities. Supplement,
7/1970.   Council and Commission, 1970.   26p.
D E F I N   4001

2153 WERNER, P., chairman
Report to the Council and the Commission on the
realisation by stages of economic and monetary union in
the Community 'Werner Report' (definitive text) (Rapport
au Conseil et à la Commission concernant la réalisation par
étapes de l'union économique et monétaire dans la
Communauté 'Rapport Werner' (texte final)).
In Bulletin of the European Communities. Supplement,
11/1970.   Council and Commission, 1970.   68p.
D E F I N   4001

2154 WESTERGÅRD, K.
Educational leave in Member States (Les congés culturels
dans les États membres).
Commission, 1977.   416p.   Studies: social policy
series, 26.
D E F I N   CH-SN-76-026-EN-C

2155 WESTERHUIS, J. R.
Premier séminaire pour cadres dirigeants de la formation
dans l'agriculture et en milieu rural. Rapport final [First
seminar for executive officials about training in
agriculture and the rural environment. Final report].
Commission, 1970.   var. pag.
F

2156 WESTPHAL, H.
The effects of national price controls in the European
Economic Community (Effets des réglementations
nationales des prix dans la Communauté économique
européenne).
Commission, 1971.   168p.   Studies:
competition–approximation of legislation series, 9.
D E F I N   8267

2157 WIEMER, H. J.
La situation sur les marchés sidérurgiques dans les pays
tiers [State of the iron and steel market in non-member
countries].
ECSC HA, 1965.   239p.   Collection: iron and steel
market, 1.
D F I N   11780

2158 WIEMER, H. J.
La situation sur les marchés sidérurgiques dans les pays
tiers. Plans d'investissement et possibilités de production
[State of the iron and steel market in non-member
countries. Investment plans and production possibilities].
ECSC HA, 1967.   145p.   Collection: iron and steel
market, 2.
D F I N   13609

2159 WIESMANN
La formation professionnelle dans les mines de fer des
pays de la Communauté [Vocational training in the iron
mines of the countries of the Community].
ECSC HA, 1959.   182p.
F   8149

2160 WIETHOFF, G.
Les aciéries [The steel-works].
Commission, 1971.   283p.   New technical processes
in the iron and steel industry: a personal training manual,
3.   Studies: vocational training.
D F I N   17433

2161 WIETHOFF, G.
Les laminoirs [The rolling mills].
Commission, 1972.   240p.   New technical processes
in the iron and steel industry: a personal training manual,
4.   Studies: vocational training.
D F I N   8349

2162 WIETHOFF, G.
Mécanisation, automatisation et techniques de mesure
dans les services des hauts fourneaux [Mechanisation,
automation and measurement techniques in blast-furnace
works].
Commission, 1969.   172p.   New technical processes
in the iron and steel industry: a personal training manual,
2.   Studies: vocational training.
D F I N   14722

2163 WIGNY, P.
L'Assemblée Parlementaire dans l'Europe des Six [The
Parliamentary Assembly in the Europe of the Six].
ECSC, 1958.   110p.
F   2017

2164 WIGNY, P.
Rechenschaft über die Gemeinschaft der Sechs [Account
of the Community of the Six / Exposé de la Communauté
des Six].
ECSC, 1957.   135p.
D   1872

2165 WIGNY, P.
Un témoignage sur la Communauté des Six [A statement on the Community of the Six].
ECSC, 1957.   121p.
F   1872

2166 WILBRANDT, H.
L'agrumculture dans les pays du Bassin méditerranéen. Production, commerce, débouchés [Citrus cultivation in the countries of the Mediterranean Basin. Production, trade, markets].
Commission, 1967.   320p.   Internal information on agriculture, 22.
D F   8740/3/VI/66

2167 WILBRANDT, H.
L'aide alimentaire de la C.E.E. aux pays en voie de développement problèmes et possibilités réeles. 10: L'utilisation d'excédents agricoles en Arabie Séoudite [Food aid from the E.E.C. to the developing countries. Problems and possibilities. 10: The use of agricultural surpluses in Saudi Arabia].
Commission EEC, 1963.   10p.
F   7829

2168 WILBRANDT, H.
L'aide alimentaire de la C.E.E. aux pays en voie de développement problèmes et possibilités réelles. 12: Élements d'un système d'évaluation des possibilités d'utilisation des excédents agricoles dans les pays en voie de développement [Food aid from the E.E.C. to the developing countries. Problems and possibilities. 12: Elements of an evaluation system of possibilities for the use of agricultural surpluses in the developing countries].
Commission EEC, 1963.   16p.
F   7829

2169 WILBRANDT, H.
L'aide alimentaire de la C.E.E. aux pays en voie de développement problèmes et possibilités réelles. 13: Organisation de l'utilisation des excédents agricoles aux

États-Unis [Food aid from the E.E.C. to the developing
countries. Problems and possibilities. 13: Organisation of
the use of agricultural surpluses in the United States].
Commission EEC, 1963.   15p.
F   7829

2170 WILBRANDT, H.
L'aide alimentaire de la C.E.E. aux pays en voie de
développement problèmes posés et possibilités réelles. 6:
Étude régionale. Turquie [Food aid from the E.E.C. to
the developing countries. Problems and possibilities. 6:
Regional study. Turkey].
Commission EEC, 1963.   61p.
F   7829

2171 WILBRANDT, H.
L'aide alimentaire de la C.E.E. aux pays en voie de
développement problèmes posés et possibilités réelles. 7:
Étude régionale. Inde [Food aid from the E.E.C. to the
developing countries. Problems and possibilities. 7:
Regional study. India].
Commission EEC, 1963.   63p.
F   7829

2172 WILBRANDT, H.
L'aide alimentaire de la C.E.E. aux pays en voie de
développement problèmes posés et possibilités réelles. 8:
Étude régionale. Tanganyika [Food aid from the E.E.C.
to the developing countries. Problems and possibilities. 8:
Regional study. Tanganyika].
Commission EEC, 1963.   25p.
F   7829

2173 WILBRANDT, H.
L'aide alimentaire de la C.E.E. aux pays en voie de
développement problèmes posés et possibilités réelles. 9:
Étude régionale. Afghanistan [Food aid from the E.E.C.
to the developing countries. Problems and possibilities. 9:
Regional study. Afghanistan].
Commission EEC, 1963.   25p.
F   7829

2174 WILBRANDT, H.
Food aid from the EEC to developing countries. Problems
and possibilities (L'aide alimentaire de la C.E.E. aux pays
en voie de développement. Problèmes posés et possibilités
réelles).
Commission EEC, 1964.   233p.   Studies:
agricultural series, 14.
D E F I N   8102

2175 WILL, G.
Technical measures of air pollution control in the iron and
steel industry. Reports and information on research work
subsidized by the ECSC as at June 1968 [Mesures
techniques contre la pollution atmosphérique dans la
sidérurgie. Rapports et information sur le travail de la
recherche subsidié par la CECA à juin 1968].
Commission, 1969.   71p.
E   15444

2176 WILLENER, A.
Niveau de mécanisation et mode de rémunération [Level
of mechanization and mode of payment].
ECSC HA, 1960.   149p.
F   2347

2177 WILLERS, B.
La spéculation ovine. 3: R.F. d'Allemagne, Pays-Bas
[Sheep specialization. 3: F.R. of Germany, the
Netherlands].
Commission, 1973.   var, pag.   Internal information
on agriculture, 103.
D F   VI/1509/73

WILMARS, C. Mertens de, *see* MERTENS DE
WILMARS, C.

2178 WILSON, J. S. G.
Credit to agriculture. 5: United Kingdom [Crédits à
l'agriculture. 5: Royaume-Uni].
Commission, 1975.   292p.   Internal information on
agriculture, 147.
E   VI/1593/75

2179 WILTZIUS, W.
Conditions de commercialisation et de formation des prix
des vins de consommation courante au niveau de la
première vente. France, Italie [Conditions for marketing
and price formation of ordinary wines at the first sale.
France, Italy].
Commission, 1969. 474p. Internal information on
agriculture, 52.
D F 1789/VI/70

2180 WILTZIUS, W.
Conditions de commercialisation et de formation des prix
des vins de consommation courante au niveau de la
première vente. Synthèse, R.F. d'Allemagne, G.D. de
Luxembourg [Conditions for marketing and price
formation of ordinary wines at the first sale. Summary,
F.R. of Germany, G.D. of Luxembourg].
Commission, 1973. var. pag. Internal information
on agriculture, 51.
D F 5305/VI/67

2181 WILWERTZ, P.
Les services de la main-d'œuvre des États membres de la
Communauté. Exposé de synthèse [Employment
exchanges in the Member States of the Community.
Summary].
Commission EEC, 1967. 131p. Studies: social
policy series, 16.
D F I N 8193

2182 WINCKEL, V. van
La consommation du vin et les facteurs qui la déterminent.
2: Belgique [Wine consumption and the factors which
determine it. 2: Belgium].
Commission, 1973. 289p. Internal information on
agriculture, 112.
F N VI/2949/73

2183 WINKLER, W.
Accès à l'exploitation agricole. Dispositions et pratiques
existant dans les États membres de la CEE en vue de

l'obtention et de l'aménagement d'une exploitation
agricole [Access to the farm. Arrangements and practices
existing in the Member States of the EEC for obtaining
and managing a farm].
Commission, 1967.   var. pag.   Internal information
on agriculture, 21.
D F   8325/VI/66

2184 WINSEMIUS, W.
Onderzoek in de Nederlandse ijzer- en staalindustrie
[Research in the Dutch iron and steel industry / Recherche
dans la sidérurgie néerlandaise].
Commission, 1967.   62p.   Collection: occupational
physiology and psychology, 3/11.
N   13749

2185 WINTER, F.
Méthodes des densités de charge, modèle d'analyse et de
prévision de la production de fruits à pépins [Methods of
load densities, analysis model and forecasts of pomaceous
fruit production].
In Agricultural statistical studies, 5.
Eurostat, 1969.   140p.
D F   15523

2186 WISCHHUSEN, L.
La production et la commercialisation de parties de
volaille [The production and marketing of poultry cuts].
Commission, 1974.   var. pag.   Internal information
on agriculture, 136.
D F   VI/3723/74

2187 WISNER, C.
Essai d'appréciation des conditions d'application et des
résultats d'une politique de réforme en agriculture dans
des régions agricoles difficiles. 2: Queyras [Attempt at
estimating the conditions from the application and results
of a reform policy in agriculture in difficult agricultural
regions. 2: Queyras].
Commission, 1975.   var. pag.   Internal information
on agriculture, 150.
F   VI/1988/75

2188 WISSELS, G., chairman
L'évolution des finances publiques dans les États
membres des Communautés européennes de 1957 à 1966
[The development of public finance in the Member States
of the European Communities from 1957 to 1966].
Commission, 1970.   262p.   Studies: economic and
financial series, 8.
D F I N   8291

2188A WÖHLKEN, E.
Objectif, évidences et limites de l'agrégation de quantités
et de valeurs [Objective, facts and limits of the aggregate
of quantities and values].
In Agricultural statistical studies, 16.
Eurostat, 1974.   82p.
D F   6641

2189 WÖHLKEN, E.
Prévisions agricoles. 2: Possibilités d'utilisation de
certains modèles, méthodes et techniques dans la
Communauté [Agricultural forecasting. 2: Possibilities of
using certain models, methods and techniques in the
Community].
Commission, 1970.   249p.   Internal information on
agriculture, 63.
D F   8433/VI/69

2190 WOITRIN
Enquête sur la situation des petites et moyennes
entreprises industrielles dans les pays de la CEE [Survey
on the situation of small and medium-sized industrial
undertakings in the countries of the EEC].
Commission EEC, 1966.   108p.   Studies:
competition series, 4.
D F I N   8183

2191 WOLFF, P. de, chairman
Perspectives pour 1975. Évolution globale et problèmes de
politique économique dans la Communauté [Prospects for
1975. Global development and economic policy problems in
the Community].
Commission, 1971.   2 vols.
D F   20791/II/1970

2192 WOOD, C. M.
Environmental impact assessment of physical plans in the
European Communities [L'imposition d'impact de
l'environnement des plans physiques dans les
Communautés européennes].
Commission, 1977.   162p.
E   ENV/37/78

2193 WORSWICK, G. D. N.
The United Kingdom economy [L'économie britannique].
Commission, 1975.   155p.   Studies: economic and
financial series, 9.
E   8461

2194 WORTMANN, H.
Economic and monetary union (L'union économique et
monétaire).
In Information: economy and finance, 43/1973.
Pr Inf, 1973.   23p.
D E F I N   BG 43-73

2195 WURDACK, G.
Pesticide residues in tobacco and tobacco products. 1:
General report (Les résidus de pesticides dans le tabac et
les produits de tabac. 1: Rapport général).
Commission, 1976.   145p.   Information on
agriculture, 14.
E F   8864

2196 WURDACK, G.
Les résidus de pesticides dans le tabac et les produits de
tabac. 2: Substances phytosanitaires employées.
Législations. Méthodes d'analyse [Pesticide residues in
tobacco and tobacco products. 2: Plant health substances
employed. Legislation. Methods of analysis].
Commission, 1977.   157p.   Information on
agriculture, 23.
F   8877

2197 WÜRDINGER, H.
Joint companies (sociétés liées, verbundene
Gesellschaften) [Sociétés liées (joint companies,
verbundene Gesellschaften)].
Commission, 1970.   63p.
E   15524/XIV/70

2198 WÜRL, D.
Untersuchung zur Konzentrationsentwicklung in der
Nahrungsmitteldistribution in Deutschland [A study of
the evolution of concentration in food distribution in
Germany / Étude sur l'évolution de la concentration dans
la distribution des produits alimentaires en Allemagne].
Commission, 1977.   307p.
D   8767

2199 ZACHER, H. F.
Rapport sur le droit économique en république fédérale
d'Allemagne [Report on the economic law in the Federal
Republic of Germany].
Commission, 1974.   179p.   Studies:
competition–approximation of legislation series, 20/1.
D F   8425

ZAHR, C. Abou-, *see* ABOU-ZAHR, C.

2200 ZAJADACZ, P.
Possibilités d'industrialisation des États africains et
malgache associés. Volume 2: Cameroun,
Congo-Brazzaville, Gabon, République centrafricaine,
Tchad (Union douanière et économique de l'Afrique
centrale) [Possibilities for the industrialization of the
Associated African States and Madagascar. Volume 2:
Cameroon, Congo-Brazzaville, Gabon, Central African
Republic, Chad (Customs and economic union of Central
Africa)].
Commission EEC, 1966.   4 vols.
F   13074/VIII/B/66, 13075/VIII/B/66, 13076/VIII/B/66,
13085/VIII/B/66

2201 ZAMARON, B.
Mémorandum sur les objectifs de 1965. Méthodes
d'élaboration et résultats détaillés [Memorandum on the
1965 objectives. Methods of elaboration and detailed
results].
ECSC HA, 1962. 540p. Collection: general
objectives for steel, 1.
D F I N 3017

2202 ZEITEL, G.
Rapport sur le choix des méthodes de comparaison de la
charge fiscale effective que supportent les entreprises
dans les divers États membres de la CEE [Report on the
choice of comparison methods for an effective tax burden
which firms can bear in the various Member States of the
EEC].
Commission, 1968. 36p. Studies: competition
series, 7.
D F 8234

2203 ZIGHERA, J. A.
Coordination of investments in transport infrastructures.
Analysis. Recommendations. Procedures (Coordination
des investissements en infrastructure de transport.
Analyse. Recommandations. Procédures).
Commission, 1974. 85p. Studies: transport series,
3.
D E F I N 8423

2204 ZIJLSTRA, J.
Politique économique et problèmes de la concurrence dans
la CEE et dans les pays membres de la CEE [Economic
policy and competition problems in the EEC and the
member countries of the EEC].
Commission EEC, 1966. 68p. Studies: competition
series, 2.
D F I N 8176

2205 ZITO, F.
L'agrumculture dans les pays du Bassin méditerranéen.
Production, commerce, débouchés [Citrus cultivation in

498

the countries of the Mediterranean Basin. Production,
trade, markets].
Commission, 1967.   320p.   Internal information on
agriculture, 22.
D F   8740/3/VI/66

2206 ZÖLLNER, H., chairman
Report on the ECSC experimental programme of
modernization of housing (Rapport sur le programme
expérimental de construction de la CECA. Modernisation
des logements).
Commission, 1977.   368p.
D E F I N   8451

2207 ZONCHELLO
Management, organization and methods in the American
iron and steel industry. E.C.S.C. fact finding mission to
U.S.A. March–April 1957 [Direction, organisation et
méthodes dans la sidérurgie des États-Unis. C.E.C.A.
mission des faits-fournitures aux États-Unis mars–avril
1957].
ECSC HA, 1958.   364p.
E   4444

2208 ZUILEN, D. van
Le travail de la soudure. Monographie des aspects
technologiques et pathologiques [Suture work.
Monograph of technological and pathological aspects].
Commission, 1969.   88p.   Collection: industrial
health and medicine, 9.
D F I N   4613

2209 ZUREK, E.
Le marché foncier et les baux ruraux. Effets des mesures
de réforme des structures agricoles. 2: R.F. d'Allemagne,
France [The land market and rural leases. Effects of
reform measures of agricultural structures. 2: F.R. of
Germany, France].
Commission, 1972.   var. pag.   Internal information
on agriculture, 82.
F   VI/537/72

2210 ZWAENEPOEL, J.
Environmental problems of city centres [Les problèmes d'environnement des centres de cité].
Commission, 1976.   88p.
E

2211 ZWAENEPOEL, O.
Intégration verticale et contrats en agriculture. 3: Belgique [Vertical integration and contracts in agriculture. 3: Belgium].
Commission, 1975.   121p.   Internal information on agriculture, 144.
F N   VI/1590/75

Subject Index

Numbers refer to the entries in the Author Index.

Accession
  Acts, *see* Acts of Accession
Accidents
  Industrial, *see* Industries,
    Accidents
  Statistics, 2079, *see also*
    Statistics
  See also Injuries; Rescue;
    Safety
Accounting
  National, 1115
  See also Auditing; Finance;
    Income, National
Accounts
  Agricultural, *see* Agriculture,
    Accounts
  Social, *see* Social accounts
  See also Budgets
Actions
  Economic, *see* Economics,
    Actions
Activities
  Economic, *see* Economics,
    Activities
Actors, 1090, *see also* Workers
Acts of Accession, 1291, *see also*
  Treaties
Administration, 10, 43, 169, 301,
  358, 583, 641, 867, 1185,
  1317, 1403, 1864, 1932, 2015,
  2143
  Economic, *see* Economics,
    Administration
  Financial, *see* Finance,
    Administration
  Fiscal, *see* Fiscal
    administration
  Legal, *see* Laws,
    Administration
  See also Management
Aeronautical industry, *see*
  Aerospace industry
Aerospace industry, 258, 260,
  604, 610, 625, 626, 961, 962,
  see also Industries
Afforestation, 96, 1039, 2073, *see*
  also Forestry
Afghanistan
  Food aid, 975, 1049, 1374, 2173
Africa, 13, 876, 1757
  Central, *see* Central Africa
  North, *see* North Africa
  West, *see* West Africa
  see also Associated African
    States and Madagascar;
    Ethiopia; Somalia;
    Tanganyika
Agreements
  Collective, *see* Collective
    agreements
Agriculture, 899–908, 1308,
  1508, 1583, 1857–9, 1882–5,
  1892–6
  Accounts, 1306, *see also*
    Accounts
  Aid, 1365, 2057, *see also* Aid
  Areas, 44, 115, 234, 457, 933,
    1027, 1058, 1175, 1426, 1502,
    1510, 1640, 1666, 1740, 1799,
    see also Areas
  Conferences, 1314, *see also*
    Conferences
  Contracts, 19, 248, 558, 1253,
    1523, 1802, 2017, 2211, *see*
    also Contracts
  Cooperation, 1241, *see also*
    Cooperation
  Credit, 45, 231, 322, 323, 401,
    402, 943, 968, 976, 1002,
    1078, 1251, 1363, 1364, 1499,
    1525, 1528, 1989, 2053, 2080,
    2111, 2178

Agriculture—*contd*

Decision making, 2148

Development, 8, 77, 304, 462, 582, 729, 1232, 1273, 1613, 1680, *see also* Development

Employment, 454, 455, 577, 578, 790, 791, 916, 917, 937, 938, 1188, 1189, 1397, 1398, 1662, 1663, 2146, 2147, *see also* Employment

Enterprises, 4, 29, 75, 166, 318, 385, 391, 446, 585, 635, 636, 721, 723, 735, 821, 825, 882, 1003, 1023, 1064, 1065, 1285, 1411, 1489, 1649, 1716, 1765, 1837, 1844, 1902, 1905, 1933, 1980, 2008, 2019, 2072, 2183, *see also* Enterprises

Forecasting, 5, 164, 189, 486, 602, 1051, 2189

Income, 59, *see also* Income

Investment, 663, 732, 795, 1638, 2084, *see also* Investment

Land, 952, *see also* Land; Reparcelling; Rural environment; Rural leases; Rural property

Machinery, 131, 1013, 1459, 1460, *see also* Machinery

Manpower, 52, 109, 344, 514, 792, 956, 957, 1104, 1207, 1208, 1511, 1591, 2032, *see also* Manpower

Manpower statistics, 1961, 1972, *see also* Manpower; Statistics

Markets, 1089, *see also* Markets

Organizations, 1309, *see also* Organizations

Pest control, 151, 211, *see also* Pests, Control

Policy, 110, 111, 197, 565, 664, 811, 899–908, 1310, 1416, 1664, 1857–9, 1882–5, 1892–6, *see also* Policy

Population, 1766, 2081, *see also* Population

Price statistics, 799, *see also* Prices; Statistics

Production, 73, 157, 320, 824, 892, 1330, 1331, 1469, 1596, 1865, *see also* Production

Production factors, 1890, 2142, 2145

Production prices, 493

Production structures, 1156

Production systems, 1361

Production techniques, 124, 257, 313, 395, 410, 449, 515, 1174, 1180, 1332, 1484, 1749, 1812, 1916, 1993

Productivity, 314, 456, 489, 752, 1183, 1853, 2070, *see also* Productivity

Products, 46, 165, 190, 263, 445, 603, 628, 720, 722, 870, 909–14, 1012, 1079, 1173, 1307, 1316, 1454, 1694, 1852, 1860–4, 2000–2, 2098, 2117, 2143, *see also* Almonds; Cereals; Feed; Fodder; Forage; Fruit; Meat; Nuts; Oils; Oilseeds; Products; Sugar; Tobacco; Vegetables

Reform, 76, 85, 90, 116, 213, 245, 340, 393, 520, 521, 627, 741, 800, 818, 1080, 1311, 1313, 1359, 1360, 1430, 1647, 1652, 1669, 1678, 1903, 2075, 2078, 2187, *see also* Reform

Revolving funds, 491, 844, 1024

Sector, 1146, 1890, 2089, 2142, 2145

Social security, 1734, *see also* Social security

Socio-economic structures, 1010, 1011, 1689, 1690

Structures, 226, 426, 594, 1425, 1455, 1639, 1651, 1665, 1890, 2068, 2142, 2145, 2209, *see also* Structures

Surpluses, 969–71, 1043–5, 1368–70, 2167–9

Training, 158, 394, 1919, 2155, *see also* Training

Vertical integration, 19, 248, 558, 1253, 1523, 1802, 2017, 2211, *see also* Integration, Vertical

Wages, 679, 846, 1015, 1582, *see also* Wages

Workers, 349, 632, 1187, *see also* Farmers; Workers

See also Animals; Farming; Fertilizers; Fishing; Forestry; Horticulture; Irrigation; Orchards

Aid, 519
  Agricultural, *see* Agriculture, Aid
  Food, *see* Food, Aid
  Migrant agricultural workers, 349, 632
  State, *see* State aid

Air, 1386
  Pollution, *see* Pollution, Air
  Pollution control, 817, 2175

Aircraft industry, *see* Aerospace industry

Alloys
  Consumption, 470, 1336, *see also* Consumption
  Iron, *see* Iron, Alloys
  See also Steels

Almonds, 440, 441, 588, 589, *see also* Agriculture, Products

Alpine areas, 883, 1718, 1719, 1745, 1746, 2102, *see also* Areas

America
  Latin, *see* Latin America
  United States of, *see* United States of America

Analysis
  Job, *see* Job analysis
  Regional, *see* Regions, Analysis
  Statistical, *see* Statistics, Analysis

Animals
  Feeding, 1198, 2040, *see also* Feed; Fodder; Forage
  Products, 49, 50, 91, 92, 149, 222, 223, 309, 510, 611, 612, 750, 751, 797, 798, 813, 814, 840, 841, 1030, 1031, 1034–6, 1158, 1229, 1230, 1254, 1401, 1402, 1500, 1501, 1572, 1573, 1633, 1634, 1821, 1822, 1835, 1836, 1854, 1855, 2025, 2026, 2109, 2125, 2126, *see also* Beef; Chicken; Dairy products; Hides and skins; Leather goods; Meat; Pork; Poultry; Products
  Slaughtering, 1171, 1399
  See also Cattle; Livestock; Piglets; Pigs; Sheep

Appeals
  Legal, *see* Laws, Appeals

Appliances,
  Domestic, *see* Domestic appliances
  Electrical industry, *see* Electrical appliance industry
  See also Equipment

Apprenticeships, 191, 1148, 1264, *see also* Training

Architectural heritage, 1737, *see also* Buildings

Areas
  Agricultural, *see* Agriculture, Areas
  Alpine, *see* Alpine areas
  Frontier, *see* Frontier areas
  Industrial, *see* Industries, Areas
  Iron and steel, *see* Iron and steel, Areas
  Mining, *see* Mines, Areas
  See also Regions; Towns

Arms control, 469

Associated African States and Madagascar, 1388, 1757

Animal products, 49, 50, 91, 92, 222, 223, 611, 612, 750, 751, 797, 798, 813, 814, 840, 841, 1030, 1031, 1034, 1035, 1229, 1230, 1401, 1402, 1500, 1501, 1572, 1573, 1633, 1634, 1821, 1822, 1835, 1836, 2025, 2026, 2125, 2126

Associated African States—*contd*
  Bananas, 148, 440, 441, 588,
    589, 1237, 1982
  Cigarillos and cigars, 590, 591,
    2003, 2004
  Electromechanical products,
    592, 593, 815, 816, 1389,
    1390, 1738, 1739, 1868, 1869
  Electronic products, 592, 593,
    815, 816, 1389, 1390, 1738,
    1739, 1868, 1869
  Export-oriented industries, 1,
    49, 50, 71, 91, 92, 218, 219,
    222, 223, 356, 440, 441,
    588–93, 611, 612, 750, 751,
    797, 798, 813–16, 840, 841,
    1030, 1031, 1034, 1035, 1117,
    1191, 1229, 1230, 1389, 1390,
    1401, 1402, 1432, 1433, 1438,
    1500, 1501, 1572, 1573, 1633,
    1634, 1738, 1739, 1797, 1821,
    1822, 1835, 1836, 1840, 1841,
    1868, 1869, 1955, 2003, 2004,
    2025, 2026, 2124–6
  Hides and skins, 324, 325,
    1751, 1752
  Iron alloys, 219, 1433, 1841
  Iron and steel production, 218,
    219, 1432, 1433, 1840, 1841
  Product marketing, 500
  Textile industrialization, 71
  Trade promotion, 324, 325,
    1751, 1752
  Tropical fruit, 440, 441, 588,
    589
  Wood, 1, 356, 1117, 1191, 1438,
    1955, 2124
  See also Burundi; Cameroon;
    Central African Republic;
    Chad; Congo (Brazzaville);
    Congo (Kinshasa); Congo
    (People's Republic);
    Dahomey; Gabon; Ivory
    Coast; Madagascar;
    Malagasy Republic; Mali;
    Mauritania; Mauritius;
    Niger; Rwanda; Senegal;
    Somalia; Togo; Upper Volta;
    Zaïre

Associated countries, 600, 1673,
  1674
Associated developing countries,
  2041
Association Councils, 2139
Associations
  Economic, *see* Economics,
    Associations
  Producer, *see* Producers'
    associations
  See also Organizations
Atomic energy, *see* Energy,
  Nuclear
Audio equipment, 22, 23, 266,
  267, 415, 566, 827, 1118,
  1327, 1328, 1988, *see also*
  Electronics; Equipment
Audio industry, 2099, *see also*
  Industries
Auditing, 9, 667–72, 1071, 1072,
  1944, 1945, 2042–52, *see also*
  Accounting
Austria
  Agricultural policy, 899, 1892
  Agriculture, 899, 1892
  Youth, 1873, 2061
  See also Western Europe
Authorities
  Public, 1838
Automation, 119, 283, 619, 856,
  857, 1068, 1119, 1120, 1352,
  1587, 1617, 1618, 1965, 2162
  Control, 858, *see also* Control
  Techniques, 120, 284, 497, 620,
    1050, 1069, 1353, 1588, 1966,
    see also Techniques
  See also Mechanization
Averages, 333, 334, 654, 688,
  1055, 1056, 1775, 1909
  See also Statistics

Bacteria, 868, 1261, 2016, *see
  also* Pollutants
Balance
  Energy, *see* Energy, Balance
Balance of payments, 1147, 1954
Balance sheets
  Feed, *see* Feed, Balance
    sheets

Supply, *see* Supply, Balance
  sheets
Bananas, 148, 440, 441, 588, 589,
  1237, 1982, *see also* Fruit
Banking, 942
Banks, 678, 693, 944, 1094, 1487,
  1488, 1914
Bargaining,
  Collective, *see* Collective
    bargaining
Barley products, 413, 1605, *see
  also* Cereals
Batteries, 21, 265, 1326, *see also*
  Electrical equipment
Beef, 492
  Carcasses, 37, 122, 167, 241,
    308, 528–30, 557, 734, 1803,
    2151, *see also* Carcasses
  Husbandry, 327, 1927
  Production, 352, 1795, *see also*
    Production
  Statistics, 279, 2027, *see also*
    Statistics
  See also Animals, Products;
    Meat
Belgium
  Administration, 301, 358, 583,
    1317, 1403
  Agricultural contracts, 2017,
    2211
  Agricultural credit, 323, 1364,
    1989
  Agricultural enterprises, 635,
    735, 1023
  Agricultural manpower
    statistics, 1961, 1972
  Agricultural products, 46, 165,
    263, 2098
  Audio equipment, 827
  Automation, 856, 857, 1119,
    1120
  Beef statistical harmonization,
    2027
  Beverages industry, 704, 954
  Brewing industry, 704, 954
  Cereal trade, 478, 482, 754,
    758, 1446, 1450, 1946, 1950,
    2090, 2094
  Chemical industry, 828

Cleaning products, 828
Coal mines, 596
Concentration, 704, 826–9, 954
Consumption, 46, 165, 263, 2098
Cooperation, 635, 735, 743,
  1023, 1132, 1428
Cotton, 829
Domestic appliances, 827
Electrical engineering
  industry, 827
Electrical equipment, 827
Employment, 1202, 2007
Factories, 856, 1120
Family budgets, 1016, 1125
Fishing industry, 743, 1132,
  1428
Flour trade, 478, 482, 754, 758,
  1446, 1450, 1946, 1950, 2090,
  2094
Food industry, 826
Handicapped, 169
Industrial areas, 301, 358, 583,
  1317, 1403
Industrial conversion, 1467
Inflation, 2058
Iron and steel areas, 1517
Iron and steel industry, 1384
Knitted and crocheted goods,
  829
Maintenance products, 828
Mergers, 635, 735, 1023
Mining areas, 1517
Mixed farming models, 39,
  378, 448, 771, 805, 1274
Non-employment incomes,
  2058
Pharmaceuticals, 828
Photography, 828
Planning, 301, 358, 583, 1317,
  1403
Ports, 478, 482, 754, 758, 1446,
  1450, 1946, 1950, 2090, 2094
Production, 46, 165, 263, 2098
Radio receivers, 827
Regional economics, 705, 2059
Regions, 1017, 2106
Rehabilitation, 169
Research, 596, 856, 1120, 1384
Sampling methods, 1961, 1972

Belgium—*contd*
  Sheep, 208, 1161, 2083, 2103
  Sintering, 856, 857, 1119,
    1120
  Slope maps, 334, 1056
  Socio-economic structures,
    1517
  Steel works, 1017, 2106
  Taxes, 635, 735, 1023
  Television receivers, 827
  Textile industry, 829
  Trade unions, 2055
  Underemployment, 168, 761,
    1201
  Unemployment, 168, 761,
    1201, 1202, 2007
  Vertical integration, 2017,
    2211
  Wine consumption, 2182
  Women workers, 2112
  Wool, 829
  Workers control, 2055
  Working conditions, 2112
  See also Benelux; European
    Atomic Energy Community;
    European Coal and Steel
    Community; European
    Communities; European
    Economic Community;
    Western Europe
Benelux, 1839
  Agricultural manpower, 792
  Agricultural production, 73,
    1330
  Cooperation, 73, 1330
  Regional development, 792
  See also Belgium;
    Luxembourg; The
    Netherlands
Beverages, 289, 525
  Industry, 69, 193, 225, 229,
    567, 704, 850, 954, 980, 1137,
    1142, 1270, 1631, 1658, *see
    also* Industries
  See also Brewing industry;
    Champagne industry;
    Drinks, Soft; Fruit, Juices;
    Spirits industry; Wine
Bicycles, *see* Cycles

Bids
  Take-over, *see* Take-over bids
Blast furnaces, *see* Furnaces,
    Blast
Bloomings, 1617, *see also* Steels
Boats
  Fishing, *see* Fishing, Vessels
Bonds
  Market policy, 2113, *see also*
    Investment
Books, 2024
Bread, 1606, 1607, 1929, 1930,
    see also Food
Bretton Woods, *see* Money,
    International systems
Brewing industry, 194, 704, 954,
    1143, 1698, *see also*
    Beverages; Industries
Britain, *see* United Kingdom
Bronchitis, 1507, *see also*
    Medicine
Budgets, 464, 1503, 2086
  Family, 17, 126, 209, 249, 250,
    460, 563, 674, 675, 1016,
    1125, 1721, 1848, 1928, 1968,
    1969, 2136, 2137
  See also Accounts
Buildings, 1318, 1319
  Costs, 1065, 2019, *see also*
    Costs
  Industrial, *see* Industries,
    Buildings
  Machinery, 1459, 1460, *see
    also* Machinery
  See also Architectural
    heritage
Burundi
  Industrial enterprises, 606,
    1168, 1550, 1561
  Industrialization, 141, 337,
    639, 1163, 1177, 1598, 1754
  See also Associated African
    States and Madagascar;
    Central Africa
Businesses
  Organization, 1342, *see also*
    Organizations
  Statistics, 6, *see also* Statistics
  See also Enterprises

Butter markets, 748, *see also*
    Dairy products; Food

Cameroon
    Industrial enterprises, 421,
        1543, 1571, 1706, 1789
    Industrialization, 1478, 1524,
        1720, 2200
    See also Associated African
        States and Madagascar;
        West Africa
Canals, 2022, *see also* Transport,
    Infrastructure
Canning
    Fish, *see* Fish, Canned
    Fruit, *see* Fruit, Canned
    Meat, *see* Meat, Canned
    Vegetables, *see* Vegetables,
        Canned
Capital
    Goods, 94, 630, 1074, 1105,
        1496, 1506, 1601, 1602, 1870,
        1876, 2054, *see also* Goods
    Markets, 963, 1891, *see also*
        Markets
    Productivity, 1070, *see also*
        Productivity
    See also Finance; Investment
Carbon monoxide poisoning, *see*
    Poisoning, Carbon monoxide
Carcasses
    Beef, *see* Beef, Carcasses
    Pig, *see* Pigs, Carcasses
    Pork, *see* Pork, Carcasses
    Poultry, *see* Poultry,
        Carcasses
Cardio-respiratory
    physiopathology, *see*
    Physiopathology,
    Cardio-respiratory
Cartels, 1315
Cattle, 149, 309, 867, 1065, 1158,
    1254, 1854, 2019, 2109, *see*
    also Animals
Censuses
    Sample livestock, *see*
        Livestock, Sample censuses
Central Africa
    Food aid, 316

See also Africa; Burundi;
    Central African Republic;
    Chad; Congo (Brazzaville);
    Congo (Kinshasa); Congo
    (People's Republic); Gabon;
    Rwanda; Zaïre
Central African Republic
    Industrial enterprises, 422,
        1545, 1564, 1703, 1790
    Industrialization, 1478, 1524,
        1720, 2200
    See also Associated African
        States and Madagascar;
        Central Africa
Cereals
    Markets, 870, 911, *see also*
        Markets
    Prices, 1637, *see also* Prices
    Products, 121, *see also*
        Products
    Storage, 930, 1505, 1874, 1975
    Trade, 97–102, 199–204,
        472–84, 754–60, 1108–13,
        1440–52, 1946–52, 2090–6,
        see also Trade
    See also Barley products;
        Wheat
Chad
    Industrial enterprises, 605,
        1167, 1544, 1559, 1763
    Industrialization, 1478, 1524,
        1720, 2200
    See also Associated African
        States and Madagascar;
        Central Africa
Champagne industry, 195, 1144,
    1699, *see also* Beverages;
    Wine
Chemical industry, 130, 828, 978,
    1924, *see also* Industries
Chicken, 1157, *see also* Animals;
    Meat; Poultry
Children, 1154, 1231, 1616, *see*
    also Youth
Cigarillos and cigars, 590, 591,
    2003, 2004, *see also* Tobacco
Cities
    Centres, 58, 290, 1107, 2122,
        2210

Cities—*contd*
  Freedom, *see* Freedom of the
    city
  See also Towns; Urban
    networks
Citrus fruit, *see* Fruit, Citrus
Civil engineering
  Equipment, 131, *see also*
    Equipment
  See also Engineering
Civil laws, *see* Laws, Civil
Civil servants, 551, 1681, 1824,
  see also Workers
Cleaning products, 828, *see also*
  Detergents; Products
Closures
  Mine, *see* Mines, Closure
Clothing industry, 53, 1099, *see*
  also Industries; Textiles
Coal
  Industry, 185, 292, 584, *see*
    also Industries
  Markets, 369, *see also* Markets
  Mines, 11, 295, 432, 443, 459,
    495, 506, 536, 596, 597, 860,
    871, 945, 1151, 1193, 1247,
    1394, 1456, 1457, 1590, 1747,
    1804, 1904, 1994, 2006, 2029,
    2116, *see also* Mines
  Organizations, 560, *see also*
    Organizations
  Research, 463, 531, *see also*
    Research
  See also Coke production;
    Energy, Sources
Coefficients of value, 1871
Coke production, 93, 993, *see*
  also Coal
Collective agreements, 431, *see*
  also Working conditions
Collective bargaining, 731, *see*
  also Trade, Unions
Combustion, 463, 531
Commerce
  Enterprises, 3, *see also*
    Enterprises
  Laws, 243, 244, 964, 965, *see*
    also Laws; Trade, Marks
  See also Trade

Commission
  European Communities, *see*
    European Communities,
    Commission
  European Economic
    Community, *see* European
    Economic Community,
    Commission
Common Assembly, *see*
  European Parliament
Common Market, *see* European
  Economic Community
Communities
  Mountain, 7, 303, 461, 581,
    728, 1272, 1612
  See also Towns
Companies, *see* Enterprises
Company laws, *see* Laws,
  Company
Compensation, 86, 351, 405, 438,
  511, 512, 932, 1081, 1233,
  1764, 1787, 1814, 1850, 2127
Competition, 86, 351, 405, 438,
  511, 512, 763, 781, 932, 1081,
  1233, 1627, 1707, 1764, 1787,
  1814, 1825, 1850, 2127, 2204
  Policy, 782–4, 787, 2085, *see*
    also Policy
Competitiveness, 161, 1036,
  1128, 1654, 1855, 2034
Compounds
  Organo-halogen, *see*
    Organo-halogen compounds
Concentration, 1758
  Agricultural machinery, 131,
    1459, 1460
  Air pollution, *see* Pollution,
    Air
  Audio equipment, *see* Audio
    equipment
  Audio industry, *see* Audio
    industry
  Batteries, *see* Batteries
  Beverages industry, *see*
    Beverages, Industry
  Brewing industry, *see*
    Brewing industry
  Building machinery, *see*
    Buildings, Machinery

Canned fish, *see* Fish, **Canned**
Canned fruit, *see* Fruit, Canned
Canned meat, *see* Meat, Canned
Canned vegetables, *see* Vegetables, Canned
Champagne industry, *see* Champagne industry
Chemical industry, *see* Chemical industry
Civil engineering equipment, *see* Civil engineering, Equipment
Cleaning products, *see* Cleaning products
Cotton, *see* Cotton
Cotton industry, *see* Cotton, Industry
Cycles, *see* Cycles
Cycles industry, *see* Cycles, Industry
Detergents, *see* Detergents
Domestic appliances, *see* Domestic appliances
Domestic appliance industry, *see* Domestic appliances, Industry
Electrical appliance industry, *see* Electrical appliance industry
Electrical engineering industry, *see* Electrical engineering industry
Electrical equipment, *see* Electrical equipment
Electronic equipment, *see* Electronics, Equipment
Enterprises, *see* Enterprises, Concentration
Food distribution, *see* Food, Distribution
Food distribution industry, *see* Food, Distribution industry
Food industry, *see* Food, Industry
Food processing industry, *see* Food, Processing industry

Food products, 14, 305, 706, 1695
Handling equipment, *see* Handling, Equipment
Hoisting equipment, *see* Hoisting equipment
Indices, 20, 264
Industrial, *see* Industries, Concentration
Knitted and crocheted goods, *see* Knitted and crocheted goods
Lifting equipment, *see* Lifts, Equipment
Lifts, *see* Lifts
Maintenance products, *see* Maintenance products
Markets, *see* Markets, Concentration
Mechanical engineering industry, *see* Mechanical engineering industry
Methodology, 1234
Motor vehicle industry, *see* Motor vehicles, Industry
Office Machinery, *see* Office machinery
Paper, *see* Paper
Paper industry, *see* Paper, Industry
Paper processing, *see* Paper, Processing
Paper products industry, *see* Paper, Products industry
Pharmaceutical industry, *see* Pharmaceuticals, Industry
Pharmaceuticals, *see* Pharmaceuticals
Photographic industry, *see* Photography, Industry
Photographic products, *see* Photography, Products
Photography, *see* Photography
Radio industry, *see* Radios, Industry
Radio receivers, *see* Radios, Receivers
Record players, *see* Record players

Concentration—*contd*
  Soft drinks industry, 193, 1142
  Sparking plugs, *see* Sparking
    plugs
  Sparkling wine industry, *see*
    Wine, Sparkling industry
  Spirits industry, *see* Spirits
    industry
  Tables, 307, 708, 866, 1697
  Television industry, *see*
    Televisions, Industry
  Television receivers, *see*
    Televisions, Receivers
  Textile industry, 63, 261, 354,
    383, 442, 615, 710, 715, 829
  Textile machinery, *see*
    Textiles, Machinery
  Tractors, 131, 1459, 1460
  Transport equipment, *see*
    Transport, Equipment
  Transport equipment
    industry, *see* Transport,
    Equipment industry
  Tyre industry, *see* Tyres,
    Industry
  Tyres, *see* Tyres
  Wool, *see* Wool
Conditions
  Economic, *see* Economics,
    Conditions
  Employment, *see*
    Employment, Conditions
  Political, *see* Politics,
    Conditions
  Working, *see* Working
    conditions
Conductivity measurements
  Electrical, *see* Electrical
    conductivity measurements
Conferences, 934, 1211, 1219,
  1732
  Agricultural, *see* Agriculture,
    Conferences
  See also Meetings
Confidentiality, 6
Congo (Brazzaville)
  Industrialization, 140, 280,
    336, 638, 1162, 1176, 1478,
    1524, 1597, 1720, 1753, 2200

  See also Associated African
    States and Madagascar;
    Central Africa; Congo
    (People's Republic)
Congo (Kinshasa)
  Industrialization, 141, 337,
    639, 1163, 1177, 1598, 1754
  See also Associated African
    States and Madagascar;
    Central Africa; Zaïre
Congo (People's Republic)
  Industrial enterprises, 424,
    1547, 1565, 1704, 1792
  See also Associated African
    States and Madagascar;
    Central Africa; Congo
    (Brazzaville)
Consultation, 1940
Consumers, 1677, 1682, 1741,
  1750, 1756
  Education, 724, *see also*
    Education
  Price indices, 1943, *see also*
    Indices; Prices
Consumption, 54, 127, 689, 1776
  Agricultural products, 46, 165,
    190, 263, 445, 603, 628, 909,
    910, 1012, 1173, 1307, 1316,
    1694, 1852, 1860, 1863, 2000,
    2098
  Alloys, *see* Alloys,
    Consumption
  Beverages, *see* Beverages
  Energy, *see* Energy,
    Consumption
  Fertilizer, *see* Fertilizers,
    Consumption
  Food, *see* Food, Consumption
  Milk, *see* Milk, Consumption
  Oils, 400, 1845
  Taxes, *see* Taxes, Value added
  Wheat, 293, 412
  Wine, see Wine, Consumption
  See also Marketing;
    Purchasing; Supply
Contaminants, *see* Pollutants
Contracts
  Agricultural, *see* Agriculture,
    Contracts

Labour, *see* Labour, Contracts
Control, 36
  Air pollution, *see* Air,
    Pollution control
  Arms, *see* Arms control
  Automatic, *see* Automation,
    Control
  Pest, *see* Pests, Control
  Pollution, *see* Pollution,
    Control
  Price, *see* Prices, Control
  Workers, *see* Workers,
    Control
Conversion
  Agricultural workers, 1187
  Coal industry, 292, 584
  Coal mines, 432, 536, 871, 945,
    1151, 1904
  Industrial, *see* Industries,
    Conversion
  Industrial enterprises, 1579
  Industrialized areas, *see*
    Industries, Areas
  Iron and steel industry, 292,
    584
  National policy, *see* Policy,
    National
  Social aspects, 33, 272, 296,
    297, 373, 451, 499, 526, 730,
    863, 1116, 1223, 1294, 1393,
    1615, 1671, 1784, 1811, 1901,
    2030, 2105
Cooperation, 95, 697, 1410, 1473,
  1849
  Agricultural, *see* Agriculture,
    Cooperation
  Agricultural enterprises, 385,
    585, 635, 723, 735, 882, 1003,
    1023, 1716, 1844, 1933, 1980,
    2008
  Agricultural production, 73,
    157, 320, 824, 892, 1330,
    1331, 1469, 1596
  Agricultural sector, 1146
  Financial, *see* Finance,
    Cooperation
  Fishing industry, *see* Fishing,
    Industry
  Technical, *see* Technical

    cooperation
  Trade union, 1407
  Youth, 1873, 2061
Corporation taxes, *see* Taxes,
  Corporation
Costs
  Building, *see* Buildings, Costs
  Coal mines, 443, 506, 1394
  Economic, *see* Economics,
    Costs
  Labour, *see* Labour, Costs
  Social, *see* Social costs
  See also Prices
Cotton, 63, 261, 354, 442, 710,
  715, 829
  Industry, 67, 134, 1437, *see*
    also Industries
  See also Textiles
Council
  European Coal and Steel
    Community, *see* European
    Coal and Steel Community,
    Council
Councils
  Association, *see* Association
    Councils
Countries
  Associated, *see* Associated
    countries
  Associated developing, *see*
    Associated developing
    countries
  Developed, *see* Developed
    countries
  Developing, *see* Developing
    countries
Court of Justice, *see* European
  Communities, Court of
  Justice
Craft enterprises, 3, *see also*
  Enterprises
Credit
  Agricultural, *see* Agriculture,
    Credit
  See also Financing
Crocheted goods, *see* Knitted
  and crocheted goods
Cultural workers, *see* Workers,
  Cultural

Currency, 104, 105, *see also*
   Money
Customs regulations, 1711, *see*
   also Regulations; Tariffs
Cycles, 132, 1032
   Industry, 24, 268, 979, 1329,
    1925, *see also* Industries

Dahomey
   Industrial enterprises, 951,
    1542, 1553, 1793, 2067
   Industrialization, 986, 992,
    1717, 1796
   See also Associated African
    States and Madagascar;
    West Africa
Dairy products, 867, 2015, *see*
   also Animals, Products;
   Butter markets; Eggs;
   Food; Milk
Damage, 86, 351, 405, 438, 511,
   512, 932, 1081, 1233, 1764,
   1787, 1814, 1850, 2127
Dates, 440, 441, 588, 589
Decision making
   Agricultural, *see* Agriculture,
   Decision making
Demand, 1186
Denmark
   Agricultural credit, 968, 1078
   Agricultural policy, 900, 1882
   Agricultural products, 910,
    1860, 2000
   Agriculture, 900, 1882
   Apprenticeships, 1148
   Audio industry, 2099
   Cereal trade, 478, 483, 754,
    759, 1446, 1451, 1946, 1951,
    2090, 2095
   Concentration, 879, 880, 983,
    984, 1076, 1077, 2099–101
   Consumption, 910, 1860, 2000
   Cooperation, 74, 181, 504,
    1382, 1453
   Domestic appliance industry,
    2099
   Economic laws, 1052, 1133
   Electrical appliance industry,
    2099

Fishing industry, 74, 181, 504,
   1382, 1453
Flour trade, 478, 483, 754, 759,
   1446, 1451, 1946, 1951, 2090,
   2095
Food distribution industry,
   879, 983, 1076, 2100
Food processing industry, 880,
   1077, 2101
Handicapped, 1932
Mixed farming models, 381,
   382, 699, 774, 775, 808, 809,
   874, 875, 1262, 1263, 1277,
   1978, 1979
Pharmaceutical industry, 984
Pollution control laws and
   practices, 967
Ports, 478, 483, 754, 759, 1446,
   1451, 1946, 1951, 2090,
   2095
Price surveys, 879, 983, 1076,
   2100
Production, 910, 1860, 2000
Radio industry, 2099
Rehabilitation, 1932
Teaching, 1693, 1977
Television industry, 2099
Trade union federations,
   1934
Women's employment, 384
See also European
   Communities; Western
   Europe
Densities
   Load, *see* Load densities
Description
   Work, *see* Work, Description
Detergents, 363, 713, 801, 1628,
   1813, *see also* Cleaning
   products
Developed countries
   Agricultural markets, 1089
Developing countries, 1195,
   1846
   Agricultural markets, 1089
   Agricultural surpluses, 970,
    1044, 1369, 2168
   Associated, *see* Associated
    developing countries

Food aid, 317, 970, 1044, 1088, 1349, 1369, 2168, 2174
See also Third World
Development
Agricultural, *see* Agriculture, Development
Economic, *see* Economics, Development
Industrial, *see* Industries, Development
Long term, 1335
Medium term, 1335
Policy, 1718, 1745, *see also* Policy
Regional, *see* Regions, Development
Regional economic, *see* Regions, Economic development
Regional policy, *see* Regions, Development policy
Research and, *see* Research and Development
See also Progress; Redevelopment; Reform; Resources
Dioxides
Sulphur, *see* Sulphur dioxide
Direct elections, *see* Elections, Direct
Disparities
Regional, *see* Regions, Disparities
Distribution
Food, *see* Food, Distribution
Food industry, *see* Food, Distribution industry
See also Marketing; Selling
Domestic appliances, 22, 23, 266, 267, 415, 566, 827, 1118, 1327, 1328, 1842, 1843, 1988
Industry, 2099, *see also* Industries
See also Appliances
Draft regulations, *see* Regulations, Draft
Drinks
Soft, 145, 193, 508, 1142, 1408, 2018, *see also* Fruit, Juices

See also Beverages
Dwellings, *see* Housing

Earnings, *see* Wages
East, 1691, 1692
Eastern Europe, 621, 1675
Transport, 601, 877
Youth, 1873, 2061
See also Europe; Union of Soviet Socialist Republics
Ecological results, 124, 257, 313, 395, 410, 449, 515, 1174, 1180, 1332, 1484, 1749, 1812, 1916, 1993, *see also* Environment
Econometrics, 51
Economic and Social Committee, *see* European Communities, Economic and Social Committee
Economics, 293, 372, 412, 464, 507, 663, 732, 795, 1503, 1638, 2084, 2086
Actions, 43, 641
Activities, 27, 30, 31, 240, 273, 392, 465, 467, 487, 717, 1221, 1222, 1518, 1576, 1661, 1668, 1906
Administration, 547, 548, 622, 623, 1623, 1624, *see also* Administration
Associations, 399, *see also* Associations
Conditions, 15, 89, 152, 232, 237, 420, 977, 1007, 1282, 1296, 1322, 1362, 1431, 1439, 1622, 1795, 2035, 2037, 2193, *see also* Poverty
Costs, 366, 2023, *see also* Costs
Development, 414, 922, 1040, 1204, 1321, 2033, *see also* Development
Energy, *see* Energy, Economy
Integration, 374, 740, 833, *see also* Integration
Laws, 294, 407, 640, 696, 1052, 1133, 1269, 1435, 2087, 2088, 2199, *see also* Laws

Economics—*contd*
Life, 542
Planning, 2020, *see also*
Industries, Location;
Planning
Policy, 763, 1127, 2191, 2204,
see also Policy
Programmes, 1305, *see also*
Programmes
Regional, *see* Regions,
Economics
Sectors, 944
Selling, 509, 1248, 1670
Structures, 70, 496, 1810, *see*
also Structures
Unions, 183, 1323, 1728, 1730,
2087, 2152, 2153, 2194, *see*
also Unions
See also Finance; Income;
Inflation; Macroeconomics,
Methods; Trade
Education, 95, 406, 697, 1154,
1231, 1410, 1473, 1616, 1806,
1849
Consumer, *see* Consumers,
Education
Leave, 227, 404, 703, 762, 985,
2062, 2121, 2154, *see also*
Employment, Conditions
Policy, 955, 1713, *see also*
Policy
Statistics, 644, 1019, 1530,
1656, *see also* Statistics
Systems, 1021, 1529, 1530,
2131, 2132, *see also*
Systems
See also Graduates; Pupils;
Schools; Students; Teachers;
Teaching
E.E.C., *see* European Economic
Community
Eggs
Price statistics, 739, 1976, *see*
also Prices; Statistics
Production, 1637, *see also*
Production
Products, 738, *see also*
Products
See also Dairy products; Food

Elections
Direct, 88, 429, 430, 595, 1387,
1589, 1880
Programmes, 915, *see also*
Programmes
See also Suffrage
Electrical appliance industry,
566, 1988, 2099, *see also*
Appliances; Industries
Electrical conductivity
measurements, 858
Electrical engineering industry,
22, 23, 266, 267, 415, 827,
1118, 1327, 1328, 1842, 1843,
see also Engineering;
Industries
Electrical equipment, 415, 827,
939, 1118, 1465, 1888, *see*
also Batteries; Radios,
Receivers; Sparking plugs;
Televisions, Receivers
Electromechanical products,
592, 593, 815, 816, 1389,
1390, 1738, 1739, 1868, 1869,
see also Products
Electronics
Equipment, 22, 23, 266, 267,
1327, 1328, *see also*
Equipment
Industry, 87, 416, 700, 1574,
see also Industries
Products, 592, 593, 815, 816,
1389, 1390, 1738, 1739, 1868,
1869, *see also* Products
Emphysema, 1507, *see also*
Medicine
Employees, 186, 187, 646, 655,
1912
Participation, *see* Workers,
Participation
See also Workers
Employers, 1999, *see also*
Workers
Employment, 147, 177, 390, 545,
645, 649, 650, 680, 896, 929,
1001, 1020, 1041, 1202, 1367,
1381, 1415, 1521, 1522, 2007,
2138
Actor, *see* Actors

Agricultural, *see* Agriculture, Employment
Conditions, 551, 1681, 1824, *see also* Education, Leave; Working conditions
Jurisdiction, 173, 270, 657, 925, 998, 1377
Musicians, *see* Musicians
Regional, *see* Regions, Employment
Sea fishing, 83, 178, 549, 887, 1783
Services, 396, 458, 845, 878, 1042, 1915, 2181
Temporary, 1325, 1819
Women, *see* Women, Employment
See also Labour; Occupations; Re-employment; Underemployment; Unemployment
Energy, 210, 397, 1138, 1140, 1235
Balance, 884, 2150
Consumption, 884, 1744, 1921, 2021, *see also* Consumption
Economy, 1708, 1712, 2036, *see also* Economics
Nuclear, 331
Policy, 26, 188, 662, 1004, 1139, 1494, 1655, *see also* Policy
Prices, 1710, *see also* Prices
Products, 1711, *see also* Products
Sources, 1303, *see also* Coal; Gas; Petroleum
Engineering
Civil, *see* Civil engineering
Electrical industry, *see* Electrical engineering industry
Mechanical industry, *see* Mechanical engineering industry
Enlargement, 288, 450, 498, 516, 1098, 1846, 2009, 2010, 2069, 2076
Enterprises, 788, 1295, 1758, 2140, 2202
Agricultural, *see* Agriculture, Enterprises
Commercial, *see* Commerce, Enterprises
Concentration, 217
Craft, *see* Craft enterprises
Horticultural, *see* Horticulture, Enterprises
Industrial, *see* Industries, Enterprises
Joint stock, 1259, 1816–18, 2197
Large scale, 149, 309, 1036, 1158, 1254, 1854, 1855, 2109
Medium-sized, 198, 586, 587, 1053
Medium-sized industrial, *see* Industries, Medium-sized enterprises
Private, 1899
Public, 2108
Small-sized, 198, 586, 587, 994, 1053
Small-sized industrial, *see* Industries, Small-sized enterprises
See also Businesses; Organizations
Environment, 58, 196, 290, 896, 1082–6, 1107, 1184, 1242–6, 1367, 1642–6, 1684–8, 2120, 2122, 2192, 2210
Protection, 1629
Rural, *see* Rural environment
See also Ecological results; Industries, Areas; Noise; Pollution
Equipment
Audio, *see* Audio equipment
Civil engineering, *see* Civil engineering, Equipment
Electrical, *see* Electrical equipment
Electronic, *see* Electronics, Equipment
Handling, *see* Handling, Equipment

Equipment—*contd*
  Hoisting, *see* Hoisting
    equipment
  Lifting, *see* Lifts, Equipment
  Mining, *see* Mines, Equipment
  Transport, *see* Transport,
    Equipment
  Transport industry, *see*
    Transport, Equipment
    industry
  See also Appliances;
    Machinery; Receivers
Errors, 624, 1630, 1960, 1971, *see*
  also Statistics
Essential oils, *see* Oils, Essential
Establishments
  Stand, *see* Stand
    establishments
Estate
  Real, *see* Real estate
Ethiopia
  Food aid, 1347
  See also Africa
Euratom, *see* European Atomic
    Energy Community
Europe, 915, 1290, 1312, 1692
  Architectural heritage, 1737
  Arms control, 469
  Auditing, 9
  Capital markets, 1891
  Carbon monoxide poisoning,
    123, 362, 1130, 1592
  Competition policy, 2085
  Consumers, 1677, 1682, 1741,
    1756
  Currency, 104, 105
  Eastern, *see* Eastern Europe
  Economic integration, 740, 833
  Economic programmes, 1305
  Energy, 397, 1138, 1235
  Energy policy, 1494
  Fees, 215, 1918
  Frontier areas, 1922
  Industrial concentration, 1626
  Institutions, 1138
  Integration, 562, 786, 789, 835,
    893, 1302, 1515, 1728
  Investment, 162
  Joint stock enterprises, 1259,

    1816–18
  Jurists, 666
  Labour market policy, 1213
  Monetary policy, 785
  Monetary system, 785
  Motor vehicles, 2079
  Nuclear energy, 331
  Patents, 106–8, 215, 637, 1917,
    1918
  Policy, 331, 469, 1357
  Political unity, 833
  Population, 123, 362, 1060,
    1130, 1592
  Ports, 1061
  Poverty perception, 1683, 1742
  Public opinion, 1103, 1743
  Regional policy, 1942
  Regulations, 215, 1918
  Research and development,
    1235
  Schools, 1609
  Science, 409, 1103, 1743
  Secondary schools, 849
  Social policy, 891
  South-Eastern, *see*
    South-Eastern Europe
  Speeches, 370, 1423
  Trade mark laws, 820
  Trade union federations, 1407
  Union, 238, 564, 1145, 2013
  Unity, 1806, 1887
  Vocational training, 1213
  Western, *see* Western Europe
  Workers' representation, 1259
European Atomic Energy
    Community, 35, 561, 726
  Scientific and technical
    research, 794
  See also Belgium; European
    Communities; European
    Parliament; France;
    Germany (Federal
    Republic); Italy;
    Luxembourg; The
    Netherlands
European Coal and Steel
    Community, 437, 1131,
    1424, 1820, 1937, 1941, 1956,
    2118, 2164, 2165, 2207

Association Councils, 2139
Auditing, 667–72, 1071, 1072, 1944, 1945, 2042–52
Business organization, 1342
Capital goods, 94, 630, 1074, 1105, 1496, 1506, 1602, 1870, 1876, 2054
Coal mines, 11, 295, 495, 860, 1247, 1747, 2006, 2029
Coal organizations, 560
Collective bargaining, 731
Conferences, 934
Consumption, 54, 127, 689, 1776
Cooperation, 95, 697, 1410, 1473, 1849
Council, 2139
Economic activities, 27, 30, 31, 240, 273, 392, 465, 467, 717, 1221, 1222, 1518, 1576, 1661, 1668, 1906
Economic integration, 374
Education, 95, 697, 1410, 1473, 1849
Employment laws, 177, 545, 929, 1001, 1381, 1415
Energy balance, 884, 2150
Energy economy, 1708, 1712, 2036
Enterprises, 2140
Exports, 94, 630, 1074, 1105, 1496, 1506, 1602, 1870, 1876, 2054
Family budgets, 126, 674, 1969, 2136
Finance, 27, 30, 31, 240, 273, 392, 465, 467, 717, 1221, 1222, 1518, 1576, 1661, 1668, 1906
High Authority, 1304, 1420, 2104
Housing, 128, 653, 691
Housing improvement, 1170, 1981, 2206
Income, 54, 127, 689, 1776
Industrial location, 246, 1338
Industries, 95, 128, 129, 159, 311, 532, 653, 690, 691, 697, 731, 753, 859, 1153, 1275,
1342, 1410, 1470, 1473, 1653, 1777, 1849, 1910, 1911, 2028, 2060, 2119
Iron and steel industry, 233, 522, 919, 953, 1584, 1881, 1962
Iron ore mines, 135, 144, 312, 1495, 2159
Labour contract laws, 171 269, 923, 995, 1205, 1375
Labour costs, 690, 1777, 1910, 1911
Labour laws, 540
Laws, 27, 30, 31, 240, 273, 392, 465, 467, 717, 1221, 1222, 1518, 1576, 1661, 1668, 1906
Legal administration, 175, 535, 927, 1206, 1379, 2133
Mergers, 436, 2140
Planning, 246, 1338
Prices, 54, 127, 689, 1776
Productivity measurements, 753, 1470, 2060
Professional organizations, 175, 535, 927, 1206, 1379, 2133
Purchasing power, 54, 127, 689, 1776
Speeches, 560, 1304, 1938
Statistical analysis, 2119
Supranationality, 2141
Technical progress, 1342
Trade unions, 242
Trainers' training, 129, 159, 311, 532, 859, 1153, 1275, 2028
Treaties, 1073, 2141
Unemployment, 174, 543, 926, 999, 1278
Vocational training, 11, 135, 144, 233, 295, 312, 495, 522, 860, 919, 953, 1247, 1495, 1584, 1747, 1881, 1962, 2006, 2029, 2159
Wages, 690, 1777, 1910, 1911
Workers, 126, 128, 653, 674, 691, 1969, 2136
Workers' income, 690, 1777, 1910, 1911, 2119

European Coal and Steel—*contd*
  Workers' protection, 174, 543,
    926, 999, 1378, 1413
  Workers' re-employment, 2104
  Workers' representation laws,
    176, 544, 928, 1000, 1380,
    1414
  See also Belgium; European
    Communities; European
    Parliament; France;
    Germany (Federal
    Republic); Italy;
    Luxembourg; The
    Netherlands
European Communities, 60, 339,
  554, 555, 834, 836, 1290,
  1333, 1388, 1497, 1516, 1673,
  1674
  Acts of Accession, 1291
  Aerospace industry, 258, 260,
    604, 610, 625, 626, 961, 962
  Agricultural accounts, 1306
  Agricultural aid, 1365, 2057
  Agricultural credit, 2111
  Agricultural decision making,
    2148
  Agricultural enterprises, 4,
    391, 723, 825, 1003, 1716,
    1844, 1933, 2008
  Agricultural forecasting, 5,
    164, 189, 602, 1051, 2189
  Agricultural machinery price
    statistics, 1013
  Agricultural policy, 110, 111,
    197, 565
  Agricultural price statistics,
    799
  Agricultural production
    factors, 1890, 2142, 2145
  Agricultural production price
    indices, 493
  Agricultural products, 722
  Agricultural reform, 1313
  Agricultural sector, 1146,
    1890, 2089, 2142, 2145
  Agricultural socio-economic
    structures, 1010, 1011, 1689,
    1690
  Agricultural structures, 1890,

    2142, 2145
  Agriculture, 1508, 1583
  Air pollution, 869
  Alpine areas, 1718, 1745
  Animal slaughtering, 1171,
    1399
  Averages, 688, 1775, 1909
  Balance of payments, 1147
  Beef carcasses, 37
  Beef production, 352
  Beverage consumption, 289,
    525
  Business statistics, 6
  Cereal trade, 484, 760, 1452,
    1952, 2096
  Civil servants, 551, 1681, 1824
  Commission, 811, 1288, 1289,
    1512–14, 1726, 1830
  Competition, 1825
  Competitiveness, 161, 1128,
    1654, 2034
  Conditions of employment,
    551, 1681, 1824
  Confidentiality, 6
  Consumer price index
    harmonisation, 1943
  Cooperation, 723, 1003, 1146,
    1716, 1844, 1933, 2008
  Corporation taxes, 1997, 1998
  Court of Justice, 570, 1172,
    1935, 2097
  Cultural workers, 822
  Development policy, 1718,
    1745
  Economic and Social
    Committee, 1940
  Economic conditions, 1622
  Economic laws, 2087
  Economic policy, 2191
  Economic union, 2087, 2152,
    2153
  Educational leave, 227, 404,
    703, 762, 985, 2062, 2121,
    2154
  Educational policy, 955,
    1713
  Educational statistics, 1530
  Educational systems, 1021,
    1529, 1530, 2131, 2132

Electronics industry, 87, 416, 700, 1574

Employees, 186, 187

Employment, 645, 680, 896, 1367, 1521

Employment jurisdiction, 173, 270, 657, 925, 998, 1377

Energy, 1140

Energy policy, 1139

Enlargement, 288, 450, 498, 516, 1098, 2076

Environment, 896, 1082–6, 1184, 1242–6, 1367, 1642–6, 1684–8, 2192

Environmental protection, 1629

Exchange rates, 84

Executives, 367

Family budgets, 250

Farmers, 352

Feed balance sheets, 1124

Finance, 1530

Financing, 960, 1474, 1733

Flour trade, 484, 760, 1452, 1952, 2096

Food policy, 580

Forestry, 1082–6, 1242–6, 1642–6, 1684–8

Gas prices, 386

General reports, 1512, 1513, 1726, 1729, 1830, 1832

Geography, 1672

Graduates, 251

Handicapped, 10, 169, 1932

Harmonized statistics, 688, 1775, 1909

Hill farming, 1718, 1722, 1745

Housing, 643, 676

Income, 16, 79, 289, 525, 613, 1239, 1798

Income taxes, 1997, 1998

Indirect taxes, 4, 391, 825

Industrial health, 1344

Industrial policy, 361

Industries, 677, 688, 1091, 1092, 1775, 1909

Inflation, 84

Inheritances, 16, 79, 613, 1239, 1798

Input-output table methodology, 326, 766, 778, 1075, 1169, 1575

Institutional structure, 1400

Institutions, 835, 893, 1147, 1302, 1479–81, 1834

Investment, 343

Iron and steel areas, 1517

Labour costs, 677, 1091, 1092

Land transport, 1059

Laws, 830, 831, 1181

Legal harmonization, 780

Long term policy, 1279, 1281

Macroeconomic methods, 4, 391, 825

Manganese, 411, 736

Manpower, 155

Manpower sample surveys, 651

Maps, 335, 575, 1057, 1517

Medical research, 1344

Medium-sized enterprises, 198, 586, 587, 1053

Mergers, 367

Methods, 5, 164, 189, 493, 602, 1051, 2189

Mining areas, 1517

Mobility, 822

Models, 5, 164, 189, 602, 1051, 2189

Monetary union, 2087, 2152, 2153

National income, 733

Non-governmental organizations, 1629

Nuclear safety, 182

Physical plans, 1184, 2192

Policy, 1278

Political conditions, 516

Political unification, 419

Pollution control laws and practices, 1267

Polyvalency, 701

Population, 155, 651, 1521

Pork production statistics, 888, 1228, 1867

Ports, 484, 760, 1452, 1952, 2096

Prices, 289, 525

European Communities—*contd*
Property laws, 776, 853, 1121
Public enterprises, 2108
Public expenditure, 220, 221, 427, 733, 1939
Public finance, 103, 2188
Pupils, 153, 252, 1021, 1529, 1530
Real estate, 205
Regional analysis, 1010, 1011, 1689, 1690
Regional development, 1155, 1276
Regional economics, 1767
Regional policy, 1126, 1155, 1276
Regional problems, 2009, 2010
Rehabilitation, 10, 169, 1932
Research and Development, 220, 221, 236, 427, 1008, 1009, 1939
Research and Development policy, 1404, 1490
Rights, 125
Seasonal variations, 1385
Small-sized enterprises, 198, 586, 587, 994, 1053
Social accounts, 847
Social indicators, 2, 1018, 2135
Social policy, 1214–16, 1218, 2014
Social protection, 847
Social security, 186, 187, 960, 1219, 1474, 1733, 1735
Social security jurisdiction, 173, 270, 657, 925, 998, 1377
Social security systems, 534
Socio-economic structures, 1517
Speeches, 368, 371
Staff regulations, 551, 1681, 1824
Statistical methods, 1385
Steel trade, 180
Students, 153, 252, 1021, 1529
Stunning, 1171, 1399
Supply, 411, 736
Suretyship laws, 513
Tariffs, 350

Taxation policy, 343
Teacher retraining, 1714
Teacher training, 1715
Teachers, 251
Teaching, 1700
Teaching systems reform, 1713
Techniques, 5, 164, 189, 602, 1051, 2189
Temporary employment, 1325, 1819
Tractor price statistics, 1013
Trade, 350, 411, 736
Training, 1713
Treaties, 367, 550, 1240, 1823
Value added taxes, 205, 994, 2089
Vegetation maps, 216, 1889
Vocabularies, 550, 551, 1240, 1681, 1823, 1824
Vocational training, 701
Vocational training systems, 2131, 2132
Wage statistics, 688, 1775, 1909
Women workers, 428
Women's employment, 1984–6
Working conditions, 428
See also Belgium; Denmark; European Atomic Energy Community; European Coal and Steel Community; European Economic Community; European Parliament;.France; Germany (Federal Republic); Ireland; Italy; Luxembourg; The Netherlands; United Kingdom
European Community, *see* European Communities
European Economic Community, 13, 89, 517, 576, 600, 601, 621, 839, 873, 876, 877, 1195, 1209, 1212, 1296, 1312, 1320, 1343, 1348, 1463, 1675, 1757, 1786, 1839, 1846, 2024, 2041

Actors, 1090
Administration, 43, 301, 358, 583, 641, 1317, 1403
Agricultural areas, 933, 1027, 1058, 1502, 1510
Agricultural conferences, 1314
Agricultural cooperation, 1241
Agricultural enterprise models, 1411
Agricultural enterprises, 29, 318, 446, 1285, 1765, 1905, 2183
Agricultural employment, 454, 455, 577, 578, 790, 791, 916, 917, 937, 938, 1188, 1189, 1397, 1398, 1662, 1663, 2146, 2147
Agricultural income, 59
Agricultural policy, 1310, 1416, 1664
Agricultural production systems, 1361
Agricultural productivity, 314, 456, 489, 752, 1183, 1853, 2070
Agricultural products, 1454, 2117
Agricultural reform, 1311, 1313
Agricultural workers' conversion, 1187
Aid, 349, 632
Animal products, 149, 309, 1036, 1158, 1254, 1854, 1855, 2109
Barley products, 413, 1605
Beef carcasses, 122, 167, 529, 557, 734, 2151
Beef production, 1795
Bond market policy, 2113
Books, 2024
Bread, 1606, 1607, 1929, 1930
Budgets, 464, 1503, 2086
Butter markets, 748
Canals, 2022
Capital markets, 963
Cartels, 1315
Cattle, 149, 309, 1158, 1254, 1854, 2109

Cereal prices, 1637
Cereal storage, 930, 1505, 1874, 1975
Chicken, 1157
Clothing industry, 53, 1099
Collective agreements, 431
Commercial enterprises, 3
Commission, 539
Compensation, 86, 351, 405, 438, 511, 512, 932, 1081, 1233, 1764, 1787, 1814, 1850, 2127
Competition, 86, 351, 405, 438, 511, 512, 763, 781, 932, 1081, 1233, 1707, 1764, 1787, 1814, 1850, 2127, 2204
Competition policy, 782–4, 787
Competitiveness, 1036, 1855
Consumers, 1750
Consumption, 293, 412
Craft enterprises, 3
Damage, 86, 351, 405, 438, 511, 512, 932, 1081, 1233, 1764, 1787, 1814, 1850, 2127
Economic actions, 43, 641
Economic conditions, 1322, 2035
Economic development, 1204, 1321, 2033
Economic policy, 763, 1127, 2204
Economics, 293, 412, 464, 1503, 2086
Egg price statistics, 739, 1976
Egg production, 1637
Egg product markets, 738
Employment, 1090
Employment services, 396, 458, 845, 878, 1042, 1915, 2181
Energy, 210
Enlargement, 1846
Enterprises, 2202
Farmers, 1905
Fertilizer consumption, 170
Financial administration, 1475
Financial cooperation, 2041
Fiscal administration, 1475
Flax, 425

EEC—*contd*

Flour quality, 1606, 1607, 1929, 1930

Food aid, 315–17, 969–75, 1043–9, 1088, 1345–9, 1368–74, 2167–74

Food consumption, 239, 287, 553, 749, 1028, 1509, 1788, 2144

Food production, 239, 287, 553, 749, 1028, 1509, 1788, 2144

Fruit preservation and processing industry, 1022

Fruit selling, 509, 1248, 1670

Fruit trade, 1005

Grading systems, 413, 1605

Horticultural products, 1236

Industrial areas, 301, 358, 583, 1317, 1403

Industrial enterprises, 3

Industrial production indices, 642

Industries, 579, 681–7, 1095–7, 1768–74, 1907

Input-output tables, 80, 81, 206, 207, 285, 286, 452, 453, 494, 765, 842, 843, 1149, 1150, 1491, 1492, 1800, 1801, 2038, 2039

Inspection, 1005

Institutions, 1482, 1483

Investment, 873

Labour laws, 1090

Landlords, 821, 1649

Large scale enterprises, 149, 309, 1036, 1158, 1254, 1854, 1855, 2109

Laws, 431, 665

Legal appeals, 43, 641

Lessees, 821, 1649

Marketing, 1157, 1236

Markets, 324, 325, 1454, 1751, 1752

Medium-sized industrial enterprises, 1953, 2190

Methods, 1411

Migrant agricultural workers, 349, 632

Migrant workers, 1676

Milk markets, 1260

Milk processing industry, 694

Monetary policy, 345

Musicians, 1090

Patents, 1828

Pension funds, 963

Petroleum refining, 398

Pigs, 149, 309, 1158, 1254, 1854, 2109

Planning, 301, 358, 583, 1317, 1403

Policy, 1195

Pork carcasses, 122, 167, 529, 557, 734, 2151

Pork production, 1637

Poultry meat production, 1637

Practice, 431

Price control, 987, 2156

Price policy, 2117

Processing, 293, 412

Production, 149, 293, 309, 412, 1036, 1157, 1158, 1254, 1854, 1855, 2109

Public purchasing, 328, 346

Publishing, 1815

Regional development, 539

Regional economic policy, 1416, 1664

Regional policy, 1129

Rights, 1676

Rural property, 1366

Small-sized industrial enterprises, 1953, 2190

Social accounts, 571, 1486, 1619

Social aspects, 1210

Social policy, 1217, 1220

Social results, 464, 1503, 2086

Social security, 133, 139, 501, 533, 959, 996, 1106, 1182, 2074, 2107

Speeches, 600, 1212

Standardization, 1005

State aid, 748

Surveys, 1953, 2190

Tax harmonization, 881

Taxes, 1905, 2202

Technical cooperation, 2041

Textile industry, 72
Towns, 408
Transport, 601, 877
Tropical oils and oilseeds
    markets, 1197
Turnover taxes, 2012
Value added tax
    harmonization, 464, 1503,
    2086
Vegetable preservation and
    processing industry, 1022
Vegetable selling, 509, 1248,
    1670
Vegetable trade, 1005
Vocational training, 3
Wage surveys, 579, 681–7,
    1095–7, 1768–74, 1907
Waterways, 2022
Wheat, 293, 412, 1606, 1607,
    1929, 1930
Wheat products, 413, 1605
Youth, 3
See also Belgium; European
    Communities; European
    Parliament; France;
    Germany (Federal
    Republic); Italy;
    Luxembourg; The
    Netherlands
European Investment Bank,
    271
European Parliament, 793, 931,
    1256, 1334, 1648, 2069, 2163
  Direct elections, 88, 429, 430,
    595, 1387, 1589, 1880
  Speeches, 34, 330, 332, 365,
    367, 371, 433–5, 560, 614,
    780–2, 832, 837, 894, 895,
    966, 1217, 1288, 1290, 1292,
    1297–1301, 1305, 1354–6,
    1358, 1417–22, 1512, 1513,
    1725, 1726, 1729, 1730, 1830,
    1832
European Parliamentary
    Assembly, *see* European
    Parliament
Exchange rates, 84
Executive officials, 158, 394,
    1919, 2155

Executives, 367
Exercise tests, 182A, 288A,
    385A, 428A, 450A, 878A,
    1155A, 1464A, 1478A,
    1648A, 1715A, 1808A,
    1819A, 2109A
Expenditure
  Public, 220, 221, 427, 733, 1939
    See also Finance; Income;
    State aid
Expenses, 2023
Export-oriented industries, *see*
    Industries, Export-oriented
Exports
  Capital goods, see Capital
    goods
  Textile industrialization,
    71
    See also Imports; Trade

Factories, 856, 1120
  Iron and steel, *see* Iron and
    steel, Factories
    See also Works
Factors
  Agricultural production, *see*
    Agriculture, Production
    factors
Family budgets, *see* Budgets,
    Family
Farm workers, *see* Agriculture,
    Workers
Farmers, 352, 1905, *see also*
    Agriculture, Workers
Farming
  Hill, 7, 303, 461, 581, 728, 883,
    1272, 1612, 1718, 1719, 1722,
    1745, 1746, 2102
  Mixed, 38–41, 375–82, 448,
    698, 699, 768–75, 802–9, 874,
    875, 935, 1196, 1262, 1263,
    1274, 1277, 1785, 1851, 1978,
    1979, 2071
    See also Agriculture
Farms, *see* Agriculture,
    Enterprises
Fats
  Supply, 720, 764, 914, 1190,
    1862, 2002

Federal Republic of Germany,
 see Germany (Federal
 Republic)
Federations
 Trade union, 1407, 1934
Feed
 Balance sheets, 1124 *see also*
  Balance sheets
 Grains, 913, 1861, 2001
 See also Fodder; Forage
Feeding
 Animal, *see* Animals, Feeding
Fees, 215, 1918, *see also* Wages
Ferrous alloys, *see* Iron, Alloys
Fertilizers
 Consumption, 170
 Price statistics, 2031
Finance
 Administration, 1475, *see also*
  Accounting; Expenditure;
  Income
 Cooperation, 2041
 Economic activities, 27, 30, 31,
  240, 273, 392, 465, 467, 717,
  1221, 1222, 1518, 1576, 1661,
  1668, 1906
 Educational systems, 1530
 Public, 103, 2188, *see also*
  Expenditure, Public;
  Income, National; State aid
 See also Capital; Insurance;
  Investment; Money
Financing, 942
 Forests, 1085, 1245, 1645, 1687
 Industrial conversion, 823,
  1580
 Investment, *see* Investment,
  Financing
 Social security, 960, 1474,
  1733, 1734
 See also Credit; Investment
Finland
 Agricultural policy, 907
 Agriculture, 907
 See also Western Europe
Firedamp, 1457, 1590
Firms, *see* Enterprises
Fiscal administration, 1475, *see
 also* Taxes

Fiscal regulations, 1711
Fish
 Canned, 1458
 Markets, 737, 885, 886, *see
  also* Markets
 See also Food; Sardines
Fishing
 Industry, 74, 82, 181, 504, 546,
  742, 743, 1132, 1382, 1427,
  1428, 1453, *see also*
  Industries
 Sea, 83, 178, 549, 887, 1783
 Small scale, 1383, 1429, 1625
 Statistics, 1250, *see also*
  Statistics
 Vessels, 547, 548, 622, 623,
  1623, 1624
 See also Agriculture
Flax, 425, *see also* Textiles
Flour
 Quality, 1606, 1607, 1929, 1930
 Trade, 97–102, 199–204,
  472–84, 754–60, 1108–13,
  1440–52, 1946–52, 2090–6
Fodder, 721, 2072, *see also* Feed;
 Forage
Food
 Aid, 315–17, 969–75, 1043–9,
  1088, 1345–9, 1368–74,
  2167–74, *see also* Aid
 Consumption, 239, 287, 553,
  749, 1028, 1509, 1788, 2144,
  see also Consumption
 Distribution, 779, 2198
 Distribution industry, 568,
  851, 879, 983, 1076, 1271,
  1659, 2100
 Industry, 224, 306, 307, 569,
  707, 708, 826, 852, 981, 991,
  1038, 1122, 1458, 1660, 1679,
  1696, 1697, 1923, 1926, *see
  also* Industries
 Policy, 580, *see also* Policy
 Processing industry, 880,
  1077, 2101, *see also*
  Industries; Processing
 Production, 239, 287, 553, 749,
  1028, 1509, 1788, 2144, *see
  also* Production

Products, 14, 305, 706, 1386,
1695, *see also* Products
See also Bread; Dairy
products; Feed; Fish; Fruit;
Meat; Nuts; Vegetables
Forage, 867, 2015, *see also* Feed;
Fodder
Forecasting
Agricultural, *see* Agriculture,
Forecasting
Foreign workers, *see*
Immigrants, Workers;
Migrants, Workers
Forestry, 1082–6, 1242–6,
1642–6, 1684–8, *see also*
Afforestation; Timber;
Wood
Forests, 1083, 1243, 1643, 1685
Private ownership, 1085, 1086,
1245, 1246, 1645, 1646, 1687,
1688
France
Administration, 301, 358, 583,
1317, 1403
Agricultural credit, 323, 1364,
1989
Agricultural enterprises, 635,
735, 1023
Agricultural machinery, 131
Agricultural manpower, 1207
Agricultural production, 157
Agricultural products, 445,
628, 1316, 1694
Agricultural reform, 76, 85,
90, 116, 213, 245, 340, 393,
520, 521, 627, 741, 800, 818,
1080, 1359, 1360, 1430, 1647,
1652, 1669, 1678, 1903, 2075,
2078, 2187
Agricultural structures, 226,
426, 594, 1455, 1651, 2068,
2209
Alpine areas, 2102
Apprenticeships, 191
Audio equipment, 415, 1118
Beef carcasses, 528
Beef statistical harmonization,
279
Beverages industry, 193, 1142

Brewing industry, 194, 1143,
1698
Cereal trade, 97–100, 199–202,
472–5, 1108–11, 1440–3
Champagne industry, 195,
1144, 1699
Chemical industry, 130
Children, 1231
Civil engineering equipment,
131
Coal mines, 536, 597
Concentration, 14, 130–2, 160,
192–5, 305–7, 415, 442, 471,
706–8, 1118, 1141–4, 1695–9
Consumption, 445, 628, 1316,
1694
Conversion, 536, 1579
Cooperation, 157, 635, 735,
743, 1023, 1132, 1428
Cotton, 442
Cycles, 132
Domestic appliances, 415, 1118
Economic administration, 547,
548, 622, 623, 1623, 1624
Economic conditions, 1296
Economic laws, 640
Economic life, 542
Education, 1231
Electrical engineering
industry, 415, 1118
Electrical equipment, 415,
1118
Family budgets, 460, 1721
Fishing industry, 743, 1132,
1428
Fishing vessels, 547, 548, 622,
623, 1623, 1624
Flour trade, 97–100, 199–202,
472–5, 1108–11, 1440–3
Food industry, 306, 307, 707,
708, 1696, 1697
Food products, 14, 305, 706,
1695
Handicapped, 169
Handling equipment, 131
Hill farming, 2102
Hoisting equipment, 131
Industrial areas, 301, 358, 583,
1317, 1403

France—*contd*
 Industrial enterprises, 1579
 Industries, 517, 576, 1343,
  1463
 Inflation, 1409
 Iron and steel areas, 1517
 Iron and steel industry, 1199
 Iron ore mines, 598, 1200
 Land markets, 226, 426, 594,
  1455, 1651, 2068, 2209
 Marketing, 727, 988, 2179
 Mechanical engineering
  industry, 131
 Mediterranean, 100, 202, 475,
  547, 548, 622, 623, 1111,
  1443, 1623, 1624
 Mergers, 635, 735, 1023
 Mining areas, 1517
 Mixed farming models, 39, 41,
  375, 376, 378, 448, 768, 769,
  771, 802, 803, 805, 935, 1196,
  1274, 1785
 Non-employment incomes,
  1409
 Office machinery, 131
 Ordinary wines, 727, 988, 2179
 Pharmaceutical industry, 160
 Pharmaceuticals, 130
 Photographic products, 130
 Planning, 301, 358, 583, 1317,
  1403
 Pollution control laws and
  practices, 357
 Ports, 97–100, 199–202, 472–5,
  1108–11, 1440–3
 Prices, 727, 988, 2179
 Production, 445, 628, 1316,
  1694
 Production prices, 573, 1395,
  1471, 1995
 Radio receivers, 415, 1118
 Reform, 226, 426, 594, 1455,
  1651, 2068, 2209
 Regional development, 1207
 Regional employment, 777
 Rehabilitation, 169
 Research, 547, 548, 597, 598,
  622, 623, 1199, 1200, 1623,
  1624
 Rural leases, 226, 426, 594,
  1455, 1651, 2068, 2209
 Sheep, 208, 1161, 2083, 2103
 Slope maps, 334, 1056
 Social life, 542
 Socio-economic structures,
  1517
 Soft drinks industry, 193, 1142
 Sparkling wines industry, 195,
  1144, 1699
 Spirits industry, 192, 1141
 Table wines, 573, 1395, 1471,
  1995
 Taxes, 635, 735, 1023
 Television receivers, 415, 1118
 Textile industry, 442
 Textile machinery, 131
 Tractors, 131
 Transport equipment
  industry, 132
 Tyre industry, 471
 Vocational training, 1231
 Women workers, 1983
 Wool, 442
 Workers, 1231
 Workers' participation, 542
 Working conditions, 1983
 See also European Atomic
  Energy Community;
  European Coal and Steel
  Community; European
  Communities; European
  Economic Community;
  Mediterranean countries;
  Western Europe
Freedom of the city, 364, 838,
 1293, 1731
Freezing
 Poultry, *see* Poultry, Freezing
 Poultry carcasses, *see* Poultry,
  Carcasses
Frontier areas, 1922
Fruit
 Canned, 1458
 Citrus, 256, 440, 441, 588, 589,
  2166, 2205
 Juices, 145, 508, 1408, 2018,
  see also Beverages; Drinks,
  Soft

Pomaceous, 2185
Preservation and processing
    industry, 1022
Production, 2005, *see also*
    Production
Selling, 509, 1248, 1670, *see
    also* Selling
Trade, 1005, *see also* Trade
Tropical, 440, 441, 588, 589,
    see also Bananas
See also Agriculture,
    Products; Almonds; Food;
    Horticulture; Orchards,
    Production
Funds
Pension, *see* Pensions, Funds
Revolving, *see* Revolving
    funds
Furnaces, 93, 993
Blast, 119, 283, 619, 1068,
    1352, 1587, 1965, 2162
Rotary, 1252, 1391, 1898
Shaft, 725, 1531, 1532
See also Iron and steel; Steels

Gabon
Industrial enterprises, 423,
    1546, 1566, 1705, 1791
Industrialization, 1478, 1524,
    1720, 2200
See also Associated African
    States and Madagascar;
    Central Africa
Gas
Prices, 386, *see also* Prices
See also Energy, Sources
General public, 1083, 1243, 1643,
    1685
General reports, 1512, 1513,
    1726, 1729, 1830, 1832
Geography, 1672
Germany (Federal Republic)
Administration, 301, 358, 583,
    1317, 1403
Agricultural contracts, 19,
    558, 1253, 1523
Agricultural credit, 976, 1002,
    1528
Agricultural enterprises, 1980

Agricultural machinery, 1459,
    1460
Agricultural manpower, 1511,
    1591, 2032
Agricultural production, 824,
    892
Agricultural products, 1012,
    1307, 1852
Agricultural structures, 226,
    426, 594, 1455, 1651, 2068,
    2209
Alpine areas, 883, 1719, 1746
Beef statistical harmonization,
    2027
Beverages industry, 225
Building machinery, 1459,
    1460
Canned fish, 1458
Canned fruit, 1458
Canned meat, 1458
Canned vegetables, 1458
Capital productivity, 1070
Cereal trade, 478, 479, 754,
    755, 1446, 1447, 1946, 1947,
    2090, 2091
Children, 1154, 1616
Coal mines, 443, 506, 871, 945,
    1151, 1193, 1394, 1904
Concentration, 224, 225, 779,
    939, 940, 1032, 1033,
    1458–60, 1465, 1466, 1842,
    1843, 1888, 2198
Consumption, 1012, 1307,
    1852
Conversion, 871, 945, 1151,
    1904
Cooperation, 82, 546, 742, 824,
    892, 1427, 1873, 1980, 2061
Costs, 443, 506, 1394
Cycles, 1032
Domestic appliances, 1842,
    1843
Economic conditions, 89
Economic development, 414,
    922, 1040
Economic laws, 2199
Economic structures, 70, 496,
    1810
Education, 1154, 1616

Germany (F.R.)—*contd*

Electrical engineering industry, 1842, 1843
Electrical equipment, 939, 1465, 1888
Family budgets, 563, 1928
Fish markets, 737, 886
Fishing industry, 82, 546, 742, 1427
Flour trade, 478, 479, 754, 755, 1446, 1447, 1946, 1947, 2090, 2091
Food distribution, 779, 2198
Food industry, 224, 1458
Handicapped, 10
Handling, 1886
Handling equipment, 1459, 1460
Herring prices, 737, 886
Hill farming, 883, 1719, 1746
Income, 443, 506, 1394
Industrial areas, 301, 358, 583, 1317, 1403
Industrial medical centres, 990, 1477
Industries, 1070
Inflation, 660, 1026, 1087
Investment, 1603, 1604
Iron and steel areas, 1517
Iron and steel factories, 990, 1477
Iron and steel industry, 524
Iron ore mines, 1192
Land markets, 226, 426, 594, 1455, 1651, 2068, 2209
Lifting equipment, 1459, 1460
Manufacturing, 1458
Marketing, 989, 1856, 2180
Mechanical engineering industry, 1459, 1460
Mergers, 1980
Mining areas, 1517
Mixed farming models, 380, 382, 698, 699, 773, 775, 807, 809, 875, 1263, 1851, 1979
Motor vehicle industry, 939, 1465, 1888
Non-employment incomes, 660, 1026, 1087

Office machinery, 1459, 1460
Ordinary wines, 989, 1856, 2180
Paper industry, 940, 1033, 1466
Paper products industry, 940, 1033, 1466
Planning, 301, 358, 583, 1317, 1403
Pollution control laws and practices, 1014, 1957
Ports, 478, 479, 754, 755, 1446, 1447, 1946, 1947, 2090, 2091
Prices, 989, 1856, 2180
Production, 1012, 1307, 1852
Production prices, 573, 1395, 1471, 1995
Radio receivers, 1842, 1843
Record players, 1842, 1843
Reform, 226, 426, 594, 1455, 1651, 2068, 2209
Regional development, 1511, 1591, 2032
Regional economic development, 414, 922, 1040
Regional economic structures, 1037, 1461, 1748, 1970, 2011
Rehabilitation, 10
Research, 524, 1192, 1193
Retail trade, 1886
Rural leases, 226, 426, 594, 1455, 1651, 2068, 2209
Sheep, 150, 2177
Social structures, 70, 496, 1810
Socio-economic structures, 1517
Surveys, 443, 506, 563, 1394, 1928
Table wines, 573, 1395, 1471, 1995
Taxes, 1980
Television receivers, 1842, 1843
Textile machinery, 1459, 1460
Tractors, 1459, 1460
Transport equipment, 1032
Tyre industry, 939, 1465, 1888
Vertical integration, 19, 558, 1253, 1523

Vocational training, 1154, 1616
Wholesale trade, 1886
Wine consumption, 702, 1866, 1974
Women workers, 1667
Workers, 1154, 1616
Working conditions, 1667
Youth, 1873, 2061
See also European Atomic Energy Community; European Coal and Steel Community; European Communities; European Economic Community; Western Europe
Glossaries, 28, 32, 78, 359, 360, 485, 744, 745, 918, 1062, 1063, 2115, *see also* Vocabularies
Goods
Capital, *see* Capital, Goods
Knitted and crocheted, *see* Knitted and crocheted goods
Leather, *see* Leather goods
See also Products
Governments
United Kingdom, *see* United Kingdom, Government
Grading systems, *see* Systems, Grading
Graduates, 251, *see also* Education; Students
Grains
Feed, *see* Feed, Grains
Gravitational models, *see* Models, Gravitational
Great Britain, *see* United Kingdom
Guidance
Vocational, *see* Vocational guidance

Halogens
Organic compounds, *see* Organo-halogen compounds
Handicapped, 10, 169, 1932
Handling, 1886
Equipment, 68, 131, 1136, 1459, 1460, *see also* Equipment
Harmonization
Beef statistics, *see* Beef, Statistics
Consumer price indices, *see* Consumers, Price indices
Legal, *see* Laws, Harmonization
Social statistics, 692
Statistics, *see* Statistics, Harmonized
Taxes, *see* Taxes, Harmonized
Value added taxes, 464, 1503, 2086
Health
Industrial, *see* Industries, Health
Heritage
Architectural, *see* Architectural heritage
Herrings
Prices, 737, 886
See also Fish
Hides and skins, 49, 50, 91, 92, 222, 223, 324, 325, 611, 612, 750, 751, 797, 798, 813, 814, 840, 841, 1030, 1031, 1034, 1035, 1229, 1230, 1401, 1402, 1500, 1501, 1572, 1573, 1633, 1634, 1751, 1752, 1821, 1822, 1835, 1836, 2025, 2026, 2125, 2126, *see also* Animals, Products
High Authority
European Coal and Steel Community, *see* European Coal and Steel Community, High Authority
Hill farming, *see* Farming, Hill
Hoisting equipment, 68, 131, 1136, *see also* Equipment; Lifts
Holland, *see* The Netherlands
Horizontal integration, *see* Integration, Horizontal
Horticulture
Enterprises, 1967, *see also* Enterprises

Horticulture—*contd*
  Products, 247, 1236, 1238, *see
    also* Products
  See also Agriculture; Fruit;
    Vegetables
Hours of work, *see* Work, Hours
  of
Household appliances, *see*
  Domestic appliances
Housing, 128, 643, 653, 676, 691
  Improvement, 1170, 1981,
    2206
  Social policy, 1211
Humidity, 858, *see also*
  Moisture; Water
Husbandry
  Beef, *see* Beef, Husbandry
Hygiene, 447, 921

Ignition, 463, 531
Immigrants
  Workers, 507, *see also*
    Workers
  See also Migrants
Imports
  Coal organizations, *see* Coal,
    Organizations
  See also Exports; Trade
Improvements
  Housing, *see* Housing,
    Improvement
Income, 16, 54, 79, 127, 289, 525,
  613, 689, 1239, 1776, 1798
  Agricultural, *see* Agriculture,
    Income
  Agricultural population, *see*
    Agriculture, Population
  Coal mines, 443, 506, 1394
  National, 733, *see also*
    Accounting, National;
    Finance, Public
  Non-employment, 18, 660,
    695, 946, 1026, 1054, 1087,
    1114, 1409, 1464, 2058
  Policy, 55, 179, 214, 1875,
    1897, *see also* Policy
  Small scale fishing, *see*
    Fishing, Small scale
  Taxes, *see* Taxes, Income

Workers, 682, 690, 1769, 1777,
  1910, 1911, 2119
  See also Expenditure;
    Finance; Profits; Wages
Indemnity
  Laws, 854, *see also* Laws
India
  Food aid, 973, 1047, 1372,
    2171
Indicators
  Social, *see* Social indicators
  Social security, *see* Social
    security, Indicators
Indices
  Agricultural production
    prices, *see* Agriculture,
    Production prices
  Concentration, *see*
    Concentration, Indices
  Consumer price, *see*
    Consumers, Price indices
  Industrial production, *see*
    Industries, Production
    indices
  Price and volume measures,
    890
Indirect taxes, *see* Taxes,
  Indirect
Industrialization, 140–3, 163,
  280, 336–8, 638, 639, 986,
  992, 1162, 1163, 1176–9,
  1478, 1524, 1597–1600, 1635,
  1636, 1717, 1720, 1753–5,
  1796, 2082, 2200
  Regional policy, 1519
  Textile, *see* Textiles,
    Industrialization
  See also Industries
Industries, 42, 95, 128, 129, 154,
  159, 311, 532, 579, 646, 653,
  655, 677, 681–8, 690, 691,
  697, 731, 753, 859, 889, 1070,
  1091, 1092, 1095–7, 1153,
  1275, 1342, 1410, 1470, 1473,
  1653, 1768–75, 1777, 1849,
  1907, 1909–13, 2028, 2060,
  2119, 2134
  Accidents, 673, 1485, 1778–82,
    see also Accidents

Aerospace, *see* Aerospace
industry
Areas, 301, 358, 583, 1317,
1403, 1611, *see also*
Environment; Towns
Audio, *see* Audio industry
Beverages, *see* Beverages,
Industry
Brewing, *see* Brewing
industry
Buildings, 1577, 1578
Champagne, *see* Champagne
industry
Chemical, *see* Chemical
industry
Clothing, *see* Clothing
industry
Coal, *see* Coal, Industry
Concentration, 20, 21, 61, 259,
264, 265, 353, 709, 714, 1234,
1326, 1626, *see also*
Concentration
Conversion, 235, 253, 254, 274,
321, 466, 488, 490, 505, 527,
538, 656, 823, 1029, 1203,
1295, 1324, 1337, 1467, 1534,
1580, 1759, 1807, 1899, 1900,
see also Conversion
Cotton, *see* Cotton, Industry
Cycles, *see* Cycles, Industry
Development, 1295, 1732, *see
also* Development;
Industrialization
Domestic appliance, *see*
Domestic appliances,
Industry
Electrical appliance, *see*
Electrical appliance
industry
Electrical engineering, *see*
Electrical engineering
industry
Electronics, *see* Electronics,
Industry
Enterprises, 3, 137, 138,
276–8, 387–9, 421–4, 605–9,
661, 718, 947–51, 1164–8,
1226, 1227, 1340, 1341,
1535–71, 1579, 1703–6,

1760–3, 1789–94, 2063–7, *see
also* Enterprises
Export-oriented, 1, 49, 50, 91,
92, 218, 219, 222, 223, 356,
440, 441, 588–93, 611, 612,
750, 751, 797, 798, 813–16,
840, 841, 1030, 1031, 1034, 1035,
1117, 1191, 1229, 1230, 1389,
1390, 1401, 1402, 1432, 1433,
1438, 1500, 1501, 1572, 1573,
1633, 1634, 1738, 1739, 1797,
1821, 1822, 1835, 1836, 1840,
1841, 1868, 1869, 1955, 2003,
2004, 2025, 2026, 2124–6, *see
also* Exports
Fishing, *see* Fishing, Industry
Food, *see* Food, Industry
Food distribution, *see* Food,
Distribution industry
Food processing, *see* Food,
Processing industry
France, 517, 576, 1343, 1463
Fruit preservation and
processing, *see* Fruit,
Preservation and processing
industry
Health, 1344
Iron and steel, *see* Iron and
steel, Industry
Location, 246, 1338, 1808, *see
also* Economics; Planning
Mechanical engineering, *see*
Mechanical engineering
industry
Medical centres, 990, 1477
Medicine, 182A, 288A, 385A,
428A, 450A, 878A, 1155A,
1464A, 1478A, 1648A,
1715A, 1808A, 1809, 1819A,
2109A, *see also* Medicine
Medium-sized enterprises,
1953, 2190
Milk processing, *see* Milk,
Processing industry
Motor vehicle, *see* Motor
vehicles, Industry
Paper, *see* Paper, Industry
Paper products, *see* Paper,
Products industry

Industries—*contd*
  Pharmaceutical, *see*
    Pharmaceuticals, Industry
  Photographic, *see*
    Photography, Industry
  Policy, 361, *see also* Policy
  Production, 2119A, *see also*
    Production
  Production indices, 642, *see*
    also Indices; Production
  Radio, *see* Radios, Industry
  Revolutions, 1303
  Small-sized enterprises, 1953,
    2190
  Soft drinks, 193, 1142
  Sparkling wine, *see* Wine,
    Sparkling industry
  Spirits, *see* Spirits, Industry
  Television, *see* Televisions,
    Industry
  Textile, *see* Textiles, Industry
  Transport equipment, *see*
    Transport, Equipment
    industry
  Tyre, *see* Tyres, Industry
  Vegetable preservation and
    processing, *see* Vegetables,
    Preservation and processing
    industry
  Wood, *see* Wood
  See also Industrialization
Inflation, 18, 84, 660, 695, 946,
    1026, 1054, 1087, 1114, 1284,
    1409, 1464, 2058, *see also*
    Economics; Prices
Information
  Scientific and technical, *see*
    Scientific and technical,
    Information
Infrastructure
  Road, *see* Roads,
    Infrastructure
  Transport, *see* Transport,
    Infrastructure
Inheritances, 16, 79, 613, 1239,
    1798
Injuries, 1782, *see also* Accidents
Input-output tables, 80, 81, 206,
    207, 285, 286, 326, 452, 453,
    494, 765, 766, 778, 842, 843,
    1075, 1149, 1150, 1169, 1491,
    1492, 1575, 1800, 1801, 2038,
    2039
Inspection, 1005, *see also*
    Standardization
Institutions, 835, 893, 1138,
    1147, 1302, 1479–83, 1834
  Monetary policy, 345
  Structures, 1400
  See also Organizations
Instruments, 243, 345, 2113
Insurance, 678, 693, 1094, 1487,
    1488, 1914, *see also* Finance
Integration
  Arms control, *see* Arms
    control
  Economic, *see* Economics,
    Integration
  European, *see* Europe,
    Integration
  Horizontal, 1156
  Price and volume measures,
    890
  Vertical, 19, 248, 558, 1156,
    1253, 1523, 1802, 2017, 2211
Internal markets, *see* Markets,
    Internal
International monetary systems,
    see Money, International
    systems
Intervention, 487
Investment, 343, 369, 1603, 1604
  Agricultural, *see* Agriculture,
    Investment
  American, 87, 162, 416, 700,
    873, 1574
  Financing, 33, 272, 296, 297,
    373, 451, 499, 526, 730, 863,
    1116, 1223, 1294, 1393, 1615,
    1671, 1784, 1811, 1901, 2030,
    2105, *see also* Financing
  Iron and steel markets, 1102,
    1594, 2158, *see also* Iron and
    steel; Markets
  Transport infrastructure, *see*
    Transport, Infrastructure
  See also Bonds, Market policy;
    Capital; Finance; Financing

Ireland
 Agricultural credit, 943
 Agricultural policy, 906, 1858
 Agricultural products, 910,
  1860, 2000
 Agriculture, 906, 1858
 Apprenticeships, 1264
 Cereal trade, 478, 483, 754,
  759, 1446, 1451, 1946, 1951,
  2090, 2095
 Concentration, 1679, 1923
 Consumption, 910, 1860, 2000
 Cooperation, 74, 181, 504,
  1382, 1453
 Economic conditions, 237,
  1007
 Economic laws, 1269
 Fishing industry, 74, 181, 504,
  1382, 1453
 Flour trade, 478, 483, 754, 759,
  1446, 1451, 1946, 1951, 2090,
  2095
 Food industry, 1679, 1923
 Handicapped, 1932
 Indemnity laws, 854
 Inflation, 695, 1464
 Mixed farming models, 381,
  382, 699, 774, 775, 808, 809,
  874, 875, 1262, 1263, 1277,
  1978, 1979
 Non-employment incomes,
  695, 1464
 Pollution control laws and
  practices, 1829
 Ports, 478, 483, 754, 759, 1446,
  1451, 1946, 1951, 2090, 2095
 Production, 910, 1860, 2000
 Rehabilitation, 1932
 Suretyship, 854
 Trade unions, 1498
 Women's employment, 384
 See also European
  Communities; Western
  Europe
Iron
 Alloys, 219, 1433, 1841, see
  also Alloys; Steels
 Ores, 135, 144, 312, 598, 725,
  1192, 1200, 1252, 1391, 1495,

  1531, 1532, 1898, 2159
  See also Iron and steel
Iron and steel
 Areas, 1517, see also Areas
 Factories, 990, 1477, see also
  Factories
 Industry, 120, 233, 284, 292,
  319, 497, 519, 522, 524, 584,
  620, 673, 817, 919, 953, 1050,
  1069, 1131, 1199, 1257, 1353,
  1384, 1424, 1485, 1584, 1588,
  1778–82, 1820, 1881, 1941,
  1956, 1962, 1966, 2175, 2184,
  2207, see also Industries
 Markets, 1101, 1102, 1593,
  1594, 2157, 2158, see also
  Markets
 Production, 218, 219, 1102,
  1432, 1433, 1594, 1840, 1841,
  2158, see also Production
 See also Furnaces; Iron; Steels
Irrigation, 663, 732, 795, 1638,
 2084, see also Agriculture
Italy
 Administration, 301, 358, 583,
  1317, 1403
 Agricultural contracts, 1802
 Agricultural credit, 231, 401,
  402, 1251
 Agricultural development, 8,
  304, 462, 582, 729, 1273,
  1613
 Agricultural enterprises, 385,
  585
 Agricultural manpower, 109,
  957, 1104
 Agricultural production, 320,
  1469, 1596
 Agricultural products, 603,
  1173
 Agricultural structures, 1425,
  1639
 Audio equipment, 22, 23, 266,
  267, 1327, 1328
 Batteries, 21, 265, 1326
 Beef carcasses, 241, 308, 1803
 Beef statistical harmonization,
  279
 Beverages industry, 69, 1137

Italy—*contd*

Cereal trade, 97, 101, 102, 199, 203, 204, 472, 476, 477, 1108, 1112, 1113, 1440, 1444, 1445

Children, 1154, 1231, 1616

Coal industry, 292, 584

Coal mines, 459, 1994

Concentration, 22–4, 62–9, 134, 261, 262, 266–8, 354, 355, 363, 710, 711, 713, 715, 716, 801, 1134–7, 1327–9, 1436, 1437, 1628, 1813

Concentration indices, 20, 264

Consumption, 603, 1173

Conversion, 292, 584

Cooperation, 82, 320, 385, 546, 585, 742, 1427, 1469, 1596

Cotton, 63, 261, 354, 710, 715

Cotton industry, 67, 134, 1437

Cycle industry, 24, 268, 1329

Detergents, 363, 713, 801, 1628, 1813

Domestic appliances, 22, 23, 266, 267, 1327, 1328

Economic administration, 547, 548, 622, 623, 1623, 1624

Economic laws, 1435

Electrical engineering industry, 22, 23, 266, 267, 1327, 1328

Electronic equipment, 22, 23, 266, 267, 1327, 1328

Fishing industry, 82, 546, 742, 1427

Fishing vessels, 547, 548, 622, 623, 1623, 1624

Flour trade, 97, 101, 102, 199, 203, 204, 472, 476, 477, 1108, 1112, 1113, 1440, 1444, 1445

Handicapped, 169

Hill farming, 7, 303, 461, 581, 728, 1272, 1612

Handling equipment, 68, 1136

Hoisting equipment, 68, 1136

Industrial areas, 301, 358, 583, 1317, 1403

Industrial concentration, 20, 21, 61, 259, 264, 265, 353, 709, 714, 1326

Inflation, 946

Iron and steel areas, 1517

Iron and steel industry, 292, 319, 584

Knitted and crocheted goods, 63, 261, 354, 710, 715

Land markets, 1425, 1639

Lifts, 68, 1136

Manufacturing, 65, 66, 68, 1135, 1136, 1436

Marketing, 727, 988, 2179

Markets, 712

Mechanical engineering industry, 68, 1136

Mergers, 385, 585

Methodology, 61, 259, 353, 709, 714

Mining areas, 1517

Mountain communities, 7, 303, 461, 581, 728, 1272, 1612

Non-employment incomes, 946

Office machinery, 66, 1436

Ordinary wines, 727, 988, 2179

Paper, 64, 262, 355, 711, 716

Paper industry, 62, 64, 262, 355, 711, 716, 1134

Paper products industry, 64, 262, 355, 711, 716

Planning, 301, 358, 583, 1317, 1403

Pollution control laws and practices, 444

Ports, 97, 101, 102, 199, 203, 204, 472, 476, 477, 1108, 1112, 1113, 1440, 1444, 1445

Prices, 727, 988, 2179

Production, 603, 1173

Production prices, 574, 1396, 1472, 1996

Radio receivers, 22, 23, 266, 267, 1327, 1328

Reform, 1425, 1639

Regional employment, 403

Regions, 712

Rehabilitation, 169

Research, 20, 264, 319, 547, 548, 622, 623, 1623, 1624

Rural leases, 1425, 1639

Sardines, 547, 548, 622, 623, 1623, 1624
Slope maps, 333, 1055
Social results, 459, 1994
Socio-economic structures, 1517
Sparking plugs, 21, 265, 1326
Structural reform, 8, 304, 462, 582, 729, 1273, 1613
Table wines, 574, 1396, 1472, 1996
Taxes, 385, 585
Television receivers, 22, 23, 266, 267, 1327, 1328
Textile industry, 63, 261, 354, 710, 715
Textile machinery, 65, 1135
Tyres, 21, 265, 1326
Vertical integration, 1802
Women workers, 146, 599, 1632
Wool, 63, 261, 354, 710, 715
Workers, 1154, 1231, 1616
Working conditions, 146, 599, 1632
See also European Atomic Energy Community; European Coal and Steel Community; European Communities; European Economic Community; Mediterranean countries; Western Europe
Ivory Coast
Industrial enterprises, 389, 949, 1540, 1568, 2065
Industrialization, 986, 992, 1717, 1796
See also Associated African States and Madagascar; West Africa

Job analysis, 1653
Joint stock companies, *see* Enterprises, Joint stock
Judgments, 243, 244, 964, 965, *see also* Laws
Juices
Fruit, *see* Fruit, Juices

Jurisdiction
Civil laws, 243, 244, 964, 965
Commercial laws, 243, 244, 964, 965
Court of Justice, 570, 1935
Employment, *see* Employment, Jurisdiction
Social security, *see* Social security, Jurisdiction
See also Laws
Jurists, 666, *see also* Laws

Knitted and crocheted goods, 63, 261, 354, 710, 715, 829, *see also* Textiles

Labour
Contracts, 171, 269, 923, 995, 1205, 1375, *see also* Contracts
Costs, 154, 677, 678, 690, 889, 1091–4, 1487, 1777, 1910, 1911, 2134, *see also* Costs
Force, *see* Manpower
Laws, 176A, 540, 544A, 928A, 1000A, 1090, 1380A, 1414A, *see also* Laws
Market policy, 1213, *see also* Markets; Policy
Organizations, 1833, *see also* Organizations
See also Employment; Occupations; Workers
Labourers, *see* Workers, Manual
Land
Agricultural, *see* Agriculture, Land
Marginal, 96, 1039, 2073
Markets, 226, 426, 594, 1425, 1455, 1639, 1651, 1665, 2068, 2209, *see also* Markets
Price statistics, 952, *see also* Prices; Statistics
Transport, 1059, *see also* Transport
Landlords, 821, 1649
Large scale enterprises, *see* Enterprises, Large scale

Latin America, 60, 1333
  Food aid, 1348
Laws
  Administration, 175, 535, 927,
    1206, 1379, 2133, *see also*
    Administration
  Agricultural enterprises, 821,
    1649
  Appeals, 43, 641
  Civil, 243, 244, 964, 965
  Collective agreements, 431
  Commercial, *see* Commerce,
    Laws
  Company, 746, 747
  Economic, *see* Economics,
    Laws
  Economic activities, 27, 30, 31,
    240, 273, 392, 465, 467, 717,
    1221, 1222, 1518, 1576, 1661,
    1668, 1906
  Employment, 177, 545, 929,
    1001, 1381, 1415
  European Community, 830,
    831, 1181, *see also* European
    Communities, Court of
    Justice
  European Economic
    Community, 665
  Harmonization, 780, 810
  Indemnity, *see* Indemnity,
    Laws
  Labour, *see* Labour, Laws
  Labour contracts, 171, 269,
    923, 995, 1205, 1375
  Pesticide residues, 48, 57, 114,
    300, 342, 659, 1702, 1879,
    2130, 2196
  Pollution control, 357, 444,
    767, 967, 1014, 1267, 1268,
    1650, 1829, 1957
  Property, *see* Property, Laws
  Rehabilitation, 10, 169,
    1932
  Residues, 867, 2015
  Selling, 509, 1248, 1670
  Suretyship, 513, 854
  Temporary employment, 1325,
    1819
  Trademark, *see* Trade, Marks

Unemployment, 174, 543, 926,
    999, 1378, 1413
  Workers' representation, 176,
    544, 928, 1000, 1380, 1414
  See also Jurisdiction; Jurists;
    Regulations; Statutes;
    Treaties
Leases
  Rural, *see* Rural leases
Leather goods, 49, 50, 91, 92,
    222, 223, 611, 612, 750, 751,
    797, 798, 813, 814, 840, 841,
    1030, 1031, 1034, 1035, 1229,
    1230, 1401, 1402, 1500, 1501,
    1572, 1573, 1633, 1634, 1821,
    1822, 1835, 1836, 2025, 2026,
    2125, 2126, *see also*
    Animals, Products; Goods
Leave
  Educational, *see* Education,
    Leave
Legislation, *see* Laws
Leisure, *see* Recreation
Lessees, 821, 1649
Libya
  Food aid, 1345
  See also North Africa
Life
  Economic, *see* Economics, Life
  Social, *see* Social life
Lifts, 68, 1136
  Equipment, 1459, 1460, *see
    also* Equipment
Linseed oils, *see* Oils, Linseed
Livestock
  Sample censuses, 624, 1630,
    1960, 1971
  See also Animals
Load densities, 2185
Location of industry, *see*
    Industries, Location
Lockouts, 172, 541, 924, 997,
    1376, 1412
Long term development, *see*
    Development, Long term
Long term policy, *see* Policy,
    Long term
Long term projections, *see*
    Projections, Long term

Luxembourg
  Agricultural credit, 323, 1364,
    1989
  Agricultural enterprises, 635,
    735, 1023
  Agricultural products, 46, 165,
    263, 2098
  Consumption, 46, 165, 263,
    2098
  Cooperation, 635, 735, 1023
  Family budgets, 17, 1848
  Handicapped, 169
  Industrial conversion, 274
  Inflation, 18
  Marketing, 989, 1856, 2180
  Mergers, 635, 735, 1023
  Non-employment incomes, 18
  Ordinary wines, 989, 1856,
    2180
  Prices, 989, 1856, 2180
  Production, 46, 165, 263, 2098
  Production prices, 574, 1396,
    1472, 1996
  Rehabilitation, 169
  Slope maps, 334, 1056
  Surveys, 17, 1848
  Table wines, 574, 1396, 1472,
    1996
  Taxes, 635, 735, 1023
  Women workers, 1255
  Working conditions, 1255
  See also Benelux; European
    Atomic Energy Community;
    European Coal and Steel
    Community; European
    Communities; European
    Economic Community;
    Western Europe

Machinery
  Agricultural, *see* Agriculture,
    Machinery
  Building, *see* Buildings,
    Machinery
  Office, *see* Office machinery
  Textile, *see* Textiles,
    Machinery
  See also Equipment

Macroeconomics
  Methods, 4, 391, 825
Madagascar
  Industrialization, 142, 163,
    338, 1178, 1599, 1635
  See also Associated African
    States and Madagascar;
    Malagasy Republic
Maintenance products, 828, 978,
  1924, *see also* Products
Malagasy Republic
  Industrial enterprises, 661,
    1340, 1552, 1555
  See also Associated African
    States and Madagascar;
    Madagascar
Mali
  Industrial enterprises, 276,
    1164, 1537, 1556, 1760
  Industrialization, 986, 992,
    1717, 1796
  See also Associated African
    States and Madagascar;
    West Africa
Man, 2120
Management
  Iron and steel industry, 1131,
    1424, 1820, 1941, 1956,
    2207
  Operational, 235, 321, 466,
    490, 505, 527, 538, 656, 1029,
    1203, 1324, 1337, 1534, 1759,
    1807, 1900
  See also Administration
Manganese, 411, 736
Manpower, 155, 156, 185, 652,
  1257
  Agricultural, *see* Agriculture,
    Manpower
  Agricultural statistics, *see*
    Agriculture, Manpower
    statistics
  Sample surveys, 633, 634, 648,
    651, 1405, 1462
  See also Labour;
    Underemployment;
    Unemployment
Manual workers, *see* Workers,
  Manual

Manufacturing, 1827
  Audio equipment, *see* Audio
    equipment
  Canned fish, 1458
  Canned fruit, 1458
  Canned meat, 1458
  Canned vegetables, 1458
  Cigarillos and cigars, 590, 591,
    2003, 2004
  Domestic appliances, 22, 23,
    266, 267, 415, 827, 1118,
    1327, 1328
  Electrical equipment, 415,
    827, 1118
  Electronic equipment, 22, 23,
    266, 267, 1327, 1328
  Handling equipment, 68,
    1136
  Hoisting equipment, 68, 1136
  Lifts, 68, 1136
  Office machinery, 66, 1436
  Paper industry, 940, 1033,
    1466
  Paper products industry, 940,
    1033, 1466
  Radio receivers, 22, 23, 266,
    267, 415, 827, 1118, 1327,
    1328
  Television receivers, 22, 23,
    266, 267, 415, 827, 1118,
    1327, 1328
  Textile machinery, 65, 1135
  Transport equipment, *see*
    Transport, Equipment
  Transport equipment
    industry, *see* Transport,
    Equipment industry
  Wood products, 1, 356, 1117,
    1191, 1438, 1955, 2124
Maps, 335, 575, 1057
  Slope, *see* Slopes, Maps
  Socio-economic structural,
    1517
  Vegetation, *see* Vegetation
    maps
Marginal land, *see* Land,
  Marginal
Market gardening, *see*
  Horticulture

Marketing
  Bananas, 148, 1237, 1982
  Chicken, 1157
  Horticultural products, 1236
  Ordinary wines, 727, 988, 989,
    1856, 2179, 2180
  Poultry, *see* Poultry
  Products, *see* Products,
    Marketing
  See also Distribution;
    Purchasing; Selling; Trade
Markets
  Agricultural, *see* Agriculture,
    Markets
  Agricultural products, 1079,
    1454
  Bond policy, *see* Bonds,
    Market policy
  Butter, *see* Butter markets
  Capital, *see* Capital, Markets
  Cereal, *see* Cereals, Markets
  Citrus fruit, 256, 2166,
    2205
  Coal, *see* Coal, Markets
  Concentration, 1234
  Egg products, 738
  Fish, *see* Fish, Markets
  Hides and skins, 324, 325,
    1751, 1752
  Internal, 812
  Iron and steel, *see* Iron and
    steel, Markets
  Italian, *see* Italy, Markets
  Labour policy, *see* Labour,
    Market policy
  Land, *see* Land, Markets
  Milk, *see* Milk, Markets
  Milk products, *see* Milk,
    Products markets
  Piglet, *see* Piglets, Markets
  Pork, *see* Pork, Markets
  Shipbuilding, *see* Shipbuilding,
    Markets
  Steel, *see* Steels, Markets
  Tropical oil and oilseed, 51,
    1197
  See also Trade
Materials
  Raw, *see* Raw materials

Mauritania
  Industrial enterprises, 277,
    947, 1535, 1557, 2063
  Industrialization, 986, 992,
    1717, 1796
  See also Associated African
    States and Madagascar;
    West Africa
Mauritius
  Industrial enterprises, 1341,
    1569
  See also Associated African
    States and Madagascar
Measurement
  Carbon monoxide poisoning,
    123, 362, 1130, 1592
  Electrical conductivity, *see*
    Electrical conductivity
    measurements
  Industrial concentration, 1626
  Mining equipment, 36
  Moisture, *see* Moisture,
    Measurement
  Productivity, *see* Productivity,
    Measurement
  Techniques, 119, 120, 283, 284,
    497, 619, 620, 1050, 1068,
    1069, 1352, 1353, 1587, 1588,
    1965, 1966, 2162
  See also Standardization
Measures
  Integrated price and volume,
    890
  Technical, *see* Technical
    measures
Meat, 49, 50, 91, 92, 222, 223,
    611, 612, 750, 751, 797, 798,
    813, 814, 840, 841, 1030,
    1031, 1034, 1035, 1229, 1230,
    1401, 1402, 1500, 1501, 1572,
    1573, 1633, 1634, 1821, 1822,
    1835, 1836, 2025, 2026, 2125,
    2126
  Canned, 1458
  Pig, 1595, 1872
  Poultry production, *see*
    Poultry, Meat production
  See also Animals, Products;
    Beef; Chicken; Pork

Mechanical engineering
    industry, 68, 131, 502, 864,
    866, 1136, 1266, 1459, 1460,
    1526, *see also* Engineering;
    Industries
Mechanization, 1258, 2176
  Blast furnaces, *see* Furnaces,
    Blast
  Stand establishments, 1084,
    1244, 1644, 1686
  See also Automation
Medicine
  Industrial, *see* Industries,
    Medicine
  Industrial centres, *see*
    Industries, Medical centres
  Research, 1344, *see also*
    Research
  See also Bronchitis;
    Emphysema;
    Physiopathology,
    Cardio-respiratory; Suture
    work
Mediterranean
  French, *see* France,
    Mediterranean
  Small scale fishing, 1383, 1429,
    1625
Mediterranean countries
  Citrus fruit, 256, 2166, 2205
  See also France; Italy
Medium-sized enterprises, *see*
    Enterprises, Medium-sized
Medium-sized industrial
    enterprises, *see* Industries,
    Medium-sized enterprises
Medium term development, *see*
    Development, Medium term
Meetings
  Summit, *see* Summit meetings
  See also Conferences
Mergers, 367, 436, 747, 1315,
    2140
  Agricultural enterprises, 385,
    585, 635, 735, 882, 1023,
    1980
  See also Take-over bids
Methodology
  Balance of payments, 1954

Methodology—*contd*
  Carbon monoxide poisoning,
    123, 362, 1130, 1592
  Concentration, *see*
    Concentration, Methodology
  Industrial concentration, 61,
    259, 353, 709, 714, 1234
  Input-output tables, 326, 766,
    778, 1075, 1169, 1575
  Surveys, 1967
  See also Models
Methods
  Agricultural enterprise
    models, 1411
  Agricultural forecasting, 5,
    164, 189, 486, 602, 1051,
    2189
  Agricultural pest control, 151,
    211
  Agricultural population
    income, 1766, 2081
  Agricultural production price
    indices, 493
  Beef, 492
  Iron and steel industry, 1131,
    1424, 1820, 1941, 1956, 2207
  Job analysis, 1653
  Long term projections, 1865
  Macroeconomic, *see*
    Macroeconomics, Methods
  Moisture measurement, 136,
    298, 616, 1992
  Multivariable statistical, *see*
    Statistics, Multivariable
    methods
  Pest control, 212
  Productivity measurement,
    753, 1470, 2060
  Regional policy, 1126
  Research, *see* Research,
    Methods
  Sampling, *see* Samples,
    Methods
  Statistical, *see* Statistics,
    Methods
  Taxes, 2202
  Wage structures, 693, 1488
  Water content, 1826, 1959
  Work description, 1653

  See also Techniques
Migrants
  Agricultural workers, 349,
    632, *see also* Agriculture;
    Workers
  Workers, 1676, *see also*
    Workers
  See also Immigrants
Migration
  Miners, 862
Milk
  Consumption, 868, 1261, 2016,
    see also Consumption
  Markets, 1260, *see also*
    Markets
  Processing industry, 694
  Production, 721, 2072
  Products markets, 912
  Residues, 867, 2015
  See also Dairy products
Mills
  Rolling, 118, 282, 347, 618,
    796, 898, 1067, 1351, 1392,
    1434, 1586, 1931, 1964, 2123,
    2161
  See also Steels
Miners, 862, *see also* Workers
Mines
  Areas, 1517
  Closure, 718
  Coal, *see* Coal, Mines
  Equipment, 36, *see also*
    Equipment
  Iron ore, 135, 144, 312, 598,
    1192, 1200, 1495, 2159
Mixed farming, *see* Farming,
    Mixed
Mobility
  Cultural workers, 822
Models
  Agricultural enterprises, 1411
  Agricultural forecasting, 5,
    164, 189, 486, 602, 1051,
    2189
  Beef, 492
  Gravitational, 1601
  Mixed farming, 38–41,
    375–382, 448, 698, 699,
    768–75, 802–9, 874, 875, 935,

1196, 1262, 1263, 1274, 1277,
1785, 1851, 1978, 1979, 2071
Pomaceous fruit production,
2185
See also Methodology;
Techniques
Moisture
Measurement, 136, 298, 616,
1992
See also Humidity; Water
Money
International systems, 417, 418
Policy, 345, 785
Systems, 785
Unions, 183, 1323, 2087, 2152,
2153, 2194, *see also* Unions
See also Currency; Finance
Motor cycles, *see* Cycles
Motor vehicles, 2079
Industry, 939, 1465, 1888, *see
also* Industries
See also Tractors
Mountain communities, *see*
Communities, Mountain
Multivariable statistical
methods, *see* Statistics,
Multivariable methods
Musicians, 1090, *see also*
Workers

National accounting, *see*
Accounting, National
National income, *see* Income,
National
National policy, *see* Policy,
National
Netherlands, The
Administration, 301, 358, 583,
1317, 1403
Agricultural credit, 45, 1499,
1525, 2053
Agricultural enterprises, 882
Agricultural products, 190
Agricultural structures, 1665
Beef statistical harmonization,
2027
Beverages industry, 229, 980,
1631
Cereal trade, 478, 481, 754,

757, 1446, 1449, 1946, 1949,
2090, 2093
Chemical industry, 978, 1924
Coal mines, 432, 1804
Concentration, 229, 230,
978–82, 991, 1038, 1122,
1123, 1631, 1924–6, 1958
Consumption, 190
Conversion, 432
Cooperation, 743, 882, 1132,
1428
Cycle industry, 979, 1925
Economic laws, 696, 2088
Electoral programmes, 915
Employers, 1999
Family budgets, 209, 249,
1968
Fish markets, 737, 886
Fishing industry, 743, 1132,
1428
Flour trade, 478, 481, 754, 757,
1446, 1449, 1946, 1949, 2090,
2093
Food industry, 981, 991, 1038,
1122, 1926
Handicapped, 10
Herring prices, 737, 886
Industrial areas, 301, 358, 583,
1317, 1403
Industrial buildings, 1578
Inflation, 1054
Iron and steel areas, 1517
Iron and steel industry, 2184
Land markets, 1665
Maintenance products, 978,
1924
Mining areas, 1517
Mixed farming models, 40,
379, 772, 806, 2071
Non-employment incomes,
1054
Paper products industry, 230,
1958
Pharmaceutical industry, 978,
982, 1123, 1924
Photographic industry, 978,
1924
Planning, 301, 358, 583, 1317,
1403

Netherlands—*contd*
Pollution control laws and
practices, 767, 1650
Ports, 478, 481, 754, 757, 1446,
1449, 1946, 1949, 2090, 2093
Production, 190
Reform, 1665
Regional industrialization
policy, 1519
Rehabilitation, 10
Research, 1804, 2184
Rural leases, 1665
Sheep, 150, 2177
Socio-economic structures,
1517
Surveys, 209, 249, 1968
Taxes, 882
Value added taxes, 464, 1503,
2086
Wine consumption, 920
Women workers, 428
Workers, 1999
Working conditions, 428
See also Benelux; European
Atomic Energy Community;
European Coal and Steel
Community; European
Communities; European
Economic Community;
Western Europe
Networks
Urban, *see* Urban networks
Niger
Industrial enterprises, 1165,
1538, 1558, 1761, 1794
Industrialization, 986, 992,
1717, 1796
See also Associated African
States and Madagascar;
West Africa
Nitrogen oxides, 2120
Noise, 2110, *see also*
Environment; Pollution
Non-employment incomes, *see*
Income, Non-employment
Non-governmental
organizations, *see*
Organizations,
Non-governmental

Non-member countries
Iron and steel markets, 1101,
1102, 1593, 1594, 2157, 2158
North Africa, 315, *see also*
Africa; Libya
Norway
Agricultural policy, 901, 1883
Agriculture, 901, 1883
See also Western Europe
Nuclear energy, *see* Energy,
Nuclear
Nuclear safety, *see* Safety,
Nuclear
Nuts, 440, 441, 588, 589, *see also*
Agriculture, Products; Food

Occupations, 1766, *see also*
Employment; Labour
Office machinery, 66, 131, 1436,
1459, 1460
Officials
Executive, *see* Executive
officials
Oils
Essential, 440, 441, 588, 589
Linseed, 400, 1845
Olive, 184, 400, 1641, 1845
Supply, 720, 764, 914, 1190,
1862, 2002
Tropical, 51, 1197
See also Agriculture,
Products; Oilseeds
Oilseeds
Tropical, 51, 1197
See also Agriculture,
Products; Oils
Olive oils, *see* Oils, Olive
Operational management, *see*
Management, Operational
Opinion
Public, *see* Public, Opinion
Orchards
Production, 1339, 1476, 1621,
see also Production
See also Agriculture; Fruit
Ordinary wines, *see* Wine,
Ordinary
Ores
Iron, *see* Iron, Ores

Organization
  Business, *see* Businesses,
    Organization
  Iron and steel industry, 1131,
    1424, 1820, 1941, 1956, 2207
Organizations
  Agricultural, *see* Agriculture,
    Organizations
  Coal, *see* Coal, Organizations
  Labour, *see* Labour
    Organizations
  Non-governmental, 1629
  Professional, 175, 535, 927,
    1206, 1379, 2133
  Regional, *see* Regions,
    Organizations
  See also Associations;
    Enterprises; Institutions
Organo-halogen compounds,
  1386
Organoleptic quality, 868, 1261,
  2016
Ownership
  Private forest, *see* Forests,
    Private ownership
Oxides
  Nitrogen, *see* Nitrogen oxides

Paper, 64, 262, 355, 711, 716
  Industry, 62, 64, 262, 355, 711,
    716, 940, 1033, 1134, 1466,
    see also Industries
  Processing, 64, 262, 355, 711,
    716, *see also* Processing
  Products industry, 64, 230,
    262, 355, 711, 716, 940, 1033,
    1466, 1958, *see also*
    Industries; Products
Participation
  Workers, *see* Workers,
    Participation
  See also Cooperation
Patents, 106–8, 215, 637, 1828,
    1917, 1918, *see also*
    Property, Laws; Trade,
    Marks
Pathology
  Suture work, *see* Suture work
  See also Medicine;

Physiopathology
Payments, 1258, 2176
  Balance of, *see* Balance of
    payments
Pensions, 185
  Funds, 963
  See also Social security
Perception
  Poverty, *see* Poverty
Pesticides
  Residues, 47, 48, 56, 57,
    112–14, 299, 300, 341, 342,
    658, 659, 1608, 1701, 1702,
    1877–9, 2128–30, 2195, 2196
  See also Pollutants
Pests
  Agricultural control, *see*
    Agriculture, Pest control
  Control, 212
Petrol, 1186
Petroleum
  Refining, 398
  See also Energy, Sources
Pharmaceuticals, 828
  Industry, 160, 503, 865, 978,
    982, 984, 1123, 1265, 1527,
    1920, 1924, *see also*
    Industries
  Products, 130
Photography, 828
  Industry, 978, 1924, *see also*
    Industries
  Products, 130, *see also*
    Products
Physical plans, *see* Plans,
  Physical
Physiopathology
  Cardio-respiratory, 1809
  See also Medicine
Piglets
  Markets, 559, 1973, *see also*
    Markets
  See also Animals
Pigs, 149, 309, 1158, 1254, 1854,
    2109
  Carcasses, 1595, 1872, *see also*
    Carcasses
  See also Animals
Pineapples, 440, 441, 588, 589

Planning
  Economic, *see* Economics,
    Planning
  Industrial areas, 301, 358, 583,
    1317, 1403
  Industrial location, 246, 1338
  See also Policy
Plans
  Physical, 1184, 2192
Plugs
  Sparking, *see* Sparking plugs
Poisoning
  Carbon monoxide, 123, 362,
    1130, 1592
  See also Pollutants
Policy, 331, 469, 1278, 1357
  Agricultural, *see* Agriculture,
    Policy
  Bond market, *see* Bonds,
    Market policy
  Competition, *see* Competition,
    Policy
  Developing countries, 1195
  Development, *see*
    Development, Policy
  Economic, *see* Economics,
    Policy
  Educational, *see* Education,
    Policy
  Energy, *see* Energy, Policy
  Food, *see* Food, Policy
  Incomes, *see* Income, Policy
  Industrial, *see* Industries,
    Policy
  Industrial location, 1808
  Labour market, *see* Labour,
    Market policy
  Long term, 1279, 1281
  Monetary, *see* Money, Policy
  National, 275, 719, 1225, 1468,
    1520, 1581, 2077
  Prices, *see* Prices, Policy
  Regional, *see* Regions, Policy
  Regional development, *see*
    Regions, Development
    policy
  Regional economic, *see*
    Regions, Economic policy
  Regional industrialization, *see*

Industrialization, Regional
  policy
Research and development,
  see Research and
  Development, policy
Scientific and technical
  research, *see* Scientific and
  technical, Research
Social housing, *see* Housing,
  Social policy
Social, *see* Social policy
Tax, *see* Taxes, Policy
Transport, *see* Transport,
  Policy
Unemployment, 1224
Wages, 55, 179, 214, 1875, 1897
See also Planning
Politics
  Conditions, 516
  Unification, 419
  Unity, 833
Pollutants, 145, 196, 508, 1408,
  2018, *see also* Bacteria;
  Pesticides; Poisoning;
  Residues; Viruses
Pollution
  Air, 869
  Control, 357, 444, 767, 817,
    967, 1014, 1267, 1268, 1650,
    1829, 1957, 2175
  See also Environment; Noise
Polyvalency, 701, *see also*
  Training
Pomaceous fruit, *see* Fruit,
  Pomaceous
Population, 123, 147, 155, 156,
  362, 390, 649–52, 1020, 1041,
  1060, 1130, 1521, 1522, 1592,
  2138
  Agricultural, *see* Agriculture,
    Population
Pork
  Carcasses, 122, 167, 529, 557,
    734, 1871, 2151, *see also*
    Carcasses
  Markets, 559, 1973, *see also*
    Markets
  Production, 1637, *see also*
    Production

Production statistics, 888,
1228, 1867, *see also*
Production; Statistics
See also Animals, Products;
Meat
Ports, 97–102, 199–204, 472–84,
754–60, 1061, 1108–13,
1440–52, 1946–52, 2090–6,
see also Transport,
Infrastructure
Portugal
Agricultural policy, 905, 1895
Agriculture, 905, 1895
Children, 1231
Workers, 1231
See also Western Europe
Potatoes
Products, 348, *see also*
Products
See also Vegetables
Poultry, 310, 941, 1159, 1249,
1991, 2186
Carcasses, 447, 921, *see also*
Carcasses
Freezing, 1826, 1959, *see also*
Freezing
Meat production, 1637, *see
also* Meat; Production
See also Animals, Products;
Chicken; Meat
Poverty, 1683, 1742, *see also*
Economics, Conditions
Power
Energy, *see* Energy
Purchasing, *see* Purchasing,
Power
Practice
Collective agreements, *see*
Collective agreements
Exercise tests, *see* Exercise
tests
Pollution control, 357, 444,
767, 967, 1014, 1267, 1268,
1650, 1829, 1957
Unemployment, 1224
Preservation
Fruit, *see* Fruit, Preservation
and processing industry
Tropical fruit, *see* Fruit,

Tropical
Vegetables, *see* Vegetables,
Preservation and processing
industry
Preserves, 440, 441, 588, 589
Prices, 54, 127, 289, 525, 689,
1776
Agricultural land, *see*
Agriculture, Land
Agricultural production, *see*
Agriculture, Production
prices
Agricultural statistics, *see*
Agriculture, Price statistics
Beef carcasses, 37, 530, *see
also* Beef; Carcasses
Cereal, *see* Cereals, Prices
Consumer index, *see*
Consumers, Price indices
Control, 987, 2156, *see also*
Control
Egg statistics, *see* Eggs, Price
statistics
Energy, *see* Energy, Prices
Fertilizer statistics, *see*
Fertilizers, Price statistics
Fishing statistics, 1250, *see
also* Fishing; Statistics
Gas, *see* Gas, Prices
Herring, *see* Herrings, Prices
Land statistics, *see* Land,
Price statistics
Linseed and olive oil, 400,
1845, *see also* Oils
Measures, 890, *see also*
Measures
Ordinary wine, 727, 988, 989,
1856, 2179, 2180
Policy, 2117, *see also* Policy
Production, *see* Production,
Prices
Spatial, 1627
Statistics, 1013, *see also*
Statistics
Surveys, 568, 851, 879, 983,
1076, 1271, 1659, 2100, *see
also* Surveys
See also Costs; Inflation;
Supply

Private enterprises, *see*
Enterprises, Private
Private ownership
Forests, *see* Forests, Private
ownership
See also Property, Laws
Problems
Regional, *see* Regions,
Problems
Processing
Food industry, *see* Food,
Processing industry
Fruit industry, *see* Fruit,
Preservation and processing
industry
Milk industry, *see* Milk,
Processing industry
Paper, *see* Paper, Processing
Vegetable industry, *see*
Vegetables, Preservation
and processing industry
Wheat, 293, 412
Wood, *see* Wood
Producers' associations, 509,
1248, 1670, *see also*
Associations
Production
Agricultural, *see* Agriculture,
Production
Agricultural factors, *see*
Agriculture, Production
factors
Agricultural prices, *see*
Agriculture, Production
prices
Agricultural products, 46, 165,
190, 263, 445, 603, 628, 909,
910, 1012, 1173, 1307, 1316,
1694, 1852, 1860, 1863, 2000,
2098
Agricultural structures, *see*
Agriculture, Production
structures
Agricultural systems, *see*
Agriculture, Production
systems
Agricultural techniques, *see*
Agriculture, Production
techniques

Animal products, 149, 309,
1036, 1158, 1254, 1854, 1855,
2109
Bananas, 148, 1237, 1982
Beef, *see* Beef, Production
Chicken, 1157
Citrus fruit, 256, 2166, 2205
Coke, *see* Coke production
Egg, *see* Eggs, Production
Food, *see* Food, Production
Fruit, *see* Fruit, Production
Industrial, *see* Industries,
Production
Industrial indices, *see*
Industries, Production
indices
Iron and steel, *see* Iron and
steel, Production
Milk, *see* Milk, Production
Orchard, *see* Orchards,
Production
Pomaceous fruit, *see* Fruit,
Pomaceous
Pork, *see* Pork, Production
Pork statistics, *see* Pork,
Production statistics
Poultry, *see* Poultry
Poultry meat, *see* Poultry,
Meat production
Prices, 573, 574, 1395, 1396,
1471, 1472, 1995, 1996
Special steel, *see* Steels,
Special
Vegetable, *see* Vegetables,
Production
Wheat, 293, 412
See also Productivity;
Products; Raw materials
Productivity
Agricultural, *see* Agriculture,
Productivity
Capital, *see* Capital,
Productivity
Measurement, 753, 1470, 2060,
see also Measurement
See also Production
Products
Agricultural, *see* Agriculture,
Products

Animal, *see* Animals, Products
Barley, *see* Barley products
Cereal, *see* Cereals, Products
Cleaning, *see* Cleaning
  products
Dairy, *see* Dairy products
Egg, *see* Eggs, Products
Electromechanical, *see*
  Electromechanical products
Electronic, *see* Electronics,
  Products
Energy, *see* Energy, Products
Food, *see* Food, Products
Horticultural, *see*
  Horticulture, Products
Maintenance, *see* Maintenance
  products
Marketing, 500
Milk markets, *see* Milk,
  Products markets
Paper industry, *see* Paper,
  Products industry
Pharmaceutical, *see*
  Pharmaceuticals, Products
Photographic, *see*
  Photography, Products
Potato, *see* Potatoes, Products
Protein, *see* Protein products
Substitute, *see* Substitute
  products
Tobacco, *see* Tobacco,
  Products
Wheat, *see* Wheat, Products
Wood, *see* Wood
See also Production; Raw
  materials
Professional organizations, *see*
  Organizations, Professional
Profits, 788, *see also* Income
Programmes, 1288, 1289,
  1512–14, 1726, 1830
  Economic, *see* Economics,
    Programmes
  Electoral, *see* Elections,
    Programmes
Progress
  Technical, *see* Technical
    progress
  See also Development; Reform

Projections
  Long term, 1865
Promotion
  Trade, *see* Trade, Promotion
Property
  Laws, 776, 853, 1121, *see also*
    Patents; Private
    ownership
  Rural, *see* Rural property
Protection
  Environmental, *see*
    Environment, Protection
  Social, *see* Social protection
  Worker, *see* Workers,
    Protection
Protein products, 720, 914, 1862,
  2002, *see also* Products
Public
  Authorities, *see* Authorities,
    Public
  Enterprises, *see* Enterprises,
    Public
  Expenditure, *see*
    Expenditure, Public
  Finance, *see* Finance, Public
  General, *see* General public
  Opinion, 1103, 1743, *see also*
    General public
  Purchasing, *see* Purchasing,
    Public
Publishing, 1815
Pupils, 153, 252, 1021, 1529,
  1530, *see also* Education
Purchasing
  Power, 54, 127, 689, 1776, *see*
    also Power
  Public, 328, 346
  See also Consumption;
    Marketing
Purification, *see* Refining

Quality
  Flour, *see* Flour, Quality
  Organoleptic, *see* Organoleptic
    quality
  Taste-standards, *see*
    Standards, Taste-quality
  See also Standardization

R & D, *see* Research and
    Development
Radios
    Industry, 2099, *see also*
        Industries
    Receivers, 22, 23, 266, 267,
        415, 566, 827, 1118, 1327,
        1328, 1842, 1843, 1988, *see
        also* Receivers
Railways
    Transport, 2023, *see also*
        Transport
Rates
    Exchange, *see* Exchange rates
Rationalization, 184, 1641
Raw materials, 470, 1336, *see
    also* Production; Products
Re-employment, 242, 2104, *see
    also* Employment
Readaptation, 242
Real estate, 205
Receivers
    Radio, *see* Radios, Receivers
    Television, *see* Televisions,
        Receivers
    See also Equipment
Record players, 1842, 1843
Recreation, 1083, 1243, 1643,
    1685
Redeployment, *see*
    Re-employment
Redevelopment, 271, *see also*
    Development
Reduction
    Iron ores, 725, 1252, 1391,
        1531, 1532, 1898
Refining
    Olive oil, 184, 1641
    Petroleum, *see* Petroleum,
        Refining
Reform
    Agricultural, *see* Agriculture,
        Reform
    Agricultural structures, 226,
        426, 594, 1425, 1455, 1639,
        1651, 1665, 2068, 2209
    Structural, 8, 44, 115, 234,
        304, 457, 462, 582, 729, 1175,
        1273, 1426, 1613, 1640, 1666,

1740, 1799, *see also*
    Structures
Teaching systems, *see*
    Teaching, Systems
See also Development;
    Progress
Regionalism, 2020
Regions
    Analysis, 1010, 1011, 1689,
        1690
    Belgium, 1017, 2106
    Development, 77, 275, 539,
        719, 792, 956, 957, 1104,
        1155, 1207, 1225, 1232, 1276,
        1468, 1511, 1520, 1581, 1591,
        1680, 2032, 2077, *see also*
        Development
    Development policy, 1577, *see
        also* Development; Policy
    Disparities, 2056
    Economic development, 414,
        922, 1040, *see also*
        Development; Economics
    Economic policy, 1416, 1664,
        see also Economics; Policy
    Economic structures, 1037,
        1461, 1748, 1970, 2011, *see
        also* Structures
    Economics, 705, 1767, 2059,
        see also Economics
    Employment, 403, 777, *see
        also* Employment
    Industrialization policy, *see*
        Industrialization, Regional
        policy
    Italy, 712
    Organizations, 468, *see also*
        Organizations
    Policy, 789, 1126, 1129, 1155,
        1276, 1942, *see also* Policy
    Problems, 2009, 2010
Regulations, 215, 637, 1325,
    1819, 1917, 1918
    Customs, *see* Customs
        regulations
    Draft, 781
    Fiscal, *see* Fiscal regulations
    Staff, *see* Staff regulations
    See also Laws

Rehabilitation, 10, 169, 1932
Reparcelling, 663, 732, 795,
    1185, 1366, 1638, 2084
Reports
  General, see General reports
Representation
  Workers, see Workers,
    Representation
Republic of Germany
  Federal, see Germany
    (Federal Republic)
Rescue, 519, see also Accidents;
    Safety
Research, 20, 264, 406, 547, 548,
    622, 623, 725, 817, 856, 1120,
    1531, 1532, 1623, 1624,
    2175
  Coal, see Coal, Research
  Coal mines, 596, 597, 1193,
    1804
  Industrial health, 1344
  Iron and steel industry, 319,
    524, 1199, 1384, 2184
  Iron ore mines, 598, 1192,
    1200
  Medical, see Medicine,
    Research
  Methods, 168, 761, 1201, see
    also Methods
  Scientific, see Science,
    Research
  Scientific and technical, see
    Scientific and technical,
    Research
  See also Research and
    Development
Research and Development, 220,
    221, 236, 427, 1008, 1009,
    1939
  Energy, 1235
  Policy, 1404, 1490, see also
    Policy
  See also Development;
    Research
Residues
  Milk, see Milk, Residues
  Pesticide, see Pesticides,
    Residues
  See also Pollutants

Resistance
  Virus, see Viruses, Resistance
Resources, 580, see also
    Development; Policy
Respiratory physiopathology
  Cardio-, see Physiopathology,
    Cardio-respiratory
Results
  Ecological, see Ecological
    results
  Short term, 1637
  Social, see Social results
Retail trade, see Trade, Retail
Retraining
  Teachers, see Teachers,
    Retraining
  See also Training
Revolutions
  Industrial, see Industries,
    Revolutions
Revolving funds
  Agricultural, see Agriculture,
    Revolving funds
Rights, 125, 1758
  Migrant workers, 1676
Roads
  Infrastructure, 1283, see also
    Infrastructure
  Transport, 1093, 2023, see also
    Transport
Rolling mills, see Mills, Rolling
Rotary furnaces, see Furnaces,
    Rotary
Rural environment, 158, 394,
    1919, 2155, see also
    Environment
Rural leases, 226, 426, 594, 1425,
    1455, 1639, 1651, 1665, 2068,
    2209
Rural property, 1366, see also
    Property
Rwanda
  Industrial enterprises, 607,
    1227, 1549, 1562
  Industrialization, 141, 337,
    639, 1163, 1177, 1598, 1754
  See also Associated African
    States and Madagascar;
    Central Africa

Safety
  Nuclear, 182
  See also Accidents; Rescue
Salaries, *see* Wages
Samples, 94, 630, 1074, 1105,
    1496, 1506, 1602, 1870, 1876,
    2054
  Livestock censuses, *see*
    Livestock, Sample censuses
  Manpower surveys, *see*
    Manpower, Sample surveys
  Methods, 1961, 1972
Sardines, 547, 548, 622, 623,
    1623, 1624, *see also* Fish
Saudi Arabia
  Agricultural surpluses, 969,
    1043, 1368, 2167
School-work transition, *see*
    Transition from school to
    work
Schools
  European, *see* Europe,
    Schools
  Secondary, 849, *see also*
    Education
  See also Education
Science, 406, 409, 1103, 1743
  Research, 1115, *see also*
    Research
Scientific and technical
  Information, 406
  Research, 794, *see also*
    Research
  See also Science
Sea fishing, *see* Fishing,
    Sea
Seasonal variations, 1385
Secondary schools, *see* Schools,
    Secondary
Sectors
  Agricultural, *see* Agriculture,
    Sector
  Economic, *see* Economics,
    Sectors
Security
  Social, *see* Social security
Selling
  Economics, *see* Economics,
    Selling

Fruit, *see* Fruit, Selling
  Vegetable, *see* Vegetables,
    Selling
  See also Marketing
Senegal
  Industrial enterprises, 278,
    948, 1536, 1567, 2064
  Industrialization, 986, 992,
    1717, 1796
  See also Associated African
    States and Madagascar;
    West Africa
Sentencing, *see* Judgments
Servants
  Civil, *see* Civil servants
Services
  Employment, *see*
    Employment, Services
Shaft furnaces, *see* Furnaces,
    Shaft
Sheep, 150, 208, 1160, 1161,
    2083, 2103, 2177, *see also*
    Animals
Shipbuilding
  Markets, 1335, *see also*
    Markets
Shoes, 49, 50, 91, 92, 222, 223,
    611, 612, 750, 751, 797, 798,
    813, 814, 840, 841, 1030,
    1031, 1034, 1035, 1229, 1230,
    1401, 1402, 1500, 1501, 1572,
    1573, 1633, 1634, 1821, 1822,
    1835, 1836, 2025, 2026, 2125,
    2126, *see also* Animals,
    Products
Shop floor, 291
Shop stewards, 1006, *see also*
    Trade, Unions
Short term results, *see* Results,
    Short term
Sintering, 856–8, 1119, 1120,
    1618, *see also* Steels
Skins, *see* Hides and skins
Slaughtering
  Animals, *see* Animals,
    Slaughtering
Slopes
  Maps, 333, 334, 1055, 1056, *see*
    also Maps

Small scale fishing, *see* Fishing, Small scale
Small-sized enterprises, *see* Enterprises, Small-sized
Small-sized industrial enterprises, *see* Industries, Small-sized enterprises
Social accounts, 571, 847, 848, 1486, 1619, *see also* Accounts
Social aspects, 1210
    Conversion, *see* Conversion, Social aspects
Social Committee
    Economic and, *see* European Communities, Economic and Social Committee
Social costs, 366, *see also* Costs
Social housing policy, *see* Housing, Social policy
Social indicators, 2, 1018, 2135, *see also* Indicators
Social life, 542
Social policy, 891, 1214–18, 1220, 2014, *see also* Policy
Social protection, 847, *see also* Protection
Social results
    Coal, 459, 1994
    Value added tax harmonization, 464, 1503, 2086
Social security, 133, 139, 186, 187, 372, 501, 533, 959, 960, 996, 1106, 1182, 1219, 1474, 1733, 1735, 2074, 2107
    Agricultural, *see* Agriculture, Social security
    Indicators, 572, 1152, *see also* Indicators
    Jurisdiction, 173, 270, 657, 925, 998, 1377, *see also* Jurisdiction
    Systems, 185, 534, *see also* Systems
    See also Pensions; State aid
Social statistics, 692, *see also* Statistics
Social structures, 70, 496, 1810, *see also* Structures

Socio-economic structures, 1517
    Agricultural, *see* Agriculture, Socio-economic structures
    See also Economics; Structures
Soft drinks, *see* Drinks, Soft
Somalia
    Food aid, 1346
    Industrial enterprises, 138, 609, 1551, 1570
    Industrialization, 143, 1179, 1600, 1636, 1755, 2082
    See also Africa; Associated African States and Madagascar
Songs, 1609
Sources
    Energy, *see* Energy, Sources
    Labour law, 176A, 540, 544A, 928A, 1000A, 1380A, 1414A
South-Eastern Europe
    Youth, 1873, 2061
    See also Europe
Soviet Union, *see* Union of Soviet Socialist Republics
Space industry, *see* Aerospace industry
Sparking plugs, 21, 265, 1326, *see also* Electrical equipment
Sparkling wine industry, *see* Wine, Sparkling industry
Spatial pricing, *see* Prices, Spatial
Special steels, *see* Steels, Special
Speeches, 34, 236, 330, 332, 364–8, 370, 371, 433–5, 560, 562, 600, 614, 780–2, 831, 832, 837, 838, 876, 894, 895, 966, 1146, 1194, 1195, 1212, 1217, 1219, 1286–8, 1290–3, 1297–1301, 1304, 1305, 1308, 1309, 1312, 1354–8, 1417–23, 1512–15, 1723–7, 1729–31, 1757, 1830, 1832, 1834, 1838, 1839, 1936, 1938, 2141
Spirits industry, 192, 1141, *see also* Beverages; Industries

Stabilization
  Pork markets, *see* Pork,
    Markets
Stables, 1065, 2019, *see also*
  Agriculture
Staff regulations, 551, 1681, 1824
Stand establishments, 1084,
  1244, 1644, 1686, *see also*
  Forestry
Standardization, 1005
  Horticultural products, 247,
  1238
  See also Measurement;
    Quality; Standards
Standards
  Steel, *see* Steels, Standards
  Taste-quality, 2005
State aid, 748, 1085, 1245, 1645,
  1687, *see also* Aid;
    Expenditure, Public;
    Finance, Public; Social
    security
Statistics
  Accident, *see* Accidents,
    Statistics
  Agricultural manpower, *see*
    Agriculture, Manpower
    statistics
  Agricultural price, *see*
    Agriculture, Price statistics
  Analysis, 2119, *see also*
    Analysis
  Beef, *see* Beef, Statistics
  Business, *see* Businesses,
    Statistics
  Educational, *see* Education,
    Statistics
  Egg price, *see* Eggs, Price
    statistics
  Fertilizer price, *see*
    Fertilizers, Price statistics
  Fishing, *see* Fishing, Statistics
  Harmonized, 654, 655, 688,
    1775, 1909, 1912
  Land price, *see* Land, Price
    statistics
  Methods, 1339, 1385, 1476,
    1621, *see also* Methods
  Multivariable methods, 1837

Pork production, *see* Pork,
  Production statistics
Price, *see* Prices, Statistics
Social, *see* Social statistics
Tax, *see* Taxes, Statistics
Wage, *see* Wages, Statistics
See also Averages; Censuses;
  Errors; Input-output tables
Statutes, 1816–18, *see also* Laws
Steels, 329, 631, 958, 1100, 1280,
  1493, 1533, 1709, 1736, 1987,
  2201
  Markets, 369, *see also* Markets
  Special, 470, 1336
  Standards, 359, 485, 744, 1062,
    see also Standards
  Trade, 180, *see also* Trade
  Works, 25, 117, 281, 552, 556,
    617, 855, 861, 872, 897, 1017,
    1066, 1350, 1585, 1805, 1847,
    1963, 2106, 2160
  See also Alloys; Bloomings;
    Furnaces; Iron and steel;
    Mills
Storage
  Cereal, *see* Cereals, Storage
Strikes, 172, 541, 924, 997, 1376,
  1412
Structures
  Agricultural, *see* Agriculture,
    Structures
  Agricultural enterprises, 75,
    166, 1064, 1489, 1902
  Agricultural production, *see*
    Agriculture, Production
    structures
  Agricultural socio-economic,
    see Agriculture,
    Socio-economic structures
  Beverages industry, 567, 850,
    1270, 1658
  Economic, *see* Economics,
    Structures
  Fruit and vegetable trade,
    1005
  Horticultural enterprises,
    1967
  Institutional, *see* Institutions,
    Structures

Milk processing industry, 694
Reform, *see* Reform,
  Structural
Regional economic, *see*
  Regions, Economic
  structures
Social, *see* Social structures
Socio-economic, *see*
  Socio-economic structures
Trade, 1601
Wage, *see* Wages, Structure
Students, 153, 252, 1021, 1529,
  see also Education;
  Graduates
Stunning, 1171, 1399
Substitute products, 1198, 2040,
  see also Products
Suffrage
  Universal, 429
  See also Elections
Sugar, 913, 1861, 2001, *see also*
  Agriculture, Products
Sulphur dioxide, 869
Summit meetings, 523, *see also*
  Conferences
Supply
  Agricultural products, 1864,
    2143
  Balance sheets, 1250, *see also*
    Balance sheets
  Cereal, 121
  Fats, *see* Fats, Supply
  Manganese, 411, 736
  Oils, *see* Oils, Supply
  Protein products, 720, 914,
    1862, 2002
  Raw materials, 470, 1336
  See also Consumption; Prices;
    Trade
Supranationality, 934, 2141
Suretyship, 513, 854
Surpluses
  Agricultural, *see* Agriculture,
    Surpluses
Surveys, 154, 443, 506, 889,
    1267, 1394, 1782, 1908, 1953,
    1967, 2134, 2190
  Family budget, 17, 209, 249,
    460, 563, 1016, 1125, 1721,
    1848, 1928, 1968
  Fishing zone, 548, 623, 1624
  Manpower sample, *see*
    Manpower, Sample surveys
  Price, *see* Prices, Surveys
  Wage, *see* Wages, Surveys
Suture work, 228, 255, 629, 1990,
  2208, *see also* Medicine
Sweden
  Agricultural policy, 902, 1884,
    1893
  Agriculture, 902, 1884, 1893
  See also Western Europe
Switzerland
  Agricultural policy, 904, 1894
  Agriculture, 904, 1894
  See also Western Europe
Systems
  Agricultural production, *see*
    Agriculture, Production
    systems
  Educational, *see* Education,
    Systems
  Grading, 413, 1605
  International monetary, *see*
    Money, International
    systems
  Monetary, *see* Money,
    Systems
  Social security, *see* Social
    security, Systems
  Teaching, *see* Teaching,
    Systems
  Vocational training, *see*
    Vocational training,
    Systems

Table wines, *see* Wine, Table
Tables
  Concentration, *see*
    Concentration, Tables
  Input-output, *see* Input-output
    tables
  See also Statistics
Take-over bids, 1610, *see also*
  Mergers
Tanganyika
  Food aid, 974, 1048, 1373, 2172
  See also Africa

Tariffs, 12, 350, 439, 537, 1283,
1504, *see also* Customs
regulations
Taste-quality standards, *see*
Standards, Taste-quality
Taxes, 385, 585, 635, 735, 882,
1023, 1905, 1980
Corporation, 1997, 1998
Enterprises, 788, 2202
Forests, 1086, 1246, 1646,
1688
Harmonized, 786, 881
Income, 1997, 1998, *see also*
Income
Indirect, 4, 391, 825
Policy, 343, *see also* Policy
Statistics, 302, *see also*
Statistics
Turnover, 2012
Value added, 205, 464, 942,
994, 1025, 1503, 2086, 2089
See also Fiscal administration
Teachers, 251
Retraining, 1714
Training, 1715, *see also*
Training
See also Education; Trainers
Teaching, 1693, 1700, 1977
Systems, 1713
See also Education
Technical and scientific
information, *see* Scientific
and technical, Information
Technical and scientific research,
see Scientific and technical,
Research
Technical aspects, 10, 169, 1932
Technical cooperation, 2041, *see
also* Cooperation
Technical measures, 817, 2175,
see also Measures
Technical possibilities, 1795
Technical progress, 1342
Techniques
Agricultural forecasting, *see*
Agriculture, Forecasting
Agricultural production, *see*
Agriculture, Production
techniques

Automation, *see* Automation,
Techniques
Measurement, *see*
Measurement, Techniques
Transport, *see* Transport,
Techniques
See also Methods; Models
Technology
Suture work, *see* Suture work
Televisions
Industry, 2099, *see also*
Industries
Receivers, 22, 23, 266, 267,
415, 566, 827, 1118, 1327,
1328, 1842, 1843, 1988
Temporary employment, *see*
Employment, Temporary
Tests
Exercise, *see* Exercise tests
Textiles
Industrialization, 71, *see also*
Industrialization
Industry, 63, 72, 261, 354, 383,
442, 615, 710, 715, 829, *see
also* Industries
Machinery, 65, 131, 1135,
1459, 1460, *see also*
Machinery
See also Cotton; Flax; Wool
Third World, 339, 554, 555, *see
also* Developing countries
Timber, 1084, 1244, 1644, 1686,
see also Wood
Tobacco, 136, 298, 616, 1406,
1992
Products, 47, 48, 56, 57,
112–14, 299, 300, 341, 342,
658, 659, 1608, 1701, 1702,
1877–9, 2128–30, 2195, 2196,
see also Products
See also Cigarillos and cigars
Togo
Industrial enterprises, 388,
950, 1541, 1560, 2066
Industrialization, 986, 992,
1717, 1796
See also Associated African
States and Madagascar;
West Africa

Towns, 408, *see also* Areas;
 Cities; Communities;
 Regions; Urban networks
Toxicology, 113, 1608, 1878, 2129
Tractors, 131, 1013, 1459, 1460,
 see also Motor vehicles
Trade, 350
 Capital goods, 1601
 Cereal, *see* Cereals, Trade
 Citrus fruit, 256, 2166, 2205
 Flour, *see* Flour, Trade
 Fruit, *see* Fruit, Trade
 Manganese, 411, 736
 Marks, 820
 Promotion, 324, 325, 1751,
 1752
 Retail, 678, 693, 1094, 1487,
 1488, 1886, 1914
 Steel, *see* Steels, Trade
 Unions, 242, 291, 1407, 1498,
 1934, 2055, *see also*
 Associations; Collective
 bargaining; Shop stewards
 Vegetable, *see* Vegetables,
 Trade
 Wholesale, 693, 1488, 1886,
 1914
 See also Commerce; Exports;
 Imports; Marketing;
 Markets; Supply
Trainers, 129, 159, 311, 532, 859,
 1153, 1275, 2028, *see also*
 Teachers
Training, 647, 1657, 1713
 Agricultural, *see* Agriculture,
 Training
 Manpower, 1257
 Rural environment, *see* Rural
 environment
 Teacher, *see* Teachers,
 Training
 Trainers, *see* Trainers
 Vocational, *see* Vocational
 training
 Vocational systems, *see*
 Vocational training,
 Systems
 See also Apprenticeships;
 Retraining

Transition from school to work,
 936, 1614, 2149, *see also*
 Vocational guidance; Youth
Transport, 12, 439, 537, 601, 877,
 1504, 1744, 1838, 1921, 2021
 Equipment, 1032, *see also*
 Equipment
 Equipment industry, 132, *see
 also* Equipment; Industries
 Infrastructure, 819, 1620,
 2114, 2203, *see also* Canals;
 Ports; Waterways
 Land, *see* Land, Transport
 Policy, 1831, *see also* Policy
 Railway, *see* Railways,
 Transport
 Road, *see* Roads, Transport
 Techniques, 28, 32, 78, 360,
 745, 918, 1063, 2115, *see also*
 Techniques
Treaties, 367, 550, 1073, 1240,
 1823, 2141, *see also* Acts of
 Accession; Laws
Tropical fruit, *see* Fruit, Tropical
Tropical oils, *see* Oils, Tropical
Tropical oilseeds, *see* Oilseeds,
 Tropical
Turkey
 Food aid, 972, 1046, 1371, 2170
 See also Western Europe
Turnover taxes, *see* Taxes,
 Turnover
Tyres, 21, 265, 1326
 Industry, 471, 939, 1465, 1888,
 see also Industries

Underemployment, 168, 761,
 1201, *see also* Employment
Unemployment, 168, 174, 543,
 761, 926, 999, 1201, 1202,
 1224, 1378, 1413, 2007, *see
 also* Employment
Unification
 Political, *see* Politics,
 Unification
Union of Soviet Socialist
 Republics
 Industrial production, 2119A
 See also Eastern Europe

Unions
Economic, *see* Economics,
Unions
European, *see* Europe, Union
Monetary, *see* Money, Unions
Trade, *see* Trade, Unions
United Kingdom, 2024
Aerospace industry, 258, 260,
604, 610, 625, 626, 961, 962
Agricultural credit, 2178
Agricultural policy, 903, 1857
Agricultural products, 909,
1863
Agriculture, 903, 1857
Association Councils, 2139
Audio equipment, 566, 1988
Balance of payments
methodology, 1954
Beverages industry, 567, 850,
1270, 1658
Books, 2024
Cereal trade, 478, 480, 754,
756, 1446, 1448, 1946, 1948,
2090, 2092
Concentration, 383, 502, 503,
566–9, 615, 850–2, 864–6,
1265, 1266, 1270, 1271, 1526,
1527, 1658–60, 1920, 1988
Concentration tables, 866
Consumer education, 724
Consumption, 909, 1863
Cooperation, 74, 181, 504,
1382, 1453
Domestic appliances, 566, 1988
Economic activities, 27, 30, 31,
240, 273, 392, 465, 467, 717,
1221, 1222, 1518, 1576, 1661,
1668, 1906
Economic conditions, 15, 152,
232, 420, 977, 1282, 1362,
1431, 1439, 2037, 2193
Economic laws, 294, 407
Electrical appliance industry,
566, 1988
Energy balance, 884, 2150
Finance, 27, 30, 31, 240, 273,
392, 465, 467, 717, 1221,
1222, 1518, 1576, 1661, 1668,
1906

Fishing industry, 74, 181, 504,
1382, 1453
Flour trade, 478, 480, 754, 756,
1446, 1448, 1946, 1948, 2090,
2092
Food distribution industry,
568, 851, 1271, 1659
Food industry, 569, 852, 1660
Government, 1224
Handicapped, 1932
Indemnity laws, 854
Industrial location, 246, 1338
Industrial location policy, 1808
Inflation, 1114
Laws, 27, 30, 31, 240, 273, 392,
465, 467, 717, 1221, 1222,
1518, 1576, 1661, 1668, 1906
Mechanical engineering
industry, 502, 864, 866,
1266, 1526
Mixed farming models, 381,
382, 699, 774, 775, 808, 809,
874, 875, 1262, 1263, 1277,
1978, 1979
Non-employment incomes,
1114
Pharmaceutical industry, 503,
865, 1265, 1527, 1920
Planning, 246, 1338
Pollution control laws and
practices, 1268
Ports, 478, 480, 754, 756, 1446,
1448, 1946, 1948, 2090, 2092
Price surveys, 568, 851, 1271,
1659
Production, 909, 1863
Radio receivers, 566, 1988
Rehabilitation, 1932
Shop stewards, 1006
Social security systems, 534
Suretyship, 854
Television receivers, 566, 1988
Textile industry, 383, 615
Unemployment policies and
practices, 1224
Women's employment, 384
See also European
Communities; Western
Europe

United States of America
  Aerospace industry, 258, 260,
    604, 610, 625, 626, 961, 962
  Agricultural aid, 1365, 2057
  Agricultural sector, 1146
  Agricultural surpluses, 971,
    1045, 1370, 2169
  Cooperation, 1146
  Food policy, 580
  Industrial location, 246, 1338
  Industrial production, 2119A
  Investment, 87, 162, 416, 700,
    873, 1574
  Iron and steel industry, 1131,
    1424, 1820, 1941, 1956, 2207
  Management, 1131, 1424,
    1820, 1941, 1956, 2207
  Methods, 1131, 1424, 1820,
    1941, 1956, 2207
  Organization, 1131, 1424,
    1820, 1941, 1956, 2207
  Planning, 246, 1338
  Re-employment, 242
  Readaptation, 242
  Workers, 242
Unity
  European, *see* Europe, Unity
  Political, *see* Politics, Unity
Universal suffrage, *see* Suffrage,
    Universal
Upper Volta
  Industrial enterprises, 387,
    1166, 1539, 1554, 1762
  Industrialization, 986, 992,
    1717, 1796
  See also Associated African
    States and Madagascar;
    West Africa
Urban centres, *see* Cities,
    Centres
Urban networks, 2056, *see also*
    Cities
U.S.A., *see* United States of
    America
U.S.S.R., *see* Union of Soviet
    Socialist Republics

Value
  Added taxes, *see* Taxes, Value

  added
  Coefficients of, *see* Coefficients
    of value
Variations
  Seasonal, see Seasonal
    variations
Vegetables
  Canned, 1458
  Preservation and processing
    industry, 1022, *see also*
    Industries; Preservation;
    Processing
  Production, 2005, *see also*
    Production
  Selling, 509, 1248, 1670
  Trade, 1005, *see also* Trade
  See also Agriculture,
    Products; Food;
    Horticulture; Potatoes
Vegetation maps, 216, 1889, *see*
    also Maps
Vehicles
  Motor, *see* Motor vehicles
Verdicts, *see* Judgments
Vertical integration, *see*
    Integration, Vertical
Vessels
  Fishing, *see* Fishing, Vessels
Viruses
  Resistance, 510
  See also Pollutants
Vocabularies, 550, 551, 1240,
    1681, 1823, 1824, *see also*
    Glossaries
Vocational guidance, 518, *see*
    also Transition from school
    to work
Vocational training, 3, 11, 25,
    117–20, 135, 144, 233, 281–4,
    295, 312, 347, 495, 497, 518,
    522, 552, 556, 617–20, 647,
    701, 796, 855, 860, 861, 872,
    897, 898, 919, 953, 1050,
    1066–9, 1154, 1213, 1231,
    1247, 1350–3, 1392, 1434,
    1495, 1584–8, 1616, 1657,
    1747, 1805, 1847, 1881, 1931,
    1962–6, 2006, 2029, 2123,
    2159–62

Vocational training—*contd*
  Systems, 2131, 2132
Volume measures, 890
Voting, *see* Elections

Wages, 55, 179, 214, 690, 1777,
  1875, 1897, 1910, 1911
  Agricultural, *see* Agriculture,
    Wages
  Statistics, 655, 688, 1775,
    1909, 1912, *see also*
    Statistics
  Structure, 42, 693, 1488, 1908,
    1913, 1914, *see also*
    Structures
  Surveys, 579, 681–7, 1095–7,
    1768–74, 1907, 1908, *see also*
    Surveys
  See also Fees; Income
Water, 1386, 1826, 1959, *see also*
    Humidity; Moisture
Waterways, 2022, *see also*
    Transport, Infrastructure
West, 1691, 1692
West Africa
  Food aid, 316
  See also Africa; Cameroon;
    Dahomey; Ivory Coast;
    Mali; Mauritania; Niger;
    Senegal; Togo; Upper Volta
West Germany, see Germany
    (Federal Republic)
Western Europe
  Agricultural policy, 908, 1859,
    1885, 1896
  Agriculture, 908, 1859, 1885,
    1896
  Economics, 507
  Immigrant workers, 507
  Shop floor, 291
  Trade unions, 291
  See also Austria; Belgium;
    Denmark; Europe; Finland;
    France; Germany (Federal
    Republic); Ireland; Italy;
    Luxembourg; The
    Netherlands; Norway;
    Portugal; Sweden;
    Switzerland; Turkey;

  United Kingdom
Western European Union, 1723,
    1724, 1727
Wheat, 293, 412, 913, 1606, 1607,
    1861, 1929, 1930, 2001
  Products, 413, 1605, *see also*
    Products
  See also Cereals
Wholesale trade, *see* Trade,
    Wholesale
Wine
  Consumption, 702, 920, 1866,
    1974, 2182, *see also*
    Consumption
  Ordinary, 727, 988, 989, 1856,
    2179, 2180
  Sparkling industry, 195, 1144,
    1699, *see also* Industries
  Table, 573, 574, 1395, 1396,
    1471, 1472, 1995, 1996
  See also Beverages;
    Champagne industry
Women
  Employment, 384, 1984–6, *see*
    also Employment
  Workers, 146, 428, 518, 599,
    1255, 1632, 1667, 1983, 2112,
    see also Workers
Wood, 1, 356, 1117, 1191, 1438,
    1955, 2124, *see also*
    Forestry; Industries;
    Timber
Wool, 63, 261, 354, 442, 710, 715,
    829, *see also* Textiles
Work, 936, 1614, 2149
  Description, 1653
  Hours of, 654, 655, 1912
  Suture, *see* Suture work
Work-school transition, *see*
    Transition from school to
    work
Workers, 126, 128, 242, 653, 674,
    682, 690, 691, 1231, 1769,
    1777, 1910, 1911, 1969, 2119,
    2136
  Agricultural, *see* Agriculture,
    Workers
  Control, 2055, *see also* Control
  Cultural, 822

Immigrant, *see* Immigrants,
  Workers
Italy, 1154, 1616
Manual, 654
Migrant, *see* Migrants,
  Workers
Netherlands, The, 1999
Participation, 542
Protection, 174, 543, 926, 999,
  1378, 1413, *see also*
  Protection
Re-employment, 2104
Representation, 176, 544, 928,
  1000, 1259, 1380, 1414
Women, *see* Women, Workers
See also Actors; Civil
  servants; Employees;
  Employers; Farmers;
  Labour; Manpower; Miners;
  Musicians
Working conditions, 146, 428,
  599, 1255, 1456, 1457, 1590,
  1632, 1667, 1983, 2112, 2116,
  see also Collective
  agreements; Employment,
  Conditions
Working population, *see*
  Manpower
Working time, *see* Work, Hours
  of
Works
  Steel, *see* Steels, Works
  See also Factories

Youth, 3, 936, 1614, 1873, 2061,
  2149, *see also* Children;
  Transition from school to
  work

Zaïre
  Industrial enterprises, 137,
  608, 1226, 1548, 1563
  See also Associated African
  States and Madagascar;
  Central Africa; Congo
  (Kinshasa)